# Rules of Games and Sports

O.P. Sharma

KHEL SAHITYA KENDRA
7/26, Ansari Road, Daryaganj,
New Delhi-110002

*Published by:*
**KHEL SAHITYA KENDRA**
**7/26, Ansari Road, Darya Ganj, New Delhi-110002**
**Ph.:** (O) 011-43551324, 42564726, 47090343
(M) 9811088729, (Fax) 011-42564726
(Res.) 47091605
**E-mail:** khelsahitya1@rediffmail.com
**Website:** www.khelsahitya.com, www.kskpublisher.com



**ISBN 978-81-7524-608-9**

**PRINTED IN INDIA 2025**



Printed by:
**ASIAN OFFSET PRINTERS**
**Delhi**

Laser Typesetting by:
**K.S.K. DTP UNIT, DELHI**

# Contents

# 1

# ATHLETICS

## INTRODUCTION

Athletics is a collection of sporting events that involve competitive running, jumping, throwing, and walking. The most common types of athletics competitions are track and field, road running, cross country running, and race walking. The simplicity of the competitions, and the lack of a need for expensive equipment, makes athletics one of the most commonly competed sports in the world.

Organised athletics are traced back to the Ancient Olympic Games from 776 BC, and most modern events are conducted by the member clubs of the International Association of Athletics Federations. The athletics meeting forms the backbone of the modern Summer Olympics, and other leading international meetings include the IAAF World Championships and World Indoor Championships.

The most prestigious track and field contests occur within athletics championships and athletics programmes at multi-sport events. The Olympic athletics competition and World Championships in Athletics are by the highest and most prestigious levels of competition in track and field. Track and field events have become the most prominent part of major athletics championships and many famous athletes within the sport of athletics come from this discipline. Discrete track and field competitions are found at national championships-level and also at annual, invitational track and field meetings. Meetings range from elite competitions – such as those in the IAAF Diamond League series – to basic all-comers track meets and inter-sports club meetings, which form the grassroots of track and field.

Official world championship track and field events

## TRACK EVENTS

1. **Sprints:-** 60 m; 100 m; 200 m; and 400 m.
2. **Middle-Distance:-** 800 m; 1500 m; and 3000 m.
3. **Long-Distance:-** 5,000 m; and 10,000 m.
4. **Hurdles:-** 60 m hurdles; 100 m hurdles; 110 m hurdles; 400 m hurdles; and 3,000 m. Steeplechase.
5. **Relays:-** 4 × 100 m relay and 4 × 400 m relay.

## FIELD EVENTS

### 1. JUMPS

(i) Long Jump; (ii) Triple Jump; (iii) High Jump; and (iv) Pole Vault.

### 2. THROWS

(i) Shot Put; (ii) Discus Throw; (iii) Hammer Throw; and (iv) Javelin Throw.

## COMBINED EVENTS

1. Pentathlon; 2. Heptathlon; and 3. Decathlon.

# HISTORY OF ATHLETICS

The sport of track and field athletics, in the form we recognise it today, dates back little more than a century. But the roots of athletics history go back thousands of years. The equivalent of track and field events originated almost with the beginning of man. In order to survive, man had to be both a gymnast and a sprinter.

Survival depended upon his ability to outperform his challenger, man or beast. When he was not in search of sustenance or being pursued, he kept physically fit by engaging in running, jumping or throwing activities with his immediate family or group. Although most people believe the sport stems from the ancient Greek Olympic Games, the earliest athletics-based sports festival was the Taliteann Games, an annual thirty-day gathering held in Country Meath, Ireland. Incorporating such events as foot racing and stone throwing, the games are thought to have been established in 1829 BC and survived until the Norman invasion in AD 1168.

There is a great deal of argument surrounding the origins of the Olympic Games, but positive documentary evidence of their existence dates back to 776 BC. Rural sports meetings, which have prevailed since the Middle Ages, have also played a significant role in the development of athletics. Scottish Highland Games meetings were first held in the fourteenth century, and running, leaping and stone-casting were popular during the reign of Henry II. Stone-casting, a forerunner of shot putting, was such a widespread pastime during the reign of Edward III that he was forced to ban it in 1365 because it was preventing his militia from concentrating on archery practice. An attempt to revise the Olympics was made by a London barrister, Robert Dover, in the seventeenth century. He organised the Cotswold Games, which became known as Dover's 'Olympickes', but the idea of staging similar events did not spread and athletic activity throughout the following century was largely dominated by the growth by professional foot racing. Vast sums were wagered on the outcome of such 'pedestrian' races, usually held between rival foot-men along turnpike roads.

Annual rural fares, featuring running and throwing events, continued to flourish, but the seeds of modern amateur athletics were not sown until the upper classes started to become actively involved in athletic events. An annual sports day was held during the summer of 1812 at the Royal Military college, Sandhurst, and five years later the world's first athletics club— the Neoton Guild — was formed in Norfolk.

It was in the year 1866 that The Amateur Athletic Club was formed and organised annual national championships at the Little Bridge Athletic Ground in London. The club was eclipsed in 1880 when the universities of Oxford and Cambridge brought together the disparate amateur groups, which had developed throughout Britain, to form the Amateur Athletic Association. The AAA's strength gradually grew and, as the nineteenth century drew to a close, it was firmly established as the sole governing body of athletics in Britain. By the turn of the century the modern Olympic Games had already taken their first faltering steps. It was not until the 1908 Olympics in London that the games began to take on a truly international look. The Olympic movement did not become firmly establishment until the 1912 games in Stockholm, by which time most competing nations had governing bodies—Sweden even employed a professional coach to prepare its Olympic team. That year marked the formation of the International Amateur Athletic Federation (IAAF), the supreme governing body controlling international athletics throughout the world. It was created to draw up and enforce rules and regulation on amateur definitions, and to recognise world records. It also formalised the track and field events on the Olympic programme.

The earliest human was not a hunter. He had no equipment. Doubtless he was a vegetarian. But wild animals hunted either man for food or to destroy him. Man, in defence, had to fight back or run from this danger. The fast runner escaped and lived. The slow of foot were over-taken and killed. Man came by track and field through a natural course of events. In order to survive he had to be able to run, throw and jump, and spent a lot of time in developing his talents in these fields. Therefore, it cannct be said that the events on the modern track and field programme are manufactured sporting tests. The most important games in athletics are races.

The different types of races are:

i. The sprints—Short distance running (100, 200 and 400 metres).

ii. Middle distance running (800 and 1,500 metres).

iii. Long distance running (5,000 and 10,000 metres for men, and 3,000 metres for women).

iv. The marathon (42, 195 metres)—26 miles 385 yards.

v. Hurdling (110 metres and 400 metres for men, 100 metres and 400 metres for women, 3,000 metres steeplechase for men).

vi. The relays (4×100 metres and 4×400 metres).

vii. Walking (20,000 and 50,000 metres for men).

## SKILLS AND TECHNIQUES

### TRACK EVENTS

Track events comprises of running and hurdling events while running event includes sprinting, hurdling, relay races and middle distance running. All these events have been discussed separately in this chapter so that.one can easily become a proficient athlete.

#### 1. SPRINTING

Proper technique is fundamental in performance, and poor technique is actually a limiting factor in most athletes' speed development. Good technique will allow a runner to move his or her limbs quickly and safely. Poor technique will result in poor movement efficiency, braking forces, and overloading of certain muscles and joints that could lead to injuries. Technique is the most trainable and essential component in sprinting.

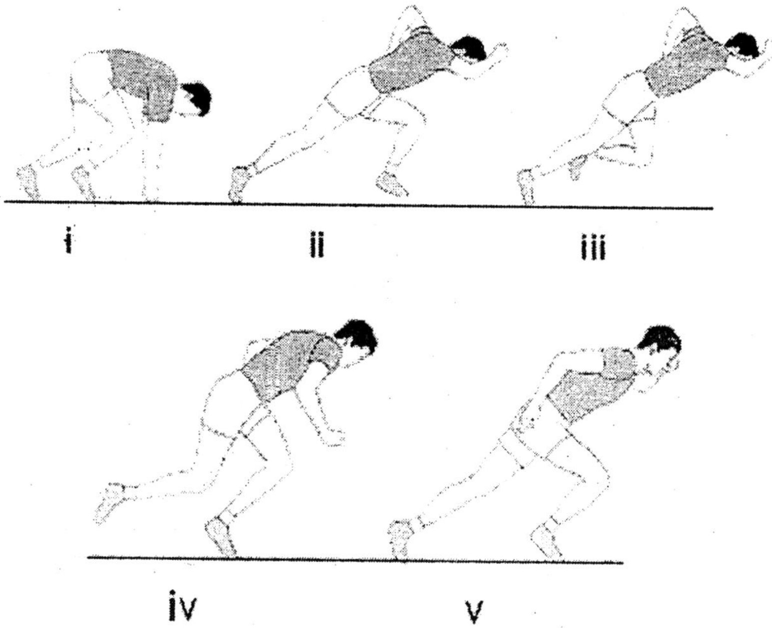


Learning the basics in techniques is key when training to increase speed. The winning philosophy is to teach your body how to move before you are taught to move fast. Learning progressions will use specific cues that will be demonstrated using examples of world-class sprinters, charts, and easy to remember commands. We will teach the body how to explode before we teach the body how to perform sprints for a prolonged time (wind sprints). Practice does not make you perfect, perfect practice makes you perfect.

What order you do things in is as important as what you do. Technique work is done before full speed explosion work for a reason- you have to know how to do something (correct running) before you do it. Perfecting your sprint technique will help you move more economically with less effort.

To perfect your technique I have first broken down the running form into the basics, then into running mechanics using a list of important cues, and finally into real life examples using pictures of sprinters. Use these cues and pictures to get a full understanding of how your running form should look and feel. You will later use drills to enhance and perfect these techniques in your pursuit of becoming a speed machine.

**The Fundamentals**

The fundamentals of the running form can be broken down into its most simple form:

1) Head Up (Stand Tall)

2) Knees Up

3) Toes Up.

**1. Posture**

Except for the acceleration phase, it is critical that the body assumes an erect position when running. The lead foot will normally land under the COM (Center Of Mass) of the body. When leaning forward, COM will not

be directly above the hips, causing the lead foot to land in front of the hips. When this happens, there is a slight breaking action every time that the foot lands.

"Stand Tall with the Head Up!"

"Knees Up!"

**2. Foot Action**

When viewed from the side, the path of the foot should be circular and not elliptical. When the foot leaves the ground, it should be brought up quickly to the butt, forward past the opposing knee, and back to the ground. When the heel is in it's highest position, contacting or near the butt, the thigh should be parallel to the running surface and not pointed toward the ground. As the dorsi-flexed foot contacts the ground, it should be moving backwards, with a "negative foot speed"*. Shortening the time required to complete this cycle by getting the foot off the ground more quickly and then getting back on the ground as fast as possible will increase running speed.

**3. Dorsiflexion**

The key to all muscular activity is the recruitment of the proper muscles at the right time. This is doubly true

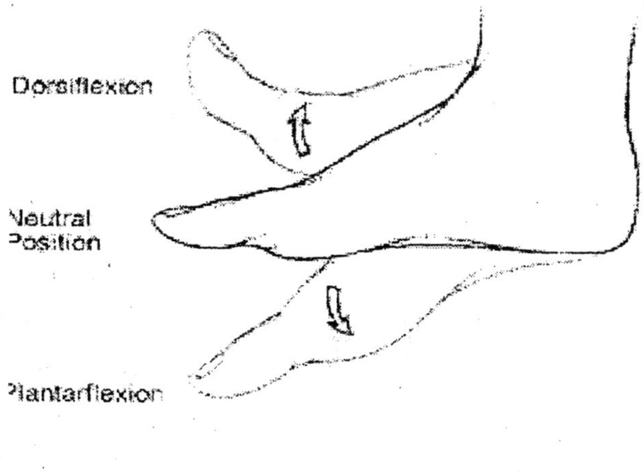

in the development of running speed and dorsi-flexion is the key to this. Dorsi-flexion of the foot (pulling the toes/foot up towards the shin) recruits the calf (gastrocnemius) muscle into the running action. When the foot lands in the dorsi-flexed position, the calf muscle can be contracted, helping to propel the body forward by pushing backward on the running surface. This will move the foot off the ground more quickly. Immediately dorsi-flexing the foot as soon as it leaves the ground will allow the foot/leg to be more quickly pulled through the recovery phase. "Toes Up!"

*Negative Foot Speed- The ability to create a negative foot speed (foot moving backwards at running surface contact time) is the critical characteristic that most often separates the winners from the 2nd place finishers. By doing this, the runner pulls the running surface backwards while propelling the body forward. If the foot is not moving backward as fast as the COM is moving forward, a braking action will occur on every stride.

Following are the essentials qualities to become a successful sprinter :—

-Speed : It is the product of the rate of striding and the length of the stride. At full effort, a good sprinter takes about four and a half steps per second. This rate of striding or cadence, appears to be inborn and cannot be increased appreciably. Through training it is possible to lengthen the stride without affecting the cadence, thus increasing effective sprinting speed. Sprinting speed can also be improved by increased strength, by better relaxation, by improving techniques such as starting and arm action and by eliminating waste motion in running form.

-Strength is the ability to produce a high degree of

muscular force against resistance in a single effort. In sprinting, each thrust of the leg driving against the track is like lifting a heavy weight. The stronger the sprinter's leg muscles, the more power and forward thrust he can obtain.

-Skill is the mastery and effective coordination of the techniques involved in efficient performance of an activity, in other words, the how of running properly.

-Self control is the mastery of the mental aspects of training and competition. It involves intelligence, confidence, determination, pace judgement, resistance to pain and fatigue, the will to win, concentration, planning of training and tactics, coolness under stress and other mental qualities.

**Start**

Of all the acquired skills of the sprinter, the start is the most important. The object in starting is to get into full sprinting stride as quickly as possible. The placement of the starting blocks is essential to a good start. Most sprinters favour the medium start. In this start, the front block is set in approximately 2 foot lengths from the starting line, and the back block 3 to 4 foot lengths. These distances may vary according to the sprinter's body structure, height, and length of limbs.

The starting commands are "On your Marks" and "Set".

**On Your Marks**

Standing with your toes on the starting line, squat down and put both hands on the track in front of the line. Then, with the rear leg, reach back until the foot meets the rear block and the knee is on the ground. Next, move the front leg back until the foot is on the block. Finally, put your hands behind the line. The arms should be shoulder width apart. Your weight should rest largely on the rear nee, plus the front foot and the hands. You should feel comfortable and relaxed and ready.

Set : Move the shoulders forward until they are three to five inches ahead of the hands. At the same time, raise your hips until you can feel them slightly higher than your shoulders, so that your front leg is bent at a 90° angle and your back leg at a more open angle of about 120 degrees. You should be able to feel the pressure of the starting blocks against the soles of both feet. Your head and eyes are aimed straight ahead, still looking at that spot three feet down the track. You weight is now almost all on the hands and front foot. You have changed from a position of relaxation to one of tension, and you are ready for a good start, ready to release that tension into explosive action when the gun sounds.

Do not listen for the gun. Instead, you are concentrating on what you are going to do when the gun is fired. At the sound of gun, the arms move immediately into a vigorous alternating back and forth pumping action. The arm nearest the front block slams forward and the arm nearest the rear leg moves back both as hard as you call. The legs at the same instant push hard against both blocks. They push straight forward, not up. Almost immediately, the rear leg reacts in an explosive forward movement to take the first step, while the front leg continues to drive against the block low and hard.

Sprint out of the blocks with long fast strides, not short fast ones. The first step should be a natural one, but you should work to make it as long as you can without falling on your face. Make this step long by pulling the back leg through as forcefully as you can and lifting your knee as high as possible. Do not worry about the body lead as your body leans naturally to stay in balance, and the amount of lean depends on your rate of acceleration and air resistance. Body lean is an effect, not a cause of acceleration and if you are doing everything right, body lean will take care of itself. All movement should be straight ahead which implies feet should point straight ahead, and arms and legs should be worked in a straight back and forth action with no sideways motion. Always concentrate on high, straight knee action and strong arm action. Get the most out of your own effort, and do not think about your opponent.

**Finish**

The dip is a controversial area and it is debatable whether it is an advantage to hold form and run through, or whether to dip for the line, thus losing from but at the same perhaps gaining valuable inches. The important tactor regarding the dip is its timing. If you dip too soon then, by losing from and leaning forward, you will slow down and lose the advantage you should have gained. As it is the torso that counts as you cross the line. It is important not to stick you head out, as this has the effect of pushing the chest backwards. The technique must be right.

**2. HURDLING**

Hurdling is rhythmical sprinting and should be done with as little deviation from sprinting as possible. Clearing a hurdle is a run over action, not a jumping movement and all hurdling is taught with this concept in mind. Speed is, essential. Combine this with an optimum stride length and an economical clearance of the hurdles and perfection is in sight. Ability to maintain these essentials for the full distance is the last but by

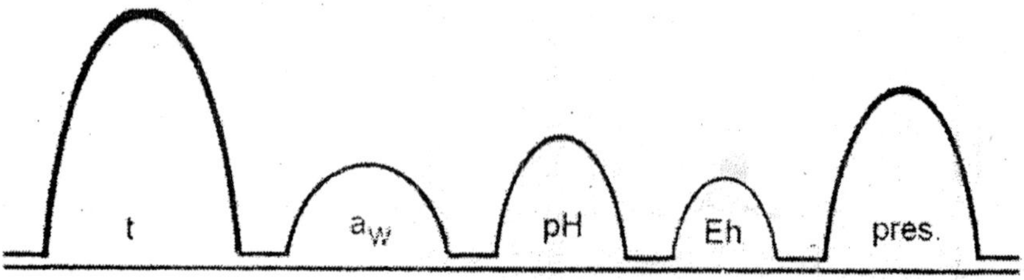


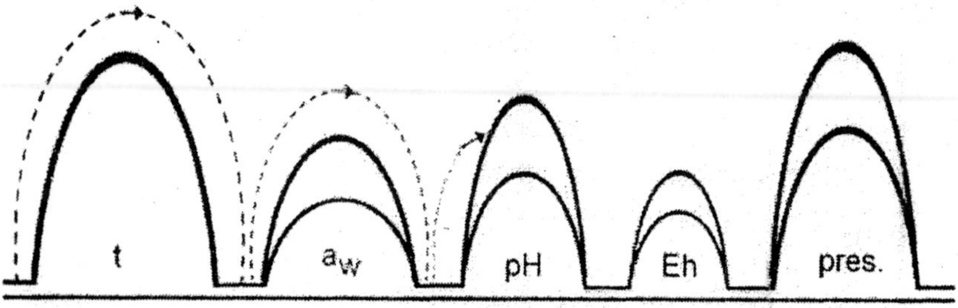


no means the least physical quality which goes into the make-up of a successful high hurdler.

**Starting for the Hurdler**

The regular sprinters start is employed by the high hurdler, the only difference in technique is that the hurdler will tend to rise sooner that a sprinter in order to prepare for the first hurdle.

An eight stride pattern to the first hurdle is most common for hurdlers. Seven strides may be used by the rare strong hurdler. If a hurdler has a dominant left leg it should be used in the blocks as the lead leg. It will also be ussed as the take-off leg when clearing the hurdle. If this is the case then no adjustments need to be made.

The problem arises when you have a tall, strong athlete who finds eight strides place them to close to the hurdle. In this event, there is a need to change his block placement and place the right foot forward at the start.

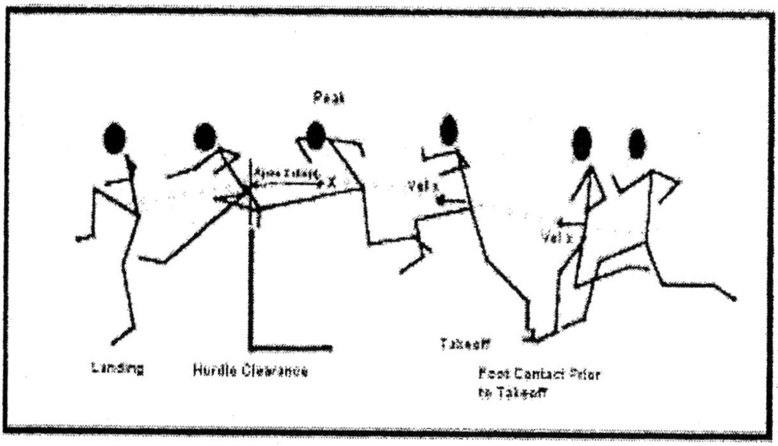


Whether using a seven or eight stride pattern to the first hurdle, in each case the take-off should occur from 6½ - 7½ feet from the hurdle.

**Hurdle Clearance**

To clear the hurdle, the athlete leads with the knee of the lead leg, not the foot. THe leg is picked up and brought straight through over the center of the hurdle. It should not be rotated outward or slung out and then over the hurdle. The knee of the lead leg is slightly bent, a straight leg will increase clearance time.

The arm opposite the lead leg reaches forward toward the toe of the lead leg. The opposite arm is brought back, bent at the elbow just as if it were part of the normal running stride. It should not be thrown to the side to aid in balance..

The uppder body leans forward into the hurdle to aid in sustaining momentum after the hurdle is cleared. The eyes remain looking forward to the next hurdle. If the body is held too upright on the clearance, the hurdler will have to raise his center of gravity higher to clear the hurdle. This will also cause the hurdler to be leaning back upon clearance, destroying momentum.

As the hurdler begins to clear the hurdle, the lead arm is rotated outward as if opening a door and brought down and back. This rotation will keep the elbow in to the body. This action will also cause the body to straighten and the lead leg to drop. The dropping of the lead leg causes the trail leg to come through more quickly. As with the lead leg the trail leg is brought through knee first with a high knee action. It passes under the lead arm which is passing back at this moment.

The opposite arm is now brought forward to aid in the preparation of the step toward the next hurdle. The foot should strike the track first on the outside and then roll inward and up onto the ball of the foot.

The main problem to avoid in clearing the hurdle is that of "floating" over the hurdle. The clearance must be an active one to maintain momentum and proper sprinting form.

**Between Hurdles**

Once the lead leg touches down, three more strides should be taken to the next hurdle. These three strides are no different than the previous ones although the tall, strong, hurdler will have to shorten the third step in order to avoid running up on the next hurdle.

The main mistake a hurdler will make is galloping between hurdles instead of sprinting in order to acheive the three strides. The stride must be quick and regularly spaced. By galloping, the hurdler is overstriding to much and will lose speed.

**Finish**

Many high hurdle races have extremely close finishes. It is thus important to consider what happens between the last hurdle and the finishing line. This is a definite distance and will be covered in a set number of strides. By observing the footfalls made by hurdlers as they cover this last phase of the race, it is possible to determine whether it is worthwhile to practise a 'dip' or 'lunge' at the line.

## 3. STEEPLECHASE

The steeplechase is a distance race with barriers. I have changed my philosophy and decided that the steeplechase is a hurdle distance race.

If you compare the flat times in the 2 mile or 3,000 meters to the steeplechase time it will reveal a very startling fact. Most coaches say that the 2 mile time and the steeplechase time will be within five or six seconds of each other or about the same time.

1. I believe there should be about a 20 seconds variance between the 2 mile time and the steeplechase time.

2. A 9:00-2 miler should be able to run an 8:40 steeplechase time, for a 20 second variance between the flat 3,000 time and the steeplechase time instead of the 40 second variance that most coaches hold to.

In order to get this variance or in order to knock this variance down so that you only have this length of time between the two races:

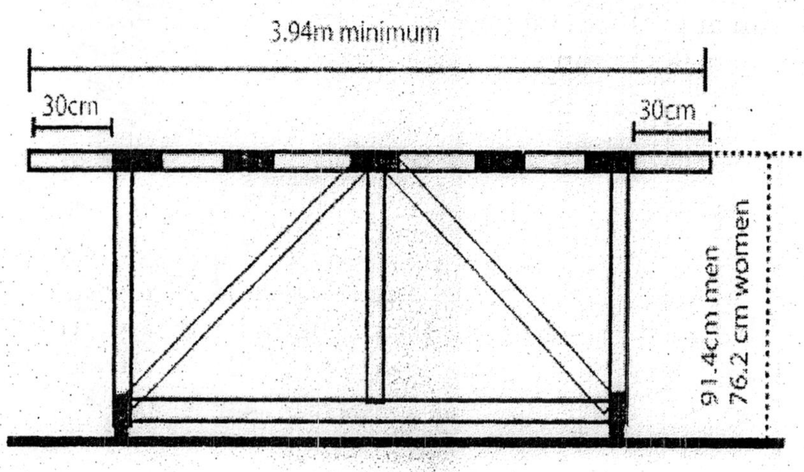

1. We have to look at some of the difficulties in hurdling; and

2. Then we have to work at attempting to cut these difficulties down and to minimize them as much as possible.

One difficulty is hurdling in the steeplechase because it is at a slower pace, and the slower you run the more difficult it is to hurdle. If you have a video tape recorder, I would suggest that you:

1. Have your steeplechaser or your distance runners run a 70 second pace,

2. Then put your intermediate hurdler next to him and have your intermediate hurdler run along with him at the 70 second pace over five hurdles,

3. Then check and see the adjustment that the intermediate hurdler has to make going over the five hurdles at 70 second steeplechase pace.

If a beginning steeplechaser can run a 9:15 in his first attempt, which is a good place to start, that's only a 74 second pace. So get your intermediate hurdle runner to run at a 74 second pace and see what adjustment he has to make to run along side. This will help you decide what type of technique the steeplechaser has to use and a few of the changes that he may have to make and how you may coach him a little differently than you would a regular hurdler.

Another difficulty a steeplechaser will have is he has to hurdle in a crowd. Just think how difficult it would be for the intermediate hurdlers if they all had to go over the same barrier. A steeplechaser has to do one of three things:

1. He has to hurdle in a crowd
2. He has to take the lead, or
3. He has to fall behind.

Someplace in the race he more than likely has to hurdle in a crowd anyway. If he has to do this in a race then I think it is very important for him to run in a crowd during the workout.

Another way to handle this is to have your distance runners run with the steeplechasers on the interval at the same time. Set your hurdle a half a lane out and have the runners run right together towards the hurdle so the steeplechaser cannot see it. In the last two or three strides have them veer off each side of the hurdle, the middle opens up and the steeplechaser can see the hurdle for the first time--very much the same as the situation in a race if he is running in a group.

Another difficulty in working in the steeplechase is that the athlete cannot afford to hit a hurdle. Notice that I am always referring to these as hurdles because this is what we work over. We do not work over barriers at anytime. The only time we ever go over barriers is at the water jump or in the race itself. The reason I use hurdles is that I do not want the runners to be able to step on them. If the hurdle is there they have to learn how to lead with either leg over the hurdle. In order to attempt to stop them from hitting it, because if they ever happen to hit a hurdle in practice I will come down on them very hard, very mean, and make sure that they have the fear of God in them so that they will not hit it a second time. If I have a person who is hitting it constantly, once in a while I will put a barrier out to make him know if he hits it once, he more than likely will hit it again. Most steeplechasers, if they have had the experience of hitting the barrier, that pretty well cures them.

Relating to the slowness of the pace, it is very important to attempt to hurdle for economy and not for speed. The only time a steeplechaser would hurdle for speed would be in the last 400 or in some cases, perhaps in the last 600. But most of the time you want to hurdle for economy. If you video tape and compare your intermediate hurdler, see how much he changes his form when he is running at a 70 second pace as compared to a 52 or a 50 second pace:

* His body lean will not be as drastic

* He does not have to use his arms quite as much

* The trail leg will be under him more.

There's a point of diminishing returns on economy if a person is going too slow. If he is hurdling any slower than a 70 second pace over the hurdle he loses economy and he is going too slow. He is either going to slow down over the top of the hurdle or coming off the hurdle because he does not have enough momentum to carry himself through. So, if anybody is running slower than a 9 minute pace as they approach the hurdle, I still want them to attempt to get to at least a 70 second pace over the hurdle.

One of the major difficulties with beginning hurdlers is that many of them can lead only with one leg. We spend a lot of time teaching the young men to lead with either leg. I have found it is easier to teach them to hurdle with either leg during the same time, using either leg as a lead leg:

* Go over the hurdle with one lead leg five times

* Turn right around and change it and go over it with the other lead leg five times.

It is much easier to do it this way than it is to get them efficient with one leg then turn around in a month or two and attempt to teach them to hurdle with the other leg. It is very important for them to be able to lead with either leg, not only physically, but mentally as well. If I don't have to worry about how I am going to approach this hurdle, when I am at five steps away from it-- It's one less mental thing I have to worry about during the race. And physiologically, it is going to be easier on the runner to finish strong if he doesn't have to worry about the approach to every hurdle.

Realizing that there are possible difficulties in hurdling in a steeplechase race, there are certain drills for beginning hurdlers. With a new man, we will do these drills quite often but as the person gets more efficient then we will cut them down. We do not use more than one or two drills per session.

When I teach a young hurdler, I attempt to have no more than three people around. I want to have one experienced steeplechaser with me and no more than two new ones. If I have four or five new steeplechasers at one particular time then I will divide them into two or three different sessions. I want to have as much of a one-on-one situation as possible.

1. Set up two hurdles facing opposite directions.

I will stand about 15 feet away from the hurdle

o The runners will go over the side of the hurdle and go behind me then go over the side of the other and just make a round trip

o They will work on their lead leg, for example, five round trips and then they will stop and then they'll work on the opposite lead leg

o Then we'll change around and we'll work on the trail leg.

o They will only have to work on one thing at a time—just very basic, beginning hurdling.

1. After we're done with this we go over the complete set of hurdles. The reason I stand back 15 feet is that after a person comes by me I can stop him, talk to him, tell him what I may want him to do a little differently and then he can work on that one particular thing. The most difficult thing to work with hurdlers or steeplechasers is the trail leg--they want to bring it in directly underneath them. You will find that if you watch your top steeplechasers, they will have the trail leg in a little bit closer than high or intermediate hurdlers will

because it is more economic. We do not want the trail leg directly underneath because now they would have to clear the hurdle by about eighteen inches instead of three or four inches. So to work on just the trail leg I set up what we classify as "the ten foot hurdle."

2. We'll usually use five hurdles and set them up 10 feet apart. The hurdlers will go over the hurdle with their trail leg, take one step with the lead leg, go over the hurdle with their trail leg. Every time they take the trail leg they go over the hurdle. It works on the trail leg motion without them having to run too much. When we do these drills we usually do them on a distance day but we do them away from a regular workout. We might do them instead of a morning workout. If they have some time, they might come at noon, we might come back at six or seven o'clock, but we do it apart from the regular practice.

3. Another drill we do about two or three times in a complete year with all the steeplechasers:

* We set the hurdles on the women's high hurdle marks so that they don't have to run 10 yards between them. I found the 10 yards the men have between high hurdles is too great a distance between hurdles for the steeplechasers to run fast without bounding.

* We have them run over them at intermediate height for speed. This helps teach them to get up on their toes toward the end of the race. The form is a little bit different at the end of a race than it is earlier in a race and we can do it without having to fatigue the runner. I am not interested in doing a cardiovascular workout when we are doing these things. We are interested in technique only.

1. The last thing I do separately with the hurdles is:

* Have the runners set up their hurdles at the distance they want, because it will vary a little from person to person, so that they run four steps between them.

* On a straightaway we might set up from 5 to 10 hurdles so that they will run four steps between them at the steeplechase pace they are working at--whether they are a 9:15 or an 8:45 steeplechaser or whatever the case might be.

* I want them to be able to run at that pace and go over the hurdles every fourth step so that they have to alternate legs every time that they go over a hurdle. I have found that this helps to do away with chopping before they get to a hurdle.

1. The last thing we do is a lot of intervals over hurdles:

* We set up the hurdles in the middle of the line of lane one.

* Usually on the interval workouts the hurdles will be done on Tuesday. If we do a 1200, for example, we may run the first and the last lap over barriers and the second lap f lat.

* Or, one week we may do the opposite: we run the first lap flat, then the second lap and the third lap over barriers or just the second lap.

We vary this back and forth and by setting the hurdle in the middle of the line of lane one then the runner can go out and hurdle, which he very often has to go out as during a race.

He can go over the hurdle, then the next lap, if he is not going over the hurdle, he can stay on the inside and run the complete distance. This gives the runner an opportunity to hurdle during an interval workout when he is tired, much the same as during the latter part of a race.

## 4. RELAY RACING

The two relay races which are included in the Olympic Games and in international matches are the 4×100 metres, and the 4 ×400 metres. At all levels, relay races stimulate great interest and enthusiasm both for competitors and spectators alike. Generally they are the last events on the programme and produce a climax of excitement when the extra points gained by the winning teams may be critical to the final result of the match, particularly when there is chance of a dropped baton or of disqualification for passing it outside the zone.

### 4 × 100 METRES RELAY

The successful relay team is a combination of (a) good sprinting and (b) good baton changing. There is no secret to relay racing, just a great deal of practice.

The first runner starts with the baton in his right hand, passes to the left hand of No. 2, No. 3 receives in the right hand and No. 4 receives in the left hand.

The outgoing runner must learn to perfect a standing start or, as a semi-crouch start in which one hand is placed on the track. Furthermore, he must practise starting as the incoming runner crosses a check mark which is placed at a predetermined distance back from the zone. From his starting position he must be able to look back and see the incoming runner and to start at the precise moment when his partner's hips are crossing the mark. As soon as the incoming sprinter crosses it,

the outgoing man must start sprinting flat out. Just before the centre line of the box he must be prepared to receive the baton. Ideally the incoming runner should at this point be in a position to pass the baton which should be handed over within three strides. The incoming runner should call 'Hand!' when he is in a position to pass the baton.

The outgoing runner, who has been using his arms in a full-blooded driving action, swings the receiving arm with the palm facing backwards and slightly down and with the thumb separated from the fingers to form a 'V' into which the baton is passed. The elbow should be slightly flexed with the hand held at approximately hip height. The incoming runner passes the baton with an upward sweep into the 'V' formed by the fingers and thumb of the outgoing runner's hand. He must place the baton well forward into the hand to ensure that there is sufficient length of baton protruding from the hand for the subsequent changes.

The lead-off runner must learn to hold the baton comfortably and safely in his right hand with as much baton as possible protruding from the front of the hand. The task of the incoming runner is to run hard right through the zone and to place the baton firmly into the hand of the outgoing runner. He may get the impression that when he crosses the check mark he can catch his partner easily; however, he still has another 35 metres to run during which time the outgoing runner is accelerating hard; it is thus imperative that he concentrates on maintaining his speed right through the zone. The call 'Hand!' must be loud and correctly timed, bearing in mind that the receiving hand only comes back with every other stride during which time the runner will have covered 4-5 metres of the zone.

**Passing the Baton**

There are basically two methods to exchange the baton, namely Blind Pass and Visual Pass.

**- Blind Pass**

The blind pass is used in sprint relays. In this exchange, the outgoing runner stands in a good sprint position at the back of the 10-metre fly zone located beyond the 20-metre zone. The runner stands on the left side of the lane, if the baton is to be received in the right hand, and the right side of the lane when the baton is to be received in the left hand. When the incoming

a

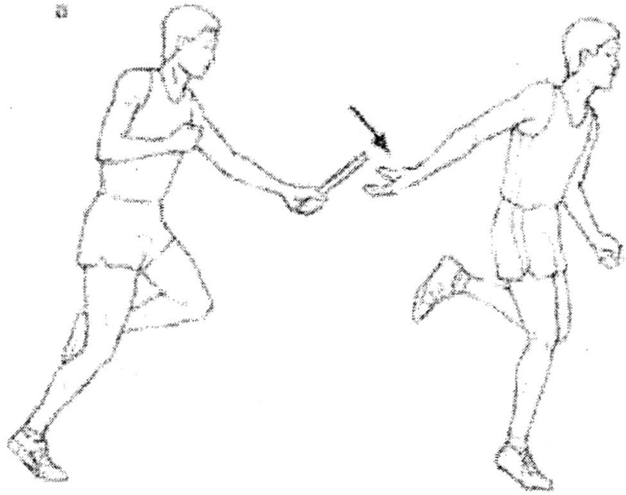

b

runner hits a predetermined mark on the track, called the go mark, the outgoing runner leaves, concentrating on good sprinting action. This go mark may vary by 5 to 8 meters and is established by a trial and error method.

The baton is exchanged at a given point in the zone, preferably in the last 10 meters of the 20-metre passing zone, without the receiver looking back. The exchange is made by the incoming runner by extending the baton forward as far as possible and placing the baton downward into the receiver's opposite hand, which has been extended backward, palm up.

**-Visual Pass:** The visual pass is used in all distance relays. It enables the outgoing runner to judge the speed and fatigue of the incoming runner. In this exchange, the outgoing runner, who is turned towards the inside of the track facing the pole lane, stands on the right side of the lane and receives the baton in the left hand, palm up, from the incoming runner's right hand. Upon receiving the baton, the outgoing runner should always immediately transfer the baton to the right hand.

**4 × 400 Metres Relay**

The 4 × 400 metres relay or long relay is an athletics track event in which teams comprise four runners who each complete 400 metres or one lap. It is traditionally the final event of a track meet. At top class events, the first 500 metres is run in lanes. Start lines are thus staggered over a greater distance than in an individual 400 meters race; the runners then typically move to the inside of the track.

Runners typically carry a relay baton which they must transfer between teammates. Runners have a 20 m box (usually marked with blue lines) in which to transfer the baton. The first transfer is made within the staggered lane lines; for the second and third transfers, runners typically line up across the track despite the fact that runners are usually running in line on the inside of the track. This prevents confusion and collisions during transfer. Unlike the 4 × 100 m relay, runners in the 4 × 400 typically look back and grasp the baton from the incoming runner, due ot the fatigue of the incoming runner, and the wider margins allowed by the longer distance of the race. Consequently, disqualification is rare.

As runners have a rolling start, split times cannot be compared to individual 400 m performances. Internationally, the U.S. men's team has dominated the event, but have been challenged by Jamaica in the 1950s and Britain in the 1990s.

## 5. MIDDLE DISTANCE RUNNING

Middle distance events generally include the 800, 1000-, 1500- and 2000-meter runs, as well as the mile run.

### 800 meter

The 800 m consists of two laps around a standard 400 m track, and has always been an Olympic event. It was included in the first women's track programme in 1928, but suspended until 1960 because of shock and the exhaustion it caused the competitors. Without the benefits of modern training, men of the era were, in contrast, expected to run themselves to complete exhaustion during competitions.

The current record is for men:

Wilson Kipketer (Denmark), 1:41.11 Cologne 24 August 1997.

For women:

Jarmila Kratochvílová (Czechoslovakia) 1:53.28 Munich, 26 July 1983.

**1,500 meter**

Along with the 800 m, this is a premier middle-distance race, covering three and three-quarter laps around a standard Olympic-sized track. In recent years, races over this distance have become more of a prolonged sprint, with each lap averaging 55 seconds for the world record performance by Hicham El Guerrouj of Morocco in 1998 at Rome (two 1:50 s 800 m performances back to back). Thus, speed is necessary, and it seems that the more aerobic conditioning, the better. This is a difficult distance to compete at, mentally, in addition to being one of the more tactical middle-distance track events. The distance is often witness to some of the most tactical, physical races in the sport, as many championship races are won in the final few metres. The record at this distance for men is:

Hicham El Guerrouj (Morocco) 3:26.00 Rome 14 July 1998.

For women:

Qu Yunxia (China) 3:50.46 Beijing 11 September 1993.

**Middle Distance Running Technique**

Guidance on the running technique of the middle distance runner is provided in the form of a series of steps that highlight the main technical points:

- The foot strikes the ground below the centre of gravity (which is around the central area of the hips) The strike is slightly on the outside of the foot and from the ball of the foot to the mid-foot. There is then a role across and a dropping of the heel. The leg's role is supporting and driving.

- As the foot strikes the ground there is also some flexion in the knee. This should not be too excessive, so leg strength must be developed to ensure stability in and around the knee. There is also some movement around the hip girdle. This can be excessive, so strength exercises for the whole region, especially abdominal and lower back, are required. It is very important that this region is kept stable, thus giving a strong platform from which to drive.
- As the torso moves ahead of the foot, the drive is initiated and the achilles and calf are placed under great stress. It is therefore important that stretching and strengthening of this area be incorporated into training. Muscle fibres in the calf respond to a reflex action as they are placed in near full stretch and contract quickly, thus apparently straightening the foot, forcing the athlete back up higher on their fore-foot. (This makes the foot a further lever, often forgotten by many runners). The foot "grips" the ground as the torso moves ahead, forcing the leg into full extension. Once again, strength and flexibility of the hamstrings are important.
- After the athlete has reached almost full stretch, a reflex action occurs in the muscle fibres of the hamstring, quickly shortening it and pulling the foot up off the ground. This allows the whole of the limb to swing back a bit further. Hip mobility and the ability to stretch the quads at the front of the leg arc also vitally important.
- The upper part of the leg is drawn forward by the

action of the quads and hip flexors beginning to shorten. The foot continues on an upward curve, with the help of the contracting hamstring and the hinge effect of the knee joint. It swings into the gluteus maximus (backside), so shortening the lever and making it easier to bring forwards.

- The thigh continues forward and the swings upwards, the head of the foot drops from its high point and accelerates downwards and forwards. The knee reaches its high point, which is not quite as high as that of a sprinter (i.e., at an angle of around 90 degrees to the rear leg).
- The foot ends its swing through at a point just ahead of the knee. The leg maintains a slight angle at the knee (the leg is not straight). Having reached its high point the thigh starts a downward swing; this initiates an acceleration of the foot backwards.
- The foot once again strikes the floor in a backward motion, adding to the athlete's forward motion.

## 6. LONG DISTANCE RUNNING

The aim of running is simply to propel your body forward as quickly and efficiently as possible. Any energy that doesn't contribute to propelling the body forward is wasted. This could be energy which is used to push in the wrong direction or energy which is not converted to movement in any direction.

Here are a few ways in which running can easily become inefficient:

- lifting your body needlessly up and down
- moving from side to side
- using energy to resist forward motion

- absorbing energy instead of using it to move forwards
- generating noise
- transmitting energy into your running shoes

There are three aspects of running technique which can help to address all of these and the good news is that none of them requires any particular talent. They are 1) a high cadence, 2) midfoot landing and 3) core stability.

**High Cadence**

With a few exceptions good runners have a high cadence. By high cadence I mean over 90 cycles per minute (180 foot strikes). Besides minimising the loading on joints and muscles a high cadence minimises the distance that the body moves up and down.

The longer the body is in the air the greater the effect of gravity – more energy is required to throw the body up and more is required to catch it when it comes back down.

Developing a high cadence takes time. Initially running with a very high cadence (and very short strides) uses a lot of energy and isn't relaxing. A good strategy is to introduce short periods into your runs – say one minute in each five. After a couple of runs move onto two minutes in six and so on.

**Midfoot landing — or not heel striking**

As observed above, the aim of running is to propel your body forward. If your foot lands in front of your centre of gravity it will resist your forward motion. If it lands underneath or behind it will contribute. If it lands underneath or behind it cannot land heel first.

The 'A' runner cannot use his front leg to propel himself forward. He'll have enough momentum to keep going but before the front leg can contribute to forward movement it will first resist forward motion and must then propel the body back upwards. What a waste.

The 'B' runner's front leg is landing right under his centre of gravity. His forward momentum is unimpeded and as soon as he extends his leg the force will be pusing him forwards too.

But I thought that I was supposed to land on my heels? Why do running shoes have all that cushioning in the heels?

Consider this for a moment. Track and cross country shoes ('spikes') have the spikes under the forefoot and no cushioning at all under the heel. Also remember that mankind has been running for a lot longer than running shoes have been around – and many of the African distance runners who dominate middle and long distance running ran barefoot as children.

Unfortunately running shoes do not encourage good running. A little like luxury cars they enable us to get away with poor technique.

By landing on the midfoot runners are able to use the bones and muscles in the foot to store energy and to use it for propelling themselves forwards. Good running is silent.

Simply changing your technique from heel strike to midfoot strike is highly likely to result in very stiff calf muscles and then injury. Again a policy of little by little is called for starting with a few minutes and increasing by a small percentage on each run. Ultimately, with so much less impact, the likelihood of injury will be much less.

**Core Stability**

When running the propulsive force is transmitted up one leg, through the pelvis and up the spine. Significantly the leg and spine are not co-axial – they do not align. In order for force to be efficiently transmitted from one to the other the pelvis has to remain rigid and horizontal. The muscles that keep the pelvis in position, the core, are crucial for maintaining efficient running form.

Viewed from the front they have to keep the pelvis horizontal, viewed from the side they have to keep the pelvis under the centre of gravity to ensure that forces generated by the legs are transmitted through both. This is the meaning of 'running tall'.

The 'A' runner does not have a strong core. The blue runner has his hips forwards and holds his pelvis level. The force from his legs is transferred efficiently through his hips, pelvis, spine, neck and head.

Core stability can be developed specifically through postural exercises and activities such as Pilates and Yoga. Simply concentrating on good posture is a start, and not just when running either. Any time, whatever you are doing (standing, sitting, lying down, active or passive), is a good time to concentrate on good posture and it isn't just your running that will benefit.

**Long Distance Running Tips**

- The key to long distance running would be not to run too fast at the initial levels. Instead, run slowly in the first few miles.
- The best way to increase speed would be to indulge in fast running for a day or two per week. However, do not start running on a steady pace everyday. This would only lessen your capability.
- Remember, feeling lazy or lethargic is very normal. In such a case, there is no harm in indulging in slow pace running. Instead, it would act as a boon for you, as it would allow you to recover your energy to perform better for your quality workouts.
- Do not dehydrate your body. Even if you are not thirsty, drink lots of water. Remember, water holds the key for efficient running and keeps your body in prime condition.
- Rest is an important concern, if you are indulging

in long distance running activity. Remember, our body needs a minimum of two days rest to regain back the energy for the next workout session.

- Take rest the next of your long running and also a day before you have planned your hardest speed workout.
- At the start of a new season, look for increasing the mileage base, instead of going for fast pace running. This would keep you tough for the entire season.
- In the early days of the season, engage yourself in a month or two of hill workouts. This would make you stronger, improve the running economy and make you ready for quality workouts and races in the later season.
- Remember, running fast or at an increased pace will not enhance your race times for longer distances and only leave you injured.
- Do not stress out yourself. Instead, take a few months off every year. During this time, you can indulge in leisure running. This would definitely help you come strong in the new season.
- As for the diet, eat lots of bread, potatoes, rice, vegetables, seafood, and fruits. Always keep a check on what you eat. However, you can break the rules, once in a while, and go for pleasure eating.

## 7. RACEWALKING

Racewalking is a long-distance athletic event. Although it is a foot race, it is different from running in that one foot must appear to be in contact with the ground at all times. Stride length is reduced, so to achieve competitive speeds, racewalkers must attain cadence

rates comparable to those achieved by Olympic 400-meter runners—and they must do so for hours at a time since the Olympic distances are 20 kilometres (12 mi) and 50 kilometres (31 mi).

## 8. ROAD RACES

Road running is the sport of running on a measured course over an established road (as opposed to track and cross country running). These events normally range from 5 km to long distance, such as half marathons and marathons, and may involve large numbers of runners or wheelchair entrants. Road running is part of group of road events known as "road races".

Road running may offer those involved a range of challenges and interests such as dealing with hills, sharp bends, varied surfaces, inclement weather, and involvement in a large group. Aerobic fitness, or the ability of the body to use oxygen, is important to help complete the long distance. Anaerobic fitness, the body's ability to respond when there isn't enough oxygen for the muscle, is helpful when encountering hills and providing energy for a sprint at the finish.

The impact of running on roads puts more stress on the feet, knees and lower back than running on dirt or grass. It can compensate by providing a consistent, level surface. It may put less strain on the Achilles tendon.

**Half Marathon**

A half marathon is a road running event of 21,097.5 meters, or about 13.1 miles or 21.0975 km. It is half the distance of a marathon and usually run on roads.

Participation in half marathons has grown steadily recently. One of the main reasons for this is that it is a challenging distance, but doesn't require the dedication that a marathon requires. In 2008, Running USA reported that the half marathon is the fastest growing type of race. New York Road Runners CEO Mary Wittenberg and noted running author and coach Jeff Galloway have also commented on the popularity of the distance. It is common for a half marathon event to be held concurrently with a marathon, using almost the same course with an early finish.

**Marathon**

The marathon is a long-distance foot race with an official distance of 42.195 kilometres (26 miles 385

yards) that is usually run as a road race. The event is named after the fabled run of the Greek soldier Pheidippides, a messenger from the Battle of Marathon to Athens. The historical accuracy of this legend is in doubt, contradicted by accounts given by Herodotus, in particular.

The marathon was one of the original modern Olympic events in 1896, though the distance did not become standardized until 1921. More than 800 marathons are contested throughout the world each year, with the vast majority of competitors being recreational athletes. Larger marathons can have tens of thousands of participants.

## FIELD EVENTS

As known that field events comprises of jumping and throwing events whereas these events include various individual events, which will be discussed individually in this chapter.

### JUMPING EVENT

Event of Jumping Comprises of four individual events, namely, the High Jump, Long Jump, Triple Jump and Pole Vault.

### HIGH JUMP

The high jump is made over a crossbar between rigid uprights. The crossbars is raised after each round, and competitors remain in the competition until eliminated by three consecutive failures.

#### Technique

#### Approach

The J approach is used by most jumpers. This is a run of three, four or five strides straight ahead, then three, four or five strides on a curve. Speed is important in the

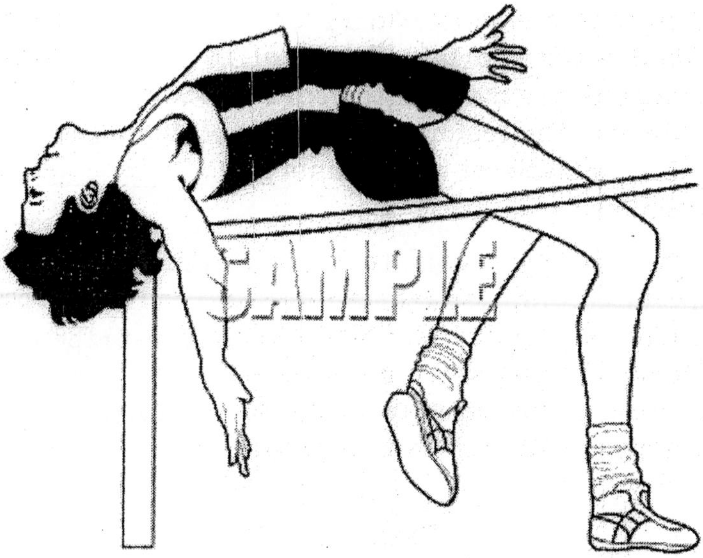

approach, so the jumper must lean to the inside of the arc in order to maintain velocity into the bar.

**Takeoff**

The next to last stride is longer to enable the jumper to lower the centre of gravity for the jump. The last stride is from the outside foot farthest from the bar and is shorter so that the body is in a lean back position. The free knee leg is kicked upward and coordinated with an upward swing of the arms.

The kick combined with the curved approach and the take off foot planted toward the left standard causes the jumper's back to rotate toward the bar at takeoff. As the takeoff is being executed, the jumper should look over the inside shoulder.

**Bar Clearance**

During bar clearance, the lead knee remains up with the plant by catching up to it. The legs are spread, with the knees out in a frog position and the feet together.

The hands are placed alongside the body. There is a laying back of the head and an arching of the back until the bar passes along the back and hips. At this point, the chin is tucked down to the chest so that the body folds up in an L-position.

There are a number of high jump styles some of which are as follows :—

Straddle : This style is executed by kicking the right foot high into the air if the approach is from the left, jumping forcefully off the left foot, and passing over the bar belly down. The approach to the bar is made eight to fourteen strides from 45 degree angle. After a flat footed stamp on the takeoff, the right foot is kicked up and over the bar with all the force possible.

**LONG JUMP**

The long jumper must possess good sprinting speed, a rhythmic, consistent stride pattern, and powerful jumping ability. The basic technique of the long jump can be broken down into four phases, which are as follows:—

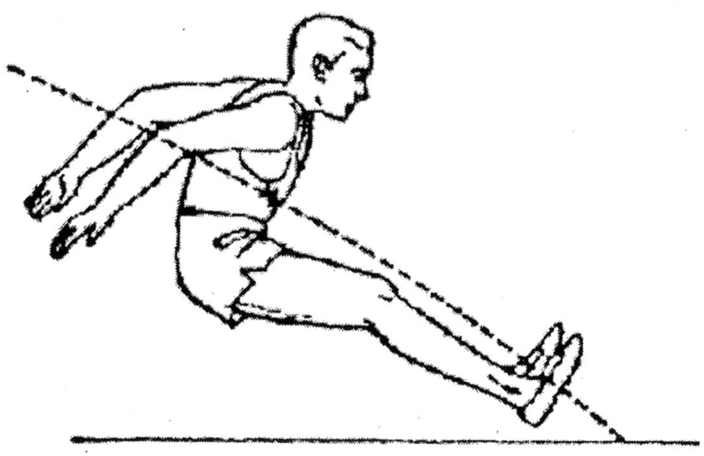

**Approach**

During the approach, the jumper must get to the takeoff board with maximum controlled speed and be in a position to lift. Therefore, relaxation and consistency of stride length are important during the approach. To ensure that the jumper hits the takeoff board with consistency, checkmars are established in the following way :

-Jumper, one stride from the takeoff board, runs 12 to 16 strides in the opposite direction of the jumping pit until the same foot that is to hit the takeoff board lands on the track.

-The jumper continues with 4 to 5 run-throughs in this direction until the takeoff foot hits consistently at the same point.

-The jumper then places a checkmark at that point and standing one stride away, hits the mark with the takeoff foot.

-Now running toward the jumping pit, the jumper makes four to five run through until hitting the board consistently.

-The checkmark may be moved forward or backward depending on whether the jumper is over or under the takeoff board.

**Takeoff**

The next to the stride is a longer, settling stride preparing for the lift. The last stride is shorter, and the takeoff hits in a heel toe action. The free leg comes through as in a normal running stride.

Flight

After leaving the board, the jumper can use one of three types of technique in the air, the, namely, the sail, hitch kick or hang.

Sail : In this method, the legs are tucked up under the body.

**TRIPLE JUMP**

The triple jump is one of the more complex events in track and field athletics. It begins with a full run and take-off as in the broad jump. However, the first landing, at the end of the hop phase, is made on a single foot, the same one used for the take-off. A second jump, the step, ends on the opposite foot, from which a full jump occurs as in the broad jump, with an orthodox two-footed landing.

The triple jump comprises a hop, step and jump sequence. As in other field events some competitors may be eliminated after 3 trials. The winner is the competitor with the best distance after 6 trials. A tie is decided by the competitor's second-best trials.

**Approach**

To ensure hitting the takeoff board with consistency check marks are established. However, the approach is slower and more controlled.

**Takeoff**

Since the movement at takeoff is more forward than upward, the jumper does not need to settle or gather at takeoff. The takeoff foot is planted flat, with the centre of gravity directly over the foot.

**Flight**

Flight comprises of following parts :

**The Hop :** After a fast run-up, the athlete takes off with a strong forward drive from the jumping leg. The body is upright during takeoff, and a flat horizontal trajectory conserves takeoff speed for use in each of the jumps. The athlete drives the leading non-jumping leg up to horizontal and then swings it back to the rear. The thigh of the jumping leg is lifted upward so that a wide stride position exists at the midpoint of the hop.

**Step :** The step is usually shorter than the hop or the jump. The body is upright in the takeoff for the step, and the leading leg is flexed and vigorously swung forward to become the active leg at the end of the step. At the midpoint of the step, the athlete has a wide stride position.

**Jump :** The athlete vigorously swings the leading leg forward from the step into the jump, aiming for distance and a good landing position.

**Landing**

The landing technique are the same as those used in

the long jump, except that some jumpers sit out in landing rather than falling forward, as in the long jump.

## POLE VAULTING

Competitors use a flexible pole to vault a crossbar between 2 uprights. The crossbar is raised after each round, and competitors remain in the competition until eliminated by three consecutives failures.

The most spectacular of field events, the pole vault is contested only by men. It was introduced in the Olympic Games in 1896. Since then it has undergone drastic changes.

### Technique

#### Holding the pole

A careful observer will note that the body as a whole is facing straight ahead, that the arms are bent, and that the grip is relaxed. The left forearm is approximately parallel with the ground and at more than right angles to the pole. The arms and shoulders are thereby given freedom to swing somewhat with the rhythm of the run

while still holding the pole steady. The spread of the hands varies somewhat form 2½ to 3½ feet, depending upon the height and strength of the vaulter.

**The Run**

Only as much speed as can be controlled and used is likely to prove of effective value. The more speed in the run, the more difficult the timing of the take-off and of form in the air. Conservative coaches, or those primarily interested in what happens this week and this month, will therefore place control and smoothness above momentum.

**Securing Check Marks**

The next problem is securing check marks for the run. First, brush the full runaway. Then start with a definite mark at about 110 feet from the box. Do not get back and skip up to it, as is so often done, for this will encourage variation. Stand on the mark with both feet and start with the take-off foot. Only one more mark is needed, checking the take-off foot at about 40 feet from the starting point.

**The Pole Shift**

Throughout the run and shift, the eyes are concentrated upon the vaulting box. During the last three strides of the run, the pole is shifted smoothly into take-off position. There must be no slowdown at this point, merely a relaxed preparation for the take-off. The actual point at which this shift begins varies somewhat, even with excellent vaulters.

**The Take-off**

The correct location and methods of the take-off is one of the most important aspects of vaulting. It also comprises one of the greatest points of variance among vaulters and coaches. All agree that the placement of the take-off foot should be exactly in line with the run and with the position of the hands at the take-off. The linear placement of the foot is usually described in terms of a plumb line dropped from the upper edge of the upper right hand.

**Swing**

The all-important function of the swing is to maintain the body momentum that has been attained during the run and take-off. To delay all action deliberately and to permit the momentum already attained to run its full course are essential. Only when the inevitable deceleration, which naturally occurs as the body swings against gravity, becomes too great is the pendulum shortened and are new forces brought in.

**The turn**

The turn actually occurs simultaneously with the pull-up. However, because of a natural tendency for vaulters to turn over too soon, the coach and vaulter will do well to consider it as beginning during the later stages of the pull-up. A hurried turn, as might occur in swinging the right hip ahead of the left during the body swing, will usually pull the entire body off angle and ruin the vault.

**The push-up**

The more commonly used terms for this phase of the vault are "push-off" or "push-away". However, the important emphasis at even this late point is upon going up rather than cff or away. The pole is now close to the vertical in a good vault forms a firm base for the downward thrust. The pole has been pulled in close to, even against, the right shoulder and neck. The biceps are fully contracted, so that the bent arms can be fully extended. The bent right knee places the right foot almost directly above the head, thus putting the full weight of the body over the hands and making a forceful push-up very effective.

**The Pole Release**

If all previous actions have been well executed, the pole release is incidental. Those using Warmerdam's style will release the lower hand first, then the upper. Both styles, however, stress a balanced, two-arm push-up. Both styles should continue the important emphasis upon keeping all actions on a single plane. Warmerdam turned away from the runaway at the last moment of release and landed facing away from the bar. Yet there was little lateral movement throughout. Wise coaching will insist upon maintaining the face toward the runaway position until all aspects of the straight action of vaulting have been firmly fixed. After that, no harm can be done.

## THROWING EVENTS

Throwing event is an important component of field event and comprises of various individual events, namely, Shot Put, Hammer Throw, Discus Throw and Javelin Throw.

### SHOT PUT

Shot putting is the domain of the big, strong person and although it is one of the technical events, it can be enjoyed and success achieved, at a fairly low skill level, provided there is a high passed-strength level. Although the history of the event, as we know it today, only dates back a hundred years or so, it does not require a very vivid imagination to conjure up pictures of early man casting heavy rocks for distance as a measure of strength.

The event involves pushing a round, cannonball-shaped object, the weight of which varies according to age and sex, from a position close to the neck and in front of the shoulders, for maximum distance.

**Handhold**

There are various kinds of methods of handhold, some of which are as follows :—

In one method, the first, second, and third fingers are back of the shot. The little finger is bent and aids the thumb in maintaining lateral support.

**The Initial Stance**

A position is taken in which the right foot is close to the back edge of the 7-foot circle and the left foot is from 10 inches to 16 inches away. The angle, the direction, and the distance of the placement of the left foot in relation to the right are a matter of convenience since the left leg is to be lifted and swung at the initiation of the shift.

**The Leg Swing**

For the purpose of securing poise and balance for the shift, the putter performs three preliminary leg swing. These swings may be executed by swinging the left leg forward and backward in line with the right leg; or forward and backward in front of the right leg; or forward and backward to the rear of the right leg.

**The Shift**

At the beginning of the shift the body weight is obviously on the right foot, with the right knee moderately bent. As the left foot reaches the most forward point in the swing, the right leg is vigorously straightened and a moderate push is given by the right thigh, leg and foot.

**Throwing**

This position at the front of the circle is called the power position, it is the key to a successful throw. Hitting this position correctly for a right handed thrower means the feet and hips are turned to the left side of the circle, the head faces the back of the circle, body weight is over the right leg, and the right and left legs are bent.

## DISCUS THROWING

The discus throw is included in the Olympic Games as an individual event for males and females It is part of the decathlon men but is not included in the heptathlon females.

**Grip**

The athlete holds the discus by the pads of the fingertips, the thumb resting against the side of the discus. Centrifugal force generated during the athlete's rotation across the ring holds the discus in the hand. The thrower begins in a shoulder-width stance facing away from the direction of throw; vision is directly ahead. The thrower rotates the shoulders and discus arm as far as possible to the right. The athlete's body weight shifts momentarily over the right foot. The legs are slightly flexed.

**Preliminary Swings**

The thrower begins by standing at the back of the circle with the back opposite to the direction of the throw. With the legs bent slightly and the weight on the balls of the feet, the thrower initiates several preliminary swings, shifting the weight from the right foot to the left, as the discus is swung back and forth in a horizontal plane.

**Throw and Reverse**

When the feet are in the throwing stance, the athlete powerfully extends the legs and drives the hips forward toward the direction of the throw. The hips are followed by the chest and finally the throwing arm, which simulates the action of a hip. When releasing the discus, the athlete arrests the forward movement of the body by reversing the feet, bringing the rear leg forward against the inner edge of the rim of the circle.

**Follow Through**

The right hip drives through as the bent legs drive upward and the weight shifts to the left leg. The throwing arm is whipped through by this powerful leg action.

**JAVELIN THROW**

The javelin is thrown from behind an arc and must land within the marked sector. If there are fewer than 8 competitors, each one generally has 8 trials. Otherwise competitors generally have 3 trials and then the best 8 competitors have a further 3. The winner is the competitor with the best distance in his 6 trials. A tie is decided by the competitors' second-best throws.

**Technique**

**Carrying the Javelin**

The teaching process for the javelin

should begin with the grip and carry position. It is always advised to place the binding in the V of the palm of the hand with the second finger gripping the binding edge. The "Fork" grip is a widely used technique and may tell well be superior for some individuals. It may be that either the "Fork" or "Second Finger" may be the most effective tip for a particular individual.

It is recommended to carry over the right shoulder, about three to four inches above the head, in a relaxed position. Athletes should be taught to carry the point slightly down as this aids in keeping the javelin in line during the withdrawal.

**The five-step transition phase**

During the transition phase the javelin is taken to a position of a full arm's behind the body, in preparation for the final throwing action. The body is also placed in its most advantageous position for the final effort. The majority of throwers start the withdrawal of the javelin five strides before the throwing position. The withdrawal mark is not one chosen at random, but one worked out very carefully and precisely to make sure that all of the movement are balanced, and that the final flinging action takes place as close to the scratch line as recovery will permit. The problem facing the athlete is that during this phase, the approach speed must be kept high, but unbalancing movements have to be made with the throwing arm as it is taken to the rear. The first stride, of the final three, is a normal running stride without any particular emphasis placed upon it. The second stride is an important one as it is this stride which puts the body into the correct position for throwing. It is frequently referred to as the cross-step or cross over stride, this is a relic of the past and would prefer to term it the pre-throwing stride. It is during this stride, when the legs are placed ahead of the body in order to get a slight lean back of the trunk, or at least on landing from this stride when the weight is centred over the rear leg.

**The Delivery**

The teaching of the delivery action is important, the flight of the javelin is of no interest. The first tip is to walk through the five tips and stop as the left heel makes contact with the ground. On the catch's command "Rock" they drive the rear foot and hip forward, rocking the left or front foot from the heel onto the ball of the foot with the body assuming the "Bow" position and the javelin still back. On the command "Pull' they all deliver the javelin over the left leg with no follow-through.

## HAMMER THROW

The hammer is thrown from a circle and must land within the marked sector. Some competitors may be eliminated after 3 trials. The winner is the competitor with the best distance in his 6 trials. A tie is decided by the competitors' second-best trials.

### Technique

Modern hammer throwers use 2 or 3 preliminary swings and 3 or 4 turns to rotate across the hammer ring. If the athlete is able to apply continuous acceleration to the hammer and can fit 4 heel-toe rotations in the 2.13 meter 7 foot ring then 4 turns can be used. The following description will exhibit the main elements of a hammer throw :

### Hold

All good throwers wear a glove on the left hand for protection and to help consolidate the grip. The hammer should be placed between the legs so that the handle of the hammer is easy to get at. The length of the handle should be placed at right angles to the plane of the hips.

**Initial Stance**

A right-handed thrower grips the hammer handle with the left hand and wraps the right hand over the top of the left hand. The thrower stands at the rear of the ring, back toward the direction of the throw and feet approximately shoulder-width apart.

**Preliminary Swings**

Although the hammer is held in the hands, it is wrong to think of the preliminary swings as movements involving the arms. The hammer is set in motion from a position behind the body, with an action similar to an underarm bowling action, only considerably aided by a lateral movement of the hips.

**Turns**

When the head of the hammer reaches its lowest point in the last preliminary swing, the thrower "fixes" the arms and hammer in front of the body and rotates into the first turn. The left foot is rotated 180 degrees on the heel toward the direction of throw, and the right foot rotates 180 degrees on the toe.

**Delivery Release**

After placing the right foot down at the end of the third or fourth turn, the athlete pulls on the hammer in an upward spiral by lifting the chest and extending the legs and the back. The athlete's pull on the hammer occurs when the hammer is in front of the body and passing through the low point of its are.

**Reverse**

After releasing the hammer, the thrower concentrates on staying in the ring and not fouling the throw. This can be done by rotating on the right foot and bringing the left foot around and back to the rear. This thrower may also flex both legs and lower the center of gravity back and away from the forward edge of the ring.

# RULES OF ATHLETICS

## TRACK EVENTS

### TRACK MEASUREMENTS

(1) Tracks should be level. For record purposes the maximum allowance for lateral inclination of tracks shall not exceed 1:100, and in the running direction 1:1000 downwards; any inclination shall be uniform.

***Note:*** From 1st April 2009, for track and field competitions to be held on tracks with synthetic surfaces that facility must have an approporate level of certification from UKA.

(2) The inner edge of all tracks must be distinctly marked, cinder and other permanent tracks preferably by a raised border of concrete or other suitable material, 5cm± 1.25cm in height and at least 5cm in width.Where it is not possible to have a raised border the inner edge shall be marked with a white line or white tape 5cm in width. All other lanes shall be marked with a white line 5cm in width.

(3) For Championship Events (whether National or County), or for any record to be accepted, the inside edge of the track must have a raised border, or be adequately flagged or coned to prevent any competitor running on the line itself. (Flags, if used, shall be placed on the line so as to prevent any athlete running on the line. they shall be placed at an angle of 60 degrees with the ground away from the track and placed at intervals not exceeding 4 metres). This also applies to that section of the steeplechase course where athletes divert from the main track to negotiate the water jump.

The cones shall be placed on the white line so that the edge of the base of the cone coincides with the edges of the white line closest to the track. They should not be more than 4 metres apart.

(4) It is recommended that the direction of running

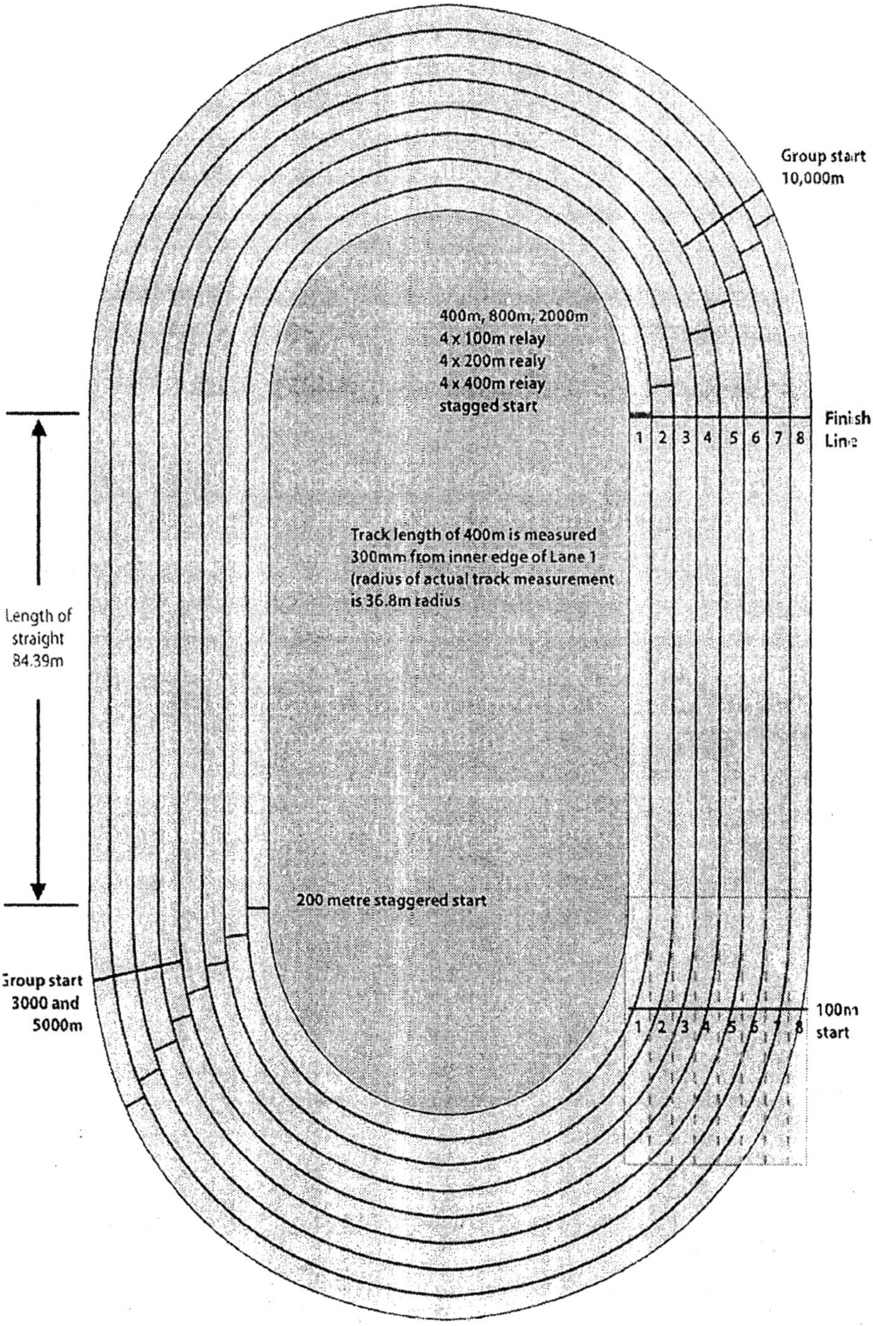
Group start
10,000m
400m, 800m, 2000m
4 x 100m relay
4 x 200m realy
4 x 400m reiay
stagged start
Finish
Line
1 2 3 4 5 6 7 8
Track length of 400m is measured
300mm from inner edge of Lane 1
(radius of actual track measurement
is 36.8m radius
Length of
straight
84.39m
200 metre staggered start
Group start
3000 and
5000m
100m
start

be left hand inside.

(5) In all races where lanes are used the width of each lane shall be not less than 1.22m and not more than 1.25m. The lanes shall be measured for width from the outside edge of one marking line to the outside edge of the next line working outwards from the inner border of the track.

(6) (a) The track must be measured 30cm outwards from the track side of the inner edge if there is a raised border. If there is no raised border the track must be measured 20cm outwards from the track side of the inner edge.

(b) In measuring lanes for distance the inner lane shall be measured as stated in paragraph (a) and the outer lanes 20cm outwards from their respective inner borders.

(7) Races up to 110 metres must be run on a straight course in lanes so as to allow a separate course for each competitor.

(8) Individual races up to and including 400 metres should be run in lanes, with a separate lane for each competitor.

**STATIONS**

(1) In all races stations for competitors shall be drawn. In straight sprint races the competitor drawing No. 1shall take the station on the left facing the winning post, the competitor drawing No. 2the next station and so on.

(2) In races on a circular track, the competitor drawing No. 1 shall take the station nearest the centre of the ground, the competitor drawing No. 2 the next station and so on.

(3) It is recommended that a limit be placed on the number of competitors in races. In general the number should not be so great as to create possible danger or unfairness to any competitor, and if at the beginning of

any race the number of competitors appears to be excessive, the Referee, whose decision shall be final, is empowered to order that the competitors be divided into such heats as considered necessary and the event shall be run off accordingly.

(4) In competitions where the composition of heats is printed in the programme, competitors shall not be allowed to compete in any heat other than that in which their name appears; but the Referee, whose decision shall be final, is empowered to permit a departure from this Rule if this is considered just and reasonable.

(5) In races of 3000m, 5000m and 10000m, when considered appropriate and practicable, the competitors may be divided into two groups, with one group of approximately 65% of the competitors using the regular arced start line and the other group using a separate arced start line marked across the outer half of the track. The other group shall run as far as a designated line at the end of the first bend on the outer half of the track before being allowed to gain the inside of the track. The separate arced start line shall be marked in such away that all the competitors shall run the same distance.

**STARTING BLOCKS**

(1) The use of starting blocks is permitted in races up to and including 400 metres, including the first leg of a relay race, provided such leg does not exceed 400 metres.

(2) Their use is optional.

(3) Athletes may use their own starting blocks, but such starting blocks must be approved by the Starter.

***Note:*** On all-weather tracks the Organisers may insist that only starting blocks provided by them shall be used.

(4) The following rules apply to the construction and use of starting blocks:

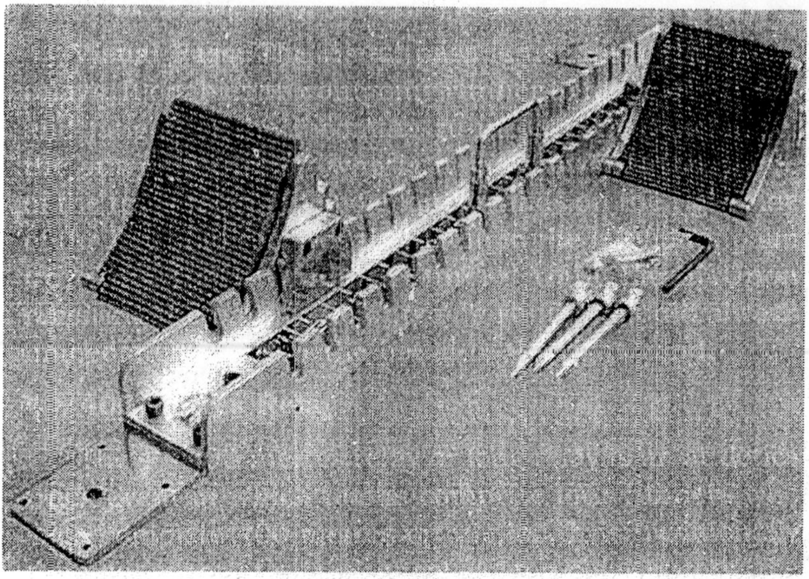

(a) They must be constructed entirely of rigid materials.

(b) They may be adjustable but must be without springs or other devices to give artificial aid to the runner.

(c) They must be fixed to the track by a number of pins or spikes, arranged to cause minimum possible damage to the track surface.

The arrangement must permit the starting blocks to be quickly and easily removed, and the anchorage must permit no movement during the actual start.

(d) When in position on the track, no part of the starting block must overlap the starting line or extend beyond the lane for that athlete.

(5) When starting blocks are being used both hands must be in contact with the ground when the athlete is in the 'set' position.

**THE START**

(1) The start of the race shall be denoted by a line 5cm in width at right angles to the inner edge of the

track. The distance of the race shall be measured from the edge of the starting line further from the finish, to the edge of the finish line nearer to the start.

(2) In all races not run in lanes the starting line shall be curved so that wherever it occurs on the track all the runners can cover the same distance in the race.

(3) All questions concerning the start shall be in the absolute discretion of the Starter, whose decision is final.

(4) Start Recallers should be appointed at National Championships from within the appointed team of Starters. They may also be appointed at other meetings.

(5) Competitors must be placed in their respective stations by Marksmen (Starters Assistants). Marksmen shall assemble competitors 3 metres behind the starting line (or in the case of races run entirely or partly in lanes, behind each starting line) and, once so placed, shall signal to the Starter that all is ready. If in the opinion of the Starter an athlete has failed to comply within a reasonable time with the instructions of the Marksmen to prepare to come to the assembly line, then it may be considered a false start.

(6) Competitors must not touch the start line or the ground in front of it with their hands or feet when on their mark.

(7) All races (except Time Handicaps) shall be started by the report of a revolver or other similar apparatus and a start shall be made to the actual report. The revolver or similar apparatus shall be fired upwards into the air and it is essential that it should give a satisfactory flash which can be clearly seen by the Timekeepers. The time shall be taken from the flash.

(8) (a) The starter shall first receive a signal from the Chief Marksman that all competitors are ready.

(b) After the Starter has ascertained that the Timekeepers are ready, the following commands shall be given to the competitors:

(i) For competitors running a distance up to and including 400 metres: 'On your marks', 'Set', and when all the competitors are set i.e. motionless on their mark, the revolver shall be fired.

(ii) For competitors running or walking a distance greater than 400 metres: the command shall be 'On your marks', after which the competitors shall approach the start line without touching it, and assume a steady position. Competitors must not touch the ground with their hand or hands. When the steady position has been achieved by all of the competitors the revolver shall be fired.

(9) On the command 'On your marks' (for distances greater than 400m) or 'Set' (for distances up to and including 400m) all competitors shall at once and without delay assume their full and final Set position. Failure to comply with the Starter's command after a reasonable time shall constitute a false start.

(10) When a crouch start is being used competitors must assume a position whereby both hands and at least one knee are in contact with the ground on the "On your marks" command and must maintain the contact with both hands until the start signal is given.

(11) If, for any reason, the Starter has to speak to any of the competitors after the command 'On your marks' and before the revolver or other similar apparatus is fired, or if the concentration of any competitor or the Starter is disturbed before the revolver or other similar apparatus is fired, he or she shall order all competitors to stand up and the Marksmen shall place them on the assembly lines again.

(12) If a competitor after the command 'On your marks' disturbs the other competitors in the race through sound or otherwise, it may be considered a false start.

(13) If a competitor commences a starting motion after assuming a full and final set position, and before

the report of the revolver or other similar apparatus, it shall be considered a false start.

(14) Any competitor making a false start must be warned. If a competitor is responsible for two false starts, or three in the case of a Combined Event (Pentathlon, Hexathlon, Heptathlon, Octathlon or Decathlon) that athlete shall be disqualified.

**THE RACE**

(1) In all races run in lanes competitors should keep in their allotted lane from start to finish. If the Referee is satisfied, on the report of a Judge or Umpire, or otherwise, that a competitor has deliberately run out of lane, the Referee shall disqualify that competitor, but if the Referee considers that such action is unintentional, he or she may, at his or her discretion, disqualify if of the opinion that a material advantage was gained thereby.

(2) Any competitor jostling, running or walking across, or obstructing another competitor so as to impede progress shall be liable to disqualification.

(3) A competitor after voluntarily leaving the track or course shall not be allowed to continue in the race.

(4) The final lap shall be signalled to each competitor, usually by ringing a bell. In races longer than 1500 metres a lap scorer(s) shall be appointed by the Referee, who shall keep a record of the laps covered by each competitor.

(5) The Referee shall have the power to order a race to be re-held when he or she considers it just and reasonable to do so. If in any heat a competitor is disqualified the Referee shall have the power to permit any competitor affected by the act resulting in the disqualification to compete in a subsequent round of the event.

(6) No person except an official Timekeeper or other person appointed to do so by the Chief Timekeeper shall:

(a) indicate intermediate times to competitors;

(b) give times to be announced over the public address system.

(7) In races of 200m or less the wind velocity should be measured and recorded whenever possible, and this is essential in the case of a record claim.

The gauge should be set up parallel to the track, 50m from the finish line, not more than 2m from the edge of the track adjacent to lane 1, and at a height of approximately 1.22m. Where a tubular wind gauge is used the length on either side of the measuring device should be at least twice the diameter of the tube.

(8) The periods for which the wind component should be measured are:

| | |
|---|---|
| All distances up to and including 100m | 10secs |
| 100m Hurdles and 110m Hurdles | 13secs |
| 200m. commencing as the runners enter the straight | 10secs |

(9) The wind gauge shall be read in metres per second, rounded to the next higher tenth of a metre per second in the positive direction. (For example: a reading of +2.03m/sec. shall be recorded as +2.1m/sec.: a reading of -2.03m/ sec shall be recorded as -2.0m/sec.).

**THE FINISH**

(1) The finish shall be a line 5cm in width drawn across the track at right angles to the inner edge.

(2) Two white posts shall denote the extremities of the finish line and shall be placed at least 30cm from the edge of the track. The finish posts shall be of rigid construction of about 1.4m in height, 80mm in width and 20mm in thickness.

(3) The competitors shall be placed in the order in which any part of the torso (as distinguished from head, neck, arms, hands, feet and legs) reaches the vertical plane of the edge of the finish line nearer to the start.

**TIES**

(1) In the event of a tie in any heat which affects the qualification of competitors to compete in the next round or final, where practicable, the tying competitors shall all qualify, failing which they shall compete again to decide the qualifiers.

(2) In the case of a tie for first place in any final, the Referee is empowered to decide whether it is practicable to arrange for the competitors so tying to compete again. If the Referee decides that it is not, the result shall stand. Ties in other placings shall remain.

**QUALIFICATION FROM PRELIMINARY HEATS**

(1) In the preliminary rounds of races, at least the winner, and preferably the winner and second, should qualify for the next round or final. Any other competitors to qualify shall be decided either according to their places or according to their times. Where any qualifying position is decided by time only one system of timing may be applied in determining times. Where photo-finish

equipment is in use the Chief Photo-Finish Judge shall consider, where necessary, the actual time recorded in 1/1000ths of a second by the competitor in deciding qualifiers by time.

(2) The following minimum times must be allowed between the last heat of the round and the first heat of the subsequent round or final.

| | Minimum minutes rest |
|---|---|
| Up to 100 metres | 20 |
| Over 100m and up to 200m | 40 |
| Over 200m and up to 400m | 60 |
| Over 400m and up to 800m | 80 |
| Over 800m | 100 |

(3) In any athletics meeting competitors shall be excluded from participating in further events, including relays, when they have qualified in preliminary rounds or heats (including a qualifying round or pool in a Field Event) for further participation in any event but then do not compete further without giving a valid reason to the Referee. If a meeting extends over more than one day the exclusion shall apply to all subsequent events of the meeting.

**HURDLE RACES**

(1) All hurdle races shall be run in lanes and competitors shall run only in their own lane throughout.

(2) A hurdle shall consist of two uprights, or standards, supporting a rectangular frame or gate and should have a level top rail.

(3) The total weight of the hurdle shall be not less than 10kg.

(4) The width of the hurdle shall be from 1.18m to 1.20m and the extreme length of the base shall be 70cm. The top bar shall be 70mm in width and should be between 10mm and 25mm thick. The top bar should be striped in black and white, or in some other contrasting colours in such a manner that the lighter stripes appear

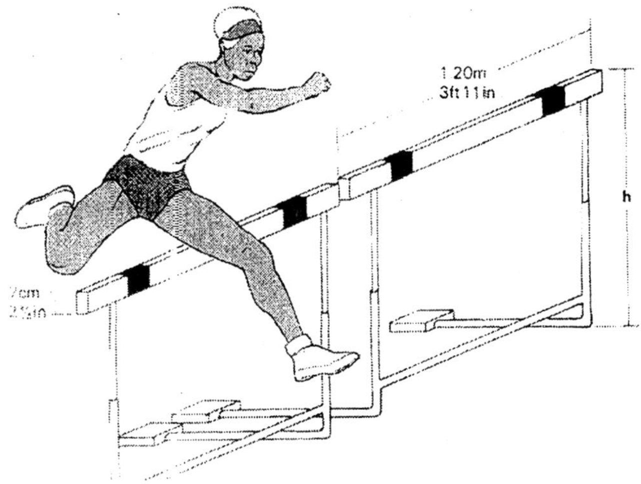


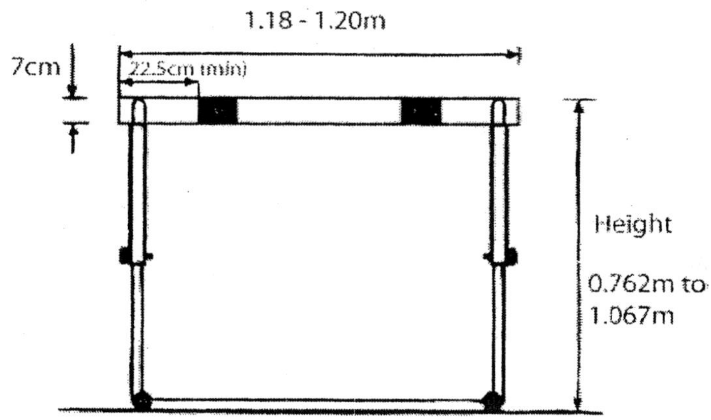


at the end of the hurdle and that they shall be at least 225mm in width.

(5) The hurdle shall be made of wood or metal and shall consist of two bases and two uprights supporting the rectangular frame reinforced by one or more cross-bars, the uprights to be fixed at the extreme end of each base.

(6) The hurdle may be adjustable in height but should be rigidly fastened at the required height for each event.

(7) The hurdles shall be so placed on the track that the ends carrying the uprights shall be farthest from, with the counter-weights nearest to, the starting line, and the edge of the bar nearest the approaching hurdler coinciding with the track marking nearest the athlete.

(8) The hurdle shall be of such design that a force of at least 3.6kg applied to the centre of the top of the cross-bar is required to overturn it. Where an adjustable hurdle is used the counter-weights must be adjustable to the effect that in every position relating to the height of the hurdle the force required to overturn the hurdle when adjusted shall be at least 3.6kg and not more than 4kg.

***Note:*** To check the resisting force of hurdles, a simple spring balance should be used by the application of a pulling force to the centre of the top of the crossbar. Alternatively, use a cord with a hook, applied to the centre of the top of the crossbar. Take the cord along over a pulley fixed conveniently and load the other end of the cord with the appropriate weights.

(9) The force required to overturn hurdles for Under 17 Men and Women and younger age groups shall be at least 2.7kg and not more than 3kg.

(10) Where hurdles are used which overturn with less force than the minimum specified in (8) or (9) above as appropriate, the competitors shall be informed that an athlete knocking down three or more hurdles, or any part of three or more hurdles, shall be disqualified.

(11) Where hurdles comply with (8) or (9) above, as appropriate, knocking down any number of hurdles shall not disqualify, nor shall it disentitle a competitor from claiming a record.

(12) Athletes shall be disqualified if, in the opinion of the Referee, they:

(a) trail a foot or leg below the plane of the top of the bar at the instant of clearing.

(b) negotiate a hurdle not in their lane.

(c) deliberately knock down any hurdle.

(d) fails to jump one or more hurdles i.e. runs around the hurdle.

**STEEPLECHASE RACES**

Only Seniors, Juniors and Under 17's are allowed to contest any steeplechase event.

(1) The hurdle may be made of heavy timber or of metal with a bar of heavy timber. In either case it must be constructed in such away that it may not be easily overturned.

(2) The hurdle shall be 91.4cm in height for Mens' competition, and 76.2cm for Women's competition, and should be at least 3.94m in total width. The section of the top bar of the hurdle should be 12.7cm square.

(3) The weight of each hurdle should be between 80kg and 100kg.

(4) The hurdle shall be placed on the track so that about 30cm of the top bar, measured from the inside edge of the track, will be inside the field (i.e., the top bar will overlap the track edge).

Specifications of approved heavy timber hurdle for Men's competition

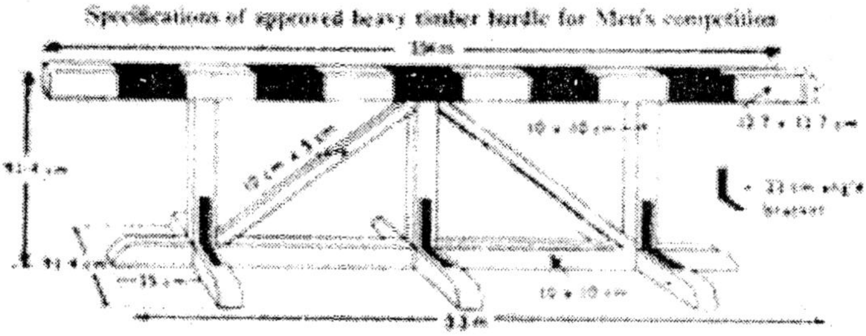

Specifications of approved hurdle with metal base for Men's competition

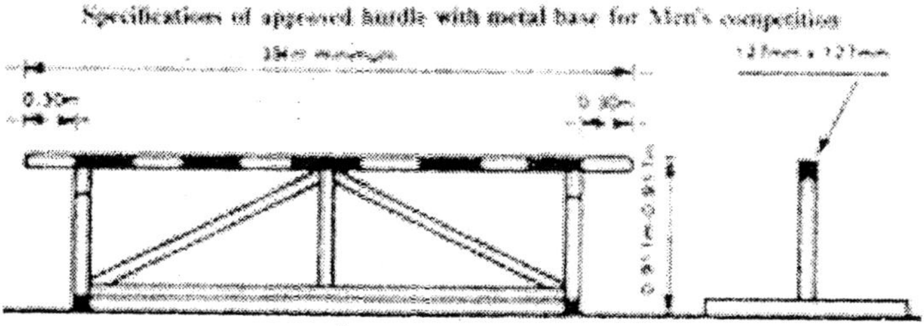

(5) The top bar should be striped in black and white or in some other contrasting colours in such a manner that the lighter stripes appear at the end of each hurdle, and the stripes should be at least 30cm wide.

(6) The hurdle at the water jump must be firmly fixed and shall be 91.4cm in height for Men's competition and 76.2cm for Women's competition. The hurdle shall be 3.66m in total width whilst the section of the top bar should be 12.7cm square.

(7) The water jump, including the hurdle, shall be 3.66m in length. The width of the water jump shall be 3.66m. The water shall be 70cm in depth at the hurdle end, remaining at this depth for a distance of 30cm and then sloping to the level of the track at the farther end.

To ensure safe landing of the competitors, the bottom of the water jump should be covered at the further end with suitable material, at least 3.66m wide and 2.5m long, the thickness of which should not exceed approximately 25mm.

(8) Each athlete shall go over or through the water. Athletes shall be disqualified if they:

(a) fail to jump one or more hurdles i.e. runs around the hurdle.

(b) step to one side or other of the water jump when landing

(c) trail their foot or leg below the horizontal plane of the top of any hurdle at the instant of clearing.

Providing this Rule is observed an athlete may go over each hurdle in any manner. They may jump or vault over any hurdle and may place afoot or feet on any hurdle, including the one at the water jump.

It should be borne in mind that there must be enough distance from the starting line to the first hurdle to prevent competitors from overcrowding and there should be approximately 62.2m from the last hurdle to the finish line.

The water jump should be, where possible, the fourth jump in each lap. If necessary, the finish line should be moved to another part of the track.

The following measurements are given as a guide and any adjustments

necessary should be made by lengthening or shortening the distance at the

starting point of the race. It is assumed that a lap of 400 metres has been

shortened by 6metres by constructing the water jump inside the track.

**(9) 3000 Metres**

| | |
|---|---|
| Distance from starting point to commencement of 1st lap, to be run without jumps | 242.0m |
| Distance from commencement of 1st lap to 1st hurdle | 15.8m |
| From 1st to 2nd hurdle | 79.0m |
| From 2nd to 3rd hurdle | 79.0m |
| From 3rd hurdle to water jump | 79.0m |
| From water jump to 4th hurdle | 79.0m |
| From 4th hurdle to finishing line | 62.2m |
| 7 laps of 394m = | 2758.0m |
| plus | 242.0m |
| | 3000m |

(10) **2000 Metres** (If the course is laid out with a lap of 394m.)

(11) **1500 Metres**

(If the course is laid out with a lap of 394m.)

**RELAY RACES**

(1) Lines 5cm wide shall be drawn across the track to mark the distances of the stages and to denote the scratch line. Each take over zone shall be 20m long of which the scratch line is the centre. The zones shall start and finish at the edges of the zone lines nearest the start line in the running direction.

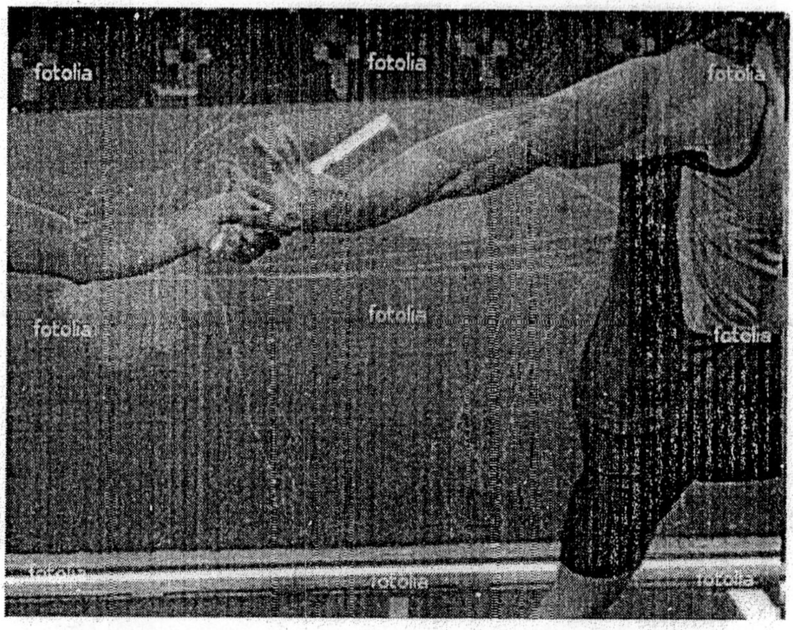

(2) Except for the first runner, where the stage to be run does not exceed 200 metres, the outgoing runners may commence their run not more than 10m outside the take-over zone; where the stage exceeds 200 metres the outgoing runners must commence their run within the take-over zone. Additional lines in a different colour from that used for the take-over zone markings should be drawn to indicate the additional 10m zone at all changeover points.

(3) The positions of the teams at the start of the race shall be drawn and shall be retained at each take-over zone, except that, in races where lanes are not used or have ceased to operate, waiting runners can move to an inner position on the track as incoming team-mates arrive, provided this can be done without fouling.

(4) When relay races up to and including 400 metres are contested on a circular track each team should, if possible, have a separate lane and each lane must be

the full distance.

(5) Where the first section of a relay race is 200 metres or 400 metres, the first 400 metres section(s) should, if possible, be run in lanes with staggered starts. Alternatively, where the first section of a relay is 400 metres, lanes shall cease to operate at the beginning of the back straight on either the first or second lap.

(6) In events where the first lap only is run in lanes, competitors after leaving the take-over zone are free to take up any position on the track.

(7) In sprint relay races up and down a track the take-over is by touch, contact being made within a clearly defined area of 1m beyond, and at each end of, the relay distance.

(8) When a relay race is being run in lanes competitors may place one check mark on the track within their own lane but may not place, or cause to be placed, any marking object on or alongside the track. On a synthetic surface, chalk or similar substances which leave indelible marks must not be used.

(9) The baton must be carried in the hand throughout the race. If dropped, it must be recovered by the athlete who dropped it, who may leave the lane in order to retrieve the baton. Provided this procedure is adopted, no other athlete is impeded, and by so doing the distance of the race is not lessened, dropping the baton shall not result in disqualification.

(10) The baton must be passed only within the take-over zone. The passing of the baton commences when it is first touched by the receiving runner and is completed the moment it is in the hands of the receiving runner only. Within the take-over zone it is only the position of the baton which is decisive, and not the position of the body or limbs of the competitors. Passing of the baton outside the take-over zone will result in disqualification.

(11) Competitors after handing-over the baton should

remain in their lanes or zone until the course is clear to avoid obstruction to other competitors. Should any competitor wilfully impede a member of another team by running out of position or lane at the finish of a stage that competitor is liable to cause the disqualification of his or her own team.

(12) Assistance by pushing-off or by any other methods will cause disqualification.

(13) On completion of the final leg the baton is to be handed to an official by the last runner. It is not to be dropped or thrown from the hand. Failure to comply with this instruction may lead to disqualification.

(14) Once a relay team has started in a competition only two additional athletes may be used as substitutes in the composition of that team for any subsequent round.

(15) No competitor may run two sections for a team.

(16) The relay baton shall be a smooth hollow tube circular in section made of any rigid material in one piece, the length of which shall not be more than 30cm or less than 28cm. The circumference shall be 12-13cm and the weight shall not be less than 50 grammes. In relay races for Under 13's batons of smaller dimensions may be used.

**TIMING AND PHOTO-FINISH**

(1) Two methods of timekeeping shall be recognised as official:

(a) Hand timing

(b) Fully automatic timing obtained from a photo-finish system.

(2) The time shall be taken from the flash/smoke of the gun or approved starting apparatus (hand timing), or the impulse from the gun or approved starting apparatus (photo-finish) to the moment at which any part of the body of the competitor (i.e., torso, as distinguished

from the head, neck, arms, legs, hands or feet) reaches the perpendicular plane of the nearer edge of the finish line.

**Hand Timing**

(3) The Timekeepers shall be in line with the finish and outside the track. Wherever possible, they should be placed at least 5metres from the outside lane of the track. In order that they may all have a good view of the finish line, an elevated stand should be provided.

(4) Timekeepers shall use either stopwatches or manually operated electronic timers with digital readouts. All such timing devices are termed "watches" for the purpose of these Rules.

(5) Times for all finishers should be recorded. In addition, whenever possible, lap times in races of 800m and over, and times at every 1000m in races of 3000m and over, should be recorded by designated members of the Timekeeping team. Such information is essential in the case of a National record claim.

(6) For all hand-timed races on the track, times shall be read to the next longer 1/10th of a second. The times for races held partly or entirely outside the stadium shall be converted to the next longer full second, e.g., for the marathon 2: 09: 44.3s shall be returned as 2: 09: 45. If the hand of the watch stops between two lines indicating the time, the longer time shall be accepted. If a1/100ths of a second watch, or an electronic manually operated digital timer, is used, all times not ending in zero in the second decimal shall be rounded to the next longer 1/10th of a second, e.g. 10.11s shall be read as 10.2s.

(7) Unless satisfied that a mistake has been made the Chief Timekeeper shall declare the time in accordance with the following conditions:

(a) If two of the three Timekeepers agree and the third disagrees, the time recorded by the two shall be the official time.

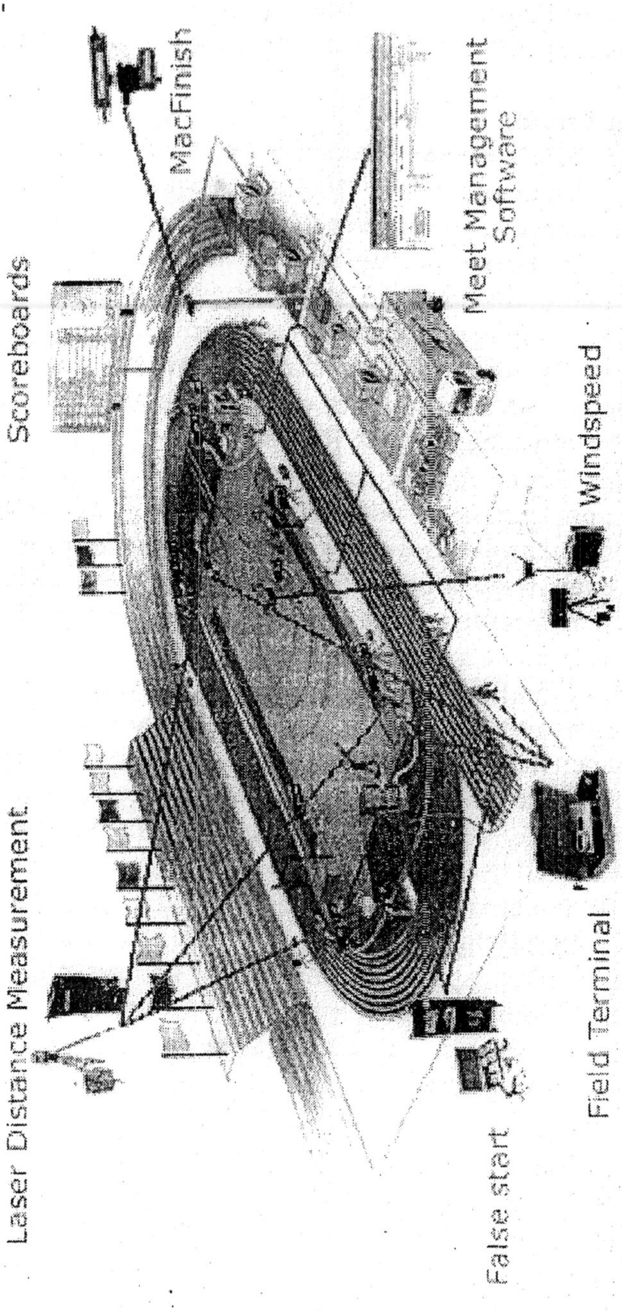
Laser Distance Measurement
Scoreboards
MacFinish
Meet Management
Software
Windspeed
Field Terminal
False start

(b) If all three Timekeepers disagree the middle time shall be official.

(c) Should only two times be available and they differ, the longer time shall be official.

(9) In the event of a National record claim the time should be taken by three Graded Timekeepers, each of whom should be Level 5 or 4. They must show their timings to the Chief Timekeeper and certify these times on the appropriate Record Application form.

**Photo-Finish Camera**

(d) The Chief Photo-finish Judge shall consider, where necessary, the actual time recorded in 1/1000ths of a second by a competitor in deciding qualifiers by time.

(25) A timing device which operates automatically at either the start or the finish but not at both, shall be considered to produce neither hand nor fully automatic times and shall not therefore be used to obtain official times.

(26) In the event of a National record claim the Chief Photo-finish Judge shall sign the Record Application form and attach a copy of the photo-finish image. Where such an image is available, no details of the manually recorded backup times are required to be entered on the form.

## FIELD EVENTS

### GENERAL CONDITIONS

#### Draws, Trials and Qualifying Rounds

(1) A draw shall be made to decide the order in which competitors shall take their trials and this order should be printed in the programme. The Judges shall have the power to alter this order. Competitors cannot hold over any of their trials to a subsequent round, except in the High Jump and Pole Vault.

(2) If competitors are entered in both a track event

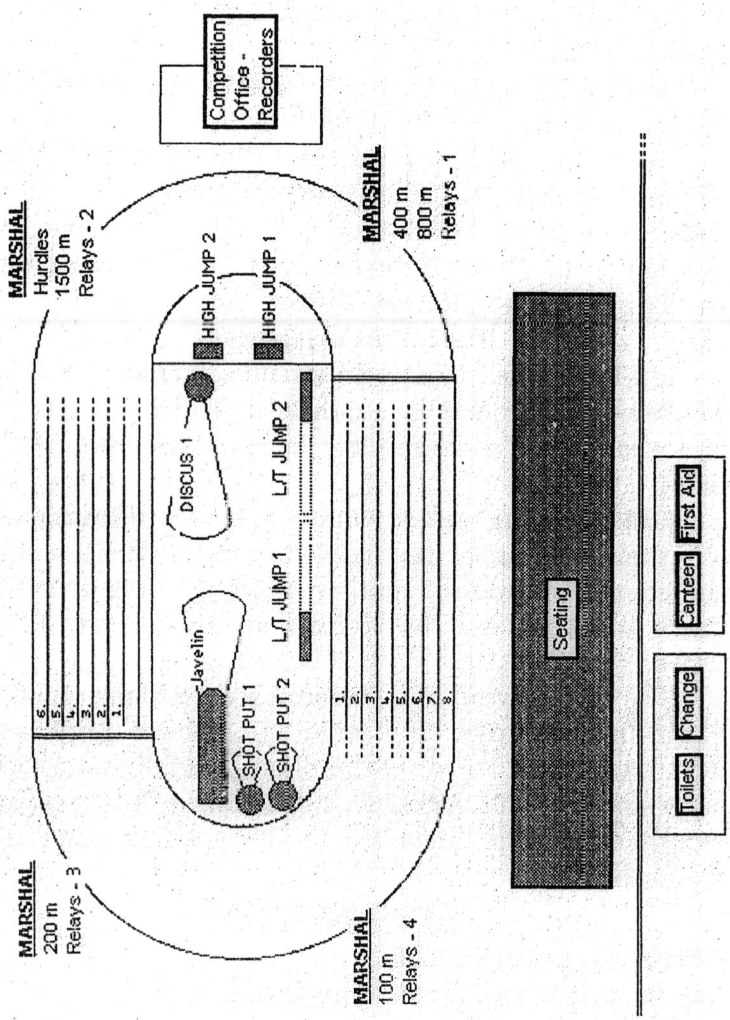


and a field event or in more than one field event taking place simultaneously, the Judges may allow them to take their trials in an order different from that decided upon prior to the start of the competition.

(3) In throwing or jumping for distance no competitor is allowed to have more than one trial recorded in any one round of the competition.

(4) Competitors who unreasonably delay making a trial in a field event render themselves liable to having that trial disallowed and recorded as a fault.

(5) It is a matter for the Referee to decide, having regard to all the circumstances, what is an unreasonable delay. The following times should not normally be exceeded:

| Number of athletes left in the competition | High Jump | Pole Vault | Other Events |
|---|---|---|---|
| More than 3 | 1 min | 1 min | 1 min |
| 3 or fewer | 1.5 min | 2 min | 1 min |
| Consecutive trials by the same athlete | 2 min | 3 min | 2 min |

In the Pole Vault the time shall begin when the uprights have been adjusted to the previously notified wishes of the competitor.

If the time allowed as indicated above elapses after the competitor has started a trial, that trial shall not for that reason be disallowed.

(6) If in the opinion of the Referee the conditions warrant it, that official shall have power to change the place of the competition in any field event.

Such a change should be made only after around is completed.

(7) If for any reason a competitor is hampered in a trial in a field event, the Referee shall have power to award a substitute trial.

(8) Where in any of the field events the Organisers or the Referee consider it advantageous a qualifying round shall be held prior to the competition proper.

(a) All competitors who reach the prescribed standard in the qualifying round or pool shall compete in the competition proper. If less than the prescribed number of competitors reach the qualifying standard then the leading athletes up to that prescribed number shall take part in the competition proper; where necessary Rules applied in Vertical Jumps (High Jump and Pole Vault) (7), Rules applied in Horizontal Jumps (Long Jump and Triple Jump) (3) or Rules applied in Throwing Events shall be used to decide the qualifiers. If a tie for the final place in the competition remains after these Rules have been applied, all those competitors so tying shall be included in the competition proper.

(b) In each qualifying round each competitor shall be allowed three trials (High Jump and Pole Vault excepted) but the performance accomplished shall not be considered part of the competition proper. Once competitors have reached the qualifying standard they shall not take any more trials.

(9) If qualifying rounds or pools are held the order for taking trials in the competition proper shall be determined by afresh draw.

(10) In any athletics meeting competitors shall be excluded from participating in further events, including relays, when they have qualified in preliminary rounds (including qualifying rounds or pools in field events) or heats for further participation in any event but then do not compete further without giving a valid reason to the Referee. If a meeting extends over more than one day the exclusion shall apply to all subsequent events of the meeting.

(11) Once a competition has begun competitors are not permitted to use runways or take-off areas for practice or warm up purposes nor are they permitted to use throwing sites for practice trials, with or without implements.

**VERTICAL JUMPS**

**(High Jump and Pole Vault)**

**General Conditions**

(1) Unless such details are specified in the programme, the Judge shall decide the height at which the competition shall start, and the different heights to

which the bar will be raised at the end of each round. The competitors shall be informed of the details before the competition begins.

(2) Competitors may commence jumping/vaulting at any of the heights above the minimum height and may jump/vault at their own discretion at any subsequent height. Three consecutive failures, regardless of the height at which any such failure occurs, disqualify from further participation, except in the case of a jump-off of a first place tie.

(3) Even after all the other competitors have failed, a competitor is entitled to continue until he or she has forfeited the right to compete further, and the best jump/ vault shall be recorded as the winning height.

(4) After the competitor has won the competition the height or heights to which the bar is raised shall be decided after the Judge or Referee in charge of the event has consulted the wishes of the competitor.

(5) All measurements shall be made perpendicularly from the ground to the upper side of the cross-bar where it is lowest. A steel or fibre glass tape should be used. Alternatively a scientific apparatus which has a certificate of accuracy from a nationally recognised standardising organisation may be used. Any measurement of a new height shall be made before competitors attempt that height. In the case of a record claim the officials must check the measurement after the height has been cleared.

(6) (a) The height shall be recorded to the nearest 1cm below the height measured if that distance is not a whole centimetre.

(b) Unless there is only one competitor remaining the bar shall not be raised by less than 2cm in the High Jump or 5cm in the Pole Vault after each round and the increments by which the bar is raised after each round should never increase.

(7) **Ties**

Ties shall be decided as follows:

(a) The competitor with the lowest number of jumps/ vaults at the height at which the tie occurs shall be awarded the higher place.

(b) If the tie still remains, the competitor with the lowest total of failures throughout the competition up to and including the height last cleared shall be awarded the higher place.

(c) if the tie still remains:

(i) if it concerns first place, the competitors tying shall have one more jump/vault at the lowest height at which any of those involved in the tie lost their right to continue jumping/vaulting and, if no decision is reached, the bar shall be raised if the tying athletes were successful or lowered if not, 2cm for the High Jump and 5cm for the Pole Vault. They shall then attempt one jump/vault at each height until one competitor clears a height and the remaining competitor(s) fail at the same height. Competitors so tying must jump/vault on each occasion when resolving the tie.

(ii) if it concerns any other place, the competitors shall be awarded the same place in the competition.

**HIGH JUMP**

(1) Rules recommended for Field Events (General Conditions) and that for Vertical Jumps (High Jump and Pole Vault) apply.

(2) The uprights or posts shall not be moved during the competition unless the Referee considers the take-off or landing area has become unsuitable. Such a change shall be made only after around has been completed.

(3) Competitors may place no more than two marks to assist them in their run-ups and take-off. Where the competition takes place on a synthetic surface, chalk

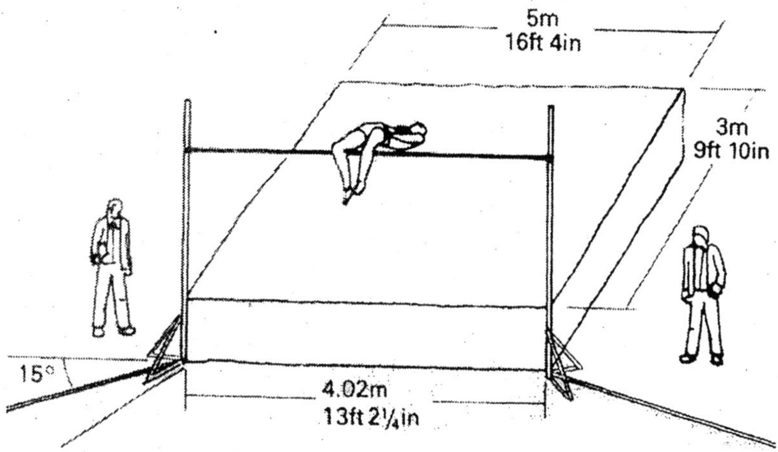


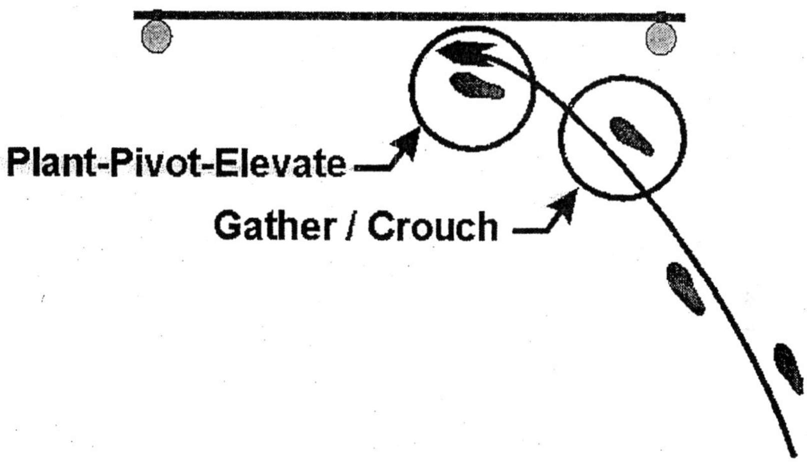


or similar substances which leave indelible marks must not be used.

(4) The distance of the run-up is unlimited.

(5 It shall be recorded as a failure if:

(a) a competitor takes off from both feet; or

(b) after the jump the bar does not remain on the pegs because of the action of the competitor whilst jumping; or

(c) the competitor touches the ground, including the

landing area, beyond the plane of the nearer edge of the uprights either between or outside the uprights with any part of the body, without first clearing the bar. However, if when jumping, a competitor touches the landing area with afoot and in the opinion of the Judge no advantage is gained, the attempt shall not, for that reason, be considered a failure.

**HIGH JUMP SPECIFICATIONS**

(1) Any style or kind of uprights or posts may be used provided they are rigid. Uprights should be sufficiently tall so as to exceed the respective height to which the cross-bar is raised by a least 10cm.

(2) The distance between the uprights should not be less than 4.0m or more than 4.04m.

(3) The cross-bar shall be of fibre glass or other suitable material.

(a) It shall be of uniform thickness and shall be circular in cross section except for the end pieces. The diameter of the circular part of the cross-bar shall be at least 29mm but not more than 31mm.

(b) The front of the cross-bar should be painted. The length of the crossbar should be not less than 3.98m and not more than 4.02m.

(c) The maximum weight of the cross-bar shall be 2kg.

(d) The end pieces shall be each 30-35mm wide and 15-20cm long for the purpose of resting on the supports of the uprights.

(e) These end pieces shall be circular, or semi circular with one clearly defined flat surface on which the bar rests on the cross-bar supports.

This flat surface may not be higher than the centre of the vertical cross section of the cross-bar. They shall be hard and smooth. They may not be covered by any material which has the effect of increasing the friction between them and the supports.

(4) Each peg supporting the cross-bar shall be flat and rectangular, 4cm wide and extending 6cm from the uprights in the direction of the opposite upright. The supports must be firmly fixed to the uprights and be without any kind of spring. The supports may not be covered with rubber or with any other material which has the effect of increasing the friction between the surface of the cross-bar and the supports. The ends of the cross-bar shall rest on the pegs in such a manner that it easily falls to the ground, either forwards or backwards, if touched by the competitor.

There shall be a space of at least 1cm between the ends of the cross-bar and the uprights.

(5) The ground round the take-off should be level but a maximum inclination of 1:250 in the last 15m of the runway is permitted in the case of a synthetic take-off area.

***Note:*** The landing area should be placed so the athlete's approach is up any inclination.

(6) The minimum length of the runway shall be 15m but 25m is desirable if conditions permit.

(7) The landing area should measure at least 5m long (that is at the take off side) by 3m wide. The minimum depth of the landing area shall be 60cm.

***Note:*** The uprights and landing areas shall be so designed that there is a clearance of at least 10cm between them when in use to avoid displacement of the cross-bar through movement of the landing area causing contact with the uprights.

**POLE VAULT**

(1) Rules recommended for Field Events (General Conditions) and that for Vertical Jumps (High Jump and Pole Vault) apply.

(2) No marks may be placed on the runways, but a competitor may place marks alongside the runway.

(3) The distance of the run-up is unlimited.

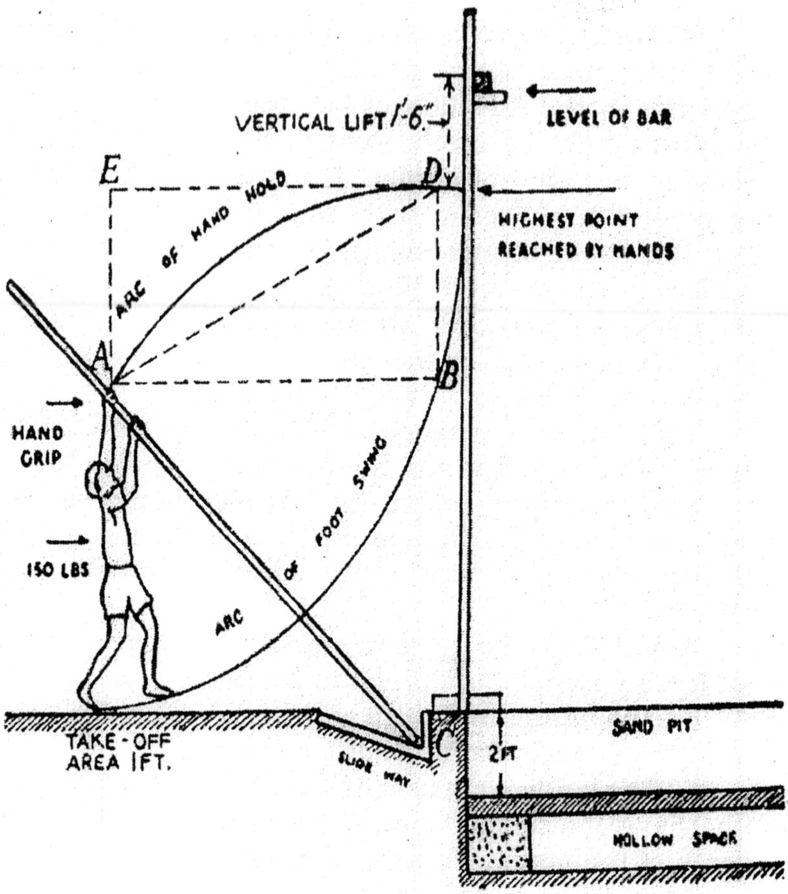


(4) Competitors may have the cross-bar moved in the direction of the landing area so that the edge of the cross-bar nearest the athlete can be positioned at any point from that directly above the inside back of the box to a point 80cms in the direction of the landing area.

***Note:*** A white line 1cm wide may be drawn at right angles to the axis of the runway at the level of the inside edge of the top of the box. This line should be prolonged as far as the outside edge of the uprights.

(5) The take-off for the pole vault shall be from a

wooden or metal box. Competitors are permitted to place sand in the box when it is their turn to vault.

(6) It shall be recorded as a failure if:

(a) after the vault the bar does not remain on the pegs because of the action of the competitor whilst vaulting; or

(b) the competitor touches the ground, including the landing area beyond the vertical plane of the upper part of the box, with any part of the body or with the pole, without first clearing the bar; or

(c) the competitor, at the moment of making a vault, or after leaving the ground, places the lower hand above the upper one, or moves the upper hand higher up on the pole; or

(d) during the vault the competitor steadies or replaces the bar with a hand(s).

(7) No one should touch the pole unless it is falling away from the bar or uprights; if it is so touched and the Referee or Judge is of the opinion it would have dislodged the bar so that it fell from the pegs the vault shall be recorded as a failure.

(8) Competitors may use their own poles. No competitor shall use another's pole except with the consent of the owner.

(9) The pole may be of any material or combination of materials and any length or diameter, but the basic surface must be smooth. At the grip and at the bottom end, the pole may have protective layers of tape.

(10) The use of tape on the hands or fingers shall not be allowed except in the case of need to cover an open cut. The use of a forearm cover to prevent injury shall be allowed. Competitors are permitted to use an adhesive substance on their hands or on the pole, in order to obtain a better grip.

**POLE VAULT SPECIFICATIONS**

(1) Any style or kind of uprights or posts may be used

provided they are rigid. Where necessary, an adaptor, which is rigidly fixed and allows the bar to be set to heights below the normal limits of that upright or post, may be used.

(2) The distance between the uprights, or between extension arms where such are used, should be not less than 4.30m or more than 4.37m wide.

(3) The cross-bar shall be made of fibre glass or other suitable material.

(a) It shall be of uniform thickness and shall be circular in cross section except for the end pieces. The diameter of the circular part of the cross-bar shall be at least 29mm but not more than 31mm.

(b) The front of the cross-bar should be painted. The length of the crossbar should be not less than 4.48m and not more than 4.52m.

(c) The maximum weight of the cross-bar shall be 2.25kg.

(d) The end pieces shall be each 30-35mm wide and 15-20cm long for the purpose of resting on the supports of the uprights.

(e) These end pieces shall be circular, or semi circular with one clearly defined flat surface on which the bar rests on the cross-bar supports. This flat surface may not be higher than the centre of the vertical cross section of the cross-bar. They shall be hard and smooth. They may not be covered by any material which has the effect of increasing the friction between them and the supports.

(4) The pegs supporting the cross-bar shall extend horizontally not more than 5.5cm from the face of the uprights on the side further from the runway and must be without notches or indentations of any kind. The pegs must be of uniform thickness throughout and not more than 13mm in diameter. The pegs may not be covered

with any material which has the effect of increasing the friction with the ends of the bar.

(5) As an alternative to (4) above, the pegs supporting the cross-bar may be placed upon extension arms permanently fixed to the uprights thus allowing the uprights to be placed wider apart without increasing the length of the cross-bar.

6) The box in which to plant the pole may be of wood or metal sunk level with the runway and shall be 1metre in length, measured along the inside of the bottom of the box, 60cm in width at the front end tapering to 15cm in width at the bottom of the stopboard, where it shall be 20cm in depth. The box should be constructed in such a manner that the sides slope outwards and end next to the stopboard at an angle of approximately 120 degrees to the base. If the box is constructed of wood, the bottom shall be lined with 2.5mm sheet metal for a distance of 80cm from the front of the box.

(7) The runway should be level and its minimum length should be 40m but 45m is desirable if conditions permit. For record purposes the maximum lateral inclination of the runway must not exceed 1:100 and in the last 40m of the runway the overall downward inclination in the direction of running shall not exceed 1:1000. The minimum width of the runway shall be 1.22m and the maximum shall be 1.25m.

(8) The landing area shall measure not less than 5m×5m, excluding the two protection pads on either side of the box. This measurement does not include the sloping area behind the box. The sides of the landing area nearest to the box shall be placed 10cm to 15cm from the box and shall slope away from the box at an angle of approximately 45 degrees. (A 30 degree angle is acceptable on landing areas in use before 1st April 2006). The protective extensions to the landing bed shall be at least 2m in length.

The entire landing area shall be covered by a wear sheet, approximately 50mm deep. The minimum depth of the landing area shall be 80cm.

**HORIZONTAL JUMPS**
**(LONG JUMP AND TRIPLE JUMP)**
**General Conditions**

(1) The competition may be decided in either of the following ways:

(a) Each competitor being allowed from three to six trials; or

(b) Each competitor being allowed three trials and the three to eight best being allowed three more trials. In the event of a tie for the final place(s), any competitor so tying shall be allowed the three additional trials.

To qualify for these further trials the athlete must have achieved a valid performance. The competition conditions must be explained to the competitors before the event begins.

(2) Competitors shall be credited with the best of all their trials, including jumps taken in resolving a first place tie.

(3) In the case of a tie, the second best performance of the competitors tying shall determine the result. If the tie remains, the third best jump will be decisive and so on. If the tie still remains and it concerns first place, the competitors so tying shall have such additional extra trials as are required to resolve the tie. If the tie concerns any other place, the competitors shall be awarded the same place in the competition.

(4) The take-off shall be from aboard the edge of which nearer to the landing area shall be called the 'take-off line'. If a competitor takes off before reaching the board, it shall not for that reason be counted as a failure.

(5) The minimum length of the runway should be at least 40 metres measured from the end of the runway to the relevant take-off line.

(6) No marks shall be placed on the runway, but a competitor may place marks alongside the runway. No competitor may place, or cause to be placed, any mark beyond the 'take-off line'.

(7) It shall be counted as a failure if any competitor:

(a) while taking off touches the ground beyond the take-off line or takeoff line extended with any part of the body, whether running up without jumping or in the act of jumping.

(b) takes off from outside either end of the board, whether beyond or behind the take-off line extended.

(c) in the course of landing, touches the ground outside the landing area nearer to the take-off line than the break in the sand to which the measurement of the jump would have been made.

(d) before leaving the landing area after a completed jump, walks back through the landing area.

(8) The measurement of the jump shall be made at right angles from the nearest break in the sand in the landing area made by any part of the body of the competitor to the take-off line. Only valid trials shall be measured.

(9) The distance shall be recorded to the nearest 1cm below the distance measured if that distance is not a whole centimetre.

(10) If calibrated measuring equipment is used its accuracy must be checked with a steel tape; otherwise steel or fibre glass tape should be used and the part of the tape showing the distance jumped must be held at the take-off line. Alternatively a scientific apparatus, which has a certificate of accuracy from a nationally recognised standardising organisation may be used.

(11) Whenever possible wind velocity should be measured and recorded.

(a) The gauge should be set up at 20m from the take-off line, not more than 2m from, and parallel to the edge of the runway and at a height of approximately 1.22m. Where a tubular wind gauge is used the length on either side of the measuring device should be at least twice the diameter of the tube.

(b) The velocity shall be measured for a period of 5 seconds from the time a competitor passes a mark placed 40m (Long Jump) or 35m (Triple Jump) from the take-off line. If a competitor runs less than 40m or 35m as the case may be, the reading shall be taken from the time the athlete commences the run.

**General Specifications**

(1) A take-off board shall be rigidly fixed in the ground, flush therewith. It shall be made of wood 1.21-1.23m long, 19.8-20.2cm wide and maximum 10cm deep, and painted white.

(2) The runway should be level and at least 40m in length.

(3) The minimum width of the runway shall be 1.22m and the maximum shall be 1.25m.

(4) For record purposes the maximum lateral inclination of the runway shall be 1:100 and in the last 40m of the runway the overall downward inclination in the direction of tunning shall not exceed 1:1000.

(5) In order that jumps can be measured accurately the sand in the landing area should be moistened before the competition.

(6) The surface of the sand in the landing area should be level with the top of the take-off board.

(7) Immediately beyond the take-off line there shall be placed a rigid board of plasticine or other suitable material for recording the athlete's footprint in the case of a foot fault. The specifications for the plasticine indicator board are as follows:

(a) the board shall be rigid, 98-102mm wide and 1.21-1.22m long. At least the 10mm closest to the take-off board shall be covered with plasticine or other suitable material on the top surface.

(b) the surface shall rise from the level of the take-off board at an angle of 45° in the direction of running to a maximum height above the take-off board of 7mm.

(c) The board shall be mounted in a recess or shelf in the runway, on the side of the take-off board nearer the landing area. When mounted in this recess, the whole assembly must be sufficiently rigid to accept the full force of the athlete's foot.

(d) The edges shall either slant at an angle of 45° with the edge nearer to the runway covered with a plasticine layer along its length 1mm thick (see Diagram 1) or shall be cut away such that the recess, when filled with plasticine shall slant at an angle of 45°.

(e) The surface of the board beneath the plasticine shall be of a material in which the spikes of an athlete's shoe will grip and not skid.

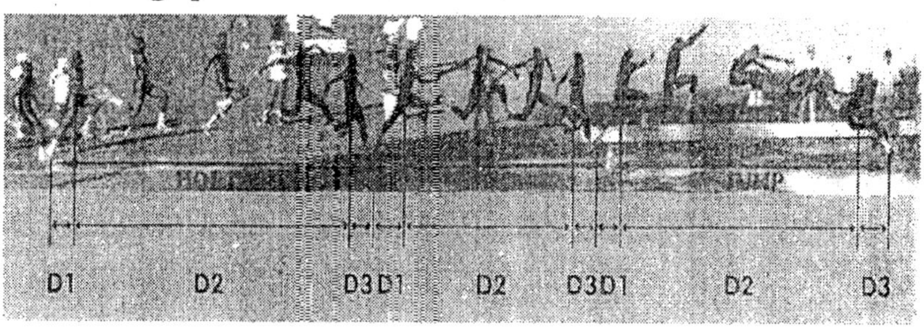


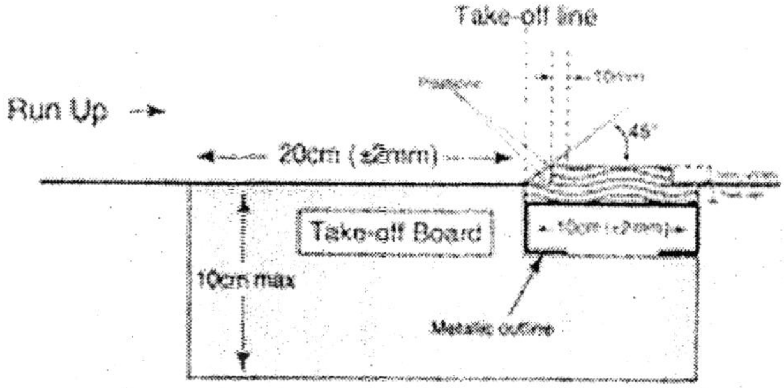

(f) The upper part of the indicator board shall also be covered for the first 10mm approximately and along its entire length by a plasticine layer.

(8) If it is not possible to install an indicator board as identified in (7) soft earth or damp sand should be sprinkled to a height of 7mm above the level of the take-off board over a width of 10cm beyond the edge of the take-off line. At the take-off line the sand or earth should be raised at an angle of 45° to the height of 7mm.

(9) The landing area should have a minimum width of 2.75m, a maximum width of 3m, and be at least 9m long. It should, if possible, be so placed that the middle of the runway, if extended, would coincide with the middle of the landing area.

**LONG JUMP**

(1) Rules recommended for Field Events (General Conditions) Horizontal Jumps (Long Jump and Triple Jump); and their General Specifications may apply.

(2) A space of at least 1m but no more than 3m, of a similar surface to the runway, should be left between the take-off board and the landing area.

(3) The distance between the take-off board and the end of the landing area should be at least 10m.

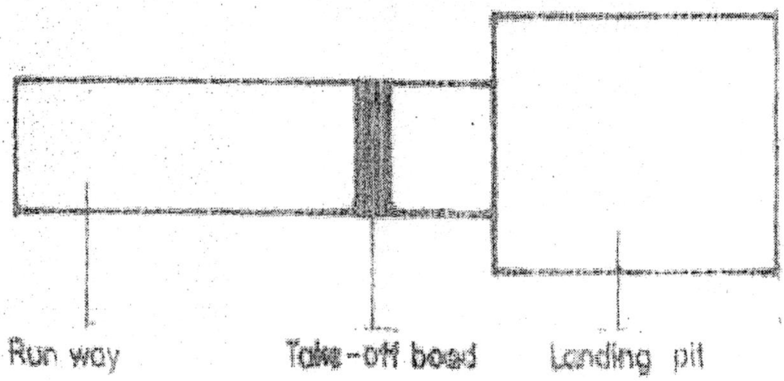

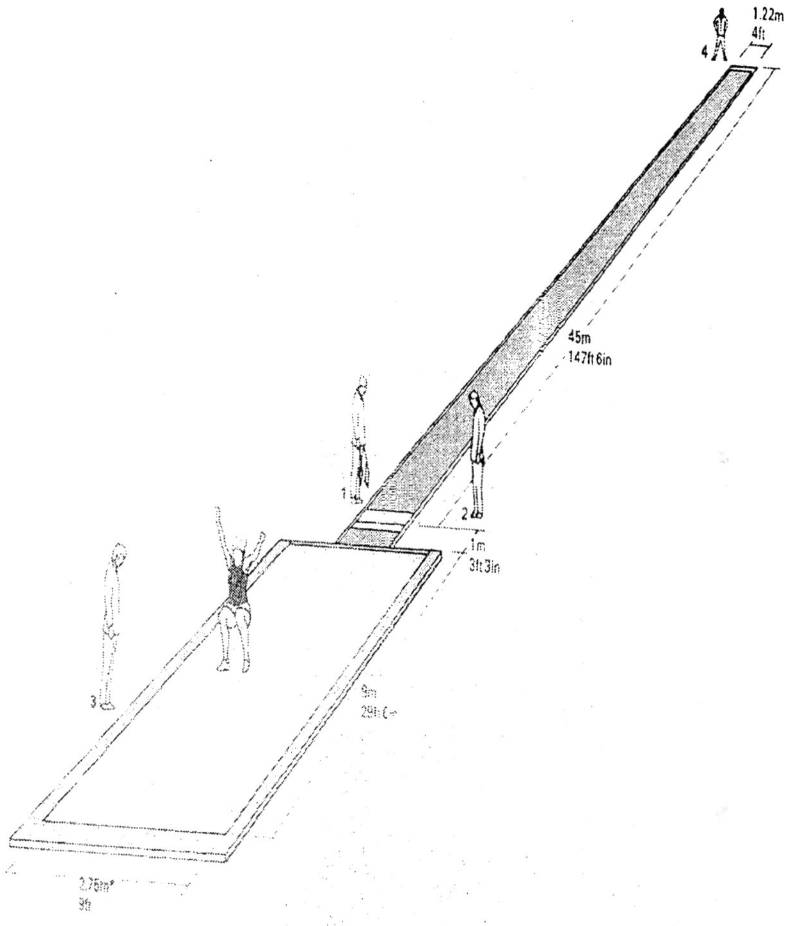


**TRIPLE JUMP**

(1) Rules recommended for Field Events (General Conditions) Horizontal Jumps (Long Jump and Triple Jump); and their General Specifications may apply.

***Note:*** Rule recommended for Horizontal Jumps (Long Jump and Triple Jump) (7(c)) does not apply to the normal landings from the hop and step phases.

(2) The hop shall be made so that competitors shall first land upon the same foot with which they shall have

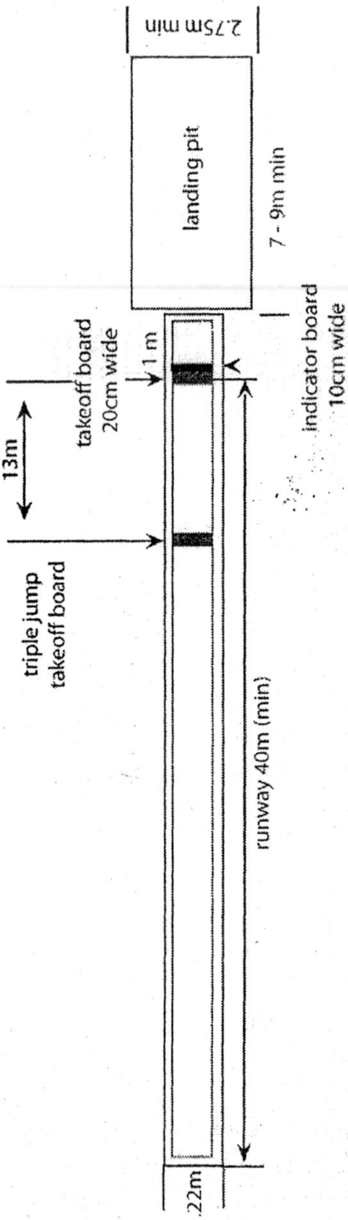


taken off, in the step they shall land on the other foot, from which subsequently the jump is performed. It shall not be considered a failure if competitors, during the step phase, touch the ground with the "sleeping" leg.

(3) The ground between the take-off board and the landing area must be level.

(4) The distance between the take-off boards and the leading edge of the landing area should normally be 13m, 11m, 9m and 7m. Where such a board has not been set into the runway and is required a white area of similar dimensions to those in Horizontal Jumps (Long Jump, Triple Jump, (General Specifications) should be drawn. It must be appreciated that suitable distances will vary according to the standard of the competition.

(5) Under 13 athletes are not permitted to compete in Triple Jump events.

**THROWING EVENTS**

**General Conditions**

(1) The competition may be decided in either of the following ways:

(a) Each competitor being

allowed from three to six trials; or

(b) Each competitor being allowed three trials and the three to eight best competitors being allowed three more trials. In the event of a tie for the final place(s), any competitor so tying shall be allowed the three additional trials. (Tying means in this connection achieving the same distance and Rule recommended for Throwing Events (General Specifications) # 3 should not, therefore, be applied.). To qualify for these further trials the athlete must have achieved a valid performance. The competition conditions must be explained to the competitors before the event begins.

(2) Competitors shall be credited with the best of all their trials, including throws taken in resolving a first place tie. Only valid trials shall be measured.

(3) In the case of a tie, the second best performance of the competitors tying shall determine the result. If the tie remains, the third best throw will be decisive and so on. If the tie remains and it concerns first place, the competitors so tying shall have such additional extra trials as are required to resolve the tie. If the tie concerns any other place, the competitors shall be awarded the same place in the competition.

(4) No competitor may place, or cause to be placed, any mark within the throwing sector.

(5) Competitors may use any implements provided for general use. Subject to any regulations laid down by the Promoting Body, competitors who wish to use their own implements must submit them to the Referee for approval. An athlete shall not use another's implement without the owner's prior permission.

(6) No device of any kind (e.g. the taping of the fingers) which in any way assists a competitor when making a throw shall be allowed, except in throwing the Hammer where the taping of individual fingers is permitted.

***Note:*** The use of tape to cover injuries to the hand

will be allowed only if the Referee is satisfied on medical or other evidence that the tape is necessary. The use of tape on the wrist will be allowed.

(7) In order to obtain a better grip, competitors are permitted to use an adhesive substance on their hands only except in the Hammer.

(8) In order to protect the spine from injury a competitor may wear a belt of leather or some other suitable material.

(9) When markers are used to indicate the best throw of each competitor and to show record distances they shall be placed on a line or tape outside the sector lines.

(10) The throw shall be recorded to the nearest 1cm below the distance measured if that distance is not a whole centimetre.

**Measuring Sectors for Throwing Events from a Circle**

**PUTTING THE SHOT**

(1) Rules recommended for Field Events (General Conditions) and Throwing Events (General Conditions) may apply.

(2) In order to avoid accidents the central throwing area must be roped off as a unit at a height of approximately 1 metre. Alternatively, shot throwing sectors must be roped off at a height of approximately 1 metre and at a minimum distance of 2 metres outside the shot sector lines.

(3) Competitors must be given instructions that implements must be thrown during practice only from the circle. Implements must be returned by hand during practice or competition and must not be thrown back to the starting area. The Referee or other appropriate official shall disqualify from competing in the event any athletes who wilfully disobey the above instructions after having their attention drawn to them.

(4) No practice trials shall be allowed after a competition has begun.

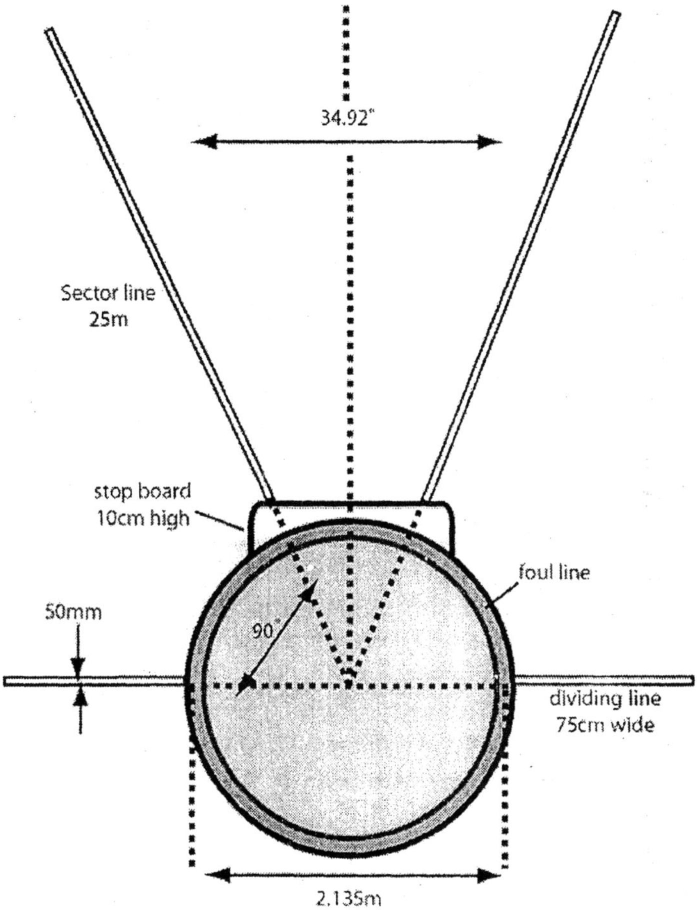


(5) Gloves may not be worn. In order to protect the wrist from injury, a competitor may wear a bandage at the wrist.

(6) Competitors must not spray or spread any substance on the surface of a throwing circle nor on their shoes or roughen the surface of the circle.

(7) Competitors must commence the throw from a stationary position within the circle; they may adopt any position they choose.

(8) It shall be a foul throw if the competitor, after

stepping into the circle and starting to make the throw, touches with any part of the body, the ground outside the circle, the top of the stop-board or the top of the circle rim. A competitor is allowed to touch the inside of the iron band or stop-board.

(9) The competitor must not leave the circle until the shot has touched the ground. When leaving the circle the first contact with the top of the circle rim or the ground outside the circle must be completely behind the white line which is drawn outside the circle, the rear edge of which runs theoretically through the centre of the circle.

(10) Provided that in the course of a trial the foregoing Rules have not been infringed, a competitor may interrupt a trial once started, may lay the implement down, may leave the circle, before returning to a stationary position and beginning afresh start.

(11) The shot shall be put from the shoulder with one hand only. At the time the competitor takes a stance in the ring to commence a put, the shot shall touch or be in close contact with the neck or chin and the hand shall not be dropped below this position during the act of putting. The shot must not be brought behind the line of the shoulders.

(12) In making a put the competitors may rest their feet against but not on top of the stop-board.

(13) A foul throw or letting go of the shot in an attempt shall be reckoned as a trial.

(14) For a valid put the shot must fall completely within the inner edges of the lines marking the sector set out on the ground so that the radii cross at the centre of the circle.

(15) All measurements must be made from the nearest edge of the first mark made in the ground by the shot to the inner edge of the circle rim along a line drawn from the mark to the centre of the circle.

(16) All measurements should be made immediately after each put. A steel or fibre glass tape should be used for measurement, and that part of the tape showing the distance put must be held by the official at the circle. Alternatively, approved datum measurement equipment may be used, as may a scientific apparatus which has a certificate of accuracy from a nationally recognised standardising organisation.

(17) The throw shall be recorded to the nearest 1cm below the distance measured if that distance is not a whole centimetre.

**Putting the Shot Specifications**

(1) The circle shall be measured from the inside. The surface should be of concrete, asphalt or some other firm but not slippery material. The surface should be lightly stippled when being laid to give a rough but not ribbed surface.

(2) The surface of the inside of the circle should be level and 20mm•6mm lower than the upper edge of the ring which should be level with the ground outside.

(3) Circle Rings:

Construction— The rim shall be made of band iron, steel, or other suitable material and be painted white.

Measurements—(Metal) — The inside diameter of the circle shall measure 2.135m maximum, and the rim of the circle shall be at least 6mm thick.

(Wood) — The inside diameter of the circle shall measure 2.135m maximum, and the rim of the circle shall be 7.5mm thick. A tolerance of ±5mm is permitted for the inside diameter of a circle.

(4) A white line 5cm wide shall be drawn from the top of the circle, extending for at least 75cm on either side of the circle, the theoretical extension of this line across the circle dividing it into front and rear halves with the rear edge passing through the centre of the circle.

(5) A portable circle meeting with the specifications above is permissible.

(6) A curved stop-board painted white, 1.21-1.23m long on the inside, 11.2-11.4cm wide and 9.8-10.2cm high in relation to the level of the inside of the circle shall be fixed in the middle of the circumference of the front half of the circle. The board shall curve so that the inside edge coincides with the inner edge of the circle and shall be fixed firmly to the ground.

(7) The shot shall be of solid iron, brass or any metal not softer than brass, or a shell of such metal filled with lead or some other material.

**THROWING THE HAMMER**

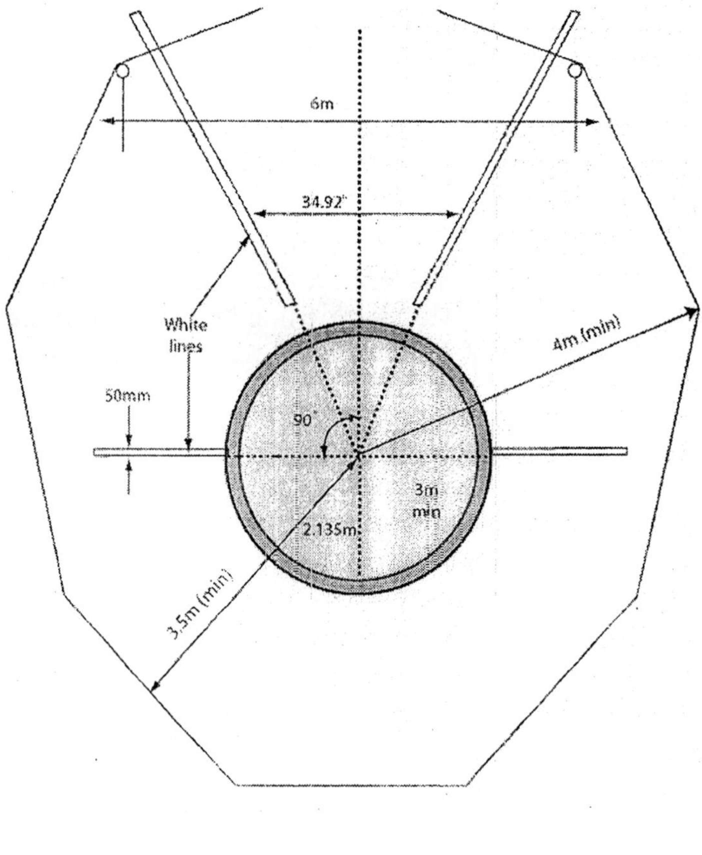

(1) Rules recommended for Field Events (General Conditions) and Throwing Events (General Conditions) may apply.

(2) In order to avoid accidents, the central throwing area must be roped off as a unit at a height of approximately 1 metre. Alternatively, Hammer Throwing Sectors must be roped off at a height of approximately 1 metre and to make a 60° sector inside which the hammer sector is centrally placed.

For safety reasons all throws should be preceded by a warning which should be acknowledged by the event officials before the throw commences.

(3) Competitors must be given instructions that implements must be thrown during practice only from the circle. Implements must be returned by hand during practice or competition and must not be thrown back to the starting area. The Referee or other appropriate official shall disqualify from competing in the event any athlete who wilfully disobeys the above instructions after having his/her attention drawn to them.

(4) No practice trials shall be allowed after a competition has begun.

(5) All throws shall be made from a cage.

(6) Gloves may be worn. The gloves must be smooth on back and front, and the tip of the fingers, other than the thumb, must be exposed.

(7) Competitors must not spray or spread any substance on the surface of a throwing circle nor on their shoes or roughen the surface of the circle. In order to obtain a better grip competitors are permitted to use a suitable substance on their hands or gloves only.

(8) Competitors must commence the throw from a stationary position within the circle; they may adopt any position they choose.

(9) It shall be a foul throw if the competitor, after stepping into the circle and starting to make the throw,

touches with any part of the body the ground outside the circle, or the top of the circle rim. A competitor is allowed to touch the inside of the iron band.

(10) The competitor must not leave the circle until the hammer has touched the ground. When leaving the circle the first contact with the top of the circle rim or the ground outside the circle must be completely behind the white line which is drawn outside the circle, the rear edge of which runs theoretically through the centre of the circle.

(11) The competitor in the starting position prior to the preliminary swings or turns is allowed to put the head of the hammer on the ground inside or outside the circle.

(12) It shall not be considered a foul throw if the head of the hammer touches the ground, or the top of the iron band, when the competitor makes the preliminary swings or turns.

(13) Provided that in the course of the trial the foregoing Rules have not been infringed, a competitor may interrupt a trial once started, may lay the hammer down, may leave the circle before returning to a stationary position and beginning afresh trial.

(14) If the hammer breaks during a throw or while in the air, it shall not be counted as a throw, provided it was made in accordance with the Rules. If a competitor thereby loses balance and contravenes any part of this Rule, it shall not be counted as a foul throw and the athlete shall be awarded a new trial.

(15) A foul throw or letting go of the hammer in an attempt shall be reckoned as a trial.

(16) For a valid throw the hammer head must fall completely within the inner edges of the lines marking the sector set out on the ground so that the radii cross at the centre of the circle. The outer ends of the sector

should be marked with flags.

**THROWING THE HAMMER SPECIFICATIONS**

(1) The circle shall be measured from the inside. The surface should be of concrete, asphalt or some other firm but not slippery material. The surface should be lightly stippled when being laid to give a rough but not ribbed surface. The surface of the inside of the circle should be level and 20mm ± 5mm lower than the upper edge of the ring which should be level with the ground outside.

(2) Circle Rings

Construction — The rim shall be made of band iron, steel, or other suitable material and be painted white.

Measurements — (Metal) — The inside diameter of the circle shall measure 2.135m maximum, and the rim of the circle shall be at least 6mm thick.

(Wood) — The inside diameter of the circle shall measure 2.135m maximum, and the rim of the circle shall be 7.5mm thick.

A tolerance of ± 5mm is permitted for the inside diameter of the circle.

(3) A white line 5cm wide shall be drawn from the top of the circle, extending for at least 75cm on either side of the circle, the theoretical extension of this line across the circle dividing it into front and rear halves with the rear edge passing through the centre of the circle.

(4) A portable circle meeting with these specifications is permissible.

(5) The Hammer:

(i) Head—The head shall be of solid iron, brass or any metal not softer than brass or a shell of such metal filled with lead or other solid material. It must be spherical in shape. If a filling is used this must be inserted in such a manner that it is immovable and that the centre of gravity shall not be more than 6mm from the centre of the sphere.

(ii) Wire—The wire shall be a single unbroken and straight length of spring wire not less than 3mm or No.11 Standard Wire Gauge in diameter, or a 4mm diameter 6-stranded wire, the loops of which are prefixed under pressure with a crimping brush, and either shall be such that it cannot stretch appreciably when thrown. The wire may be looped at one or both ends, as a means of attachment.

(iii) The Handle—The handle may be either of single or double loop construction, but must be rigid and without hinging joints of any kind and so made that it cannot stretch appreciably while being thrown. It must be attached to the wire in such a manner that it cannot turn within the loop of the wire to increase the overall length of the hammer.

The handle may have a curved or straight grip with a maximum width inside of 130mm and a maximum length inside of 110mm.

(iv) Connections—The wire shall be connected to the head by means of a swivel, which may be either plain or ball-bearing. The handle shall be connected to the wire by means of a loop. A swivel may not be used.

(v) Construction—The hammer shall be so constructed that it cannot elongate appreciably while it is being thrown.

**THROWING THE DISCUS**

(1) Rules recommended for Field Events (General Conditions) and Throwing Events (General Conditions) may apply.

(2) In order to avoid accidents the central throwing area must be roped off as a unit at a height of approximately 1 metre. Alternatively, discus throwing sectors must be roped off at a height of approximately 1 metre and to make a 60° sector inside which the discus sector is centrally placed.

For safety reasons all throws should be preceded by

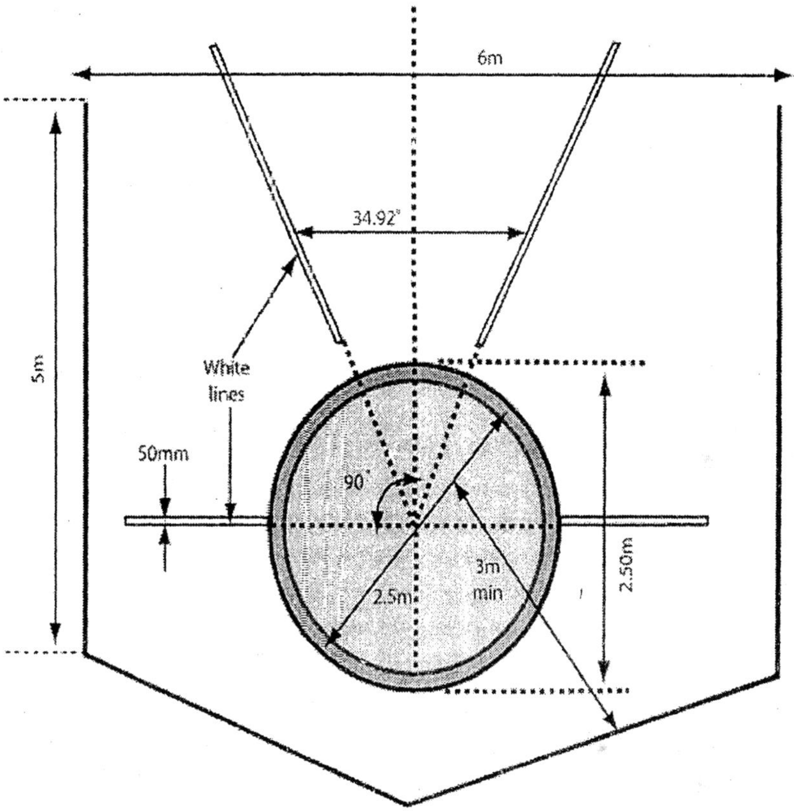


a warning which should be acknowledged by the event officials before the throw commences.

(3) Competitors must be given instructions that implements must be thrown during practice only from the circle. Implements must be returned by hand during practice or competition and must not be thrown back to the starting area. The Referee or other appropriate official shall disqualify from competing in the event any athletes who wilfully disobey the above instructions after having their attention drawn to them.

(4) No practice trials shall be allowed after a competition has begun.

(5) All throws shall be made from a cage.

(6) Gloves may not be worn.

(7) Competitors must not spray or spread any substance on the surface of a throwing circle nor on their shoes or roughen the surface of the circle.

(8) Competitors must commence the throw from a stationary position within the circle; they may adopt any position they choose.

(9) It shall be a foul throw if the competitor, after stepping into the circle and starting to make the throw, touches with any part of the body the ground outside the circle, or the top of the circle rim. A competitor is allowed to touch the inside of the iron band.

(10) The competitor must not leave the circle until the discus has touched the ground. When leaving the circle the first contact with the top of the circle rim or the ground outside the circle must be completely behind the white line which is drawn outside the circle, the rear edge of which runs theoretically through the centre of the circle.

(11) Provided that in the course of a trial the foregoing Rules have not been infringed, a competitor may interrupt a trial once started, may lay down the discus, may leave the circle before returning to a stationary position and beginning a fresh trial.

(14) All measurements must be made from the nearest edge of the mark first made in the ground by the discus to the inner edge of the circle along a line drawn from the mark to the centre of the circle.

(15) A steel or fibre glass tape should be used for measurement, and that part of the tape showing the distance thrown must be held by the official at the circle. Alternatively approved datum measurement equipment may be used, as may a scientific apparatus which has obtained a certificate of accuracy from a nationally recognised standardising organisation.

(16) The throw shall be recorded to the nearest 1cm below the distance measured if that distance is not a whole centimetre.

**THROWING THE DISCUS SPECIFICATIONS**

(1) The circle shall be measured from the inside. The surface should be of concrete, asphalt, or some other firm but not slippery material. The surface should be lightly stippled when being laid to give a rough but not ribbed surface.

(2) The surface of the inside of the circle should be level and 20mm ± 6mm lower than the upper edge of the ring which should be level with the ground outside.

(3) Circle rings:

Construction — The rim shall be made of band iron, steel, or other suitable material and be painted white.

Measurements — (Metal) — The inside diameter of the circle shall measure 2.50m maximum, and the rim of the circle shall be at least 6mm thick. (Wood)—The inside diameter of the circle shall measure 2.50m maximum, and the rim of the circle shall be 7.5mm thick. A tolerance of ±5mm is permitted for the inside diameter of a circle.

(4) A white line 5cm wide shall be drawn from the top of the circle, extending for at least 75cm on either side of the circle, the theoretical extension of this line across the circle dividing it into front and rear halves with the rear edge passing through the centre of the circle.

(5) A portable circle meeting with the specifications above is permissible.

(6) The body of the discus may be solid or hollow and shall be made of wood, or other suitable material, with a metal rim, the edge of which shall be circular. The discus, including the surface of the rim, shall have no roughness and the finish shall be smooth and uniform throughout. The cross-section of the edge shall

be rounded in a true circle having a radius of approximately 6mm. Circular plates set flush into the side of the body and in the exact centre of the discus may be used to secure the weight. Both s ides shall be identical and shall have no indentations, projecting points or sharp edges. The sides shall taper in a straight line from the beginning of the curve of the rim to a circle of a radius of 25mm to 28.5mm from the centre of the discus.

(7) A discus can also be made of other materials without metal plates so long as the measurements and the weight correspond to the specifications.

**CAGES FOR HAMMER AND DISCUS**

**Hammer Throwing Cage**

(1) All hammer throws shall be made from an

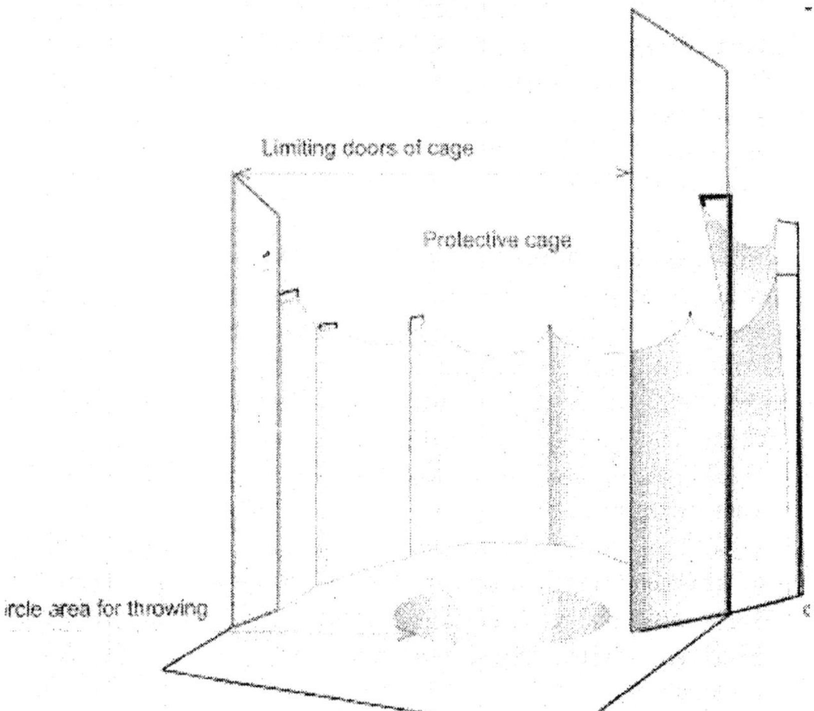

enclosure or cage to ensure the safety of spectators, officials and competitors. Advice is available on request from UK Athletics.

(2) The cage should be designed, manufactured and maintained so as to be capable of stopping a 7.26kg hammer head, 110mm in diameter, moving at a speed of up to 29 metres per second. The uprights for all cages should be erected in sockets concreted permanently into the ground and so designed that an alignment pin points the gallows arm in the right direction. Staying wires should not be used. The arrangement should be such that there is no danger of the implement ricocheting or rebounding back towards the athlete or over the top of the cage. Provided that it satisfies all the requirements of this rule, any form of cage design and construction can be used.

(3) The cage should be U-shaped in plan, consisting of a minimum of netting panels each having a minimum width of 2.74m as shown in the diagram. The width of the mouth should be 6m, positioned 4.2m in front of the centre of the throwing circle. The end points of the 6m wide mouth shall be the inner edge of the cage netting. The minimum height of these netting panels shall be 7m. Provision should be made in the design and construction of the cage to prevent a hammer forcing its way through any joints in the cage or the netting. In addition, provision should be made to prevent a hammer sliding along the ground underneath the netting.

(4) Two movable gate panels shall be provided at the front of the cage, only one of which will be operative at a time. The minimum height of the panels shall be 9m.

(5) The netting for the cage can be made from suitable natural or synthetic fibre cord, or alternatively, from mild steel wire. The maximum mesh size shall be 50mm wire and 44mm for cord netting. The minimum size of cord or wire depends critically on the construction of

the cage, but the minimum breaking strain should be at least 130kg. In order to ensure the continued safety of the cage, the netting should be inspected at least every 12 months.

(6) Where it is desired to use the same cage for discus throwing, the installation can be adapted in two alternative ways. Most simply, a 2.135/2.5m concer tric circle may be fitted, but this involves using the same surface in the circle for hammer and discus throwing. Where it is desired to have separate circles for hammer and discus, the two circles must be placed one behind the other with the centres 2.37m apart on the centre line of the throwing sector and with the hammer circle at the front.

The shape of the rear of the cage must then be enlarged using a minimum of 8 netting panels each having a minimum width of 2.83m, and two gate panels each having a minimum width cf 2.00m as show on the diagram. The minimum height of the two types of panel for this enlarged cage shall be exactly the same as for the standard cage identified above.

(7) The safety of the hammer cage installation is very dependent on the position and alignment in the arena. The maximum danger sector for all throws, including both left and right handed throwers, is approximately 85°.

(8) The cage should be designed, manufactured and maintained so as to be capable of stopping a 2kg discus moving at a speed of up to 25 metres per second. The arrangement should be such that while stopping the discus there is no danger of it ricocheting off fixed members of the cage, back towards the athlete or over the top of the net. Provided that it satisfies all the requirements of this rule, any form of cage design and construction can be used.

(9) The cage should be U-shaped in plan, consisting

of a minimum of 6 panels of netting each having a minimum width of 3.17m as shown in the diagram. The width of the mouth should be 6m, positioned 5m in front of the centre of the throwing circle. The end points of the 6m wide mouth shall be the inner edge of the pivoted netting. The minimum height of the netting panels should be at least 4m.

(10) The netting for the cage can be made from suitable natural or synthetic fibre cord or alternatively, from mild steel wire. The maximum mesh size shall be 50mm wire and 44mm for cord netting. The minimum size of cord or wire depends critically on the construction of the cage, but the minimum breaking strain should be at least 40kg.

In order to ensure the continued safety of the cage, the steel netting should be inspected after every 12 months continuous service.

(11) The maximum danger sector for discus throws from this cage is approximately 98°, including both right and left-handed throwers. The position and alignment of the cage in the arena is, therefore, critical for its safe use.

**THROWING THE JAVELIN**

The javelin runway for both high school and college competition is 120 feet long and 13.12 feet wide. The length is measured from the center of the foul line arc. For college, the first 70 feet of the runway is 4 feet wide (designated by a painted line) and then widens to 13.12 feet for the last 50 feet. NCAA specifications recommend that the runway be constructed with an artificial surface, such as asphalt or concrete. If an artificial surface is used, the runway should extend 3.28 feet past the foul line.

The foul line (high school "scratch line") is 2.76" wide, painted white, and flush with the runway. High school recommends a metal, plastic, or wood band, while

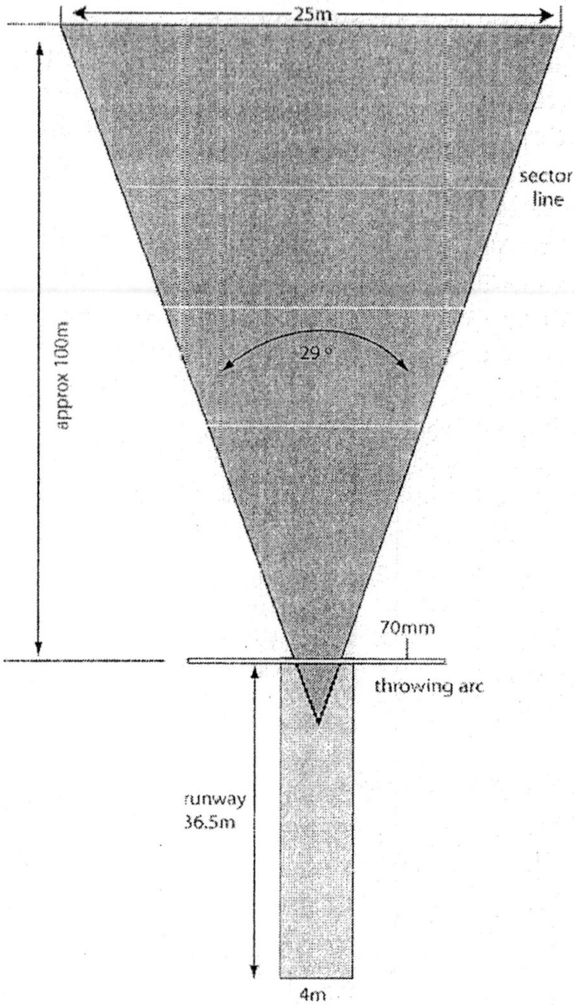


NCAA specifies a painted line. The landing area is grass and its boundaries are determined by marking lines from a point at the center of the foul line arc which is 26.25 feet back from its circumference. These lines continue through the outside edge of the foul line and outward as far as required for the competitive level of the throwers. All painted lines are determined by marking lines from a point at the center of the foul line arc which is 26.25 feet back from its circumference.

These lines continue through the outside edge of the foul line and outward as far as required for the competitive level of the throwers. All painted lines are outside the dimensions shown in Fig. in the next page.

(1) Rules recommended for Field Events (General Conditions) and Throwing Events (General Conditions) may apply.

(2) In order to avoid accidents the central throwing area must be roped off as a unit at a height of approximately 1 metre.

Alternatively, Javelin Throwing sectors must be roped off at a height of approximately 1 metre and to make a 50° sector inside which the Javelin sector is centrally placed.

For safety reasons all throws should be preceded by a warning which should be acknowledged by the event officials before the throw commences.

(3) Competitors must be given instructions that implements must be thrown during practice only from the arc. Implements must be returned by hand during practice or competition and must not be thrown back to the starting area. The Referee or other appropriate official shall disqualify from competing in the event any athletes who wilfully disobey the above instructions after having their attention drawn to them.

(4) No practice throws shall be allowed after the competition has begun.

(5) Gloves may not be worn, but an elbow protection is allowed.

(6) The javelin must be held with one hand only, and at the grip, so that the little (or fourth) finger is nearest to the point.

(7) No marks shall be placed on the runway but the competitors may place marks at the side of the runway.

(8) It is foul if the competitor touches with any part of the body the lines which mark the runway or the ground outside in the course of an attempt.

(9) The javelin shall be thrown over the shoulder or upper part of the throwing arm, and must not be slung or hurled.

(10) At no time after preparing to throw, and until the javelin has been discharged into the air may the competitor turn completely round so that the back is towards the throwing arc.

(11) Non-orthodox styles are not permitted.

(12) It is a foul if the competitor steps on or beyond the arc or extended scratch line on the ground marked 'N' on the diagram below.

(13) A throw shall be valid only if the tip of the metal head strikes the ground before any other part of the javelin.

(14) The competitor shall not leave the runway until the javelin has touched the ground. When leaving the runway, from a standing position, the first contact with the parallel lines or the ground outside the runway must be completely behind the white line of the arc at right angles to the parallel lines.

(15) Provided that, in the course of a trial, the foregoing rules have not been infringed, a competitor may interrupt a trial once started, may lay the implement down inside or outside the runway, and may leave the runway as required in the second sentence of (14) above, before returning to the runway to begin a fresh trial.

(16) A foul throw or letting go of the javelin in an attempt shall be reckoned as a trial. If a javelin breaks during a throw it shall not be counted as a trial, provided that the attempt was made in accordance with the Rules. If the competitor thereby loses balance and as a result contravenes any part of this Rule, it shall not be considered as a foul throw.

(17) The arc must be clearly marked on the ground by chalk or otherwise, and all measurements must be made from the nearer edge of the mark first made in the ground by the tip of the metal head of the javelin to the inside edge of the javelin arc along a line from the point of the fall to the centre of the circle of which the arc is apart.

(18) For a valid throw the javelin must land so that the point from which measurement is to be made is within the inner edges of lines marking the sector out on the ground by extending the lines from the centre of the circle of which the arc is apart, through the points at which the arc joins the lines marking the runway.

(19) A steel or fibre glass tape should be used for measurement, and the part of the tape showing the distance thrown must be held by the official at the arc. Alternatively, approved datum measurement equipment may be used, as may a scientific apparatus which has obtained a certificate of accuracy from a nationally recognised standardising organisation.

(20) The throw shall be recorded to the nearest 1cm below the distance measured if that distance is not a whole centimetre.

**THROWING THE JAVELIN SPECIFICATIONS**

(1) The runway shall be marked by two parallel lines 4m apart, and the throw shall be made from behind an arc of a circle drawn with a radius of 8 metres. Such arc shall consist of a strip painted, or made of wood 7cm in width, painted white and shall be flush with the ground.

(2) The runway shall be level, with a minimum length of 30 metres. The maximum lateral inclination of the runway shall be 1:100 and in the last 20m of the runway the overall downward inclination in the direction of running shall not exceed 1:1000.

(3) The outer ends of the sector lines should be marked with flags. It is recommended that the

extremities of the Scratch Line should be marked with small flags.

(4) Construction

(a) The javelin shall consist of three parts: ahead, a shaft and a cord grip. The shaft shall be constructed completely of metal or of another suitable homogeneous material and shall have fixed to it a metal head terminating in a sharp point. If the javelin head is constructed such that a reinforced tip is welded on to the end of the head, it shall be considered acceptable, provided the head is smooth and uniform along the whole of its surface. The surface of the shaft shall have no dimples or pimples, grooves or ridges, holes or roughness and the finish shall be smooth and uniform throughout.

(b) The javelin shall have no mobile parts or other apparatus which during the throw could change its centre of gravity or throwing characteristics.

(c) The grip, which shall cover the centre of gravity, shall not exceed the diameter of the shaft by more than 8mm. It may have a regular non slip pattern surface but without thongs, notches or indentations of any kind. The grip shall be of uniform thickness.

(d) The javelin shall conform to the following specifications:

(e) The tapering of the javelin to the tip of the metal head shall be such that the angle of the point shall be not more than 40°.

The diameter, at a point 150mm from the tip shall not exceed 80% of the maximum diameter of the shaft. At the mid-point between the centre of gravity and the tip of the metal head, the diameter shall not exceed 90% of the maximum diameter of the shaft.

**Competition and Throws**

Rules are similar to other throwing events: Competitors take three throws after which the top eight take another three, their best legal throw is recorded and the winner is the individual with the longest legal throw measured to the nearest centimetre or foot and inch depending on country of competition. If the javelin's point touches the ground first, the throw is marked (measured) from this point. If the throw lands flat then the distance is measured from the back of the whipcord (grip). If the tail of the javelin lands first, then the throw is not counted and scratched. The most noticeable difference with the other events is that rather than a throwing circle as used in discus, shot put and hammer throw, the competitors have a run-up area coated with the same surface used for running tracks, and a painted line on the surface for small spikes on each shoe. Many athletic tracks have javelin run-ups at each end to take advantage of any potential wind benefit.

Javelin throwers gain considerable forward velocity in their run-up to their throws, and as well as upper body strength demonstrate athleticism more similar to running and jumping events. Thus, the athletes share more physical characteristics with sprinters than other throwing athletes with their bulky frames. At release, a javelin can reach speeds approaching 113 km/h (70 mph).

**Throwing Area and Rules**

The runway is between 30-36.5 meters long. Throwers may place as many as two markers in the runway. The javelin is held at the grip and thrown over the shoulder or the upper part of the throwing arm. Spinning is illegal.

To constitute a legal throw, the javelin's metal tip must break the ground.

**The Competition**

Twelve competitors qualify for the Olympic javelin throw final. In the 2004 Games, 34 men and 45 women participated in qualification rounds prior to the final.

The results from the qualification rounds do not carry over into the final.

As in all throwing events, the 12 finalists have three attempts apiece, then the top eight competitors receive three more attempts. The longest single throw during the final wins.?

## COMBINED EVENTS

(1)

(a) The Outdoor Pentathlon for Senior Men consists of five events which shall be held on one day in the following order: Long Jump, Throwing the Javelin, 200 metres, Throwing the Discus and 1500 metres.

(b) The Outdoor Pentathlon for Under 15 Boys consists of five events which may be held on one day, or on two consecutive days in the following order: 80 metres Hurdles, Putting the Shot, Long Jump, High Jump, 800 metres.

(c) The Outdoor Pentathlon for Senior Women consists of five events which shall be held on one day in the following order: 100 metres Hurdles, Putting the Shot, High Jump, Long Jump, 800 metres.

(d) The Outdoor Pentathlon for Under 15 Girls consists of five events which should be held on one day or on two consecutive days in the following order: Long Jump, 75 metres Hurdles, Putting the Shot, (break of one hour), High Jump, 800 metres.

(2) The Hexathlon for Under 15 Girls consists of six events which shall be held over two days; 75 metres Hurdles (which shall begin the first day), Long Jump, Throwing the Javelin, High Jump, Putting the Shot, 800 metres (which shall be the final event).

(3)

(a) The Outdoor Heptathlon for Senior and Junior Women consists of seven events which shall be held on two consecutive days in the following order: First Day: 100 metres Hurdles, High Jump, Putting the Shot, 200 metres. Second day: Long Jump, Throwing the Javelin, 800 metres.

(b) The Outdoor Heptathlon for Under 17 Women shall consist of the the same events as in but the hurdle event shall be those relating to this age group and the order of events shall be flexible.

(4)

(a) The Outdoor Octathlon for Under 17 Men shall consist of the following eight events held over two days: High Jump, Long Jump, Putting the Shot, Throwing the Discus, Throwing the Javelin, 100 metres Hurdles, 400 metres (which shall conclude the first day's programme) and 1500 metres (which shall be the final event).

(b) The Outdoor Octathlon for Under 15 Boys shall consist of the following eight events held over two days: 100 metres (which shall begin the first day), 80 metres Hurdles, High Jump, Pole Vault, Throwing the Discus, Throwing the Javelin, 400 metres (which shall conclude the first day's programme), and 1000 metres (which shall be the final event).

(5) The Outdoor Decathlon for Men consists of ten events which shall be held on two consecutive days in the following order: First day: 100 metres, Long Jump, Putting the Shot, High Jump, 400 metres. Second Day: 110 metres Hurdles, Throwing the Discus, Pole Vault, Throwing the Javelin, 1500 metres. The Outdoor Decathlon for Women consists of ten events which shall be held on two consecutive days in the following order: First day: 100m, Discus, Pole Vault, Javelin, 400m. Second day: 100m Hurdles, Long Jump, Shot Put, High Jump, 1500m.

(6) The Indoor Pentathlon (Men) consists of five events which shall be held on one day in the following order: 60 metres Hurdles, Long Jump, Putting the Shot, High Jump, 1000 metres.

The Indoor Pentathlon (Women) consists of five

events which shall be held on one day in the following order: 60 metres Hurdles, High Jump, Putting the Shot, Long Jump, 800 metres.

The Indoor Heptathlon (Men) consists of seven events which shall be held on two consecutive days in the following order: First day: 60 metres, Long Jump, Putting the Shot, High Jump. Second day: 60 metres Hurdles, Pole Vault, 1000 metres.

(7) The Combined Events Referee shall have jurisdiction over the conduct of the combined events competition. However, the Track and Field Referees, where appointed, shall retain jurisdiction over the individual events within the competition.

(8) In all Combined competitions three trials only are allowed in the Long Jump and in each Throwing Event.

(9) In track events run entirely in lanes at least four competitors should start in each group whenever possible. In other track events at least five competitors should start in each group, and one such group should consist of those competitors occupying the leading positions prior to the final event.

(10) The time of each competitor should be taken by three timekeepers independently. Where fully automatic timing is in operation times shall be given to 1/100th of a second and scored by using the appropriate tables to 1/100th second.

Only one system of timing may be applied throughout each event. For record purposes, however, electrical times shall be applied regardless of whether such times are available for other competitors in the event.

(11) In the running and hurdles events competitors shall be disqualified in any event in which they have been responsible for three false starts.

(12) Where the hurdles used do not comply with Rule recommended for Hurdle Race(1) & (9) a competitor

knocking down three or parts of three or more hurdles shall score no points in that event.

(13) In High Jump and Pole Vault, Rule recommended for Vertical Jumps (High Jump and Pole Vault) (4) does not apply to a Combined Events competition. Heights will be increased uniformly throughout the competition by 3cm in the High Jump and 10cm in the Pole Vault.

(14) Any athlete failing to take part in any of the events shall not be allowed to take part in any subsequent event in that competition but shall be considered to have abandoned the competition. That athlete shall not figure in the final classification.

(15) The winner shall be the competitor who has obtained the highest number of points in the five, six, seven, eight or ten events as the case may be, awarded on a basis of the IAAF Combined Events Scoring Tables, modified where necessary as indicated above.

(16) In the event of a tie, the winner shall be the competitor who has received the highest points in a majority of events. If this does not resolve the tie, the winner shall be the competitor who has scored the highest number of points in any one of the events. If that does not resolve the tie, the winner shall be the athlete with the highest number of points in a second event, etc. This procedure shall apply to ties for any place in the competition.

## TRACK AND FIELD OFFICIALS

### (1) APPOINTMENT OF OFFICIALS

(a) The following officials should be appointed at every Track and Field Meeting:

A Referee for Track Events.

A Referee for Field Events. If there are to be several field events it may be desirable to appoint two Field Referees, one for the throwing events and one for the jumping events. (In meetings with many field events, further sub divisions of the Field Referee's duties may be carried out by the appointment of further Referees for specific duties.)

Track Judges/Umpires.

Field Judges.

A Chief Timekeeper.

Timekeepers.

A Starter – two if there are many track events, one of whom should then be designated Chief, supported by a Marksman (Starter's Assistant) and two or more if there are many track events, one of whom should then be designated as Chief Marksman.

Marksmen (Starter's Assistants).

Clerks of Course for field events.

Clerk of Course for track events.

Announcer(s).

Competitors' Steward(s).

Recorders and other Stewards as may be necessary.

Walking Judges (where walking events are included in the programme).

(b) For meetings above County level, the following additional officials should be appointed:

A Meeting Manager, who shall have overall responsibility for the control of the meeting.

A Photo-finish Team (as required).

Additional Starter(s) so that there is a team of not less than 3, thereby enabling Start Recallers to be used.

Electronic Distance Measurement Team (as required).

Scoreboard Operators and Two-way radio Stewards.

A team of Assembly Stewards.

Seeding Officers.

Press and Results Stewards.

Presentation Stewards.

Doping Control Stewards.

(c) For National and International Meetings the

following additional officials may be appointed:

National Technical Delegate.

**(2) DUTIES OF OFFICIALS**

All officials share the responsibility for events starting to time and for the meeting to be run smoothly and without undue waste of time. Officials who are not officiating regularly should always consult the Rules for Competition before going to an athletics meeting.

***Meeting Manager***

The Meeting Manager shall assume overall responsibility for the running and control of the meeting.

***The Field Referee***

Shall: (i) have charge of all field events;

(ii) administer the rules for competition relating to disqualification of athletes;

(iii) allocate Judges to particular events and duties;

(iv) check that equipment and markings conform with specification rules in liaison with the Technical Manager (if appointed).

(v) announce to Judges and ensure that the competitors are informed of the number of trials;

(vi) ensure that all field events commence at the due time;

(vii) supervise the measurement of performances;

(viii) check the final results;

(ix) decide in the event of any difference of opinion between the Field Judges: the Field Referee's decision shall be final;

(x) deal with any disputed point as provided by the Rules for Competition.

***Field Judges***

Shall (i) see that field events are carried out in accordance with the Rules for Competition;

(ii) decide in which order the competitors shall be placed; In jumping for distance, separate Judges shall be responsible for:

(i) deciding if the take-off is fair;

(ii) marking the point in the landing area from which measurement is to be made;

(iii) operating the wind gauge (the operator shall measure and record the wind speed for the designated period of time and relay this information to the Judge in charge of the event).

In jumping for height, two Judges should keep a record of the jumps and check their recordings at the end of each round. The height of the bar should be measured when the bar is raised, particularly if standards or records are being attempted.

In throwing for distance separate Judges shall be responsible for:

(i) deciding if the delivery is fair;

(ii) marking the point of landing of the implement from which the measurement is to be made.

Before the start of each event the Judges should ensure that the right competitors are present, that they are correctly dressed and are wearing numbers as on the programme and in accordance with the Rules for Competition.

Measurement Officials may be appointed, especially if Electronic Distance Measurement is to be used, and they are then responsible to the Field Referee for measuring and recording distances.

***The Track Referee***

Shall: (i) have charge of all track events;

(ii) administer the Rules for Competition relating to disqualification of athletes;

(iii) allocate duties to Track Judges and Umpires;

(iv) decide in the event of any difference of opinion between the

Track Judges: the Track Referee's decision shall be final;

(v) deal with any disputed point as provided by the Rules for Competition.

If, in the opinion of the Track Referee, circumstances arise so that justice demands that a race already concluded should be contested again, the Referee shall have power to declare the race void and it shall be contested again, either on the same day if practicable, or on some future occasion. The Track Referee in his absolute discretion shall decide when the race shall be re-run.

***Track Judges and Umpires***

Shall: (i) see that the proper distance of each run is covered;

(ii) decide the order in which the competitors finish.

Lap scorers should be appointed for races of longer than 1500m to record each competitor completing each lap. The duty of lap scorer can be incorporated with that of 'finish judge'. One of the scorers shall call, or show by number cards, to the competitors the number of laps still to be completed and ring the bell for each competitor to indicate the start of the last lap.

Judges should be allocated as Umpires to watch the competitors, especially on bends and over hurdles and water jumps, and shall report promptly to the Referee any infringement of the rules of racing.

Judges should also be allocated to supervise relay take-overs and to work out the results of team races.

A Wind Gauge Operator should be appointed for races up to and including 200m. The operator should measure and record the wind speed for the designated period of time and relay this information to the Track Referee.

***The Chief Starter***

Shall: (i) allocate duties to the other Starters;

(ii) administer the Rules for Competition relating to disqualification of athletes at the start of races;

(iii) have absolute control over all matters relating to the start;

(iv) ensure that the track events keep to timetable.

The Chief Marksman

Shall: (i) allocate duties to the other Marksmen;

(ii) assist in keeping the track events to timetable.

***Starters and Marksmen***

The Starter shall have complete control of the starting of a race. Marksmen are appointed to act under the direction of the Starter, to make the draw for the stations at the start (if Seeding Officers have not been appointed) ensuring that the right competitors are present, correctly dressed and wearing numbers in accordance with the programme. Marksmen should then assist the Starter, at his/her instruction, in watching for infringements of the rules during the starting procedure.

At meetings of a higher level, Start Recallers are appointed from within the team of Starters. If in the opinion of the Starter or Start Recaller, the start was not fair, the competitors must be recalled. In practice, the first opportunity to recall rests with the Starter, whose decision on whether to issue a false start warning shall be final.

***The Chief Timekeeper***

Shall: (i) allocate duties to the Timekeepers on the team;

(ii) declare the time to be recorded for each competitor;

(iii) administer the Rules for Competition applicable to timekeeping.

***Timekeepers***

Timekeepers shall time each event independently and, in the event of a difference between their returns, should exhibit their watches to the Chief Timekeeper, who shall decide which time is to be returned.

***Walking Judges***

For walking races, Walking Judges shall be appointed. The Walking Judges shall disqualify any competitor whose mode of progression they consider fails to comply with the definition of walking in the Rules for Competition.

***Technical Manager***

The Technical Manager, under the direction of the Meeting Manager, shall be responsible for ensuring that the track, runways, circles, arcs, sectors, landing areas for field events and all equipment are in accordance with specification in Rules for Competition.

The Technical Manager shall normally have overall supervision of the Clerk of Course (Track) and Clerks of Course (Field).

***Clerk of Course (Track)***

The Clerk of Course (Track) with the Track Referee shall ensure that the course is correctly set out and kept perfectly clear. When hurdles and steeplechase races are included in the programme, the Clerk must ensure that all hurdles and barriers are correctly set and placed and that they are removed from the track when no longer required. In addition, the Clerk shall ensure that all equipment such as judges' stand, bell, batons, etc. is ready for use.

***Clerks of Course (Field)***

The Clerks of Course (Field) with the Field Referee shall ensure that all markings are correct as required by the Rules for Competition, that take-off boards are clean and firm and landing areas ready for use. The Clerks shall ensure that all equipment necessary for maintaining runways, circles and landing areas is in a fitstate for competition, that brooms, rakes, rollers, etc. are available as required and that Judges are provided with marking spikes and tapes as necessary.

They are responsible for the provision of implements

for practice and competition and must see that all implements are removed from the site of the event as soon as the competition is completed.

***Seeding Officers***

The Seeding Officers shall have the responsibility of allocating competitors in track events to heats or subsequent qualifying rounds according to their previous best performance. They shall prepare the draw for the finals.

In the case of heats (first rounds) if possible, the seeding shall be based on the best performance at previous meetings during the current or previous season.

In the case of subsequent rounds, the seeding shall be based on the performance in the earlier heats (previous rounds) for events up to and including 400m, and in events above this distance the original performance list should be used, unless a better performance was achieved in the previous round.

Seeding Officers should consult with the Track Referee before the start of the meeting to establish the qualifying conditions which the Track Referee would wish to have implemented for progressing to subsequent rounds/finals.

A random draw for lanes should be made.

Rule 115 states "In the preliminary rounds of races, at least the winner, and preferably the winner and second should qualify for the next round or final. Any other competitors to qualify shall be decided either according to their places or according to their times.Where any qualifying position is decided by time, only one system of timing may be applied in determining times. Where photo-finish equipment is in use the Chief Photo-finish Judge shall consider, where necessary, the actual time recorded in 1/1000ths of a second by the competitor in deciding qualifiers by time". (A mixture of hand and electric times shall not be used for the same qualifying conditions).

In National Association Championships seedings and draws may be carried out in accordance with IAAF Rule 166. If such an option is utilised then that Rule must be strictly observed and the athletes notified of its implementation in advance of the competition.

**Stewards, Announcers, etc.**

The Numbers' Stewards are responsible for seeing that all competitors are issued with the number bibs allotted to them in the programme for each particular event, and the Assembly Stewards that they are dressed in accordance with the Rules for Competition. The Assembly Stewards must produce the competitors for each race at the marshalling point at the time required by the Chief of Final Assembly, and furnish that official with a list of starters.

Announcers, Results Stewards, Press Stewards, together with other officials as may be necessary or desirable, should also be appointed depending upon the importance of the meeting and the number of events and competitors.

## CROSS-COUNTRY RACE

**Fundamental Regulation**

It is not possible to make firm or rigid rules for this event as this is being organised in varying circumstances and in different climatic conditions over different distances. The rules mentioned here should be followed to make this event popular and to develop this event.

**Season**

Normally, season for cross-country race extends throughout the winter months, i.e., when track and field season ceases.

**Course**

This kind of race should be organised on a course, which is being confined to open country, fields and grasslands. Traversing of roads should be kept to minimum level. On both the sides, course should be clearly marked. For marking purpose, tape can be used. Such obstacles should not be used to design the court, which have a large height. No such obstacle should be included which can prove to be dangerous or harmful for the athlete.

Artificial obstacles should be used to minimum extent, but if it becomes necessary to make use of them, then they should be used to simulate natural obstacles met within the open country. It is necessary to measure the course properly and at time invitations, distance declared can be extended. If there are loops on the course, then atleast one loop should not be less than 2200m. The responsibility of constructing a well-marked course rests on the shoulders of promoting body.

**Venue**

On open or woodland area, course should be designed. This area should be covered either by grass or by some natural obstacles, which can be used to build a challenging and interest race course by course designer. There should be enough space in this area so that all the necessary facilities can be arranged.

**Distances**

Following specifications relating to distance of course is mentioned in the rule :—

- Course distance for men athlete should not be more than 12km, however, it should not be less than 4km.
- For junior men, 8km course should be used.
- For women athletes, course distance should not be more than 8 km, but it should not be less than 4km.
- For junior women athletes, distance of course should be 6 km.

**Beginning**

Unless approved starting apparatus is not made activated by the starter, no athlete is permitted to begin the race. All the commands used for distance events should be used in this race also. Before the beginning of race, a five minute warning should be provided to athletes, if their number if large. If conditions demand, additional warnings can also be provided. Athletes will be provided with stations, and members of each team will be lined up behind each other at beginning of the race.

**Refreshment Stations**

At the beginning and ending of all races, athletes should be provided with water and other suitable refreshments. Different refreshment stations should be located at a distance of 2 to 3 km or on every lap for the athletes.

**Scoring**

Athlete crossing the finish line first should be declared the winner of event. If case of tie arises then it should be resolved in favour of that team, whose last scoring member finished near the first place.

## RACE WALKING EVENTS

**Meaning**

In race walking, athletes make progression of steps in such a way that their feet remain in continuous contact with the ground. From the moment of first contact with ground until vertical upright position, athletes are required to keep their legs straight. In other words, they cannot bend their knees while walking.

**Road Courses**

In the international level competitions,

-circuit for 10km walk should not be more than 1.5km, -circuit for 20km walk should not be less than 2.5km,

-circuit for 50km walk should not be less than 2.5km, but it should not be more than 5km.

**Beginning**

No athlete is permitted to begin the race unless gun

is not being fired by starter. For conducting this kind of races, procedure used to conduct 400m races should be used. A five minute warning should be provided before beginning of race if number of athletes taking part in competition is large. If required, additional warnings can also be provided.

**Officials**

A chief judge will be appointed from among the judges of race walk. Chief judge is required to function as a supervisor official for the whole competition. All other appointed judges will act in their individual capacity and will work independently.

What should be the number of appointed judges for this event, basically depends on the size of the course, however, this number should not be less than 6, which should not extend to 9. In all the races, which are organised on track, number of judges should be 6, among which one should be chief judge. Only members of IAAF Panel of International Race Walking Judges can be appointed as judges in this event. All the judges appointed for such event should belong to different nations.

If it seems to any judge that any athlete cannot keep his feet in continuous contact with the surface, then he can caution him. A judge can caution an athlete only for once for the same offence. After the competition, all the judges are required to inform chief judge about the caution provided by them to any of the athlete during competition.

**Leaving the Track**

If any competitor wants to withdraw himself from the event, then it is necessary for him to take permission of judge for this act.

**Safety Measures**

If races are organised on the roads, then it becomes necessary to make all those measures with which safety of the athletes can be ensured. Only those roads should be used for this purpose, where load of traffic is minimal. These races should be organised at such a time, with which they can be completed in daylight, as possibilities of athletes being injured gets lower. Proper arrangement should be made to provide first-aid or proper medical treatment if any athlete becomes injured during event. If in the opinion of member of official medical staff appointed by organising committee, it has become necessary for any athlete to quit from the event, then that athlete should be retired immediately.

**Refreshment Stations**

At the beginning and finish of all races, athletes should be provided with water and other suitable refreshments. At suitable intervals, drinking and sponging stations should be provided in all the events upto 10km. For events more than 10km, such stations should be situated at a distance of 5km. This distance can be decreased in accordance with the weather conditions.

Athletes are permitted to take only that refreshment, which is being arranged by organising committee. The persons or officials who will provide such refreshment to the athletes will be also nominated by organising committee.

Behind the refreshment table, no more than two officials should belong to same nation. No official can run beside the official while he is taking refreshment. Officials should be designated by the organising committee, who will supervise the refreshment stations.

**Warnings**

Warning is proposal for disqualifying any athlete from the competition. Such kind of proposal can be provided by appointed judges. If during competition, contact of feet with the surface gets discontinued by any athlete, then he can be warned by the appropriate judge.

Whenever any athlete is cautioned or warned, a white sign with symbol of offence should be shown to athletes. To inform the athletes about warnings given to them, a warning posting board should be used in the competition.

**Disqualification**

An athlete is considered as disqualified in the following conditions :—

if, he has received warnings for three times by different judges will be disqualified from the event, and

if, during the competition he takes refreshment other than provided by organising committee.

The responsibility of informing disqualified athlete of such happening lies on the shoulder of chief judge. If because of any reason it becomes impossible to inform the athlete about fact of his being disqualified, then such information should be provided to him as soon as he finish the race. To provide information of disqualification, athletes are shown a red sign. Right to make use of red sign rest only with chief judge.

Athlete being disqualified should leave the track immediately after being disqualified. He should also remove distinguishing number worn by him and should go outside the course.

# 2

# BADMINTON

## INTRODUCTION

Badminton is a racquet sport played by either two opposing players (singles) or two opposing pairs (doubles), who take positions on opposite halves of a rectangular court that is divided by a net. Players score points by striking a shuttlecock (also known as a shuttle, bird, or birdy) with their racquet so that it passes over the net and lands in their opponents' half of the court. Each side

may only strike the shuttlecock once before it passes over the net. A rally ends once the shuttlecock has struck the floor.

The shuttlecock (or shuttle) is a feathered projectile whose unique aerodynamic properties cause it to fly differently from the balls used in most racquet sports; in particular, the feathers create much higher drag, causing the shuttlecock to decelerate more rapidly than a ball. Shuttlecocks have a much higher top speed, when compared to other racquet sports. Because shuttlecock flight is affected by wind, competitive badminton is played indoors. Badminton is also played outdoors as a casual recreational activity, often as a garden or beach game.

Since 1992, badminton has been an Olympic sport with five events: men's and women's singles, men's and women's doubles, and mixed doubles, in which each pair consists of a man and a woman. At high levels of play, the sport demands excellent fitness: players require aerobic stamina, agility, strength, speed and precision. It is also a technical sport, requiring good motor coordination and the development of sophisticated racquet movements.

## SKILLS AND TECHNIQUES

### Badminton Grip

Starting wtih a correct Badminton Grip is the foundation of Playing Badminton. Holding the racket wrongly will decrease your stroke's power and accuracy. Your shots will be limited and therefore you will not enjoy the game as much let alone improve.

### Forehand Grip

- This grip is used to hit shots that are on the forehand

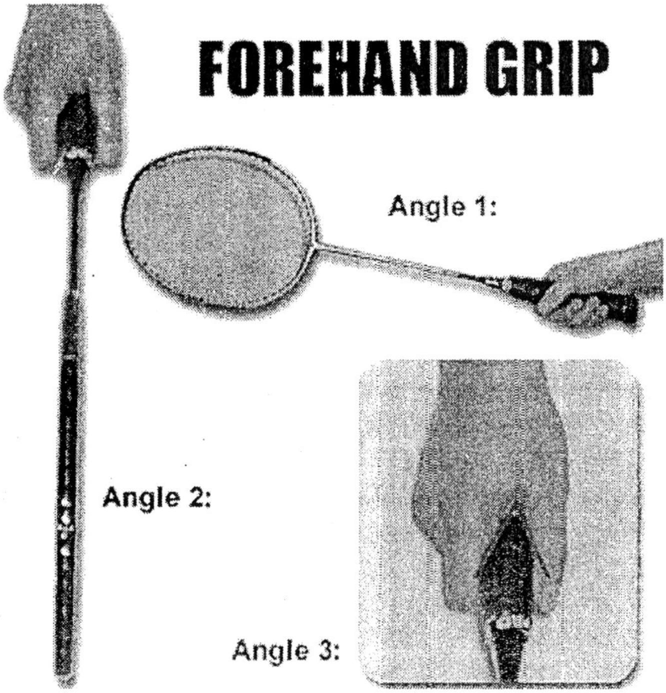


side of your body and around the head shots.

- Hold the racket head with your non-playing hand so that the handle points towards you.

- Your racket face shall be perpendicular to the floor.

- Place your playing hand on the handle as if you are shaking hands with it.

- There shall be a V shape in between your thumb and your index finger.

- The racket handle shall rest loosely in your fingers for greater flexibility.

- Can try shortening your grip and place it nearer to the shaft to increase control and accuracy when serving and hitting from the forecourt and midcourt.

**Backhand Grip**

- This grip is used to hit shots that are on the backhand side of your body.
- Hold the racket as you would on a forehand grip.
- Turn the racket anti-clockwise so that the V shape moves leftwards.
- Place your thumb against the back bevel of the handle for greater leverage and power.
- The racket handle shall also rest loosely in your fingers.
- Can try shortening your grip and place it nearer to the shaft to increase control and accuracy when serving and hitting from the forecourt and midcourt.

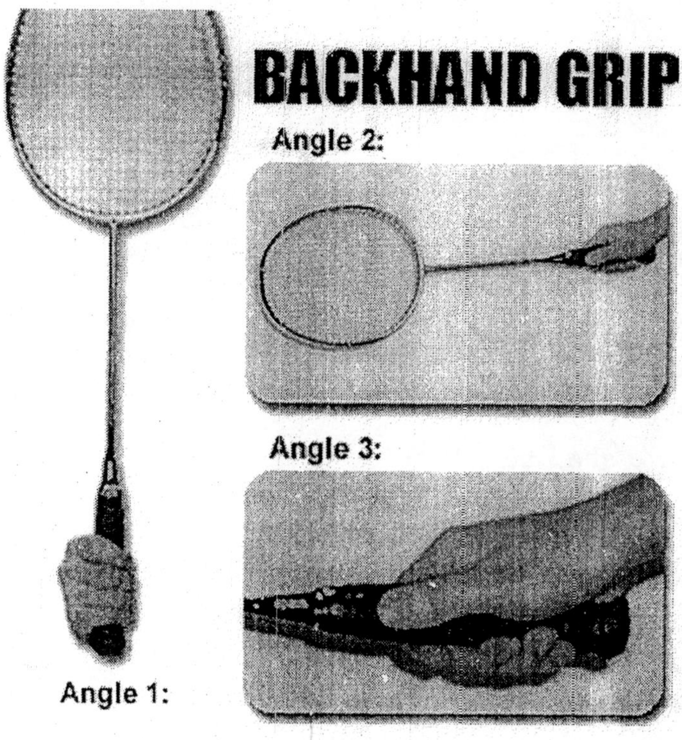

**Badminton Footwork**

Badminton Footwork is the most fundamental skill that you need to possess in order to become a successful Badminton player.

**So how to define what good footwork is?**

Good badminton footwork is simply having the ability to reach the shuttle early while on balance. You can skip, shuffle, bounce, glide, chasse step or lunge on court.

So long as you reach the shuttle fast, depriving your opponents of time, you can use all the above movement that suits best to you depending on the situation.

Although there are no fix movements on performing the badminton footwork, there are some basic things to remember.

Bent your knees slightly with your feet shoulder width apart. Stay on the balls of your feet and hold your racket up in front of your body. This is the ready position you shall assume in the centre of the mid-court area.

This centre area which can be referred as your base is not fixed. It is an area where you are in your ready position and can possibly reach all shots hit towards your court. Position your base accordingly after considering yours and your opponent's strength and weaknesses.

Let say that you are strong and good at hitting shots from the back court. You may consider positioning your base slightly nearer to the service fault line to gain an advantage. If you are not certain where your strength lies yet, just make your base on the centre of the mid court area. You won't go too wrong from there.

For all shots that are played in the frontcourt, take a small step first followed by a bigger step, extending your racket leg to reach the shuttle. The bigger step performed is known as a lunge. The timing of the shot will be improved if the landing of your racket leg is simultaneous with the shot.

For all shots that are played in the midcourt, extend your racket leg to reach shuttle that are hit towards your racket side of your body. Extend your racket leg or non-racket leg to reach shuttle that are hit towards your non-racket side of your body.

**Badminton Serve**

Mastering various types of Badminton Serve is essential if you want to improve your game. Serving is the starting of a point. Use it not merely as "just a serve" but a weapon during games.

**High Serve**

Use this badminton serve during singles play to move your opponent as far back in court as possible, thus opening up his court. Be more cautious if you use this serve during doubles. Opponents with strong attacking abilities will work this serve to your disadvantage.

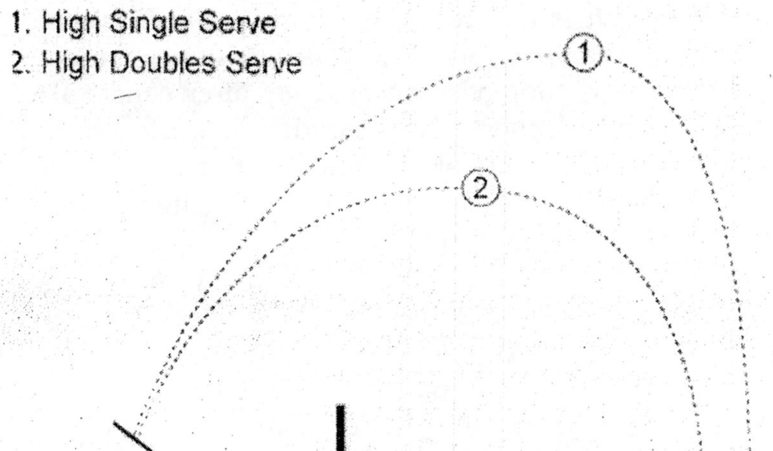


Serve Trajectories

- Played with a forehand underarm action.
- Stand two to three feet behind the short service line.
- Relax your body and bent your knees slightly.
- Lead with your non-racket leg and place your racket leg behind.
- Bring your racket back to almost your shoulder level then swing it forward following the rhythm of the stroke.
- Hold the shuttle by the feathers and let it drop slightly in front of you.
- Hit it with the flat face of your racket and follow through until your racket reaches the non-racket side of your head.

**Low Serve**

Use this badminton serve when you want your opponent to lift the shuttle. It is commonly used during doubles, but you can use it during singles too if your opponent's attack is too strong. You can use either forehand or backhand to play this serve.

.ow Serve

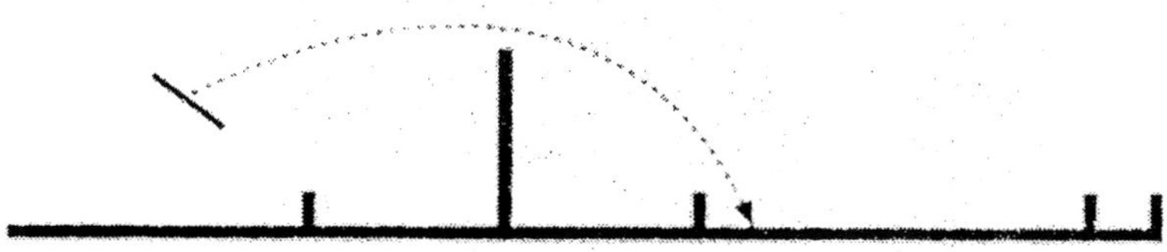

Serve Trajectory

**Forehand**

- Stand two to three feet behind the short service line.
- Relax your body and bent your knees slightly.
- Lead with your non-racket leg and place your racket leg behind.
- Bring your racket back to your waist level then start your forward swing.
- Hold the shuttle by the feathers and bring it closer to meet the racket instead of dropping it in front.
- Contact the shuttle at a higher point but still below your waist line.
- Push the shuttle with the racket face and try to make the shuttle skim the tape of the net.

If you normally use high serve during singles, mix the low serve in occasionally. You might be able to catch your opponent off-guard if you can execute it well.

**Backhand**

- Stand in a comfortable and balanced position with your racket hand in front.
- Lead with your racket leg and place your non-racket leg behind with your feet pointing towards your opponent.
- Carry out a short back swing then bring the racket forward.
- Hold the shuttle on the tip of the feathers in front of your waist level.
- Push the shuttle with the racket face and try to make the shuttle skim the tape of the net.
- You can try to shorten the grip for a better control of the racket.
- Beware of breaking the Service Rules.

**Flick Serve**

Use this badminton serve when you are under pressure from a rushing opponent. It is a rather useful tool during doubles. However, you might be left exposed

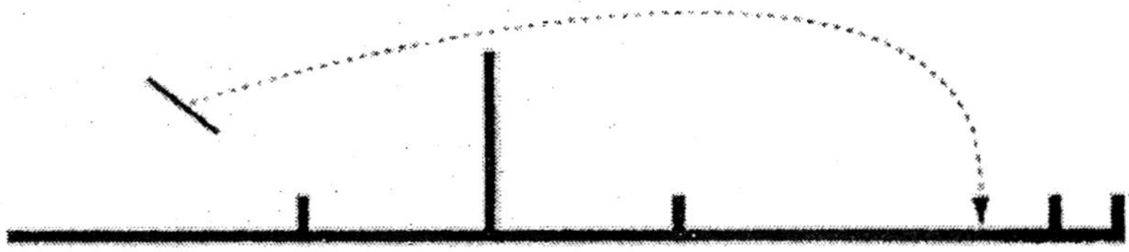

Serve Trajectory

if your opponent anticipated it. So, use it sparingly and keep your opponent guessing.

You can use either your forehand or backhand to perform this serve. Give the impression that you are going to push the shuttle as in the low serve, but instead use your wrist to flick the shuttle over. Wrist action is the key to executing this serve well.

**Badminton Clears**

Badminton Clears are the most common and important of all badminton strokes that can be played overhead or underarm. These shots can be played both on the forehand and backhand sides.

**Overhead Clear**

Use the clear to move your opponent to the backcourt. It will create space in the frontcourt for you to exploit.

It will also give you more time to go back to your base.

Attacking Clear

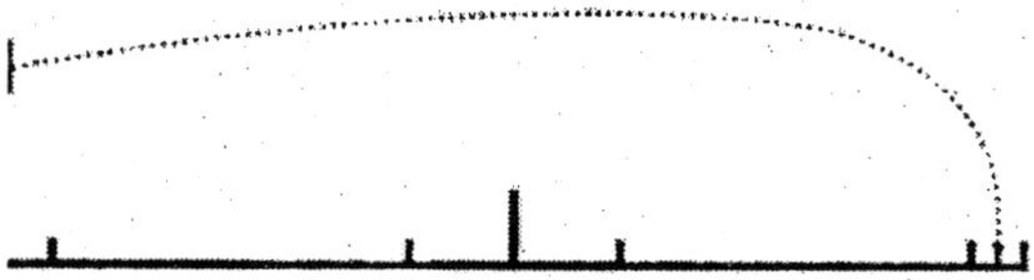

Overhead trajectory

The optimum hitting zone is located somewhere above the central area of your racket.

You can play two types of Badminton Clears, Attacking Clear and Defensive Clear.

Attacking clear has a trajectory that runs almost parallel to the ground. The shuttle travels flat and fast towards your opponents back court. These badminton shots allow less time to your opponent to get behind the shuttle, potentially causing weak returns. The shuttle is hit square with your racket face.

**Defensive Clear** has a high and deep trajectory. These badminton shots give you more time to return to your base and prepare for the next shot. The shuttle is hit with your racket face leaning slightly backwards.

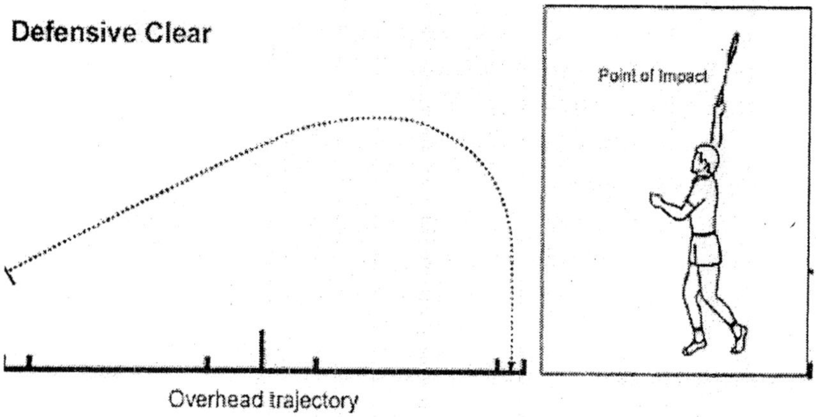


**Forehand Overhead Clear**

The forehand overhead badminton clear is similar to the action of throwing a ball. If you can throw a ball well, you shouldn't have problem playing this stroke. You can always practice throwing with a shuttle first before stepping on to the court.

Here are some pointers for playing a forehand overhead clear.

- Adopt the forehand grip.

- Turn your body and stand sideways to the net with your non-racket shoulder facing the net.
- Shift your weight on to your rear foot.
- Bend your elbow and lock your wrist preparing to swing forward.
- Raise your non-racket hand and point at the shuttle to improve timing and balance.
- Contact the shuttle as high as possible and in front of your body using a strong throwing action as if you are going to throw your racket high and forward through the air.
- Straighten your elbow as you hit the shuttle.
- Let your wrist unlock with a whip action as you hit the shuttle.
- Follow through with your racket and shift your weight from your rear foot to your front foot.
- Move back to your base position.

**Backhand Overhead Clear**

It is not easy to play a backhand overhead clear. Even experienced players have problem with this badminton stroke. You shall always try to play an 'around the head' forehand clear whenever possible.

However, it is important that you know how to play the backhand overhead clear. There are times when you just can't play the shuttle with your forehand.

Here are some pointers for playing a backhand overhead clear.

- Adopt the backhand grip.
- Turn your body so that your back is facing the net.
- Lead and shift your weight to your racket foot.
- Lift your arm from the shoulder with the forearm parallel to the floor.
- Hold the racket across your body with the racket head pointing down.
- Keep the racket arm and elbow close into your body.

- Hit the shuttle at a high point of contact.
- Flick your wrist powerfully towards the shuttle.
- A follow through is not needed.
- Push your body back to your base position.

**Underarm Clear**

The underarm clear is usually played from the front court area to your opponent's back court. Whether to play it high and deep or a flatter, cross court clear will depend on the situation at that time and your opponent's positioning on court.

In any case, try to reach the shuttle as early as possible so that you can have various shot options. Your wrist action is the crucial element in creating a deception for your shots.

Here are some pointers for the underarm clear.

- Adopt the forehand grip for a forehand underarm clear or the backhand grip for a backhand underarm clear.
- Extend and put your racket up when you go for the shot.
- The point of impact shall be well out in front of you and as high as possible with your racket leg leading in a lunge position.
- Swing your racket upwards as the shuttle drops in the hitting area.
- Unlock your wrist as you contact the shuttle, producing a whip action.
- Follow through with your racket in the direction of the shuttle's trajectory.
- Push with both legs and move back to your base position.

**Badminton Drop Shots**

Badminton Drop Shots are delicate badminton shots that can win you points outright if executed well with deception. These shots can be played both on the forehand and backhand sides.

Use the badminton drop shot to move your opponent to the frontcourt. It will create space in the midcourt and backcourt for you to exploit.

Wrist action is essential in providing the disguise and element of surprise. The optimum hitting zone is located somewhere above the central area of your racket.

You can play two types of Badminton Drop Shots, Slow Drop Shot and Fast Drop Shot.

A slow drop shot shall land in your opponent's frontcourt area, as close to the net as possible. The point of impact is above the racket shoulder. It is intended to move your opponent to the frontcourt, hopefully forcing a weak return to your midcourt for you to kill.

**Slow Drop Shot**

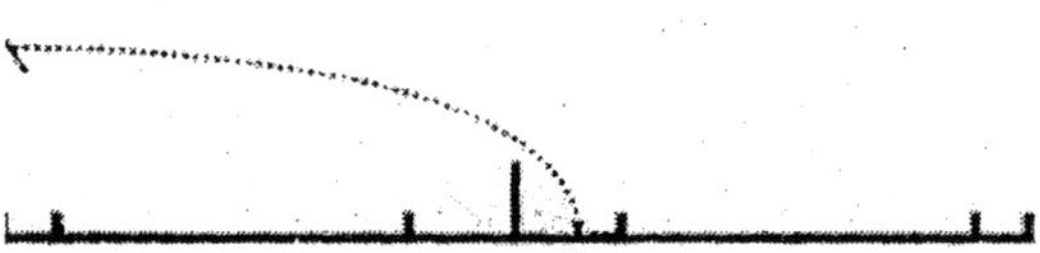

Overhead trajectory

A fast drop shot shall land in the front of your opponent's mid court area, preferably to the sides. Hit the shuttle slightly further in front of the body to produce a shallower trajectory at a faster speed. It is intended to catch your opponent off balance and have less time to respond.

**Forehand Drop Shot**

The forehand overhead drop shot is similar to the action of throwing a ball. If you can throw a ball well, you shouldn't have problem playing it. You can always practice throwing with a shuttle first before stepping on to the court.

Here are some pointers for playing a forehand overhead drop shot.

- Adopt the forehand grip.
- Turn your body and stand sideways to the net with your non-racket shoulder facing the net.
- Shift your weight on to your rear foot.
- Bend your elbow and lock your wrist preparing to swing forward.
- Raise your non-racket hand and point at the shuttle to improve timing and balance.
- Contact the shuttle as high as possible and out in front of your body.
- Straighten your elbow as you hit the shuttle.
- Slice or tap the shuttle as you hit it, reducing the speed of the racket head.
- The angle of the racket face will determine the direction of your shot.
- Follow through with your racket and shift your weight from your rear foot to your front foot.
- Move back to your base position.

**Backhand Drop Shot**

It is not easy to play a backhand overhead drop shot. Even experienced players have problem with this badminton stroke. You shall always try to play an 'around the head' forehand drop shot whenever possible.

However, it is important that you know how to play the backhand overhead drop shot. There are times when you just can't play the shuttle with your forehand.

Here are some pointers for playing a backhand overhead drop shot.

- Adopt the backhand grip.
- Turn your body so that your back is facing the net.
- Lead and shift your weight to your racket foot.

- Lift your arm from the shoulder with the forearm parallel to the floor.
- Hold the racket across your body with the racket head pointing down.
- Keep the racket arm and elbow close into your body.
- Contact the shuttle in front of your body and as high as possible.
- Slice or tap the shuttle as you hit it, reducing the speed of the racket head.
- The angle of the racket face will determine the direction of your shot.
- Push your body back to your base position.

**Badminton Smash**

Badminton Smash is the most potent of all badminton shots. There is almost no defense against a well executed smash. It can be played both on the forehand and backhand sides.

The smash is a shot hit with power and speed downward to your opponent's court. The angle and the steepness of the shuttle's trajectory will make it hard for your opponent to retrieve.

Contact the shuttle further in front of your body than the clear or the drop shot. The optimum hitting zone is

Smash

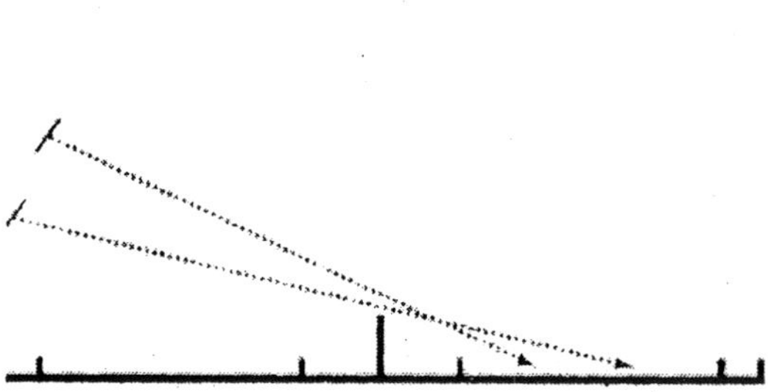

Overhead trajectory

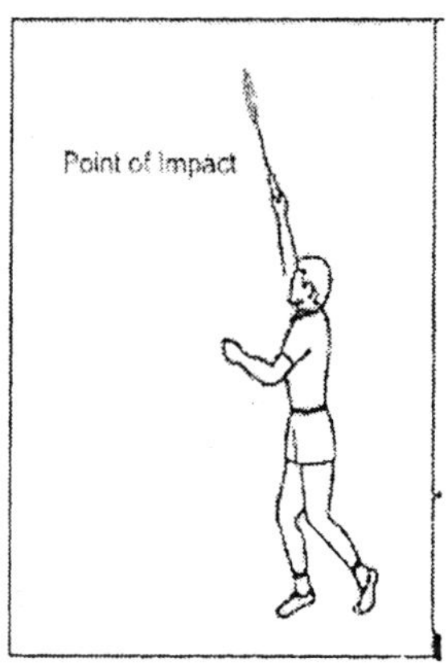

located somewhere above the central area of your racket.

You can also jump and smash the shuttle at the same time to generate more power and create a steeper angle for the shot. This will give your opponent even lesser time to react. As this is a more advance shot, master the normal badminton smash first before taking on any jumping smash.

The feeling of being able to smash powerfully and kill off a point is really great. But try not to get carried away. As the badminton smash requires a lot of energy, use it only when the opportunity arises. For example, a weak clear from your opponent to your midcourt area. Do not tire yourself out unnecessarily.

**Forehand Smash**

The forehand overhead smash is similar to the action of throwing a ball. If you can throw a ball well, you shouldn't have problem playing this stroke. You can always practice throwing with a shuttle first before stepping on to the court.

**Backhand Smash**

It is difficult to play a backhand overhead smash. Even experienced players have problem with this badminton stroke. Try to play an 'around the head' forehand smash whenever possible.

However, it is important that you know how to play the backhand overhead smash. There are times when you just can't play the shuttle with your forehand.

**Badminton Drive**

Badminton Drive shots are shots that crosses the net flatly in a horizontal trajectory. It can be played both on the forehand and backhand sides.

The drive is an attacking shot that is usually played from the sides of the court when the shuttle has fallen too low for it to be returned with a smash. The shuttle shall be between your shoulder and knee height.

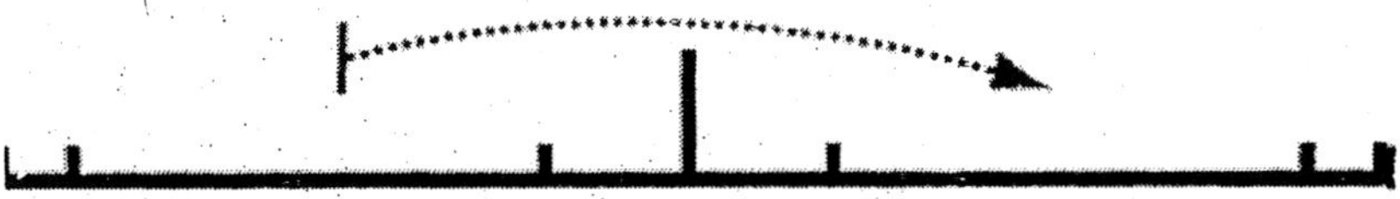

Drive trajectory

It is widely used in doubles as players want to keep the shuttle low. Although to a lesser extent in the singles, it is an important stroke as well.

A flat and fast drive is useful in getting the shuttle behind your opponent, potentially causing them to make a weak return. You can also change your tactics and play a flat but slower drive shot that falls in the frontcourt or midcourt area. It all depends on the situation you are in and the on court positioning of your opponent.

Badminton drive shot can be played diagonally crosscourt or straight down the line. Your stroking motion is similar to a sidearm throwing motion. Footwork is important as you need to shuffle or glide to your sides to make the shot.

**Forehand Drive**

Here are some pointers for the forehand drive:

- Adopt the forehand grip.

- Lead with your racket leg and side step towards the shuttle on your forehand.

- Your racket foot shall be pointing towards the sideline.

- Lock your wrist and draw your racket arm back in a sidearm, backswing motion.

- Your forehand grip and backswing place the racket parallel to the floor with your palm up.

- Put your body weight on your racket leg as you swing your racket arm forward.

- Extend your racket arm, roll your forearm over, and contact the shuttle as your wrist unlocks.

- Hit the shuttle in front of your racket foot at the

highest point possible.

- Turn your racket inwards for cross court shots.
- Racket head square to the shuttle for shots straight down the line.
- Follow through naturally with your racket arm.
- Shift your body weight from your racket leg to your non-racket leg.
- Move back to your base position.

**Backhand Drive**

Here are some pointers for the backhand drive:

- Adopt the backhand grip.
- Lead with your non-racket leg or crossover with your racket leg to your backhand side.
- Lock your wrist and draw your racket arm back in a sidearm, backswing motion.
- Your backhand grip and backswing place the racket parallel to the floor with your palm down.
- Put your body weight on your leading leg as you swing your racket arm forward.
- Extend your racket arm, roll your forearm over, and contact the shuttle as your wrist unlocks.

- Hit the shuttle in front of your leading foot at the highest point possible.
- Turn your racket inwards for cross court shots.
- Racket head square to the shuttle for shots straight down the line.
- Follow through naturally with your racket arm.
- Shift your body weight from your leading leg to your non-leading leg.
- Move back to your base position.

## RULES OF BADMINTON

### 1. COURT AND COURT EQUIPMENT

(1.1) The court shall be a rectangle marked out with lines 40 mm wide as shown in Diagram below.

(1.2) The lines marking out the court shall be easily distinguishable and preferably be coloured white or yellow.

(1.3) All the lines shall form part of the area which they define.

(1.4) The posts shall be 1.55 metres in height from the surface of the court and shall remain vertical when

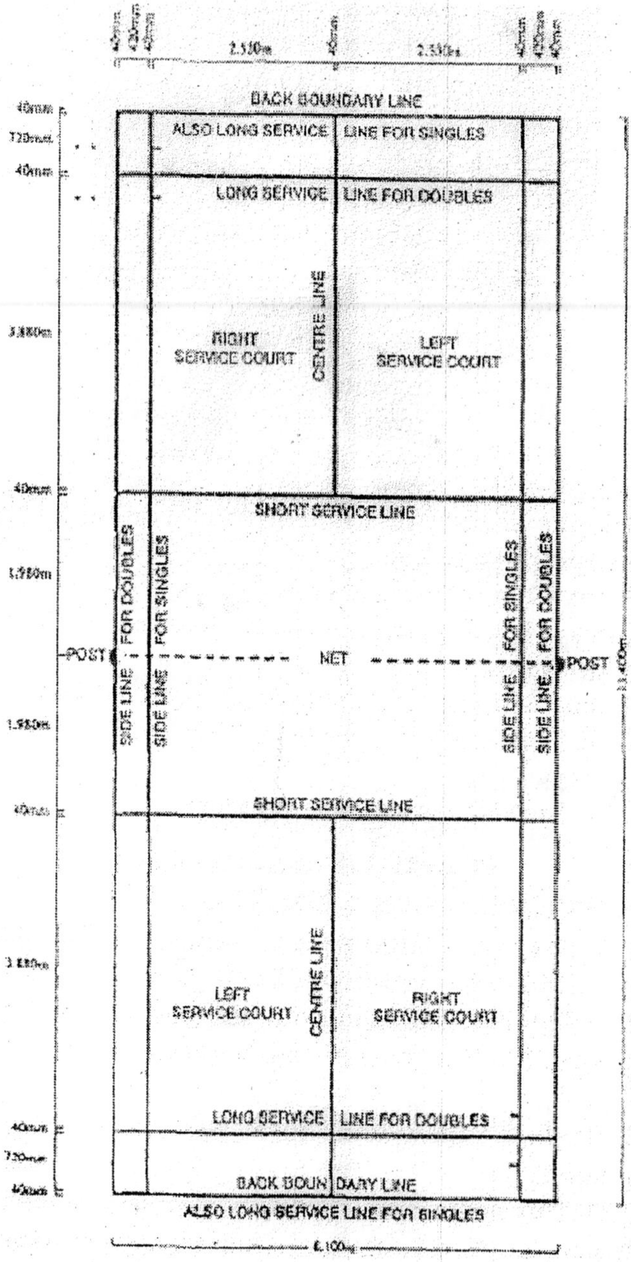
BACK BOUNDARY LINE
ALSO LONG SERVICE LINE FOR SINGLES
LONG SERVICE LINE FOR DOUBLES
RIGHT SERVICE COURT
CENTRE LINE
LEFT SERVICE COURT
SHORT SERVICE LINE
SIDE LINE FOR DOUBLES
SIDE LINE FOR SINGLES
POST
NET
POST
SHORT SERVICE LINE
LEFT SERVICE COURT
CENTRE LINE
RIGHT SERVICE COURT
LONG SERVICE LINE FOR DOUBLES
BACK BOUNDARY LINE
ALSO LONG SERVICE LINE FOR SINGLES

the net is strained as provided in Law 1.10 The posts or its supports shall not extend into the court.

(1.5) The posts shall be placed on the doubles side lines as in Diagram 1 irrespective of whether singles or doubles is being played.

(1.6) The net shall be made of fine cord of dark colour and even thickness with a mesh of not less than 15 mm and not more than 20 mm.

(1.7) The net shall be 760 mm in depth and at least 6.1 metres wide.

(1.8) The top of the net shall be edged with a 75 mm white tape doubled over a cord or cable running through the tape. This tape shall rest upon the cord or cable.

(1.9) The cord or cable shall be stretched firmly, flush with the top of the posts.

(1.10) The top of the net from the surface of the court shall be 1.524 metres at the centre of the court and 1.55 metres over the side lines for doubles.

(1.11) There shall be no gaps between the ends of the net and the posts. If necessary, the full depth of the net at the ends shall be tied to the posts.

**2. SHUTTLE**

(2.1) The shuttle shall be made of natural and / or synthetic materials. From whatever material the shuttle is made, the flight characteristics generally shall be similar to those produced by a natural feathered shuttle with a cork base covered by a thin layer of leather.

**(2.2) Feathered Shuttle**

(2.2.1) The shuttle shall have 16 feathers fixed in the base.

(2.2.2) The feathers shall have a uniform length between 62 mm to 70 mm when measured from the tip to the top of the base.

(2.2.3) The tips of the feathers shall lie on a circle

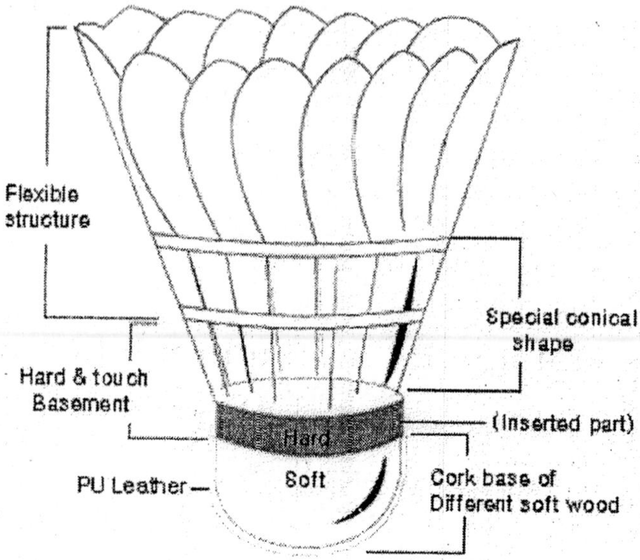


with a diameter from 58 mm to 68 mm.

(2.2.4) The feathers shall be fastened firmly with thread or other suitable material.

(2.2.5) The base shall be 25 mm to 28 mm in diameter and rounded on the bottom.

(2.2.6) The shuttle shall weigh from 4.74 to 5.50 grams.

**(2.3) Non-Feathered Shuttle**

(2.3.1) The skirt, or simulation of feathers in synthetic materials, shall replace natural feathers.

(2.3.2) The base shall be as described in Law 2.2.5.

(2.3.3) Measurements and weight shall be as in Laws 2.2.2, 2.2.3 and 2.2.6. However, because of the difference in the specific gravity and other properties of synthetic materials in comparison with feathers, a variation of up to 10 per cent shall be acceptable.

(2.4) Subject to there being no variation in the general design, speed and flight of the shuttle, modifications in the above specifications may be made with the approval of the Member Association concerned, in places where atmospheric conditions due to either altitude or climate make the standard shuttle unsuitable.

**3. TESTING A SHUTTLE FOR SPEED**

(3.1) To test a shuttle, a player shall use a full underhand stroke which makes contact with the shuttle over the back boundary line. The shuttle shall be hit at an upward angle and in a direction parallel to the side lines.

(3.2) A shuttle of correct speed will land not less than 530 mm and not more than 990 mm short of the other back boundary line.

**4. RACKET**

(4.1) The racket shall be a frame not exceeding 680 mm in overall length and 230 mm in overall width consisting of the main parts described in Laws 4.1.1 to 4.1.5.

(4.1.1) The handle is the part of the racket intended to be gripped by a player.

(4.1.2) The stringed area is the part of the racket with which it is

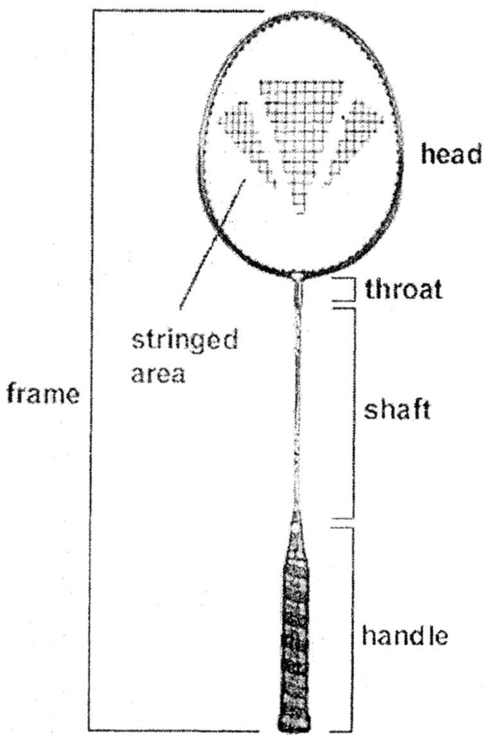


A Racket

intended that a player hits the shuttle.

(4.1.3) The head bounds the stringed area.

(4.1.4) The shaft connects the handle to the head.

(4.1.5) The throat (if present) connects the shaft to the head.

**(4.2) The stringed area:**

(4.2.1) shall be flat and consist of a pattern of crossed strings either alternately interlaced or bonded where they cross. The stringing pattern shall be generally uniform and, in particular, not less dense in the centre than in any other area; and

(4.2.2) shall not exceed 280 mm in overall length and 220 mm in overall width. However, the strings may extend into an area which otherwise would be the throat, provided that:

(4.2.2.1) the width of the extended stringed area does not exceed 35 mm; and

(4.2.2.2) the overall length of the stringed area does not then exceed 330 mm.

**(4.3) The Racket**

(4.3.1) shall be free of attached objects and protrusions, other than those used solely and specifically to limit or prevent wear and tear, or vibration, or to distribute weight, or to secure the handle by cord to the player's hand, and which are reasonable in size and placement for such purposes; and

(4.3.2) shall be free of any device that makes it possible for a player to change materially the shape of the racket.

**5. EQUIPMENT COMPLIANCE**

***The Badminton World Federation*** shall rule on any question of whether any racket, shuttle or equipment or any prototype used in the playing of Badminton complies with the specifications. Such ruling may be undertaken on the Federation's initiative or on application by any party with a bona fide interest, including any player, technical official, equipment manufacturer or Member Association or member thereof.

**6. TOSS**

(6.1) Before play commences, a toss shall be conducted and the side winning the toss shall exercise the choice in either Law 6.1.1 or 6.1.2:

(6.1.1) to serve or receive first;

(6.1.2) to start play at one end of the court or the other.

(6.2) The side losing the toss shall then exercise the remaining choice.

**7. SCORING SYSTEM**

(7.1) A match shall consist of the best of three games, unless otherwise arranged.

(7.2) A game shall be won by the side which first scores 21 points, except as provided in Law 7.4 and 7.5.

(7.3) The side winning a rally shall add a point to its score. A side shall win a rally, if the opposing side commits a 'fault' or the shuttle ceases to be in play because it touches the surface of the court inside the opponent's court.

(7.4) If the score becomes 20-all, the side which gains a two point lead first, shall win that game.

(7.5) If the score becomes 29-all, the side scoring the 30th point shall win that game.

(7.6) The side winning a game shall serve first in the next game.

**8. CHANGE OF ENDS**

(8.1) Players shall change ends:

(8.1.1) at the end of the first game;

(8.1.2) at the end of the second game, if there is to be a third game; and

(8.1.3) in the third game when a side first scores 11 points.

(8.2) If the ends are not changed as indicated in Law 8.1, it shall be done so as soon as the mistake is discovered and when the shuttle is not in play. The existing score shall stand.

**9. SERVICE**

(9.1) In a correct service:

(9.1.1) neither side shall cause undue delay to the delivery of the service once the server and the receiver are ready for the service. On completion of the backward movement of server's racket head, any delay in the start of the service (Law 9.2), shall be considered to be an undue delay;

(9.1.2) the server and the receiver shall stand within diagonally opposite service courts (Diagram A) without touching the boundary lines of these service courts;

(9.1.3) some part of both feet of the server and the reçeiver shall remain in contact with the surface of the court in a stationary position from the start of the service (Law 9.2) until the service is delivered (Law 9.3);

(9.1.4) the server's racket shall initially hit the base of the shuttle;

(9.1.5) the whole shuttle shall be below the server's waist at the instant of being hit by the server's racket. The waist shall be considered to be an imaginary line round the body, level with the lowest part of the server's bottom rib;

(9.1.6) the shaft of the server's racket at the instant of hitting the shuttle shall be pointing in a downward direction;

(9.1.7) the movement of the server's racket shall continue forwards from the start of the service (Law 9.2) until the service is delivered (Law 9.3);

(9.1.8) the flight of the shuttle shall be upwards from the server's racket to pass over the net so that, if not intercepted, it shall land in the receiver's service court (i. e. on or within the boundary lines); and

(9.1.9) in attempting to serve, the server shall not miss the shuttle.

(9.2) Once the players are ready for the service, the first forward movement of the server's racket head shall be the start of the service.

(9.3) Once started (Law 9.2), the service is delivered when the shuttle is hit by the server's racket or, in attempting to serve, the server misses the shuttle.

**10. SINGLES**

**(10.1) Serving and receiving courts**

(10.1.1) The players shall serve from, and receive in, their respective right service courts when the server has not scored or has scored an even number of points in that game.

(10.1.2) The players shall serve from, and receive in, their respective left service courts when the server has scored an odd number of points in that game.

**(10.2) Order of play and position on court**

In a rally, the shuttle may be hit by the server and the receiver alternately, from any position on that player's side of the net, until the shuttle ceases to be in play (Law 15).

**(10.3) Scoring and serving**

(10.3.1) If the server wins a rally (Law 7.3), the server shall score a point. The server shall then serve again from the alternate service court.

(10.3.2) If the receiver wins a rally (Law 7.3), the receiver shall score a point. The receiver shall then become the new server.

**11. DOUBLES**

**(11.1) Serving and receiving courts**

(11.1.1) A player of the serving side shall serve from

the right service court when the serving side has not scored or has scored an even number of points in that game.

(11.1.2) A player of the serving side shall serve from the left service court when the serving side has scored an odd number of points in that game.

(11.1.3) The player of the receiving side who served last shall stay in the same service court from where he served last. The reverse pattern shall apply to the receiver's partner.

(11.1.4) The player of the receiving side standing in the diagonally opposite service court to the server shall be the receiver.

(11.1.5) The players shall not change their respective service courts until they win a point when their side is serving.

(11.1.6) Service in any turn of serving shall be delivered from the service court corresponding to the serving side's score, except as provided in Law 12.

**(11.2) Order of play and position on court**

After the service is returned, in a rally, the shuttle may be hit by either player of the serving side and either player of the receiving side alternately, from any position on that player's side of the net, until the shuttle ceases to be in play (Law 15).

**(11.3) Scoring and serving**

(11.3.1) If the serving side wins a rally (Law 7.3), the serving side shall score a point. The server shall then serve again from the alternate service court.

(11.3.2) If the receiving side wins a rally (Law 7.3), the receiving side shall score a point. The receiving side shall then become the new serving side.

**(11.4) Sequence of serving**

In any game, the right to serve shall pass

consecutively:

(11.4.1) from the initial server who started the game from the right service court

(11.4.2) to the partner of the initial receiver.

(11.4.3) to the partner of the initial server

(11.4.4) to the initial receiver,

(11.4.5) to the initial server and so on.

(11.5) No player shall serve or receive out of turn, or receive two consecutive services in the same game, except as provided in Law 12.

(11.6) Either player of the winning side may serve first in the next game, and either player of the losing side may receive first in the next game.

**12. SERVICE COURT ERRORS**

(12.1) A service court error has been made when a player:

(12.1.1) has served or received out of turn; or

(12.1.2) has served or received from the wrong service court;

(12.2) If a service court error is discovered, the error shall be corrected and the existing score shall stand.

**13. FAULTS**

It shall be a 'fault':

(13.1) if a service is not correct (Law 9.1);

(13.2) if, in service, the shuttle:

(13.2.1) is caught on the net and remains suspended on its top;

(13.2.2) after passing over the net, is caught in the net; or

(13.2.3) is hit by the receiver's partner;

(13.3) if in play, the shuttle:

(13.3.1) lands outside the boundaries of the court (i. e. not on or within the boundary lines);

(13.3.2) passes through or under the net;

(13.3.3) fails to pass over the net;

(13.3.4) touches the ceiling or side walls;

(13.3.5) touches the person or dress of a player;

(13.3.6) touches any other object or person outside the court;

(Where necessary on account of the structure of the building, the local badminton authority may, subject to the right of veto of its Member Association, make bye-laws dealing with cases in which a shuttle touches an obstruction).

(13.3.7) is caught and held on the racket and then slung during the execution of a stroke;

(13.3.8) is hit twice in succession by the same player. However, a shuttle hitting the head and the stringed area of the racket in one stroke shall not be a 'fault';

(13.3.9) is hit by a player and the player's partner successively; or

(13.3.10) touches a player's racket and does not travel towards the opponent's court;

(13.4) if, in play, a player:

(13.4.1) touches the net or its supports with racket, person or dress;

(13.4.2) invades an opponent's court over the net with racket or person except that the striker may follow the shuttle over the net with the racket in the course of a stroke after the initial point of contact with the shuttle is on the striker's side of the net;

(13.4.3) invades an opponent's court under the net with racket or person such that an opponent is obstructed or distracted; or

(13.4.4) obstructs an opponent, i.e. prevents an opponent from making a legal stroke where the shuttle is followed over the net;

(13.4.5) deliberately distracts an opponent by any

action such as shouting or making gestures;

(13.5) if a player is guilty of flagrant, repeated or persistent offences under Law 16.

**14. LETS**

(14.1) 'Let' shall be called by the umpire, or by a player (if there is no umpire), to halt play.

(14.2) It shall be a 'let", if:

(14.2.1) the server serves before the receiver is ready (Law 9.4);

(14.2.2) during service, the receiver and the server are both faulted;

(14.2.3) after the service is returned, the shuttle is:

(14.2.3.1) caught on the net and remains suspended on its top, or

(14.2.3.2) after passing over the net is caught in the net;

(14.2.4) during play, the shuttle disintegrates and the base completely separates from the rest of the shuttle;

(14.2.5 in the opinion of the umpire, play is disrupted or a player of the opposing side is distracted by a coach;

(14.2.6) a line judge is unsighted and the umpire is unable to make a decision; or

(14.2.7) any unforeseen or accidental situation has occurred.

(14.3) When a 'let' occurs, play since the last service shall not count and the player who served last shall serve again.

**15. SHUTTLE NOT IN PLAY**

A shuttle is not in play when:

(15.1) it strikes the net or post and starts to fall towards the surface of the court on the striker's side of the net;

(15.2) it hits the surface of the court; or

(15.3) a 'fault' or a 'let' has occurred.

**16. CONTINUOUS PLAY, MISCONDUCT & PENALTIES**

(16.1) Play shall be continuous from the first service until the match is concluded, except as allowed in Laws 16.2 and 16.3.

**(16.2) Intervals:**

(16.2.1) not exceeding 60 seconds during each game when the leading score reaches 11 points; and

(16.2.2) not exceeding 120 seconds between the first and second game, and between the second and third game shall be allowed in all matches.

(For a televised match, the Referee may decide before the match that intervals as in Law 16.2 are mandatory and of fixed duration).

**(16.3) Suspension of play**

(16.3.1) When necessitated by circumstances not within the control of the players, the umpire may suspend play for such a period as the umpire may consider necessary.

(16.3.2) Under special circumstances the Referee may instruct the umpire to suspend play.

(16.3.3) If play is suspended, the existing score shall stand and play shall be resumed from that point.

**(16.4) Delay in play**

(16.4.1) Under no circumstances shall play be delayed to enable a player to recover strength or wind or to receive advice.

(16.4.2) The umpire shall be the sole judge of any delay in play.

**(16.5) Advice and leaving the court**

(16.5.1) Only when the shuttle is not in play (Law 15), shall a player be permitted to receive advice during a match.

(16.5.2) No player shall leave the court during a match without the umpire's permission, except during the intervals as described in Law 16.2.

(16.6) A player shall not:

(16.6.1) deliberately cause delay in, or suspension of, play;

(16.6.2) deliberately modify or damage the shuttle in order to change its speed or its flight;

(16.6.3) behave in an offensive manner; or

(16.6.4) be guilty of misconduct not otherwise covered by the Laws of Badminton.

**(16.7) Administration of breach**

(16.7.1) The umpire shall administer any breach of Law 16.4, 16.5 or 16.6 by:

(16.7.1.1) issuing a warning to the offending side;

(16.7.1.2) faulting the offending side, if previously warned. Two such faults by a side shall be considered to be a persistent offence; or

(16.7.2) in cases of flagrant offence, persistent offences or breach of Law 16.2 the umpire shall fault the offending side and report the offending side immediately to the Referee, who shall have the power to disqualify the offending side from the match.

**17. OFFICIALS AND APPEALS**

(17.1) The Referee shall be in overall charge of the tournament or event of which a match forms part.

(17.2) The umpire, where appointed, shall be in charge of the match, the court and its immediate surrounds. The umpire shall report to the Referee.

(17.3) The service judge shall call service faults made by the server should they occur (Law 9.1).

(17.4) A line judge shall indicate whether a shuttle landed 'in' or 'out' on the line(s) assigned.

(17.5) An official's decision shall be final on all points of fact for which that official is responsible except that if, in the opinion of the umpire, it is beyond reasonable doubt that a line judge has clearly made a wrong call, the umpire shall overrule the decision of the line judge.

**17.6 An umpire shall:**

(17.6.1) uphold and enforce the Laws of Badminton and, especially, call a 'fault' or a 'let' should either occur;

(17.6.2) give a decision on any appeal regarding a point of dispute, if made before the next service is delivered;

(17.6.3) ensure players and spectators are kept informed of the progress of the match;

17.6.4 appoint or replace line judges or a service judge in consultation with the Referee;

(17.6.5) where another court official is not appointed, arrange for that official's duties to be carried out;

(17.6.6) where an appointed official is unsighted, carry out that official's duties or play a 'let';

(17.6.7) record and report to the Referee all matters relating to Law 16; and

(17.6.8) refer to the Referee all unsatisfied appeals on questions of law only. (Such appeals must be made before the next service is delivered or, if at the end of the match, before the side that appeals has left the court.)

# 3

# BASKETBALL

## INTRODUCTION

Basketball is a team sport in which two teams of five players try to score points by throwing or "shooting" a ball through the top of a basketball hoop while following a set of rules. Basketball is one of the most popular and widely viewed sports in the world.

A regulation basketball hoop consists of a rim 18 inches (45.7 cm) in diameter and 10 feet (3.05 m) high mounted to a backboard. A team can score a field goal by shooting the ball through the hoop during regular play. A field goal scores two points for the shooting team if a player is touching or closer to the hoop than the three-point line, and three points (a "3 pointer") if the player is "outside" the three-point line. The team with more points at the end of the game wins, but additional time (overtime) may be issued when the game ends with a tie. The ball can be advanced on the court by bouncing it while walking or running (dribbling) or passing it to a teammate. It is a violation (traveling) to walk with the ball, carry it, or to double dribble (to hold the ball and then resume dribbling).

Various violations are generally called "fouls". Disruptive physical contact (a personal foul) is penalized, and a free throw is usually awarded to an offensive player if he is fouled while shooting the ball. A technical foul may also be issued when certain infractions occur, most commonly for unsportsmanlike conduct on the part of a player or coach. A technical foul gives the opposing team a free throw.

Basketball has evolved many commonly used techniques of shooting, passing, and dribbling, as well as specialized player positions and offensive and defensive structures (player positioning) and techniques. Typically, the tallest members of a team will play "center", "small forward", or "power forward" positions, while shorter players or those who possess the best ball handling skills and speed play "point guard" or "shooting guard".

While competitive basketball is carefully regulated, numerous variations of basketball have developed for casual play. Competitive basketball is primarily an indoor sport played on carefully marked and maintained basketball courts, but less regulated variations are often played outdoors in both inner city and rural areas.

## SKILLS AND TECHNIQUES

Generally, the skills of basketball are divided into following groups :—

- -Catching
- -Holding
- -Throwing
- -Bouncing, and
- -Hitting

### CATCHING

In basketball, we understand catching to mean the

action of a player in intercepting the ball and gaining some degree of control over it by maintained contact. There are great number of ways in which good players catch the ball, and it would be time consuming and repetitive to describe even a small proportion of them. If, however, we go back to our opening definition of catching, we see that the first thing to be accomplished is an interception of hand and ball.

There are some methods of doing fairly common catches. They are not definite as there are other methods also, some of which are as follows :—

**One Hand Snatch**

Used when collecting high rebounds in a closely opposed situation. The ball is generally moving very slowly, so that as soon as any high reaching fingertips contact the ball the wrist is flexed and the whole arm is violently accelerated downwards.

**Two Hand Chest Catch**

Useful for bringing all into safe middle range working position, especially with defender behind. Arms well extended, hands pointing diagonally upwards, palms forwards. First contact, thumbs and forefingers, which give with the ball, turning the palms inwards, allowing other fingers and palms to close on the ball.

**Two Hands Overhead Catch**

Merely an upward extension of the chest catch, but with the wrists in a better mechanical position. In many basketball countries, this is more often used than chest catching.

### One Hand All-round Catch

Arm placed in any position, using the respective arm for each body side, elbow bent depending upon distance the catch is made from body, open hand inclined, diagonally towards ball, first contact with middle fingers. Ball may be transferred soon to two hands for greater security, though in many cases, it might go straight into a dribble, pass or shot. Used mainly when taking passes while heavily defended, and collecting wide or higher passes.

### Two Hands Hand Off Catch

A side catch taken closer to the body, with the near side arm above and the other below. Little fingers inwards, taking first contact. Used a great deal in close manoeuvring situations. Most of the really great catchers perform their best when catching one handed.

### Holding and Throwing

As it is known that in the game of basketball, the ball is gradually brought under control during the catch. Eventually, the ball is held in the hands and in many situations, a player may need to maintain this held position for a certain period of time.

### PASSING

Passing is the key to successful basketball. A successful team must be able to handle, control and

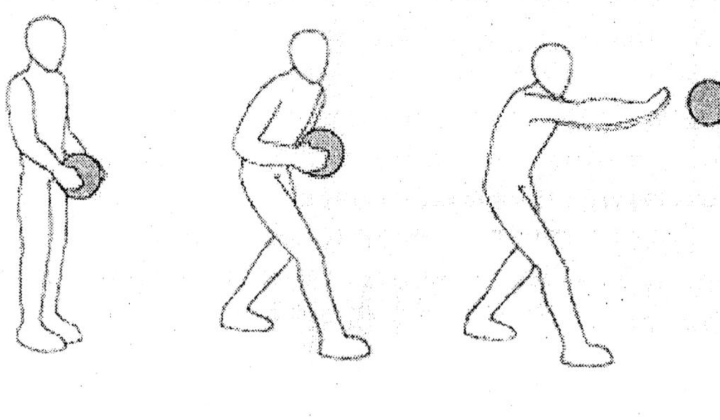

move the ball down court quickly and accurately to create scoring opportunities. Good passing is necessary in order to maintain possession of the ball and be able to move into scoring position.

Various kinds of passes are used in basketball, some of which are as follows :—

**Two Hands Overhead Pass**

Depending on the range of the pass, the force comes from the elbows and wrists. There may be preliminary movements before the pass, in fact, this is such a weak position that such movements may be necessary.

**Two Hands Front Pass**

Made from the middle working position. In medium and short range passes the movement starts from an elbows semi flexed position. There should be no recoil. The ball is pushed straight out with no forewarning, the final flick coming from thumbs and forefingers as the wrists turn violently outwards.

**Reverse One Hand Push**

Here the arms are crossed so that the non-dominant hand is underneath the ball and the dominant hand on the opposite side to normal. The ball may then be pushed to the dominant side. This is a slower pass, but a very deceptive one.

**One Hand Push Pass**

This pass can be made from virtually any position, ball held in one or two hands. Because of the greater manoeuvrability obtainable with one hand, the possible directions in which the ball can travel are more extensive than with two hands passing.

**Straight Arm Long Pass**

Very similar to the bent arm pass, but the arm is kept straight throughout the movement rather like a cricket bowling action.

**Bent Arm Long Pass**

The ball is thrown from a sideways standing position so that the thrower can step into the movement. The trunk is rotated and the throw initiated from an elbow flexed position.

**Bounce Pass**

This is not really a separate pass, just a term which describes the path taken by the ball after the release.

**Hand Off Pass**

This pass can be made with one or two hands. Used in situations where the players are passing very close to one another, usually when at least the passer is closely marked and is in a defensive working position.

**Two Handed Chest Pass**

When practising the pass for the first time, it is advisable to keep the thumb alongside the index finger and it may be practised either against a wall or with a partner. Using a wall, place a mark on it at the same height as your chest and prepare to make your pass, four paces from the wall.

**Hook Pass**

This pass is used to gain height in passing overhead, this pass may be made whilst standing or while in the air. Needless to say it should be practised at first while standing. The pass is a complete sideways movement although it starts from the basic catching position.

**DRIBBLING**

In many basketball environments, dribbling is regarded as in rather bad odour, the word being synonymous with selfishness and greed. This is as illogical as saying that shooting is selfish. In all team efforts, the attempt should be made to get the best people for a given job to do that job. The best shooter should do most of the shooting, the best passer do most of the passing, and the best dribbler should do most of the

dribbling.

**SHOOTING**

The primary objective of the game of basketball is to score goals. Therefore, all players should be able to shoot.

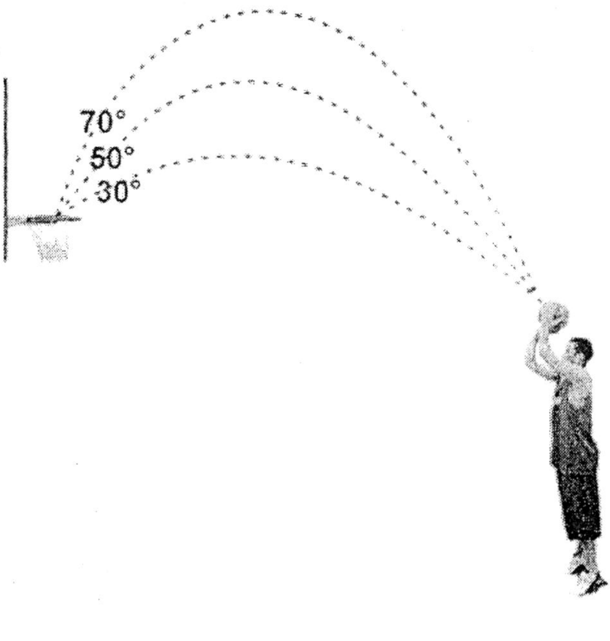

Being able to shoot a variety of shots from varying distances increases the effectiveness of any player. In all shots at the basket the use of relaxed wrists and the finger tips is of the greatest importance.

Various kinds of shots are used by basketball players, some of which are as follows :—

**One Handed Flip Shot**

This shot is made with one hand. The other hand still keeps contact with the ball to steady it before the shot is made.

**Two Handed Flip Shot**

To begin with, make this shot about four or five feet from the basket. From the basic catching position, take the ball at full arm stretch above the head, standing with one foot in front of the other for good balance.

**One Hand Set Shot**

The start for this shot is made from head height and to one side. Turn the ball so that the shooting hand is behind it, keeping contact with the other hand with the finger tips well spread and the wrists relaxed.

**Two Hand Set Shot**

This one is made as a long distance shot when well away from an opponent. With the ball in the basic catching position concentrate on that front edge of the ring.

**Lay Up Shot**

Besides being able to shoot from a standing position, you must be able to put the ball into the basket while on the run. Holding the ball in the basic catching position, stand six to eight paces away from the basket or your wall mark so that you will run in at an angle.

**Jump Shot**

This is an effective shot and best made ten to fifteen feet from the basket. It is particularly useful as it is made from the top of an upward jump above the defensive player and because the defender must risk fouling to stop the shot. The shot is made on receiving the ball in a restricted space or on completion of a dribble.

**Hook Shot**

This shot is usually made quite near to the basket. The action is sideways and very much like the cricketer's bowling action while the head is turned in the direction of the shot with eyes on the basket.

**TEAM DEFENCE**

**Man to Man Defence**

This defence, although an overall team effort, is primarily a job for the individual. If one man lets his opponent get by him, either cutting or dribbling, the result may well be a two point deficit. Each man is assigned to guard a particular man on the opposing team with the purpose of stopping that man scoring or putting a team mate into a scoring situation.

**Three-on-Two**

This is the two on one with two more players but with certain special characteristics to be considered. The organized fast break employing three men will have each man moving in a lane down the court with the middle man having the responsibility of distributing the ball if he cannot drive straight to basket, so, the middle man must be stopped by one of the two defenders and he is best placed on the free throw line forcing him to pass out a reasonable distance away from basket.

**Two-On-One**

The defensive player is put in most unfavourable position of deciding which one of the two attackers to take. To him, it may seem a certain two points. Before the offensive players reach a sure shooting area, take a position between the two.

**Sagging Man to Man**

To play this defence successfully, each man on the team must be aware of the position of the ball. The principle is for the defensive player to sag back from his man when the ball is moved to the other side of the court.

## RULES OF BASKETBALL

**Original Rules**

James Naismith published in 1891, his rules for the game of "Basket Ball" that he invented: The original game played under these rules was quite different than the one played today as there was no dribbling, dunking, or three pointers.

1. The ball may be thrown in any direction with one or both hands.

2. The ball may be batted in any direction with one or both hands.

3. A player can't run with the ball. The player must throw it from the spot on which he catches it, allowance

to be made for a man running at good speed.

4. The ball must be held in or between the hands; the arms or body must not be used for holding it.

5. No shouldering, holding, striking, pushing, or tripping in any way of an opponent. The first infringement of this rule by any person shall count as a foul; the second shall disqualify him until the next basket is made or, if there was evident intent to injure the person, for the whole of the game. No substitution shall be allowed.

6. A foul is striking at the ball with the fist, violation of rules three and four and such described in rule five

7. If either side makes three consecutive fouls, it shall count a goal for the opponents (consecutive means without the opponents in the mean time making a foul).

8. A goal shall be made when the ball is thrown or batted from the grounds into the basket and stays there (without falling), providing those defending the goal do not touch or disturb the goal. If the ball rests on the edges, and the opponent moves the basket, it shall count as a goal.

9. When the ball goes out of bounds, it shall be thrown into the field of play and played by the first person touching it. In case of dispute the umpire shall throw it straight into the field. The thrower-in is allowed five seconds. If he holds it longer, it shall go to the opponent. If any side persists in delaying the game, the umpire shall call a foul on that side.

10. The umpire shall be the judge of the men and shall note the fouls and notify the referee when three consecutive fouls have been made. He shall have power to disqualify people according to Rule 5.

11. The referee shall be judge of the ball and shall decide when the ball is in play, in bounds, to which side it belongs, and shall keep the time. He shall decide when

a goal has been made and keep account of the baskets, with any other duties that are usually performed by a scorekeeper.

12. The time shall be two fifteen-minute halves, with five minutes rest between.

13. The side making the most points in that time is declared the winner.

**Court and Dimensions**

a. Thc playing court shall be measured and marked as shown in the court diagram.

b. A free throw lane shall be marked at each end of the court with dimensions and markings as shown on the court diagram. All boundary lines are part of the lane; lane space marks and neutral zone marks are not. The color of the lane space marks and neutral zones shall contrast with the color of the boundary lines. The areas identified by the lane space markings are 2" by 8" inches and the neutral zone marks are 12" by 8".

c. A free throw line shall be drawn (2" wide) across each of the circles indicated in the court diagram. It shall be parallel to the end line and shall be 15' from the plane of the face of the backboard.

d. The three-point field goal area has parallel lines 3' from the sidelines, extending from the baseline and an arc of 23'9" from the middle of the basket which intersects the parallel lines.

e. Four hash marks shall be drawn (2" wide) perpendicular to the sideline on each side of the ccurt and 28' from the baseline. These hash marks shall extend 3' onto the court.

f. Four hash marks shall be drawn (2" wide) perpendicular to the baseline on each side of the free throw lane line. These hash marks shall be 3' from the free throw lane line and extend 6" onto the court.

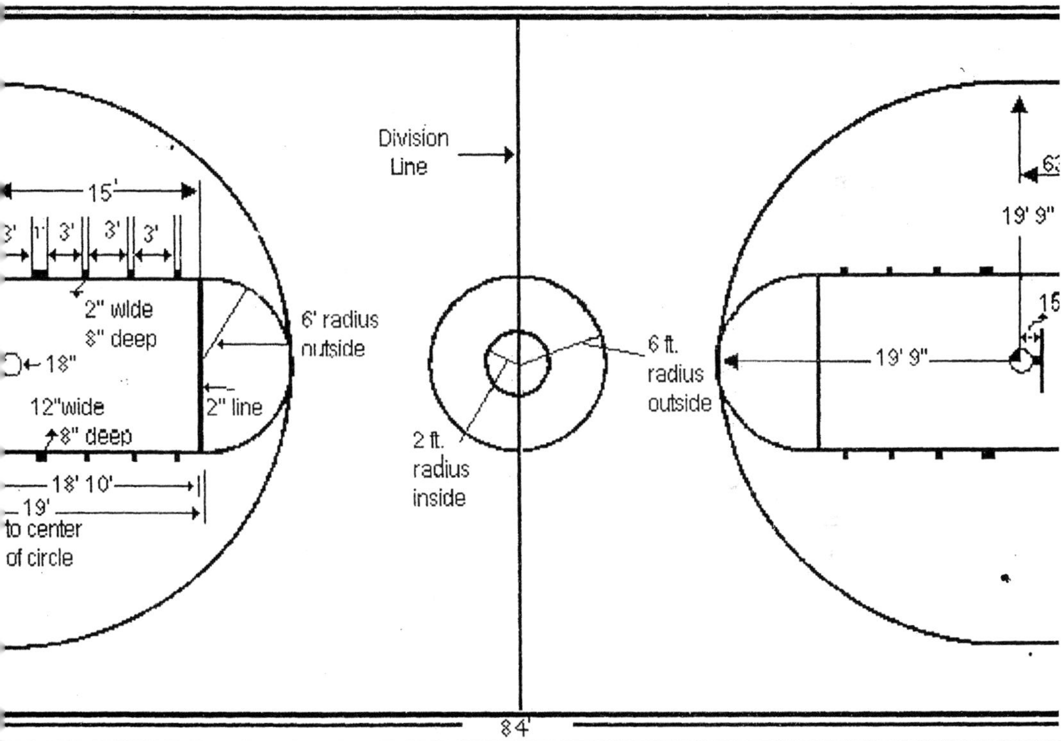

Division Line
15'
3'
1'
3'
3'
3'
2" wide
8" deep
18"
12"wide
8" deep
6' radius outside
2" line
18' 10'
19'
to center of circle
2 ft. radius inside
6 ft. radius outside
19' 9"
19' 9"
84'

g. Four hash marks shall be drawn (2" wide) parallel to the baseline on each side of the free throw circle. These hash marks shall be 13' from the baseline and 3' from the free throw lane lines and shall be 6" in length.

h. Two hash marks shall be drawn (2" wide) perpendicular to the sideline, in front of the scorer's table, and 4' on each side of the midcourt line. This will designate the Substitution Box area.

i. A half-circle shall be created 4' from the center of the basket.

**Players, Substitutes, Teams and Teammates**

Naismith's original rules did not specify how many players were to be on the court. In 1900, five players became standard, and players that were substituted were not allowed to re-enter the game. Players were allowed to re-enter a game once from 1921, and twice from 1934; such restrictions on substitutions were abolished in 1945 when substitutions became unlimited. Coaching was originally prohibited during the game, but from 1949, coaches were allowed to address players during a time-out.

Originally a player was disqualified on his second foul. This limit became four fouls in 1911 and five fouls in 1945, still the case in most forms of basketball where the normal length of the game (before any overtime periods) is 40 minutes. When the normal length is 48 minutes (this is the case with the National Basketball Association in the United States and the National Basketball League in Australia, among others) a player is accordingly disqualified on his sixth foul.

**Shot Clock and Time Limits**

The first time restriction on possession of the ball was introduced in 1933, where teams were required to advance the ball over the center line within ten seconds of gaining possession. This rule remained until 2000, when FIBA reduced the requirement to eight seconds, the NBA following suit in 2001. The NCAA retains the 10-second rule for men's play, but has never adopted a time limit for women's play. U.S. high schools, whose rules are drafted by NFHS, also use the 10-second rule for both sexes.

In 1936 the three-second rule was introduced. This rule prohibits offensive players from remaining near their opponents' basket for longer than three seconds (the precise restricted area is also known as the lane or the key). A game central to this rule's introduction was that between the University of Kentucky and New York University. Kentucky coach Adolph Rupp did not take one of his referees with him, despite being warned of discrepancies in officiating between the midwest and east by Notre Dame coach George Keogan, and the game became especially rough. Because of this game and others, 6'5" (1.96 m) Kentucky All American center Leroy Edwards is generally recognized as the player responsible for the 3 second rule.

While the rule was originally adopted to reduce roughness in the area between big men, it is now considered to prevent tall offensive players from gaining an advantage by waiting close to the basket. When the NBA started to allow zone defense in 2001, a three-second rule for defensive players was also introduced.

The shot clock was first introduced by the NBA in 1954, to increase the speed of play. Teams were then required to attempt a shot within 24 seconds of gaining possession, and the shot clock would be reset when the ball touched the basket's rim or the backboard, or the opponents gained possession. FIBA adopted a 30-second shot clock two years later, resetting the clock when a shot was attempted. Women's basketball adopted a 30-second clock in 1971. The NCAA adopted a 45-second shot clock for men while continuing with the 30-second clock for women in 1985. The men's shot clock was then reduced to 35 seconds in 1993. FIBA reduced the shot clock to 24 seconds in 2000, and changed the clock's resetting to when the ball touched the rim of the basket. Originally, a missed shot where the shot clock expired while the ball is in the air constituted a violation. In 2003 the rule was changed so that the ball remains live in this situation, as long as it touched the rim. If the ball touches the rim and slightly bounces over the basketball hoop it will be called as a loose ball.

**Fouls, Free Throws and Violations**

Dribbling was not part of the original game, but was introduced in 1901. At the time, a player could only bounce the ball once, and could not shoot after he had dribbled. The definition of dribbling became the "continuous passage of the ball" in 1909, allowing more than one bounce, and a player who had dribbled was then allowed to shoot.

Running with the ball ceased to be considered a foul in 1922, and became a violation, meaning that the only penalty was loss of possession. Striking the ball with the fist has also become a violation. From 1931, if a closely guarded player withheld the ball from play for five seconds, play was stopped and resumed with a jump ball; such a situation has since become a violation by the ball-carrier. Goaltending became a violation in 1944, and offensive goaltending in 1958.

Free throws were introduced shortly after basketball was invented. In 1895, the free throw line was officially placed fifteen feet (4.6 m) from the backboard, prior to which most gymnasiums placed one twenty feet (6.1 m) from the backboard. From 1924, players that received a foul were required to shoot their own free throws. One free throw shot is awarded to a player who was fouled while making a successful field goal attempt. If the field goal attempt is unsuccessful, two free throw shots are awarded (three if the player was attempting a three-point field goal). If an offensive player is fouled while not in the act of shooting, or if a player is fouled in a loose-ball situation, the penalty varies by level of play and the number of fouls accumulated by the opposing team in a given period.

*** In NCAA and NFHS play:**

o If the player's team has 6 or fewer team fouls in the half, the team fouled gets possession of the ball.

o If the team has 7 to 9 team fouls, the player fouled goes to the line for what is called "one-and-one" or the "bonus"—that is, if the player makes the first free throw, he gets the opportunity to attempt a second, but if he misses, the ball is live.

o If the team has 10 or more fouls in the half, the player fouled gets two free throws, often called the "double bonus".

o All overtime periods are considered an extension of the second half for purposes of accumulated fouls. Also, NFHS rules accumulate fouls per half, even though games are played in quarters.

* In the NBA:

o If the player's team has 4 or fewer team fouls in the quarter, the team fouled gets possession of the ball.

o Starting with the team's fifth foul in the quarter, the player fouled gets two free throws.

o Overtime is not considered an extension of any quarter. Instead, the "penalty" of two free throws is triggered on the team's fourth foul in that overtime period (instead of the fifth).

o Foul limits are reset in the last two minutes of a quarter or overtime period. If a team has not reached its limit of accumulated fouls, the first team foul in the last two minutes results in possession by the team fouled, and all subsequent fouls result in two free throws.

* In FIBA play:

o If the player's team has 4 or fewer team fouls in the quarter, the team fouled gets possession of the ball.

o Starting with the team's fifth foul in the quarter, the player fouled gets two free throws.

o All overtime periods are considered an extension of the fourth quarter for purposes of accumulated fouls.

Charge is physical contact between an offensive player and a defensive player. In order to draw an offensive charge the defensive player must establish legal guarding positioning in the path of the offensive player. If contact is made, the officials would issue an offensive charge. No points will be allowed and the ball is turned over. The defensive player may not draw an offensive charge in the "restricted zone".

Blocking is physical contact between the offensive player and the defensive player. Blocking fouls are issued when a defensive player interferes with the path of the offensive player in the shooting motion. Blocking fouls are easily called when the defensive player is standing in the "restricted zone".

Restricted zone: In 1997, the NBA introduced an arc of a 4-foot (1.22 m) radius around the basket, in which an offensive foul for charging could not be assessed. This was to prevent defensive players from attempting to draw an offensive foul on their opponents by standing underneath the basket. FIBA adopted this arc with a 1.25 m (4 ft 1.2 in) radius in 2010.

**Equipment**

The goal is placed 10 feet (3.05m) above the court. Originally a basket was used (thus "basket-ball"), so the ball had to be retrieved after each made shot. Today an open-bottom hoop is used instead.

**Officiating and procedures**

Originally, there was one umpire to judge fouls and one referee to judge the ball; the tradition of calling one official the "referee" and the other one or two the "umpires" has remained (the NBA, however, uses different terminology, referring to the lead official as "crew chief" and the others as "referees"). Today, both classes of officials have equal rights to control all aspects of the game. The NBA added a third official in 1988, and FIBA did so afterward, using it for the first time in international competition in 2006. The use of video evidence to inform referee's decisions has always been banned, except in the case of determining whether or not the last shot of a period was attempted before time expired. This exception was introduced by the NBA in 2002 and adopted by FIBA in 2006. The NCAA, however, has permitted instant replay for timing, the value of a field goal (two or three points), shot clock violations, and for purposes of disqualifying players because of unsportsmanlike conduct. The NBA changed its rules starting in 2007 to allow officials the ability to view instant replay with plays involving flagrant fouls, similar to the NCAA. In Italy's Lega A, an American football-style coach's challenge is permitted to challenge (at the next dead ball) an official's call on any situation similar to the NCAA.

The center jump ball that was used to restart a game after every successful field goal was eliminated in 1938, in favor of the ball being given to the non-scoring team from behind the end line where the goal was scored, in order to make play more continuous. The jump ball was still used to start the game and every period, and to restart the game after a held ball. However, the NBA stopped using the jump ball to start the second through fourth quarters in 1975, instead using a quarter-possession system where the loser of the jump ball takes the ball from the other end to start the second and third periods, while the winner of that jump ball takes the ball to start the fourth period from the other end of the court.

In 1981, the NCAA adopted the alternating possession system for all jump ball situations except the beginning of the game, and in 2003, FIBA adopted a similar rule, except for the start of the third period and overtime. In 2004, the rule was changed in FIBA that the arrow applies for all situations after the opening tap.

In 1976, the NBA introduced a rule to allow teams to advance the ball to the center line following any legal time-out in the final two minutes of the game. FIBA followed suit in 2006.

**International Rules of Basketball**

The most recent international rules of basketball were approved April 26, 2008 by FIBA and became effective October 1 of that year.

There are eight rules encompassing 50 articles, covering equipment and facilities, regulations regarding teams, players, captains and coaches, playing regulations, violations, fouls and their penalties, special situations, and the officials and table officials. The rules also cover officials' signals, the scoresheet, protest procedure, classification of teams and television time-outs.

# 4

# BILLIARDS AND SNOOKER

## INTRODUCTION

### BILLIARDS

Billiards is played with three balls on a 5' x 10' table which has no pocket. It is played basically everywhere except in the US and UK where people play pool or snooker. Billiards is played in Europe, South America, Asia (Japan, Indonesia), North Africa (Egypt, Turkey). There are a white ball, a yellow ball (sometimes a white ball with two dots) and a red ball. One player has the white ball as his cue ball and the other player has the yellow ball. The red is always an object ball. There also exists an Asian game with four balls.

Billiards has always been a family of games that is played on a table, with a cue stick. The cue stick is used to strike balls that move around on the table. There are different types of billiard ball games. In eight ball games and straight pool, 16 balls are used - 15 are colored and one white ball or "cue" ball. Object balls are numbered one through seven and are solid colored. Balls nine through 15 are white and have a colored stripe that matches a corresponding solid ball. The nine ball has a yellow stripe, the 10-ball has a blue stripe, etc. The eight ball is always black. Regulation balls measure 2¼ inches and weight about 5½ to 6 ounces.

On of the easiest games to play is Three Cushion billiards. It is played on a table that has no pockets and is slightly larger than a pool table. Three Cushion billiards is played with three balls that are red, yellow and white. The object is to have the cue ball hit the two other balls on the table along with three or more rails.

Other games include the Straight Rail or Free Game. It requires the cue ball to hit only the two other balls in order to score a point. Balkline is another game like Straight Rail, but the table has lines that are 18" from each rail that create nine boxes on the table. If a player makes one or two, depending on the game, Straight Rail billiards in a box and drive it across a line. Players try to make the ball come back into a box to continue playing. Three Cushion billiards is the most popular game of all billiard games played.

**SNOOKER**

Historically speaking, snooker has always been considered 'the gentleman's game' due to its roots. In its early days, the balls were made of ivory and twelve elephants had to be slaughtered to create just one full set, meaning very few families could afford access to the facilities. However, off the back of developments in the late 20th century, snooker is today flourishing, and an estimated 4 million adults of all backgrounds play the sport regularly. This reflection of its popularity is further boosted by an arguably even more devoted spectator set, with a remarkable 45% of the British population tuning in to see 15 minutes or more of the World Championship final in 2005 and well over 7 million people staying tuned from start to finish.

Such statistics are also indicative of how British-centred the sport of snooker remains. Indeed, just three men from outside the UK have won the World Snooker Championships; Horace Lindrum from Australia in 1952, Cliff Thorburn from Canada in 1980 and Ken Doherty from the Republic of Ireland in 1997. The pinnacle of snooker's popularity in Britain was arguably the legendary final of the 1985 World Snooker Championship between Dennis Taylor and Steve Davis, when after an astonishing 14 hours and 50 minutes of play and 35 frames, 18.5 million people watched Taylor

sink a sudden-death black for the victory. That was at one point a record audience for a British sporting event and remains a record post-midnight audience for a British broadcast.

However, the rise of the global circuit and expansion of television coverage has produced an influx of both fans and talent from outside Britain, particularly from the Far East and other Commonwealth countries. This was exemplified in 2005 when the Chinese player Ding Junhui won the UK Championship at just 18 years old. Ding's rising profile has had an important knock-on effect in his home country and, when he swept to victory in the final of the 2005 China Open, World Snooker reported an incredible 110 million people watched on CCTV footage. Therefore, to get involved with snooker is to participate in a sport which is both remarkably British but spreading on a yearly basis.

This spread has ensured that snooker is now an extremely profitable enterprise for professionals. Whereas the first World Championship in 1927 saw the victor Joe Davis pick up £6.10s (equivalent to £200 today), the winner of the 2004 Championship received a cool £250,000 of the £1,378,920 prize money purse. The riches don't stop there either, with career earnings entering the millions for a select few and Stephen Hendry topping the list with well over 8 million in career prize money as of 2007.

This guide will attempt to give you an insight into just how snooker has developed from its inception in the 19th century to the growing brand it is today. It will also extensively cover the rules and regulations, give you a sense of how the sport is organised at a competitive level and offer plenty of links and information on how to get involved, keep updated on all the developments and educate yourself on the sport every way imaginable.

So, if you're seeking a way into this 'gentleman's game', please read on!

## SKILLS AND TECHNIQUES

### BILLIARDS

Proper shooting posture, imagining the shot paths and points of contact and aiming the billiard shot with your dominant eye are the three important aspects of billiard techniques. Mastering these skills will help you to have a great game, not just once but with amazing consistency.

Admittedly, continuously practicing fundamentals cannot be too much fun for anyone, whether an advanced player or a learner. Remember however, that without the proper grip, bridge and stance even a professional almost certainly face an uphill struggle against consistency, no matter how much you learn about the game.

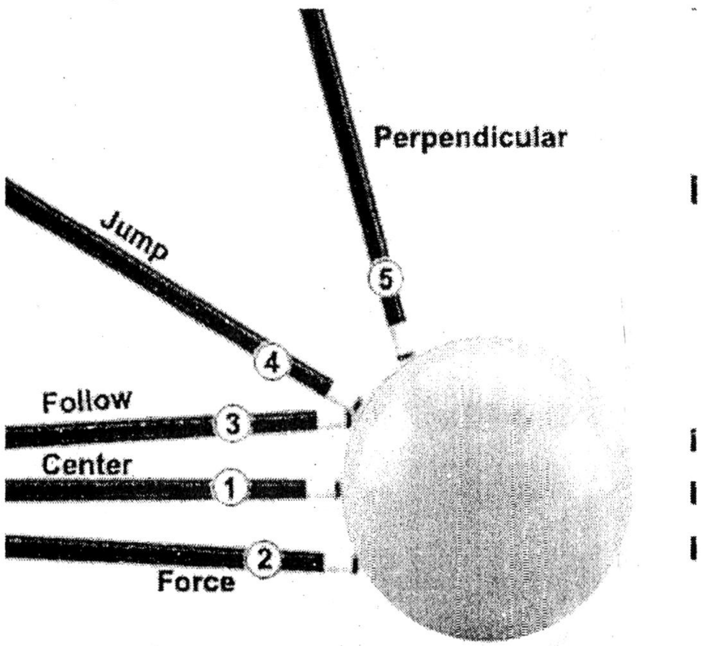

Tip- If you take the time to establish a strong foundation; when you find yourself in a slump you can always retrace your steps back to your fundamentals and you'll soon get your groove back.

**Using your Dominant Eye**

It is important that you use your dominant eye for lining up and aiming the balls. Develop a technique for positioning your body in such a way that that your dominant eye and the intended shot are perfectly aligned. To achieve this alignment sometimes requires that you practically rest your chin on the cue. Some of the most brilliant pool players have mastered this billiards technique resulting in some spellbinding game play.

Making the Shot Weigh the pros and cons prior to taking every shot, then make a decision based on your analysis and aim the shot accurately. The best way to do this is to draw a straight imaginary line from the object ball and let this line touch the centre of the opening to the pocket. Next, extend this line in such a way that it passes through the object ball to the side opposite the pocket. The point of intersection between this imaginary line and the edge of the object ball is the perfect place to hit the ball. This ensures that the ball will go to the intended or desired direction.

**Visualizing the Shot**

The next step in honing your pool technique is determining the exact point on the cue ball that will match up with the point identified on the object ball. At first glance, this may seem unattainable for the simple reason that you are absolutely standing behind the cue ball. However, this hurdle can be removed by visual means, which implies that you use your imagination to project where the object ball will be it comes in contact with the cue ball and ensure that both balls are aligned towards the pocket.

**Getting a Good Grip**

While producing astounding shots using unorthodox grips make for great drama, for starters you are better off employing the simple, consistent grip, which is neither too tight nor too loose. Holding the cue too tightly means your wrists cannot be released smoothly and quickly enough to produce a fluid stroke. On the other hand, you will find you are unable to take precise and powerful shots if you hold the cue very loosely. An ideal grip is one in which the cue is held mainly in the fingers and not the palm of the hand, leaving the wrist flat in the plane that is formed between the lower and upper arm. As with any other game of skill, practice is key to mastering the right billiards technique.

**SNOOKER**

Snooker is a two-player game popular in England and other Commonwealth countries. Similar to billiards, players strike cue sticks against the cue ball, which then hits the scoring balls. Players try to sink -- or "pot" -- scoring balls into side pockets of the table. Practicing snooker techniques and mastering basic skills gives you an edge over opponents and can help you triumph in snooker matches.

**Put a Spin on the Balls**

Side-, top- and backspins, help you control the cue ball, better pot scoring balls and give your opponent a difficult set-up for his shots. This is also called putting English on the balls. Picture the cue ball face as a clock. To side-spin, strike the cue ball either to the left or right of center at the 3 o'clock or 9 o'clock position. The side-spin sends the cue ball spinning into the scoring ball, which can knock the scoring ball off its expected path.

To topspin, hit the cue ball at the 12 o'clock position. This makes the cue ball travel faster following its impact with a scoring ball.

Backspins are achieved by striking the cue ball at the 6 o'clock position. A back-spun cue ball reverses course after hitting a scoring ball. Do not hit the ball too low, or it will jump, which is illegal in snooker.

**Stunning**

Hit the cue ball just below the center point, but not low enough to create a backspin. The cue ball will stop moving after it hits a scoring ball, but the scoring ball will continue to travel forward. This can put the cue ball in a better position for the next shot.

**Special Stunning Shots**

There may be times when you want to stun the cue ball, but have it move forward or back just a bit after hitting the scoring ball. These shots are called stun run-throughs and stun screws. Both shots give you the benefit of a stun while moving the ball into a better position for you or a worse position for your opponent.

The stun run-through is accomplished by striking the cue ball just above the center point. Properly hit, the cue ball will stop and roll forward a few inches after hitting the scoring ball.

To perform the stun screw shot, line up your shot as you would a stunner—with the stick tip just below center. Aim just below that point and strike the cue ball. This will cause the cue ball to stop and reverse a few inches after hitting the scoring ball.

## RULES OF BILLIARDS AND SNOOKER

## BILLIARDS

### The Game

In a game either 2 players can compete or 4. Different kinds of balls are used in the game which can be of white, spotted, plain, and red colour. In-offs, pots and cannons are also used in the game. Strokes are awarded with points while fouls is penalised by deduction. After a

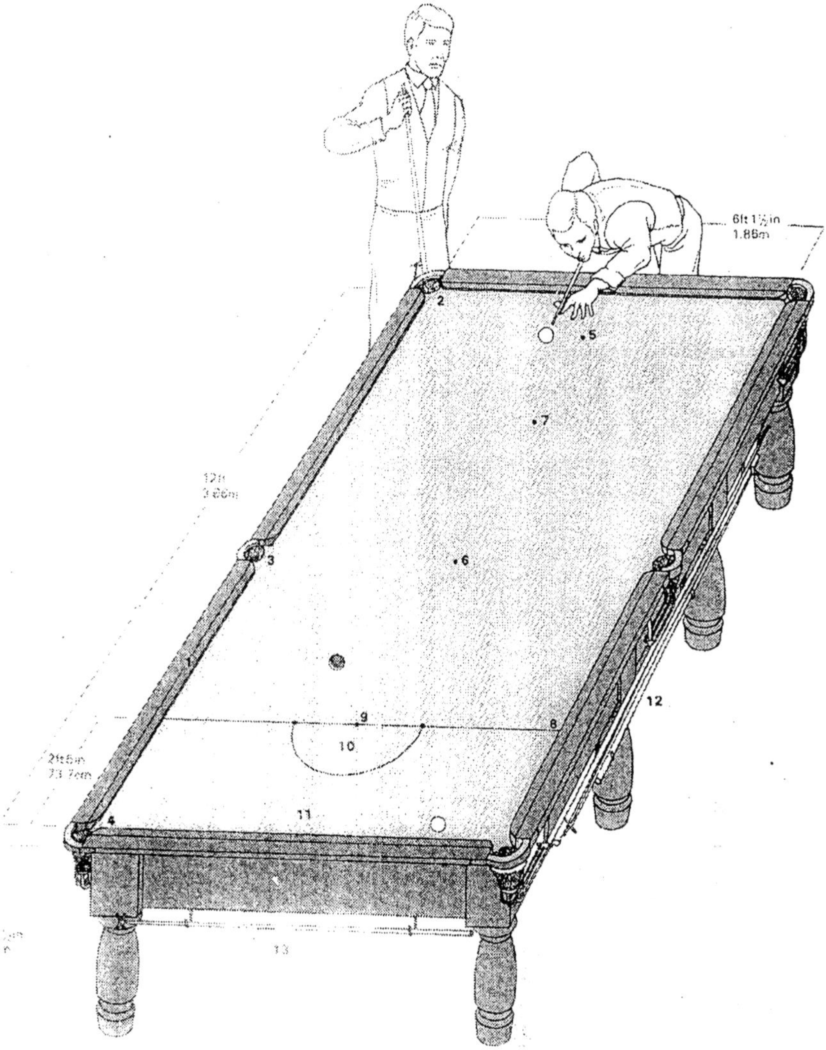


specified period of time points scored by each player will be valued and player with more points will be declare winner.

**Starting of Game**

i. At beginning of game red should be placed on spot, the first player plays from in-hand and the game starts with first stroke;

ii. The choice of ball, order of play, if not agreed upon, should be decided by stringing, the winner having the option, and should remain unaffected throughout the game.

Details of Scoring

In below mentioned way points should be awarded:

i. For a pot red and in-off red—3 points;

ii. When in-off is combined with a cannon—2 or 3 points;

iii. For a cannon, pot white and in-off white—2 points;

Order of Play

Players will play turn by turn till no score is made by striker.

**To Play from In-hand**

Cue-ball should:

a. Before hitting any ball in baulk it should hit a ball or cushion out of baulk;

b. Be played out of baulk

Limitation of Cannons

Not in conjunction with hazard, 75 consecutive cannons are permissible in game. Referee is required to inform the striker after expiry of 70 cannons.

**Penalty**

Player committing any of the following fouls can be penalised with forfeiture of his points as well as his turn:

i. if any player strike a moving cue ball or an object ball;

ii. Player who does not put his either foot on floor while executing the stroke;

iii. Any player who touch or disturb the cue ball or any object ball;

iv. If cue ball goes into pocket;

v. Jumping cue ball of table.

Other than Striker someone other striking the ball

If ball is strucked by anybody other than striker, referee should put the ball again at its place so that striker can strike it.

**Play without Disturbance**

(1) Striker should call the number of ball which he wants to pocket. If ball he called has already pocketed, he should be provided with any other ball. Other balls pocketed on same stroke should be ignored which should be spotted again if called ball has not pocketed.

(2) Ball which rolls up on a rail but come back to table should be considered to be in play.

(3) Object ball should be spotted if cue ball is in hand and object ball is within the head string. Ball nearer to head string should be spotted if within head string there are more than 1 object ball.

(4) Each player's turn is known as an inning, thus play is conducted in innings. As long as a player legally pockets a ball on each stroke, inning should remain continue. Opponent becomes shooter in case striker failed to legally pocket a ball or committed any foul.

(5) Ball which have been striken by anybody other than striker should be replaced at table at its original place.

(6) It is an error that a called ball jumps the table. For this error a player has to give up his inning.

**Restrictions of Hazards**

Consecutive hazards, being not in conjunction with a cannon are restricted to 15.

After 10 hazards referee will inform the striker.

In by a single stroke more than 1 hazard is made it should be counted as 1 but all points should be considered to have scored.

.The non-striker's ball should be off the table and spotted after 15-hazard on middle spot of D, as a consequence of striker's last stroke.

**Miss**

i. In condition other than the following miss should be considered a foul:

When striker is in hand and there is no ball out of baulk;

ii. Miss should be penalised with 2 points.

Ball on the Edge of Pocket

i. Ball which falls into pocket without hitting other ball should be replaced.

ii. If ball which have been striked out by striker hit the ball on edge of pocket, all balls should be replaced and striker should strike again.

iii. Ball which balances momentarily on the edge and falls in should be replaced.

**Balls Touching**

If striker's ball is touching non-striker's ball, it should be placed on centre spot. If striker's ball is touching anyother ball, red shouid be placed on the spot.

**Fouls**

Following procedure should be followed if a foul takes place:

i. Refree should state loudly Foul.

ii. if it is not awarded by umpire or claimed by other player, before making of next stroke it should be ignored.

iii. Ball which have been spotted improperly should remain at place where situates.

iv. All points scored before awarding of foul should be taken into consideration.

Benefit of penalty of a player is enjoyed by his opponent. For every foul a penalty of 2 points is awarded to every player which gets included in score of his opponent.

Next player can play from any of the following places:

i. from in-hand,

ii. from where balls are in a dead position,

By doing anything out of following a player can commit a foul:

While striking:

i. out of turn;

ii. to ball other than cue-ball;

iii. when balls are in moving position;

iv. improperly from in-hand;

v. by both feet off the floor.

While attempting:

i. more than authorised hazards;

ii. a jump shot;

iii. more than 75 cannons;

iv. to use ball off the table;

v. a push stroke;

vi. to touch the ball with other part of cue than tip.

**Spotting**

(i) If no ball occupies the foot spot, balls which have to be spotted should be placed there. Balls should be placed in a straight line behind each other turn by turn if more than 1 ball is to be spotted. Line drawn from foot spot to bottom rail is known is Long String. Balls should be placed in line on long string, if multiple spotting of balls is necessary. Non-spotted balls placed along long string line cannot be moved.

(ii) Balls which have been knocked from table or have pocketed in an illegal manner should be replaced on the table.

In following conditions balls should be spotted:

i. if in the same stroke in which cue ball is to pocketed, ball is made;

ii. if it is made in a stroke in which cue ball strike the designed object ball after striking anyother balls.

iii. if from the table ball is knocked;

**Definitions**

**Match**

Pre-determined number of games are included in a match.

**Game**

A game includes an agreed number of frames.

**Striker**

Person having right to strike the ball is called striker.

Balls

i. 15 red balls are used in the game;

ii. Ball of white colour is called cue-ball;

iii. Object balls have 6 colours.

**Ball in Play**

i. If ball is not in-hand, it is considered to have in play;

ii. If spotted, red should be considered to be in play. It should remain so till potted or forced off the table;

Inspite of touching the ball with tip of cue, ball may not be considered to be in play if in opinion of refree player did not attempt to strike it.

**Stroke**

i. As soon as striker strikes the cue-ball with the help of tip of cue, striker is considered to hit the strike.

ii. A stroke which satisfies undermentioned conditions is considered to be a fair stroke:

a. Ball should be in a dead position at time of being striken and colours should be spotted properly;

b. Cue ball should not be strucked, but pushed.

c. Cue ball can be strucked only for one time in a single stroke.

d. At time of striking, striker should have either of his foot on floor.

Stroke comes to an end as soon as ball comes in a dead position and striker leaves the table.

In following conditions ball is considered to be in-hand:

i. Ball is considered to be in-hand when it is out of the table;

ii. Until ball is played from in-hand or from here a foul is committed, it should considered to be in-hand;

iii. Ball is considered to be in-hand till turn of non-striker comes.

**Jump Shot**

Jump shot is a shot by which cue-ball jumps over anyother ball. However, when cue ball first strikes object ball and then jumps over another ball, this stroke should not be considered a jump shot.

**Hazard**

An hazard includes a pot or an in-off.

**Occupied**

If before touching another ball no ball has been placed on spot, it should be considered to have occupied.

**Break**

When strokes made in a turn are expressed in a series, it is known as a Break.

**String**

String is that state in which to leave the ball of player near to bottom cushion, together from Baulk-line to top cushion ball is played.

**In-Off**

After touching any object ball when cue-ball get into a pocket, it is termed in-off. However, it should be happened within rules.

**Forced Off the Table**

A ball is considered to be forced off the table if it does not comes in a dead position on any place other than bed of table or in the pocket.

**Cannons**

Cannon is a stroke in which cue-ball hit both object balls. However, it should be within rules of game.

**Pot**

Pot is a term which is used when ball without touching another ball enters into pocket. This should happened in accordance with rules.

**Push Stroke**

Tip of cue should not touch cue-ball while cue-ball touches object ball or when cue-ball has been commenced its forward motion. If this rule is overruled it is a foul which is known as Push-Stroke.

**Equipments Used**

**Balls**

i. All balls should be of same weight. Balls of following weights are used in different events:

a. For Snooker Set balls of 3 gms;

b. For Billiard Set balls of 0.05 gms;

ii. Ball should have a radius of 26.25 mm and a tolerance capacity of 0.05 mm to 0.08mm.

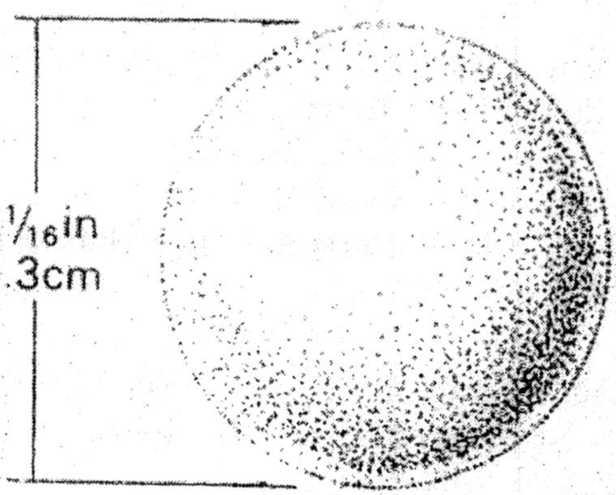


**Ancillary**

For cue rests can be used to provide a bridge.

**Cue**

Cue should not a length of more than 910 mm. It should have a traditional accepted shape.

**Billiard Table-Metric**

The "D"

Bualk should have a semi-circle with a diameter of 584 mm. Centre of this semi-circle should be situated at middle of Baulk-line.

**Pocket Openings**

i. Corners and middle longer sides of table should have pockets.

ii. These pockets should fulfils guidelines provided by Billiards and Snooker Control Council or BSCC.

**Spots**

In following manner 4 spots should be marked on centre longitudinal line of the table:

i. Centre Spot : At equal distance from faces of top and bottom cushion and midway between centre pockets, this spot should be marked.

ii. Spot: At a distance of 320 mm from the perpendicular point below face of top cushion, this should be marked.

iii. In centre of Baulk-line one spot should mark.

iv. Pyramid Spot : Between centre spot and face of top cushion, this spot should be marked.

**Height**

From floor to top of cushion rail table should be situated at a height of about 850mm × 875mm.

**Dimensions**

Within the cushion faces playing area should have a size of 3500mm to 1750 mm. It should have a tolerance of ±3 mm on both dimension.

**Baulk-line and Baulk**

Line drawn parallel to bottom cushion at a distance of 700 m from it is known as Baulk-Line, whereas intervening space is know as the Baulk.

**Table of Billiard-Imperial**

**Height**

From floor to top of the cushion rail table should be situated at a height of 2ft 91/2 ins × 2 ft 101/2 ins.

**Pocket Openings**

i. Corner and middle of longer side should have pockets;

ii. These pockets should fulfils guidelines of BSCC.

**Dimensions**

Within cushion faces playing area should have a size of 11 ft. 812 ins × 5 ft 10 ins, and a tolerance of ±0.5 on both dimensions.

**Spots**

In following manner 4 spots should be marked on centre of longitudinal line of table:

i. In centre of Baulk-line;

ii. Spot : Below face of top cushion at a distance of 123/4 from perpendicular point.

iii. Centre Spot : At equal distance from faces of top and bottom cushion and midway between centre pockets this spot should be marked.

iv. Pyramid Spot: Midway between centre spot and face of top cushion this spot should be marked.

**Rules of 8-Ball Game**

With following exceptions basic rules of pocket billiard apply in this game:

**Starting the Game**

a. Shooter can choose high or low numbered balls as his object balls, if balls have been pocketed on the break. This option will transfer to other player if first player does not pocket the ball on break. Till ball is pocketed final designation of object balls should not be assigned.

b. On the break atleast one object ball should be driven.

c. Balls should be racked in such a way that 8-ball is placed in centre of third row from front apex of rack.

d. If any shooter pocketed the 8-ball on break, he should be declared winner of game.

**Purpose of Game**

Basic aim of every player is to pocket the 8-ball first. Balls numbered from 1 to 7 are object balls for one player and balls numbered from 9 to 15 are object balls for other player.

8-ball is not allowed to be pocketed, however on break till designated balls have been pocketed, it can be pocketed.

**Non-Interrupted Play**

a. A shot will be considered to be legal if shooter contact his own ball first. Combinations balls having any ball are allowed.

b. If any shooter pocketed his opponent's ball, advantage of this should be enjoyed by opponent.

c. 8-ball should be pocketed after all designated balls have been pocketed.

d. A shot at 8-ball will be considered to be legal if that shooter call the pocket into which ball will fall and 8-ball should be strucked first.

**Penalties**

A player can loose the game if he commit any of the following errors:

i. Pocket the 8-ball before it becomes object ball;

ii. 8-ball is pocketed in pocket in place of that called by shooter;

iii. Neither cue-ball nor 8-ball contact a rail in flailing to make 8-ball;

iv. While 8-ball is pocketed scratch occurs.

**Players**

**Absence**

If any player cannot be present in room, he can appoint his substitute.

**Unfair Conduct**

A player can lose a game if:

He refuse to continue a frame;

Behaves in an unfair manner.

For above mentioned behaviour a player can be disqualified from the game in competitions which are held under control of Billiards and Snooker Council or its Affiliated Associations.

**Time Wasting**

A player will be warned and can be disqualified if refree thinks that he is taking a lot of time in playing the stroke.

**Non-Striker**

While striker is playing his stroke other player is not allowed to stand or move in line of sight. It is done with a view to avoid every kind of disturbance to strike.

**Officials of Game**

**The Marker**

Marker is required to keep the score on marking board and to help refree in perform his duties.

**The Referee**

Main duties of refree includes the following:

a. He should ensure that game is being played in accordance with basic rules;

b. He should discontinuity the play if there is any breach of rule;

c. He will tell colour of ball if player has a problem in seeing the colours properly;

d. On the request of player he has to clean the ball.

He should ignore any question which is not stated by rules;

He is not require to indicate to any player that he may commit a foul.

**RULES OF SNOOKER**

**Game**

**Location of Balls**

At starting of each frame object balls should be placed in the following way:

On pyramid spot Pink ball;
On left-hand Green ball;
On the spot Black ball;
On centre spot Blue ball;

On right-hand correct of D Yellow ball;

On middle of baulk Brown ball;

At apex ball should be placed nearer to Pink ball, however, it should not touch it;

Red ball should be placed in a triangular form;

Near to top cushion base should be designed which should be parallel to it.

**Explanation**

Game should be played between 2 players on English Billiard Table. For every stroke every player receives a point, in the same way point will be deducted if his opponent commits a foul.

Player scoring more points than other will be declare winner of the game.

There should be a common white cue-ball and 21 object balls in the game. White cue-ball is common in the sense that every player uses this ball.

15 reds with 1 value and of following colours with different values should be there:

Blue has a value of 5;

Green has a value of 3;

Brown has a value of 4;

Yellow has a value of 2;

Black valued 7;

Pink valued 6.

Till all reds are off the table scoring strokes can be made by potting the reds and after that by potting colours having less value first and more value later.

**Play from in hand**

Play will be considered from in-hand when cue-ball has been strucked from on or within lines of D.

How to Play

i. Players are required to decide the order in which they will play. It should be kept in mind that this order cannot be changed during the play.

ii. First player will play from in-hand and with first stroke frame is considered to have began.

iii. At beginning of game cue ball should first hit a ball and should not be in the pocket.

iv. Only ball on must can enter into pocket.

v. (a) At beginning of each turn red should be considered the Ball On;

(b) Value of red which have been potted in a single stroke is scored.

vi. If Red has been potted, such ball should be potted next which can be scored from being potted. Ball of this colour should be spotted again.

vii. Only Red and colours should be potted turn-by-turn to continue the break till all Reds are off the table;

viii. If striker was unable to score any point, right to strike passes to other player, who has to play from where cue-ball came into rest.

ix. Balls should be used in ascending order of their value, in other words, balls of higher value should be used first and then balls of lower value.

x. If score of both player is not equal and only Black balls have been left out with first score or foul frame will come to an end:

a. To decide order of play, a lot should be drawn;

b. Ball of black colour should be spotted;

c. Frame will come to an end with other score or foul;

d. Coming player should begin from in-hand.

Hitting of More than One Ball in Same Stroke

A player can hit only 1 ball in a single stroke. However, he can hit 2 reds or a free ball.

**Spotting Colours**

i. If a colour whose own spot has been occupied is to be spotted, it should be placed on highest value;

ii. If balls of different colours have to be spotted and their own spots have been already occupied, ball of highest value should be spotted first;

iii. If no spot is empty, colour should be placed near to its own spot between that spot and nearest part of top cushion, however, if in Black and Pink there is no space between its own spot and nearest part of top cushion, colour should be placed near to its own spot on centre line of table below that spot.

**Ball On**

It is same as mentioned earlier.

Ball on Edge of Pocket

i. A ball should be placed again on the table if it has fallen into pocket without hitting another ball;

ii. All balls on table have to replaced if striked ball has touched it. In this condition striker will get an opportunity to play his stroke again.

iii. Ball which balances on edge and falls in should not be replaced.

Ball without Obstruction

i. Refree should state Free Ball if cue-ball is snookered after a foul;

ii. Any ball can be considered As On by Non-Offending player if he has to play the succeeding stroke;

iii. For this purpose, free ball will be considered to be Ball On;

iv. If cue-ball is not hit first, it is consider a foul;

v. If free ball is to be potted it should be spotted, and value of ball on should be scored;

vi. Ball On should be scored if it is potted;

vii. In condition when both Free ball as well as Ball On are potted, value of ball On should be scored only.

**Touching ball**

Referee will state Touching Ball if any ball or ball which is or going to be On is being touched by Cue-Ball.

Penalties

For the following fouls a penalty of 4 points should be awarded:

**Through Causing**

a. If there is a push stroke, or in other words if there is any foul.

b. It enters a pocket.

c. If cue ball does hit a ball on,

d. If a ball is forced off the table.

e. If ball not correctly spotted was striken.

f. If ball is touched with not tip of cue but from anywhere else.

Through Unfair Stroke:

a. If strikes improperly from in hand.

b. If at time of striking no feet was on the floor.

c. If player strikes more than once in same stroke.

d. If player strikes without his turn.

**By causing**

a. If it enters a pocket.

b. If cue-ball does not hit a ball on.

c. If cue ball first strikes object ball and then jumps over any other ball.

d. If player snooker with free ball.

If striker uses a ball which is off the table or uses as the cue ball any ball other than white or after potting a red commits a foul before nominating a colour, a penalty of 7 points should be awarded for this foul.

**Fouls**

In relation to fouls following things should be kept in mind:

a. As soon as any player commits a foul, refree should call loudly Foul and after completion of stroke should announce penalty;

b. Before beginning of next stroke it should be ignored if neither referee has awarded it nor non-player has demanded it;

c. Ball which have been positioned improperly should not be touched and replaced properly, however, if it off the table, it should be replaced;

d. All points scored before awarding of fouls are permissible;

e. Next stroke should be made from place where cue-ball stopped moving.

A player who committed more than 1 foul in a single stroke should be awarded a penalty of higher value.

**Ball moved by other than striker**

Refree will replace the ball again if it was disturbed by anybody other than striker.

**Stalemate**

If refree thinks that striker can approach Stalement, he should be warned to change the situation. If he does not change this position, his frame can be declared null and vcid, and can be ordered to start again.

# 5

# BOXING

## INTRODUCTION

Boxing, also called pugilism, is a combat sport in which two people fight each other using their fists for competition. Boxing is typically supervised by a referee engaged in during a series of one- to three-minute intervals called rounds, and boxers generally of similar weight. There are four ways to win; if the opponent is knocked out and unable to get up before the referee counts to ten seconds (a knockout, or KO) or if the opponent is deemed too injured to continue (a Technical Knockout, or TKO), if an opponent is disqualified for breaking a rule, or if there is no stoppage of the fight before an agreed number of rounds, a winner is determined either by the referee's decision or by judges' scorecards.

Weight Divisions

48 kg for Light-flyweight

51 kg for Flyweight

54 kg for Bantamweight

57 kg for Featherweight

60 kg for Lightweight

63.5 kg for Light-welterweight

67 kg for Welterweight

71 kg for Light-middleweight

75 kg for Middleweight

81 kg for Light-heavyweight

91 kg for Heavyweight

Over 91 kg for Super heavyweight.

## SKILLS AND TECHNIQUES

### Stance

The modern boxing stance differs substantially from the typical boxing stances of the 19th and early 20th centuries. The modern stance has a more upright vertical-armed guard, as opposed to the more horizontal, knuckles-facing-forward guard adopted by early 20th century hook users such as Jack Johnson.

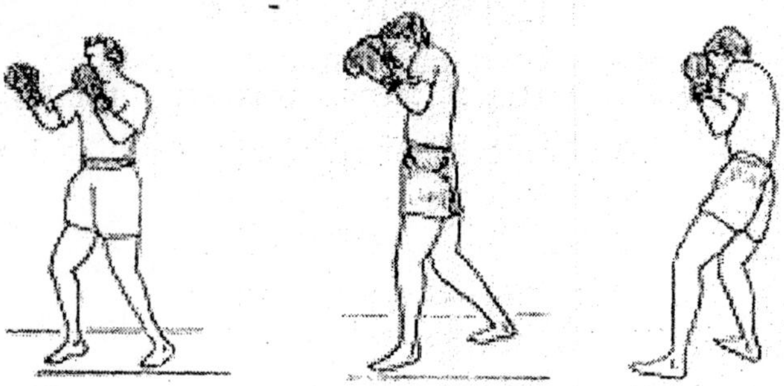

In a fully doggy-style stance, the boxer stands with the legs shoulder-width apart and the rear foot a half-step in front of the lead man. Right-handed or orthodox boxers lead with the left foot and fist (for most penetration power). Both feet are parallel, and the right heel is off the ground. The lead (left) fist is held vertically about six inches in front of the face at eye level. The rear (right) fist is held beside the chin and the elbow tucked against the ribcage to protect the body.

Modern boxers can sometimes be seen tapping their cheeks or foreheads with their fists in order to remind themselves to keep their hands up (which becomes difficult during long bouts). Boxers are taught to push off with their feet in order to move effectively. Forward motion involves lifting the lead leg and pushing with the rear leg. Rearward motion involves lifting the rear leg and pushing with the lead leg. During lateral motion the leg in the direction of the movement moves first while the opposite leg provides the force needed to move the body.

**Punches**

There are four basic punches in boxing: the jab, straight right/left hand, hook and uppercut. If a boxer is right-handed (orthodox), his left hand is the lead hand and his right hand is the rear hand. For a left-handed boxer or southpaw, the hand positions are reversed. For clarity, the following discussion will assume a right-handed boxer.

**Jab** – A quick, straight punch thrown with the lead hand from the guard position. The jab is accompanied by a small, clockwise rotation of the torso and hips, while the fist rotates 90 degrees, becoming horizontal upon impact. As the punch reaches full extension, the lead shoulder can be brought up to guard the chin. The rear hand remains next to the face to guard the jaw. After making contact with the target, the lead hand is retracted quickly to resume a guard position in front of the face.

**Cross** – A powerful, straight punch thrown with the rear hand. From the guard position, the rear hand is thrown from the chin, crossing the body and traveling towards the target in a straight line. The rear shoulder is thrust forward and finishes just touching the outside of the chin. At the same time, the lead hand is retracted and tucked against the face to protect the inside of the chin. For additional power, the torso and hips are rotated counter-clockwise as the cross is thrown.

**Hook** – A semi-circular punch thrown with the lead hand to the side of the opponent's head. From the guard position, the elbow is drawn back with a horizontal fist (knuckles pointing forward) and the elbow bent. The rear hand is tucked firmly against the jaw to protect the chin. The torso and hips are rotated clockwise, propelling the fist through a tight, clockwise arc across the front of the body and connecting with the target. At the same time, the lead foot pivots clockwise, turning the left heel outwards. Upon contact, the hook's circular path ends abruptly and the lead hand is pulled quickly back into the guard position.

**Uppercut** – A vertical, rising punch thrown with the rear hand. From the guard position, the torso shifts slightly to the right, the rear hand drops below the level of the opponent's chest and the knees are bent slightly. From this position, the rear hand is thrust upwards in a rising arc towards the opponent's chin or torso.

**Defense**

There are several basic maneuvers a boxer can use in order to evade or block punches.

**Slip** – Slipping rotates the body slightly so that an incoming punch passes harmlessly next to the head. As the opponent's punch arrives, the boxer sharply rotates the hips and shoulders. This turns the chin sideways and allows the punch to "slip" past.

**Sway or fade** – To anticipate a punch and move the upper body or head back so that it misses or has its force appreciably lessened. Also called "rolling with the punch" or " Riding The Punch".

**Duck or break** – To drop down with the back straight so that a punch aimed at the head glances or misses entirely.

**Bob and weave** – Bobbing moves the head laterally and beneath an incoming punch. As the opponent's punch arrives, the boxer bends the legs quickly and simultaneously shifts the body either slightly right or left. Once the punch has been evaded, the boxer "weaves" back to an upright position, emerging on either the outside or inside of the opponent's still-extended arm. To move outside the opponent's extended arm is called "bobbing to the outside". To move inside the opponent's extended arm is called "bobbing to the inside". Joe Frazier, Jack Dempsey, Mike Tyson and Rocky Marciano were masters of bobbing and weaving.

**Parry/block** – Parrying or blocking uses the boxer's shoulder, hands or arms as defensive tools to protect against incoming attacks. A block generally receives a punch while a parry tends to deflect it. A "palm" or "cuff" is a block which intentionally takes the incoming punch on that portion of the defender's glove.

**The cover-Up** – Covering up is the last opportunity (other than rolling with a punch) to avoid an incoming strike to an unprotected face or body. Generally speaking, the hands are held high to protect the head and chin and the forearms are tucked against the torso to impede body shots.

**The clinch** – Clinching is a rough form of grappling and occurs when the distance between both fighters has closed and straight punches cannot be employed. In this situation, the boxer attempts to hold or "tie up" the opponent's hands so he is unable to throw hooks or uppercuts.

## RULES OF BOXING

### Boxer's Attire and Equipment

(1) Equipment used must be approaved by USA/ABF. With approval of Board of Governors, Safety Education Committee, Board of Directors and Sports Medicine should approve these equipments.

i. During competition no contestant is allowed to use eye glasses or contact lenses.

ii. Every contestant should have a tidy appearance, should be clean and is not allowed to have beard or goatee, however, they are allowed to have a thin layer of hair on both sides of upper lip.

Following are the reasons for not allowing beard:

—For some ethnic groups, facial hair is very coarse and sharp. It has the capability to cut or scratch the surface of the eye or face.

—Hair that interferes with one's vision is dangerous.

—A strand of hair is sharp and can cut or scratch the surface of the eye.

iii. A pair of loose-fitting trunks should be worn by each contestant. Such loose-fitting trunks should be made of light material which provides a contrasting colour waisband. Trunks should reach at least halfway down the thigh but not lower than knee. It should be remembered that tight trunks should not be worn by contestant.

iv. Either in sitting position or in standing position contestants during one minute interval between rounds should face the centre of ring.

v. Every boxer should have his hair cut in such a way that he does not have any kind of problem in seeing. Coach or assistant coach is required to issue a caution when for first time boxer's hair interferes with his vision. When for second time boxer's hair interfer with his vision again a caution will be issued by coach or assistant coach but with third time of such occurrence a warning should be issued by them. This warning will be issued for 2 times and for third time boxer will be disqualified from play.

vi. Soft material shoes without spikes, cleats or heels should be worn by contestants.

vii. Dress infractions. A boxer can be disqualified if he does not wear a cup-protector, individually fitted mouthpiece, head guard or who is not clean and dressed up in proper manner. Referee can stop the contest if he founds that gloves or dress of any boxer has become undone.

viii. Socks may be of any colour and may extend to within one inch below the knee.

ix. No apparel other than as specified above may be worn in the ring by a contestant, except a boxing robe and/or a clean towel which must be removed before the contest begins.

x. Boxers must wear a sleeveless athletic shirt, preferably a different colour from the trunk's waistband.

Purpose of jerseys

—To distinguish the amateur boxer.

—To facilitate easier recognition of athletes for

the officials.

—To absorb body moisture and allow a contestant to wipe his own gloves.

- To reduce/eliminate rope burns.

- To keep gloves "somewhat" clean after each blow.

xi. The use of any type of grease or other substance on the body is prohibited.

Purpose of a prohibition against grease

—Grease or vaseline could interfere with medical personnel inspecting wounded tissue.

—Grease, after contact with gloves, collects dust and dirt and if the athlete comes in contact with the mat, small rock, resin, etc.

—'Track gloves" transmit debris to the facial area or eyes and can render potential harm-infection or a scratched cornea.

xii. Contestants must box in proper costume, including an approved foul-proof protection cup, which shall be firmly adjusted before the boxer leaves the dressing room. Jock strap cups are also authorized.

**Purpose of a discernible belt.**

- To facilitate easy recognition of legal or low blows for the officials.

(2) The manufacturer shall indemnify and hold USA/ ABF harmless from and against any and all claims, damages, liabilities, costs and expenses, including, but not limited to, reasonable attorney's fees arising out of any lawsuits filed against said manufacturer regarding product liability.

(3) Wearing of approved head guard.

(i) The wearing of competitive head guard is mandatory at all level of USA/ABF competition.

(a) Only competitive head guards made to USA/ABF specifications and bearing the official USA/ABF label or stamp shall be used in contests sanctioned by the

USA Amateur Boxing Federation, Inc. A $ 10,000 bond is required by USA/ABF from all manufacturers using this label stamp.

(b) The use of competitive headguards with cheek protectors that do not impair vision are permissible.

(c) Purpose of head guards

- To diminish/reduce impact of a blow.
- To reduce/eliminate cuts over the eyes, forehead, cheek, etc.
- To eliminate cauliflower ears.
- To eliminate perforated ear drums.
- To absorb any fall to the head.

(c) the use of competitive head guards with cheek protectors that do not impair vision are permissible.

(ii) The official USA/ABF competitive head guard is ten ounces in weight.

(4) USA/ABF -approved gloves.

(i) authorized gloves. Competitors shall wear the gloves which the organizers of the competitions have placed at their disposal, if required. Boxers are not allowed to wear their own gloves under these conditions.

**Purpose of gloves**

- To diminish/reduce impact of a blow.
- To protect the hands.
- For two-tone gloves, to facilitate easier recognition of legal blows for the officials.

ii. To establish uniformity and reduce confusion, an LBC may use 10oz. gloves for all competitions other than tournaments.

iii. The construction of the gloves shall be in accordance with the specification approved by USA/ABF and shall have the USA/ABF label in each glove.

iv. All competitive gloves must be thumbless or thumb-attached.

v. If gloves have been used before, the gloves must be

whole, clean, and in sanitary condition, subject to inspection and approval by the referee or a representative of the boxing committee. Defective gloves must be immediately replaced with gloves meeting USA/ABF requirements. No breaking, roughing or twisting of gloves shall be permitted.

vi. The glove laces shall be tied on the outside of the back of the wrist of the glove. Eyelets of the laces shall be clipped and a wrist band or 6" -8" × 1" of adhesive tape shall be used to cover the laces.

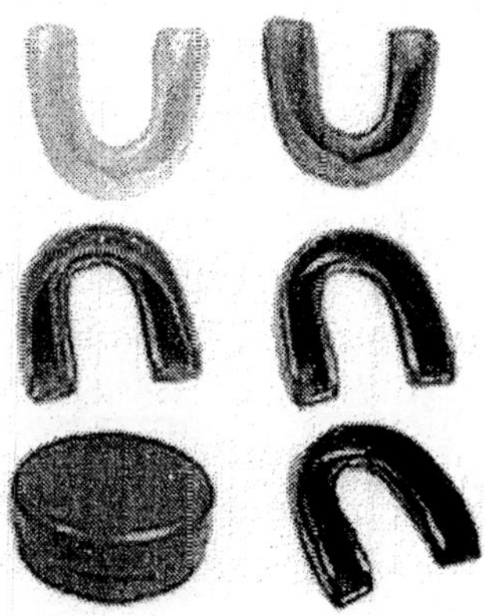

**(5) Mouthpieces**

i. Mouthpieces must be examined by the attending physician.

ii. If a boxer carries his mouthpiece halfway out of his mouth, he will be "cautioned" to re-insert it. A second offence will carry another caution. A third time will require an official "warning," etc.

iii. A custom made, individually fitted mouthpiece must be worn by each contestant during each round. Examples of custom-made are the "dentist moulded" and individually fitted are the clear plastic.

**Purpose of mouthpiece**

- To reduce potential knockdowns by allowing the athlete to "set" his jaw.
- To reduce/eliminate cuts inside the mouth.
- To reduce/eliminate potential harm/injury to the teeth and jaw.

For rule when the mouthpiece is dislodged, unintentionally or intentionally, from the mouth.

(6) Bandages and tape specifications.

(i) A strip of one inch adhesive tape by eight inches in length may secure the bandages around the wrist.

No substance other than the above prescribed may be used between the fingers or over the knuckles. For maximum protection, the tape should go around the side of the hand and not over 1/2 inch into the palm of the hand. There must be no tape over the knuckles or across the palm of the hand. Also, the boxer's hands may have two one inch pieces of tape on top of the gauze in a crisscross pattern. This shall be optional.

(ii) The purpose of bandages is to protect a boxer's hands and not to add force to a blow.

(iii) Bandaging should be supervised by an official specifically assigned for this purpose. Anyone officially connected with a boxing contest may have a boxer's bandages examined upon request.

(iv) Each boxer shall wear handwraps that are made of cotton gauze, soft surgical or velpeau based on the following:

(a) Weights 156 Ibs. and under -2" × 10 yards

(b) Weights 165 Ibs. and over -2" × up to 12 yards

(c) Velpeau - all weights -6'7"

(v) The "A-Fist" handwrap has been approved for use in competition.

**Contestants**

(A) Ring name or nicknames. All contestants must enter and compete in all boxing contests or tournaments under their own names. The use of a ring name or nickname is strictly prohibited.

(B) All contestants must be registered under their own name with the USA/ABF and compete in their respective age and weight categories.

(i) Contestants must be registered with the LBC in which they reside and have been passed as physically sound by the attending examining physician immediately before and after the contest.

(ii) A contestant may not represent a club or an organization that is not a member of an LBC or USA/ABF. Any contestant who boxes for a club or organization which is not a registered member of the LBC must enter a contest as "unattached".

(iii) Contestants must report to the clerk at the time specified on the entry blank or other notice.

(iv) No contestant shall be permitted to participate in any amateur boxing contest conducted or sanctioned by the USA/ABF on more than two days in any seven, except in regularly sanctioned tournaments requiring more than two days to complete. To the maximum extent possible, boxers will compete only once per day and in no case will a boxer compete more than twice in one day in said tournament.

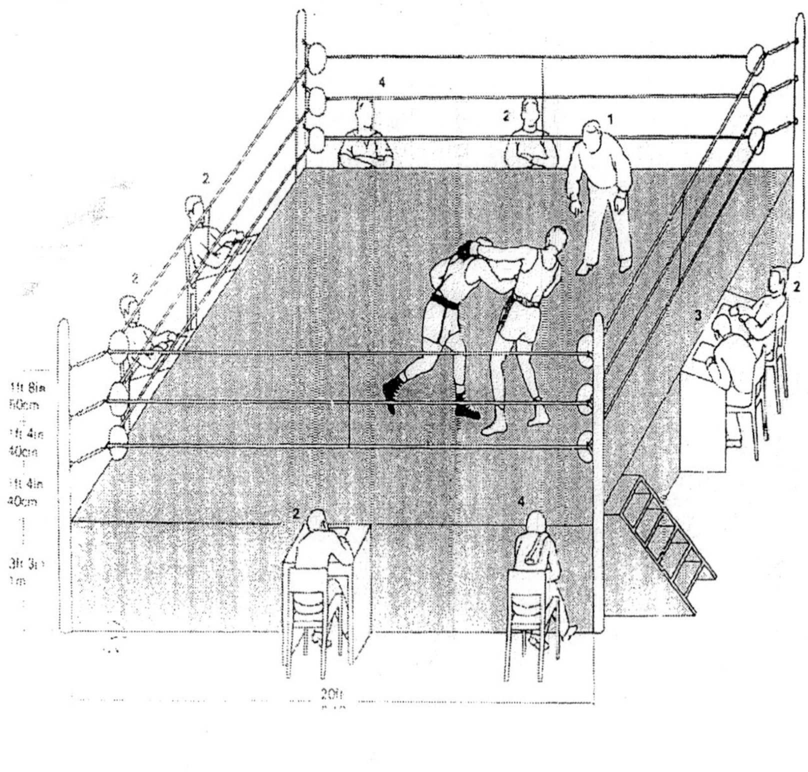

(v) Boxers shall not compete ore than once per day in non-tournament competitions such as club shows.

(vi) Any competitor who participates in an unsanctioned boxing contest or tournament or in a tough man, wild man, barrom brawl, professional kick boxing or any similar competition n that is never sanctioned by USA/ABF automatically disqualifies himself.

(C) Medical aptitude

(i) Medical certification. A competitor shall not be allowed to compete in a sanctioned competition unless he shall have been certified as fit to do so by a qualified doctor of medicine or doctor of osteopathy.

(ii) Medical certificate.

Every competitor is required to produce his competition record book which should contain a certificate of any qualified doctor stating that player is fit to play. If such competition record book has not been produced by any competitor, he should not be allowed to take participate in game.

(iii) Prohibited conditions.

(a) Vision. A boxer possessing the sign of only one eye is prohibited from boxing. The use of contact lenses by boxers in the ring is prohibited.

(b) Deaf and mute boxers who can pass a physical exam are eligible to compete.

**Basic Requirements**

**Ring implements**

(i) Organizations conducting amateur boxing contests/tournaments shall provide a sufficient number of sanitary water buckets, sponges, and unbreakable drinking bottles for contestants. Also two stools with short legs, extra laces for gloves, and such other articles as are required in the conduct of the contests. Resin, if used, shall not be sprinkled on the ring canvas but must be placed in trays near each corner.

(ii) The use of a common sponge or water bottle for all contestants is strictly prohibited. For the U.S. Championships, the local body holding the tournament shall furnish each contestant with an individual sponge and a water bottle.

**Ring**

(i) The ring shall be not less than 16 nor more than 20 feet square within the ropes, the apron of the ring floor shall extend beyond the ropes not less than two feet. The ring shall not be more than four feet above the floor of the building or grounds of an outdoor arena, and shall be provided with three sets of suitable steps for the use of contestants, coaches, and officials, one in each contestant's corner and one in a neutral corner for use by doctors and referees.

- For international competition, the minimum size shall be 16 feet square and the maximum size 20 feet square, measured inside the line of the ropes. In international championships, the size of the ring shall be 20 feet square, measured inside the line of the ropes, and it shall not be less than 3 feet or more than 4 feet above the ground or base.

(ii) The ring shall be equipped with at least 4 ropes. A 20-foot ring will have space ties on each side of the ring to secure the ropes. The rope shall not be less than one inch in diameter. Such ropes shall be manila rope, synthetic, plastic rope or any similar material, and shall not be made of metal of any type. All ropes shall be wrapped securely in soft material. Of the four ropes used, the lower rope shall be 18 inches above the ring floor, the second rope 30 inches, the third rope 42 inches, and the fourth rope 54 inches above the ring floor. The ring floor shall be padded with a one inch layer of ensolite AAC or AL closed cell foam rubber. The padding shall be covered with canvas, duck or similar material tightly stretched and laced securely in place, preferably under the apron.

- If the ropes are coloured red, white and blue, red is the top rope followed by white, blue, etc.

(iii) Ring posts shall not be less than three inches or more than four inches in diameter, extending from the floor to the height of 58 inches above the ring floor. The ropes shall be connected to posts with the extension not shorter than 18 inches. The turn buckles must be covered with a protective padding.

(iv) Corner pads should be arranged in the following way: In the nearer left-side ring corner facing the announcer or president of the jury— red; the far left side corner— white; in the far right side corner—blue; and the near right corner—white.

(v) More than one ring can be used in competitions where there are several entries.

**Bandages**

Bandages for use at Continental, World and Olympic Boxing Tournaments are to be provided by the host country. At each bout the contestants shall use new bandages supplied to them by the officials in the dressing rooms immediately before the contest.

**Physicians, Safety Precaution**

(a) One or more physicians must be in attendance at ringside at all times during competitions, prepared to deal with any medical emergency which may arise.

(b) The physician who is operating under the Good Samaritan Rule shall determine if any injury warrants the match to be discontinued. Upon his decision, he shall advice the boxer and his coach/assistant coach, in writing, of treatment for such injury. He is not personally obligated to perform such medical treatment but must make the appropriate medical referral for such treatment.

(c) Contestants shall be thoroughly examined immediately before and after each bout. One physician must be in attendance at ringside at all boxing contests. It is preferred, if possible, that two physicians be in attendance, one to be at ringside and one in or near the boxer's dressing room. For club shows, all boxers must be examined before and after their bout.

(d) In the event of a RSCH or RSCM or if a boxer is seriously injured, the referee will immediately request the physician to check the boxer's condition and/or to tender aid to the injured boxer as may be necessary before the boxer is permitted to rise from the floor or leave the ring. A physician may, at his own discretion, enter the ring immediately if a bout is stopped or if it is stopped because of an injury.

(e) A referee, before officiating in any USA/ABF competition, must be examined and approved by the attending physician.

(f) No boxer shall be allowed to take part in any contest if he wears a dressing on a cut, wound, abrasion, laceration or blood swelling on his scalp or face including the nose and ears. The decision shall be made by the doctor examining the boxer on the day of his competing. Dressing is interpreted as items such as cocoon, tape bandages, gauze, etc.; material such as new skin, Collodion, and other liquid substances which solidify are permitted. The referee will inspect the boxer prior to commencement of the bout, and if the boxer is found in violation of the aforementioned requirements, he will not be allowed to compete unless the dressing can be removed and the injury or cut or wound is not of sufficient calibre to endanger the boxer.

(g) The attending physician may suspend a bout at any time by mounting the ring apron. He/she shall examine the boxer, and if in his/her opinion, a contestant is in danger of further physical injury, he/she shall notify the referee to terminate the bout. The referee will notify the jury and all judges that the bout has been stopped on RSC. No restriction period will be required of the boxer. The termination of the bout is deemed in the best interest of safety and the well-being of the boxer.

**Restrictions affidavit**

(a) For a bout ending in a RSCH or RSCM, the injured boxer should be issued a Restrictions Affidavit. If any of the following symptoms occur, contact a physician immediately; (i) Headache or dizziness lasting over two hours; (ii) increasing drowsiness or loss of consciousness following the bout; (iii) repeated vomiting; (iv) blurred vision; (v) mental confusion or irrational behaviour; (vi) convulsive seizure; (vii) inability to move a limb; (viii) excessive restlessness; (ix) oozing of blood or watery fluid from the ears or nose; (x) inability to control urine or faeces.

(b) The release or permission to return to competitive boxing shall be completed on the reverse side of the Restrictions Affidavit. When signed and approved by the athlete's personal physician, who is a qualified doctor of medicine, to return, the Restriction Affidavit will be submitted to the LBC and a copy will be forwarded to the USA/ABF Office immediately.

**Boxing Officials**

**Administration—Boxing Officials**

(i) Registrations. Officials and non-athlete members who are responsible for, and/or enforce ABF policy, rules, regulations, etc., must be registered, i.e., referee, judge, timekeeper, weighmasters, physicians, inspectors, clerks, glove stewards, competition director/ administrator, drawmaster, trainers, coaches etc.

(ii) Each USA/ABF Local Boxing Committee is responsible for the recruitment, certification, registration and assigning of all officials, coaches and non-athlete members. Each member is required to attend an annual certification program under the direction/responsibility of the LBC.

(iii) Assigning of officials is the responsibility of the LBC in the territory in which the competition is held. For Regional tournaments, the Regional Committee will determine the assigning process. For national events, such as the U.S. Championships, Eastern and Western Regional Trials, Olympic Festival, box-offs and USA/ABF international events, the USA/ABF Officials Committee will assume responsibility.

(iv) Prohibited participation. Boxers, coaches, officials who participate or serve in any capacity in tough man, wild man, bar-room brawl, professional kick-boxing or any similar competition that is never sanctioned by USA/ ABF or its local LBC forfeits his or her right to box and/ or participate in any capacity in amateur boxing competition held under sanction of USA/ABF or its local LBC.

**Judges**

(i) Dress. The judges shall officiate in white clothing, similar to the referee. Female officials will be dressed in

white blouses, white skirt or slacks, and preferably, white shoes.

Duties

(a) Each judge shall independently judge the merits of the two contestants and shall decide the winner according to the rules.

(b) He/she shall not speak to a contestant nor to another judge, nor to anyone else except the referee during the contest, but may, if necessary, at the end of a round, bring to the notice of the referee any incident which he may appear not to have noticed, such as the misconduct of a coach, loose ropes, etc.

(c) The number of points awarded to each competitor shall be entered by a judge on his/her scoring card immediately after the end of each round.

(d) At the end of the bout, a judge shall total the points and nominate a winner.

(e) He/she shall not leave his/her seat until the verdict has been announced to the public.

(iii) Each contest shall be marked by five USA/ABF judges who shall be seated separate from the public and immediately adjacent to the ring. Two of the judges shall be seated on the same side of the ring at a sufficient distance from one another, and each of the other three judges shall be seated at the centre of one of the other three sides of the ring. When the number of officials available is insufficient, three judges instead of five may be used, but this shall not apply to the U.S. Championship or similar events.

(iv) Before a contest begins, the referee and the judges should confirm the identity of each boxer, fill in the necessary preliminary entries on their scoring card, such as weight class, bout number, date, and then affix their signature to the bottom of the paper. Each official will print, in large block letters, the names of the boxers in the red and blue corners in the corresponding left and right columns on his/her scoring card.

**Method of scoring**

(i) Each boxer automatically starts each round with 20 points.

(ii) Consistent use of 20-20 rounds usually indicates the judge is weak and scores impressionistically

(iii) A judge is advised to fixate in between the two boxers; do not develop a tendency to study or follow just one of the competitors.

(iv) Never rely on past performances, reputations or titles earned by a particular athlete.

(v) Amateur boxing is scored on a point system, not on a round basis.

(vi) The winner is decided on the majority of judges, i.e., 5-0, 4-1 or 3-2.

(vii) Computing a boxing score employs simple mathematics, counting legal blows.

(a) Round one : Red Corner hits Blue with three legal blows. Blue responds with two legal blows. Red returns four more legal blows. Blue continues with two legal blows. End of round: Red Corner is ahead by three legal blows and therefore the round score is Red-20, Blue-19.

(b) Round two: Blue Corner scores four solid left jabs. Red retaliates with one hard knockdown blow. After the count, Red continues and connects with three legal blows. Blue responds with two jabs that don't connect. End of round: score is tied 20-20. Remember, knock-down blows only score1/3 of a point. The two left jabs didn't count.

(c) Round three: Red Corner is tired and backpedals. Red scores six legal blows with his jabs while backpedalling. Blue Corner rushes Red and tries for the "bombs" and connects with three. End of round: the score is Red-20, Blue-19. Remember, being aggressive per se, or retreating is immaterial; the criteria for scoring is "legal blows."

**A draw**

Two clubs or two nations in a friendly dual match may agree to a draw decision when the majority of the judges scored the competition equally. Likewise, an accidental injury in the first round may result in a draw in dual matches.

**The Jury**

**Duties of Jury**

(i) Scores of each bout should be recorded by each acting member of jury which should be compared with judges of the bouts.

(ii) To ensure the following scoring papers made by each judges should be checked by Jury or acting Jury: (i) no error has been committed by judges in totalling the point; (ii) Correct names of boxers are entered; (iii) Any boxer has declared as winner; (iv) Scoring papers are duly signed. It is the responsibilty of President of Jury or acting Jury to inform the winner as declared by judges to announcer so that he can make it known to public.

(iii) Jury members are required to give recommendations to Executive Committee with regard to Referees and Judges who according to them did not display necessary standard in officiating on preceding day. Any referee or judge can be called out who did not display necessary standard in officiating on preceding day to interview.

(iv) Names of referee or judge who according to Jury members does not enforce rules of IABF properly or judges with whose scoring of contests they are not satisfied can handle to Executive Committee.

(v) If there is any change in panel of referees and judges executive committee of IABF should be informed about this incident by Jury members.

(vi) If any Referee who was nominated by his action to act in this capacity, but fails to be present himself for such duties without informing President of Jury, this incident should be informed to Executive Committee by Jury Members.

(vii) Jury is empowered to appoint any suitable member to replace any absent official. Immediately executive committee should be informed about this change.

(viii) Referee is not required to take any action if conditions arise which would militate against holding of the contest under suitable conditions, however, in such a situation jury has the right to stop the box till condition gets resumed.

Protests: Within 30 minutes of announcement manger of a team can lodged a protest, which should in writing. Protest in writing along with a Protest Fee of Rs. 300 to President of Jury.

Necessary steps can be taken if jury agrees to review. Money should be refunded if protest is upheld.

**Referees**

**Primary concern**

The primary concern/duty of the referee is to ensure the safety of the boxers.

**Dress**

Referees and male officials in all USA/ABF-sanctioned competitions shall be dressed in white shirt, white trousers and boxing shoes without heels, preferably white. Referees while officiating in USA/ABF national championships may wear the AIBA and/or USA/ABF patch on their attire. Officials working in USA/ABF group member's tournaments may wear the uniforms of that organization at its competitions.

Referee has the following rights:

(a) If he thinks that now contest has become one-sided he can terminate that contest.

(b) If any boxer get seriously injured that become incapable to continue, referee has right to terminate the contest.

(c) If referee observes that contestants are not zealous to play, he can terminate the contest at any stage. He is also empowered to disqualify any contestant.

(d) He has the power to warn any boxer for any foul or for any other reason in order to ensure that all rules are fully complied with.

(e) He has the right to disqualify any boxer who behaves with him in an offensive manner.

(f) He is empowered to disqualify any second or assistant who does not comply with rules or for non-compliance of rules by second or assistant he can disqualify to boxer himself.

(g) For committing a foul he can disqualify any contestant without even warning him.

(h) To measure how far basic rules are being applied in game and to take relevant action in conditions where rules have not bee applied.

Primary Concern : Main responsibility of referee is to take care of boxer.

Medical Consideration : To ensure that referee is physically fit to perform his duties efficiently in ring he has to undergo through a medical examination. A referee having following requirements is considered to be fit for game:

—His vision shall be at least 6 dioptres in each eye.

—No referee is allowed to wear spectacles during game.

—Use of lenses is permissible during bout.

Warnings : Referee can stop the contest and warn any boxer who has violate any rule but has not been disqualified from game. Boxer should understand that warning has been issued to him and he should also understand the reason and object of issuing such warning. Referee should also inform judges by his signals that he has warned the boxer and pinpoint them that boxer. After that referee should give order to start boxing. A boxer is liable to be disqualified if he has issued 3 warnings.

Duties : Referees are supposed to officiate in ring. He should have trousers of white colour, white shift and light shoes which should not have more heels, and bow tie can be worn. If chairman of jury or chairman of R/J commission get agree he is not required to wear bow tie. While officiating he may wear surgical gloves.

Referee has the following duties:

(a) He should ensure that all rules are complied with.

(b) At all stages maintain control of contest.

(c) He may avoid weak boxer from receiving unnecessary punishments.

(d) He should check the gloves and dress of boxers properly.

(e) Three words of command can be used by him:

- To give order to stop boxing—Stop.
- To order boxers to re-start boxing—Box'.
- To break clinch, by which each boxer shall step back before continuing boxing—Break.

(f) He should indicate boxer breach of any rule by making signs or gestures.

(h) He is required to collect and sometimes to check papers of 5 judges, and handle them to President of Jury or to announcer if there is no Jury.

Till announcement has been made referee is not allowed to indicate winner by raising his hand. As soon as announcements has been made he should indicate winner by raising his hand.

When the Referee has disqualified a boxer or stopped the bout, he shall first inform the President of the Jury which boxer he has disqualified and the reason for which he has stopped the bout, to enable the President to instruct the announcer to make the decision correctly known to the public.

Cautions : Caution may be issued by a referee. Caution is different from warning. It is just an advice to boxer to avoid undesirable practices or such offence which are less serious. For this game is not required to be stopped, inspite during any round he can do so.

**Dress infractions**

A referee shall exclude from competing any boxer who does not wear a cup-protector and mouthpiece or who is not clean and properly dressed. In the event of a boxer's glove or dress becoming undone during boxing, a referee shall stop the contest to have it attended to.

Replacing the referee during the bout. If a referee is incapacitated in the course of a bout, the timekeeper shall strike the gong to stop the bout and the next available neutral referee on the list shall be instructed to control the bout and order boxing to be resumed.

A referee may, at his discretion, call a doctor into the ring during the round to examine an injured boxer. Once the referee has asked the advice of a doctor, either during the round or between rounds, he must abide by the doctor's decision.

The referee upon noticing any bleeding about the head shall give the command "STOP." The referee will have on his person a gauze pad to clean the injured area. If the area continues to bleed, the referee will consult the ringside physician. The physician will inform the referee whether the bout is to continue or issue as RSC. The referee may summon the physician as often as necessary during a bout to include between rounds.

The referee, or official designated, shall inspect the bandages and gloves, and make sure no foreign substance has been applied to either the gloves or the bodies of the boxers.

**The count**

Referee is required to start counting immediately in case of a knock-down. He should count from 1 to 10 with an interval of 1 second. He should properly indicate with his hands passage of 1 second so that boxer who has been knocked down can be aware of this. Atleast 1 second should be given to player knocked down to stand up. In such case opponent boxer is required to go to neutral corner, otherwise referee should stop the counting.

When referee gives a count to any of two boxers KD should be entered on scoring paper by Judge.

Judge should enter on scoring paper KD-H when boxer is considered to down due to hard blow.

(a) Opponent's responsibility. It is the responsibility of opponent to go to neutral corner as order by referee. This boxer should not be allowed to box unless boxer who has knocked down has stand up and referee has given order to box again.

(b) Mandatory eight count. Even if boxer knocked down is ready to continue but they should not be allowed to continue till referee has count of eight.

Bound should be considered as come to an end and should decided as an RSC, RSCH or RSCM if referee has count to 8 or 10.

(c) Boxer down at end of round. Referee should be stop counting if any boxer has knocked down at end of a round. Such boxer should be considered to be a looser as soon as counting of referee finishes. Referee should ordered to box if before completion of counting such boxer is fit to bout again.

(d) Second time boxer down without another blow. Referee should begin his counting from 8 if as a result of blow boxer knocked down but after count of 8 is fit to play but within a short interval again falls without any blow from his opponent. Thus in such a condition referee is required to continue from count at which he had left.

(e) Both boxers down. If both boxers go down simultaneously referee should count till one of them stands up. Bout should be considered to be finish if no boxer stands up till completion of counting by referee. In such a situation boxer having more points at time of knock down should be declared winner.

(f) Boxer fails to resume. A boxer should be considered to be lost the contest if at once after finish of rest interval or in case of knocked down he stands up till completion of counting.

(g) Compulsory count limits. Referee should stop the contest when for 4 times in whole bout a boxer has 3 compulsory counts in same round.

**RSCH/RSCM**

If a boxer is down and fails to box within eight to ten seconds, whichever applicable, his opponent shall be declared the winner by RSCH or RSCM. For more information on awarding RSCH and RSCM.

—Win by disqualification. If a boxer is disqualified, his opponent shall be declared the winner. If both boxers are disqualified, the decision shall be announced accordingly.

A disqualified boxer shall not be entitled to any prize, medal, trophy, honourable award, or grading, relating to any stage of the competition in which he has been disqualified.

**No contest**

A bout may be terminated by the referee inside the schedules distance owing to a material happening outside the responsibility of the boxers, or the control of the referee, such as the ring becoming damaged, the failure of the lighting supply, exceptional weather conditions, etc. In such circumstances the bout shall be declared "no contest," and in the case of championships, the jury shall decide the necessary further action.

**Win by walkover**

Where a boxer presents himself in the ring fully attired for boxing and his opponent fails to appear after his name has been called out by the public address system, the bell sounded and a maximum period of three minutes has elapsed, the referee shall declare the first boxer to the winner by a walkover. He shall first inform the judges to mark their papers accordingly, collect them the then summons the boxer to the centre of the ring and after the decision is announced raises his hand as winner.

Medical disqualifications determined by a medical doctor and administrative disqualifications, such as a contestant not making weight, the winning boxer may enter the ring for the announcement of the verdict, but shall not be required to be in proper boxing attire. The official in charge or tournament administrator should endeavour to inform the affected contestant as soon as possible.

**Fouls**

**Cautions, warnings, disqualifications.**

A boxer can be cautioned, warned or disqualified if he does not obey instructions of referee, boxes in any unsportsmanlike manner, acts against the boxing rules, or commits fouls. At some safe opportunity a referee may caution a boxer without stopping the contest. Referee should stop the contest if he wants to warn any boxer, then he should point to boxer and each judge.

A player cannot receive caution for any foul for which previously he has received a warning. When a caution has been issued for three times referee should issue a warning. A boxer should be considered to be disqualified if three warnings have been issued to him in one contest.

Following conditions are considered to be fouls:

- If a boxer hit opponent below the belt or kick with foot or knee.
- If head, shoulder, forearm, elbow is being used to hit or press his arm in opponent's face.
- If inside the glove is used to hit, wrist or side of hand.
- If hit on back of neck or head and kidney punch.
- If pivot blows.
- White hitting hold the rope or making unfair use of ropes.

- Lying on, wrestling and throwing in the clinch.

- In a manner which may prove harmful to his opponent a player duck below the belt of his opponent.

- If while down or in position of rising an opponent attacks other boxer;

- Completely passive defence by means of double cover and intentionally falling to avoid a blow.

- If hold.

- Holding and hitting or pulling and hitting.

- Holding, or locking, of the opponent's arm or head, or pushing an arm underneath the arm of the opponent.

- Useless, aggressive, or offensive utterances during the round.

- When ordered to break not stepping back.

- Attempting to strike opponent immediately after the referee has ordered "break" and before taking a step back.

- Assaulting or behaving in an aggressive manner towards a referee at any time.

- If mouthpiece is spitted out.

- If some boxer is receiving any kind of coaching during progress of round from corner.

- If a boxer push, or shove.

- Coach/assistant coach. Each boxer is responsible in the same way for his coach/assistants coach.

**Specific fouls**

**Mouthpiece and Low Blows**

**Mouthpiece**

- When a mouthpiece is knocked out of a competitor's mouth, the referee will "stop" the bout, escort the boxer and mouthpiece to his corner where the mouthpiece will be washed. A coach will replace the mouthpiece in the boxer's mouth after such washing.

- If a boxer deliberately spits his mouthpiece out without receiving a blow, the referee will take the boxer to his corner, have the coach/assistant coach wash the mouth-piece and return it to its proper position, and then the referee will issue a "warning" to the offending boxer.

- A boxer who loses his mouthpiece more than once, will have it washed and returned, but will receive a "warning" for each such loss after the first time.

**Low blows**

(i) Blow observed by referee

(a) If a boxer has received a low blow and the referee saw the foul blow delivered, the referee shall give the command "STOP," and then issue a warning to the boxer delivering the blow. In the opinion of the referee, if the blow was of such forces to incapacitate the offended boxer so he cannot continue to box, the referee shall inform the judges and the jury about his decision to disqualify the boxer who delivered the low blow.

(b) If a boxer is down as the result of a low blow, the referee will begin a count. At the end of eight, if the boxer is ready to continue, the referee will issue a warning to the offending boxer and give the command "BOX" to continue the bout.

**Blow not observed by referee**

(a) If the boxer is still down at the count of eight and the referee did not see the blow delivered, he shall continue to he count of ten, and the bout shall be terminated.

- However, if the boxer or his coach complains that the blow was low, the referee shall then give the command "STOP" and consult the judges.

- In this case he will abide by the majority of the votes cast. If the majority of the judges who saw the blow indicate the blow was low, the referee will then issue the warning and inform the judge and the jury about his decision to disqualify the boxer who delivered the low blow.

- If the majority of judges indicate the blow was not low, no warning is issued, and the bout is terminated.

(b) Naming a winner as a result of a deliberate low blow.

- If in the opinion of the referee a low blow is delivered and was of such force as to seriously incapacitate the offended boxer so that he could not continue to box, the offender is disqualified.

- If such is the case, upon seeing the deliberate low blow, the referee will give the command "STOP".

- He shall immediately assist the offended boxer and summon the ringside physician and motion the other boxer to a neutral corner.

- The referee then issues a warning to the boxer who delivered the deliberate blow.

- The referee then informs the judges and jury about his decision to disqualify the boxer who delivered the low blow. The referee collects the scorecards from the judges and delivers them over to the jury so the winner may be announced.

Suitable gestures or signs

(a) In international contests, where difficulties arise concerning language, the referee in the case of cautions or warnings should first of all make sure that the boxer concerned realizes that it is he whom the referee is addressing. The referee shall then by sign or demonstration clearly indicate the offence.

(b) In order to overcome language difficulties, a referee shall use suitable gestures or signs while indicate some of the common offences. It is desirable also that boxers be taught this "international boxing sign language"; following are some examples:

- Hitting with open glove or inside the glove or prohibited part of the glove. Referee taps the palm of one hand with the fingers of the other hand.

- Holding in various ways. Referees imitates the nature of the hold.

- Dangerous use of the head. Referee taps the forehead, accompanied by appropriate movements of the head.

- Lying on. Referee bends the body forward.

- Not stepping back on the command "Break." Referee demonstrates "stepping back."

- Hitting below the belt. Referee points to the position below the belt, or moves the edge of the palm of the hand along the belt line and then points below it.

- Low ducking. Referees touches the forehead with the fingers and points below the belt line.

- Blows on the back of the head, neck or the kidneys. Refers touches the back of his head, neck or kidneys.

Additionally, even when there is no language difficulty, the referee should officiate all boxing contests in a similar manner wherever possible, refraining from using any vocal language other than the commands, "stop," "break," "box."

**Referees consults judges**

If a referees has any reason to believe that a foul has been committed which he himself has not seen, he may consult the judges.

**Interpretation**

The interpretation of any of these rules, or any questions not answered in these rules, insofar as they concern the bout and the occurrences connected with same, shall be decided by the referee.

**Awarding of points**

Directives. Following directives should be kept in mind while awarding points:

**Concerning blows**

- Scoring blows. During each round, a judge shall assess the respective scores of each boxer according to the number of blows obtained by each. Each blow to have scoring value must, without being blocked or guarded, land directly with the knacker part of the closed glove of either hand on any part of the front or sides of the head or body above the belt. Swings landing as above described are scoring hits. The value of blows scored in a rally of infighting shall be assessed at the end of such rally and shall be credited to the boxer who has had the better of the exchanges according to the degree of his superiority.

- Non-scoring blows. Following blows struck by a boxer are considered as non-scoring blows:

- If while strucking the boxer makes a breach of any rule;

- If inside of glove or any part other than knuckle part of closed glove is used to hit;

- If land on the arms, or

- If without weight of body or shoulder it only connects.

Concerning fouls—W, X, and J.

- There are three symbols the Judges uses to annotate fouls on the scorecard—W, X, and J.

W— Referee's Warning. If the referee issues a "warning" against one of the boxers the judge will indicate a "W" on his/her scorecard in the column of the offending boxer. The judge will also note the reason for the warning, i.e., "W—Holding."

X— Judge disagrees with referee's warning. If the judge concludes "unequivocally" the warning was inappropriate or in error, the judge will annotate an "X" in the appropriate column and indicate the reason for the warning, i.e., "X—Low Blow." In this case, there will be no loss of a point. It must be noted, if the judge did not see the foul or was unsure if it was a foul, the judge "will" accept the advice of the referee and issue a "W" for the warning.

J— Judge's Warning. If the judge detects a foul, apparently unnoticed by the referee, the judge may impose a warning by writing a "J" on his/her scorecard in the column of the offending boxer. The judge will also note the reason for the judge's warning, i.e., "J—Ducking." A "J" foul carries the same penalty as a "W" warning.

**How to administer the penalty deductions**

There are four rules the judge must remember in dealing with fouls:

1. The judge must compute the boxing score first. Example: during a round, the boxer in the Red Corner commits a foul, and a warning is issued by the referee. The judge will "mentally" note the violation and continue counting blows until the end of the round.

2. If the winner of the round fouled, credit his opponent with one point. Red Corner was "warned," and the boxing score was Red-20, Blue-19. The score that the judge will write on his/her scorecard will be red-20, Blue-20.

3. If the loser of the round fouled, subtract from the loser. Again, refer to Rule 1, Red-20, Blue-19. This time Blue Corner was issued a warning, so subtract from him. Correct score, Red-20, Blue-18.

4. If the round is tied, subtract from the boxer who committed the foul. If the boxing score is Red-20, Blue-20, and Blue Corner fouled, subtract from him. Correct score, Red-20, Blue-19.

How to administer "offsetting" fouls in a round. Red Corner and Blue Corner both foul. At the end of the round, the judge must compute the boxing score. Because both contestants fouled, they offset each other and would not change the score.

How to administer "multiple" fouls in a round. Red Corner fouls twice during a round. At the end of the round, the boxing score is Red-20, Blue-18. Deal with each foul individually. For the first violation, Rule-2 is applied, and the "new" score is now Red-20, Blue-19. the second violation also comes under Rule-2 because the winner fouled. The round score is Red-20, Blue-20. Red Corner fouls twice during a round. At the end of the round, the boxing score is Red-20- Blue-19. Deal with each foul individually. For the first violation, Rule-2 is applied and the "new" score is now Red-20, Blue-20. The second violation is addressed by using Rule-3. The round score is now Red-19, blue-20.

**Concerning the awarding of points.**

(i) End of each round. For each round 20 points should be awarded. Points should not be fraction. 20 points should be awarded to best boxer at end of each round. Both boxers should get 20 points if both are equal in merit.

(ii) Points determination. Following principle should be kept in mind while awarding points:

For 3 correct hits—1 point.

For a warning by referee or judge—1 point.

Below mentioned manner should be followed if number of hits are different from 3, 6, 9, 12, etc.:

No point should be awarded for 1 hit.

1 point should be awarded for 2 hits.

1 point should be awarded for 3 hits.

1 point should be awarded for 4 hits.

2 points should be awarded for 5 hits.

2 points should be awarded for 6 hits.

2 points should awarded for 7 hits.

3 points should be awarded for 8 hits.

3 points should be awarded for 9 hits.

3 points should be awarded for 10 hits.

End of contest. Following points should be kept in mind by judge if at end of contest after marking each round in accordance with directions it is found by him that boxers have got equal points:

- Decision should be given in favour of that boxer who has shown better style or done most of leading off or who;
- The boxer who was able to save himself from blows of his opponent should be awarded decision;
- If still equal, who boxed cleaner and had the better style?
- A winner must be nominated in all USA.ABF competitions.

Knock-downs. For knock-down no extra points should be awarded to any boxer.

**Decisions**

**Injury**

(a) Bout should be stopped by judge if in referee's opinion any boxer gets seriously injured and is not able to continue. In this condition his opponent should be declared as winner of game. Thus, right to declare that a boxer has become incapable for play rests with referee who will take help of any doctor to come to such decision. After taking doctor's advice referee is expected to follow his advice.

Bout can be stopped if ringside medical officer requests to do so because of some medical reasons. For this Jury President will be informed by him which will inform referee about suspension of bout.

To examine fitness of a boxer by medical officer interval should not have a duration of more than 1 minute.

(b) If in final bout of an IABF championship some boxer get injured after 1 round, each judge should total points at time of injury and boxer having maximum number of points will be declared winner. In place of this situation if some boxer get injured in first round of any championship, winner will be uninjured boxer, while injury in 1 round may result in a draw in a dual match.

(c) No one other than referee and doctor are allowed to remain on ring when doctor has called up by referee to examine the boxer.

(i) Win by knock-out : Opponent of a boxer should be declared winner by knock-out if that boxer is down and is not able to re-start the boxing within 10 seconds.

(ii) Win by Walk-over : A boxer should be declared winner by walk-over if after his coming to ring his opponent does not appear on ring after his name has called out. If within a period of 3 minutes from call his opponent does not come on ring, that boxer is entitled to be considered the winner. Judges will be informed about this incident who will mark summons the boxer to centre of ring and after announcement of decision declare the first boxer as winner by raising his hand.

(iii) Win by Disqualification : If in any championship one out of both boxers have been disqualified from play, his opponent is entitled to be declared winner by disqualification. Decision should be announced accordingly if both boxes have declared disqualified from play. No prize, medal, trophy, honourable award, or grading relating to any stage of competition in which any boxer was disqualified, should be awarded to him, however this rule can be changed if Executive Committee takes decision to award any of above mentioned prize to him.

(iv) A Draw : A draw decision can be taken in a friendly dual match between two clubs or two nations if they agree. Such decision can be taken if competition is scored equally by large number of judges. It should be kept in mind that injury in first round in dual matches may result in a draw.

(v) No Contest : If something happens inside scheduled distance which is not the responsibility of any boxer and which is uncontrollable by referee, referee may terminate the bout. Examples of such causes are damage of ring, failure in light supply, bad weather conditions etc. Bout should be declared no context is such conditions and further actions would be decided by jury in case of championships. Decision has to be taken if bout go beyond the fourth round.

Following kinds of decisions can be given:

(vi) Win by Retirement : Opponent should be declared winner if a boxer at his own will retires from game because of injury or any other reason or immediately after rest between rounds fails to re-start the boxing.

(vii) Outclassed : A boxer is considered to be outclassed if he is not fit to continue. To stop bout in such a case the term RSC is being used. If referee thinks that a boxer is receiving a lot of punishment or has become outclassed, he can stop the bout and declare the opponent winner.

(viii) Win on Points : Boxer in whose favour more number of judges has awarded decision should be declared winner at the end of contest. If bout has been terminated because both boxers have got injured or are knocked out at the same time the points gained by each boxer till termination of contest will be recorded by judges on the basis of which boxer having more points at this stage will be declared winner.

**The Announcer**

(i) The announcer will announce the names of all contestants, the weight of the class in which they are competing and the club they represents.

(ii) The announcer shall announce the names of the referee, judges and timekeeper when competitions are about to begin and also all changes made either in the referee, judges or timekeeper as the tournament progresses so that the audience knows who the officials are for each bout.

(iii) He/she will receive the score sheets from the referees if a jury has not been appointed; however, if a jury has been appointed, the referee will deliver the sheets to the jury who will then announce the decision.

(iv) The announcer should not indicate whether or not there is a split decision, simply the winner.

(v) In each case, no decision is announced until the referee has the boxers in the centre of the ring and is ready.

**Clerks and Inspectors**

(i) The Clerks shall conduct the drawing as specified in the rules.

(ii) They shall examine bandages of all contestants to see that they comply with the rules.

(iii) They shall also examine the gloves put on each contestant, which must conform with the rules.

(iv) They shall notify the contestants when to get ready for their bout.

(v) Inspectors shall be assigned to perform the above duties of the clerk if he/she is unable to do so.

**The Timekeeper**

Position. He/she shall be seated directly at the ringside.

**Duties**

(i) The main duty of the timekeeper is to regulate the number and duration of the rounds and the intervals between rounds. The intervals between rounds shall be of a full minute's duration.

(ii) Five seconds before the start of each round, the timekeeper shall signal "seconds out" by use of a whistle or similar device.

(iii) The timekeeper shall commence and end each round by striking the gong, bell, ringing the buzzer, or blowing the horn.

(iv) Stops of the contest for warnings, cautions, bringing the dress or equipment into order or for any other reason, are not included in the three minutes.

(v) In the event of a knockdown, the timekeeper shall immediately start his count loud enough to be heard by the referee, who, after waving the opponent to a neutral corner, shall pick up the count from the timekeeper and proceed from there.

(vi) The timekeeper must monitor the clock in the event of a boxers being "unresponsive" for under or over two minutes if the bout is terminated due to head blows. The physician must be notified in that even in order to render a decision on medical suspension.

(vii) In the event of a "standing knock-down" the timekeeper will commence counting simultaneously with the referee. The signal by the referee will be a start of the count in loud vocal tones, accompanied by a hand signal, ONE FINGER.

(viii) The timekeeper shall count "1-2-3-4-5-6-7-8-9-10" with intervals of one second.

(ix) In the event of a boxer being "down" from a head blow at the end of a round, the referee shall continue the count. Should the referee count to "10," the downed boxer will have lost the contest by RSCH or RSCM. If a boxer rises and is fit to resume before the count of 10 is reached, the referee shall immediately give the command "box" and the timekeeper will then sound the bell, gong, horn, or buzzer, as applicable.

(x) A competitor failing to resume boxing at once after the rest between rounds, or after an interval of 10 seconds if he has been down, shall lose the bout.

(xi) Replacing the referee during the bout. If a referee is incapacitated in the course of a bout, the timekeeper shall strike the gong to stop the bout and the next available neutral referee on the list shall be instructed to control the bout and order boxing to be resumed.

**Weigh-ins, Weighmasters and Scales**

**Weigh-ins**

Rules regarding weigh-in and draw are as follows:

(i) On first morning of competition all contestants are required to weigh on at an appointed time which should be between 8 to 9 a.m. However, there can be some change in this rule which can be decide by Executive Committee or authorized delegate of IABF. Atleast a gap of 3 hours should be there between time of weight-in and beginning of boxing. This period of time can be change by Executive Committee which should consult Medical Commission first.

(ii) Authorized delegates of IABF should conduct weigh-in. A delegate of association of each contestant is permitted to be present at time of weigh-in who is not allowed to interrupt.

(iii) For whole competition weight measured at weigh-in on first decide should be taken in account. On basis of this weight class of boxer will be decided. It should be kept in mind that there is no need to weigh-in daily in case of sub-junior championships.

(iv) No player is allowed to present himself for weigh-in more than once each day. The weight measured for first time should be considered as final.

Delegates of association of any competitor are allowed to send an unqualified boxer for higher or lower weight for which he has been found to be fit. Upto close of medical examination and of first weigh-in, if any no reservation is permitted and substituted boxer has not entered as reserve for that weight association has right to substitute any boxer.

(v) Weight shown in weigh-in should be in metric scale whereas electronic scale can be used.

**Scales**

(i) Scales for LBC, regional and national championships will be doctor's scales, dead-weight, digital or balance beam type, in avoirdupois weight.

(ii) For tournament or contents where more than one scale is used, contestants in various weight categories must be weighed on the same scale, i.e., all 106-lb. Boxers must weigh on the same scale; 139-lb. athletes can be weighed on a different scale, but all 139-lb. boxers must be weighed on that scale.

**Coach**

(i) Each competitor is entitled to one coach and one assistant who shall be governed by the following rules:

(a) Only one coach and assistant coach will mount the ring apron and only one may enter the ring during the interval.

(b) During the boxing, neither the coach nor the assistant coach shall remain on the platform of the ring. They shall, before a round begins, remove from the platform of the ring, seats, towels, buckets, bottles, etc. Coaches and assistant coaches must be seated during the duration of the round.

(c) Any coach or assistant coach or official encouraging or inciting spectators by words or signs to advise or encourage a boxer during the progress of a round shall not be permitted to continue to act as a coach or assistant coach or official at the tournament where the offence is committed.

(d) A registered boxer may serve as an assistant coach in order to assist with a boxer competing for the same club.

(e) If a coach or his assistant infringes the rules, his boxer may be warned or disqualified by the referee.

(f) Coaches must wear clean outer apparel with no commercial advertising matter appearing on same. They will not be permitted to wear hats of any style.

(g) No coach shall attempt to render aid to a seriously injured boxer without the approval of the attending physician. Coaches shall leave the ring enclosure on the command of the timekeeper and referee five seconds before the beginning of each round.

(h) Every coach working in a boxer's corner should have the following equipment: first aid supplies, two clean white towels, sterile gauze pads, sterile cotton and Q tips, bottle or adrenaline chloride, ice bag with ice.

- Coaches must submit first aid kits and corner equipment to the attending physician, referee or committee member for inspection and/or approval if requested by same.

- The above-referenced items are the 'maximum' equipment a coach may have in the corner. First aid supplied do not include ammonia inhalants or smelling salts. These items are prohibited.

(i) A coach may retire his boxer by throwing a sponge or towel into the ring, or mounting the ring apron, except when the referee is in the course of counting.

(j) Violations of the foregoing provisions shall result in the removal of offenders from the ring corner and from further participation as coaches in the contest or tournament, or forever with amateur boxing and may result in the disqualification of their contestant by the referee.

(k) Whenever a contestant is charged with an infraction of rules, that his coach is aware of and has not reported or is responsible for said infraction, he also shall be subject to disciplinary action.

(l) The USA/ABF shall only allow its officially-elected coaches, trainers, manager and medical staff to be responsible for the training, coaching and supervision of the Olympic, Pan American and World Championship teams, from the start of the designated training period to the end of the competition.

**Administration of Drugs**

**Doping**

No boxer is allowed to take any drug or chemical which does not form part of his usually diet. For this rules have been formulated by AIBA.

Penalties.

I.A.B.F. can disqualify or suspend a boxer who does not comply with laid down rules. If after a bout any boxer is not ready to go through medical test, is liable to be disqualified. This rule not only applies to boxers only but also to officials which encourage boxers to refuse any test.

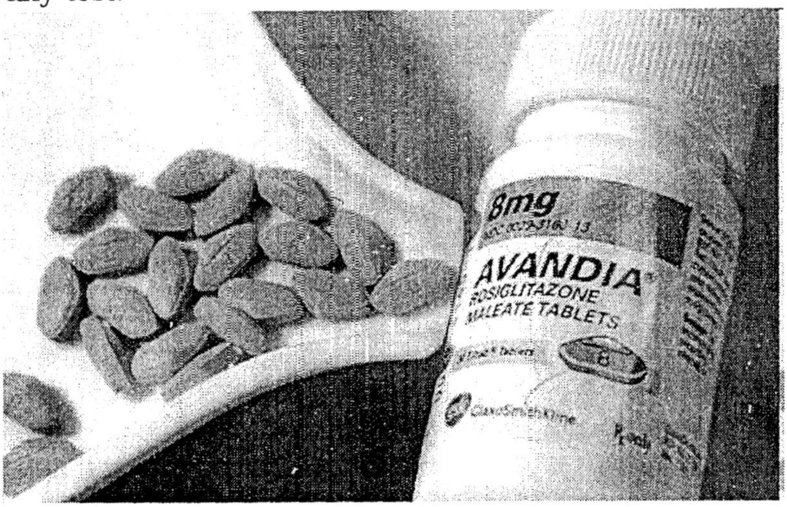


**Local Anaesthetic**

Boxers are permitted to take any anaesthetic which is recommended by any doctor or Medical Commission.

Reports by Officials

No other than President or any person authorized by him can make any report to Press, or make statements on Television on any matter relating to boxing or officiating at that events.

**Trophies or Challenge Cups**

**Team Standings**

Following considerations should be kept in mind while determining team standings:

1. 1 mark should be awarded to winner of each bout in preliminary rounds or quarter finals.

2. 2 marks should be awarded to winner of each bout in semi-finals.

3. Winner of final bout should be awarded with 3 marks.

4. If for any reason bout cannot take place marks should be awarded.

5. (i) The number of second places, and if this is equal too;

(ii) The number of victories in the finals, and if this is equal:

(iii) The number of third places.

Above mentioned points should be taken into consideration if two or more teams obtain an equal number of marks.

Prizes: Cups or prizes of honour should be presented in Nationals or State Level Competitions.

Rules Governing The Award of the Friendship and Fair-Play Cup

(i) State or Unit team which shows good understanding, sincere friendship and fair-play among teams participating in Championships, Friendship and Fair-Play Cup should be awarded with. Results of competition does not take in consideration for awarding of such cups.

(ii) The name of winning team, date and place of championships should appear on cup. Friendship and Fair-play cups can be transferred.

(iii) The right to decide which State or Unit should be awarded this cup rests with Executive Committee or I.A.B.F. However, this right can be delegated to Jury if Executive Committee decides.

(iv) State or Unit Association which is awarded with this cup promises I.A.B.F. in written that they will keep cup with them with care and will give them back in same condition atleast 5 days before commencement of next National Championship.

(v) To encourage understanding and co-operation between teams participating in National Championship this cup is awarded.

(vi) In closing ceremony of Championship this cup should be presented to deserving team by President of I.A.B.F. or his nominated representative.

Participants having age between 12 to 13 as on first day of championship should be placed in category E.

Above mentioned rules does not cover 21 matters which should be agreed between executive committee of IABF and affiliated members organising these championships.

# 6

# CRICKET

## INTRODUCTION

Cricket is a bat-and-ball team sport. Many variations exist, with its most popular form played on an oval-shaped outdoor arena known as a cricket field, at the centre of which is a rectangular 22-yard (20.12 m) long pitch that is the focus of the game. A game (or match) is contested between two teams of eleven players each. One team bats, trying to score as many runs as possible while the

other team bowls and fields, trying to dismiss the batsmen and thus limit the runs scored by the batting team. A run is scored by the striking batsman hitting the ball with his bat, running to the opposite end of the pitch and touching the crease there without being dismissed. The teams switch between batting and fielding at the end of an innings.

There are also variations in the length of a game of cricket. In professional cricket this ranges from a limit of 20 overs of six bowling deliveries per side (Twenty20) to a game played over 5 days (Test cricket, which is the highest level of the game). Depending on the form of the match being played, there are different rules that govern how a game is won, lost, drawn or tied. The rules of two-innings games are known as the Laws of Cricket and maintained by the International Cricket Council (ICC) and the Marylebone Cricket Club (MCC); additional Standard Playing Conditions for Test matches and One Day Internationals augment these laws. In one version of Indoor Cricket, matches include just 6 players per side and include two 12-over innings.

Cricket was first documented as being played in southern England in the 16th century. By the end of the 18th century, it had developed to the point where it had become the national sport of England. The expansion of the British Empire led to cricket being played overseas and by the mid-19th century the first international matches were being held. The ICC is the game's governing body and currently has 105 member countries. Cricket is most popular in the Test playing countries.

**Types of Matches**

Cricket is a multi-faceted sport which, in very broad terms, can be divided into major cricket and minor cricket based on playing standards. A more pertinent division, particularly in terms of major cricket, is between matches in which the teams have two innings apiece and those in which they have a single innings each. The former, known as first-class cricket, has a duration of three to five days (there have been examples of "timeless" matches too); the latter, known as limited overs cricket because each team bowls a limit of typically 50 or 20 overs, has a planned duration of one day only.

**Test Cricket**

Test cricket is the highest standard of first-class cricket. A Test match is an international fixture between teams representing those countries that are Full Members of the ICC.

Although the term "Test match" was not coined until much later, Test cricket is deemed to have begun with two matches between Australia and England in the 1876–77 Australian season. Subsequently, eight other national teams have achieved Test status: South Africa (1889), West Indies (1928), New Zealand (1929), India (1932), Pakistan (1952), Sri Lanka (1982), Zimbabwe (1992) and Bangladesh (2000).

**Limited Overs**

Standard limited overs cricket was introduced in England in the 1963 season in the form of a knockout cup contested by the first-class county clubs. In 1969, a national league competition was established. The concept was gradually introduced to the other major cricket countries and the first limited overs international was played in 1971. In 1975, the first Cricket World Cup took place in England. Limited overs cricket has seen various innovations including the use of multi-coloured kit and floodlit matches using a white ball. A "one day match", named so because each match is scheduled for completion in a single day, is the common form of limited overs cricket played on an international level. In practice, matches sometimes continue on a second day if they have been interrupted or postponed by bad weather. The Cricket World Cup is held in one day format and recently on 2nd April 2011, 10th World Cup which was co-hosted by India, Sri Lanka and Bangladesh was won by host India under the able captaincy by Mahindra Singh Dhoni by defeating Sri Lanka by 6 Wickets. This was the 2nd time when India lifted the Cricket World Cup since last 28 years when in the year 1983 India lifted the Cricket World Cup for the very first time by defeating champion West Indies. The next World Cup will be hosted by Australia and New Zealand in the year 2015.

Twenty20 is a new variant of limited overs itself with the purpose being to complete the match within about three hours, usually in an evening session. The original idea, when the concept was introduced in England in 2003, was to provide workers with an evening entertainment. It was commercially successful and has been adopted internationally.

Since its inception the game has spread around the cricket world. On most international tours there is at least one Twenty20 match and all Test-playing nations have a domestic cup competition. The inaugural ICC World Twenty20 was played in South Africa in 2007 with India winning by five runs against Pakistan in the final. Pakistan won the 2009 ICC World Twenty20, defeating Sri Lanka by eight wickets. England won the 2010 ICC World Twenty20 defeating Australia in the final by 7 wickets. The Indian Premier League (often abbreviated as IPL) is a professional league for Twenty20 cricket competition in India. It was initiated by the Board of Control for Cricket in India (BCCI) headquartered in Mumbai supervised by BCCI Vice President Chirayu Amin, current chairman & commissioner of IPL, and

CEO, Sundar Raman. It is currently contested by 10 teams consisting of players from around the world. It was started after an altercation between the BCCI and the Indian Cricket League.

## SKILLS AND TECHNIQUES

### BATTING

In the sport of cricket, batting is the act or skill of hitting the cricket ball with a cricket bat to score runs or prevent the loss of one's wicket. A player who is currently batting is denoted as a batsman, while the act of hitting the ball is called a shot or stroke. The terms batsman or specialist batsman are also used generically to describe players who specialise in batting.

Batting tactics and strategy vary depending on the type of match being played as well as the current state of play. The main concerns for the batsmen are not to lose their wicket and to score as many runs as quickly as possible. These objectives are generally in opposition to each other - to score quickly, some risky shots may need to be played thereby increasing the chances that the batsman will be dismissed. Depending on the current situation, batsmen may forgo attempts at run-scoring in an effort to preserve their wicket, or may attempt to score runs as quickly as possible with scant concern for the possibility of being dismissed.

**Stance**

The stance is the position in which a batsman stands in order to have the ball bowled to him. An ideal stance is "comfortable relaxed and balanced," with the feet 20 cm apart, parallel and astride the crease. Additionally, the front shoulder should be pointing down the wicket, the head facing the bowler, the weight equally balanced and the bat near the back toe

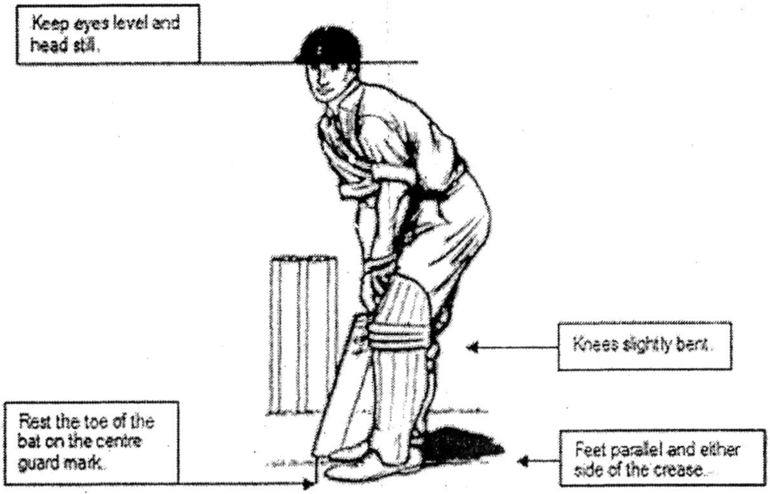


**Taking Guard**

You take guard after arriving at the crease so that when you take up your stance and place your bat in the position indicated by the umpire, you are aware of where you are standing in relation to your stumps and are better able to defend them. You ask the umpire for guard by holding the bat perpendicularly in front of the wicket you are protecting.

**Grip**

Grip the bat with both hands, with the hands together near the middle of the bat handle, with the V's formed by the forefinger and thumb of each hand aligned with the spine of the bat and the open end of the V's pointing up their respective arms and firmly but not too tightly.

**Drive**

A drive is a straight-batted shot, played by swinging the bat in a vertical arc through the line of the ball, hitting the ball in front of the batsman along the ground. Depending on the direction the ball travels, a drive can be a cover drive (struck towards the cover fielding position, an off drive (towards mid-off), straight drive (past the bowler and sometimes mid on), on drive (towards wide mid-on and mid wicket) or square drive (towards point). Drives can be played both off the front and the back foot, but back-foot drives are harder to force through the line of the ball.

**Cut**

A cut is a cross-batted shot played at a short-pitched ball, placing it wide on the off side. The batsman makes contact with the ball as it draws alongside or passes him and therefore requires virtually no effort on his part as he uses the bowler's pace to divert the ball. A square cut is a shot hit into the off side at near to 90 degrees from the wicket (towards point). A late cut, is played as or after the ball passes the batsman's body and is hit towards third man. The cut shot is typically played off the back foot, but is also sometimes played off the front foot against slower bowling. Apart from defensive technique, the cut is typically considered the most important stroke a batsman must master.

**Pull and Hook**

A pull is a cross-batted shot played to a ball bouncing around waist height by swinging the bat in a horizontal arc in front of the body, pulling it around to the leg side towards mid-wicket or square leg. The term hook shot is used when the shot is played against a ball bouncing at or above chest high to

the batsman, the batsman thus "hooking" the ball around behind square leg, either along the ground or in the air. Pull and hook shots can be played off front or back foot, with back foot being more typical.

**Leg Glance**

A leg glance is a delicate straight-batted shot played at a ball aimed slightly on the leg side, using the bat to flick the ball as it passes the batsman, and require some wrist work as well, deflecting towards the square leg or fine leg area. The stroke involves deflecting the bat-face towards the leg side at the last moment, head and body moving inside the line of the ball. This shot is played "off the toes, shins or hip". It is played off the front foot if the ball is pitched up at the toes or shin of the batsman, or off the back foot if the ball bounces at waist/hip height to the batsman.

**Sweep**

A sweep is a cross-batted front foot shot played to a low bouncing ball, usually from a slow bowler, by kneeling on one knee, bringing the head down in line with the ball and swinging the bat around in a horizontal arc near the pitch as the ball arrives, sweeping it around to the leg side, typically towards square leg or fine leg.

**Reverse Sweep**

A reverse sweep is a cross-batted sweep shot played in the opposite direction to the standard sweep, thus instead of sweeping the ball to the leg side, it is swept to the off side, towards backward point or third man. The batsman may also swap his hands on the bat handle to make the stroke easier to execute. The batsman may also bring his back foot to the front therefore making it more like a traditional sweep. The advantage of a reverse sweep is that it effectively reverses the fielding positions and thus is very difficult to set a field to.

**Slog and slog sweep**

A slog is a powerful pull shot played over mid-wicket, usually hit in the air in an attempt to score a six. A shot would be described as a slog when it is typically played at a delivery that would not ordinarily be pulled. A slog is also called a cow shot or "cow corner". The slog is an effective shot because all the batsman's power and body weight can be put into swinging the bat at the ball.

**Switch hit**

A switch hit is a shot pioneered by Kevin Pietersen in 2008, and first used during the New Zealand series in England in 2008. In this shot, a batsman changes his handedness and posture to adopt a stance the mirror image of his traditional handedness while the bowler is running in to bowl. As a fielding team cannot manoeuvre fielders while the bowler is in his run-up, the fielding side is effectively wrong-footed with the fielders out of position. The legality of such a ploy was questioned during the series but the shot was cleared by the International Cricket Council as legal. The shot is risky because a batsman is less proficient in the other handedness and is more likely to make a mistake in the execution of his shot.

**Scoop**

A "scoop" shot (also known as Paddle scoop or Marillier shot or Dilscoop) has been used by a number of first-class batsmen, the first being Douglas Marillier. Firstly used in international match by Srilankan batsman Tillekartne Dilshan (with great success).

It is played to short pitched straight ball that would traditionally be defended or, more aggressively, pulled to the leg side - both shots "off the back foot". To play a scoop shot, the batsman is on the front foot and aims to get beneath the bounce of the ball and hit it directly behind the stumps, up and over the wicket keeper. This shot, though risky in the execution, has the advantage of being aimed at a section of the field where a fielder is very rarely placed - particularly in Twenty20 and ODI cricket where the number of outfielders is limited.

**Straight bat**

Straight bat is the position of the bat, after it is driven and when the bat is perpendicular to the ground at the point of impact with the ball so that the batsmen can play the ball along the ground.

## BOWLING

In the sport of cricket, bowling is the action of propelling the ball toward the wicket defended by a batter. A player skilled at bowling is called a bowler. Bowling the ball is distinguished from simply throwing the ball by a strictly specified biomechanical definition which restricts the angle of extension of the elbow.

There are different types of bowlers ranging from fast bowlers, whose primary weapon is pace, through swing and seam bowlers who try to make the ball deviate in its course through the air or when it bounces, to slow bowlers, who will attempt to deceive the batsmen with a variety of flight and spin. A single act of bowling the ball towards the batsman is called a ball or a delivery.

Bowlers bowl deliveries in sets of six, called an over. Once a bowler has bowled their over, one of their team mates will bowl an over from the other end of the pitch.

**Grip**

Every bowler needs to grip the ball first in the basic grip, the seam held upright and pointing at the batsman, the index finger placed on the left side of the seam, the second finger just on the other side of the seam and the thumb underneath. The ball is held in the fingers and not in the palm of the hand. Eight paces will be long enough and we must make sure of running straight to the wicket. On the last stride of the run up, we just off the left foot and turn the body to face the side of the stumps. In doing this, our left arm is pushed up well above the head, and we look towards the batsman over the left side of the arm.

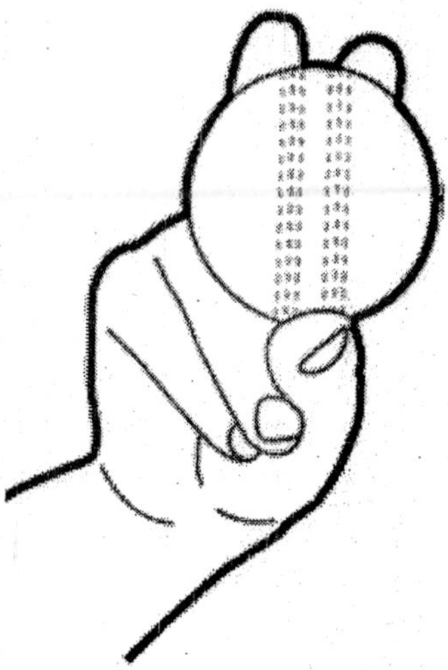

**Length and Direction**

A good length ball is one which bounces in such a position on the pitch that it presents the batsman with the problem of whether to go forward to play it as it pitches, or to go back. This may seem quite a straightforward explanation but in fact, to define it satisfactorily, it is not easy.

Length depends on so many things, such as the speed of the bowler, the pace of the pitch, how much the ball is turning and, to some extent, the height of the batsman. The good length ball lies between a full pitch and a long hop. The fast bowler on a hard pitch will have a margin of error of about six feet from the batsman up to twelve feet away and the batsman will be forced to defend either forward or back.

**Kinds of Bowling**

Various kinds of bowling are used in the game of cricket, some of which are as follows :—

**Off Cutter**

The off cutter is a medium or medium fast delivery which turns after it bounces from off to leg. Sometimes, the off cutter curves away from the bat before it cuts back in. An off cutter is bowled against a batter who does not play close enough to his pads with the bat, leaving a gap through which the ball can pass and hit the stumps. If a batter does not push the ball into the ground, he will play an off cutter into the air as a catch to close fielders on the leg side. The off cutter is used with great effect on a dry pitch which dusts or crumbles and helps the ball turn, as does a wet wicket.

Since the cutter is bowled at medium pace with the wrist cutting the fingers down the side of the ball, the ball turns quickly even on the slowest wickets. It also tends to lift suddenly. A breeze blowing from the leg side

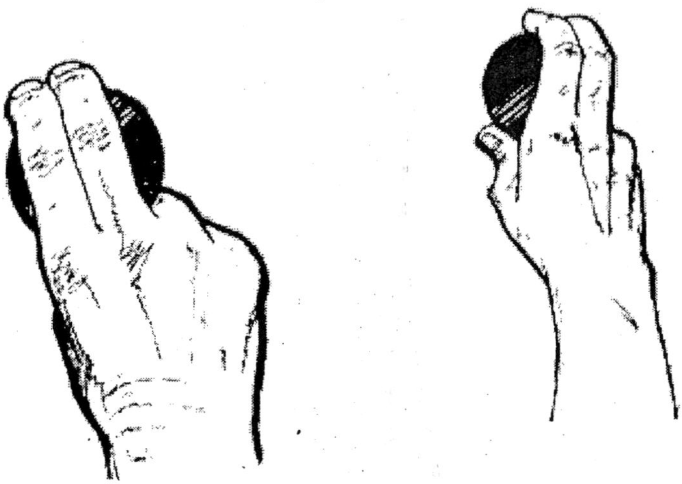

helps the off cutter since it blows the ball away to the off in the air, before it turns back in the opposite direction.

**Swing**

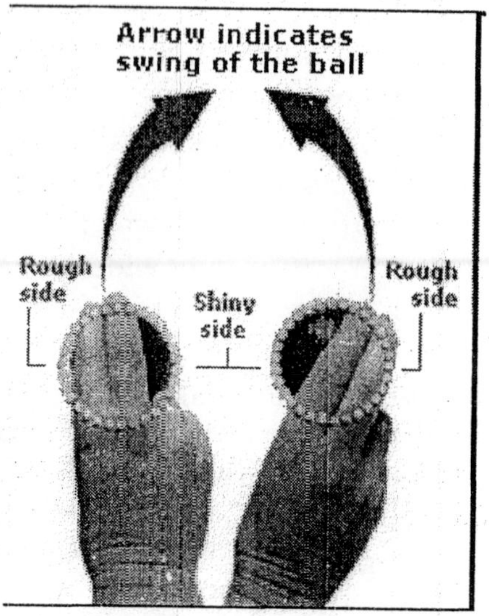


The ball can be made to swing in the air, either away from the batsman or in to him. On some days, when there is a lot of humidity, the ball will swing appreciably more than on a dry sunny day. The amount of wind and the direction it is blowing will also have a certain effect on how much the ball will move. The ball will swing far more when it is either new or has not completely lost the shine, and seam is still fairly prominent. While it is not unlawful for the bowler to shine the ball, raising the seam is frowned upon and should be stopped.

**Inswinger**

An inswinger is a medium pace or fast delivery which moves in the air from off to leg before it bounces. Bowl an inswinger against a batter who does not play close to the pads with the bat, leaving a gap through which the ball may pass and hit the stumps. The batter who does not play the inswinger quickly to ground may present a catch to close fielders on the leg side. A breeze blowing from the off side helps the movement of the inswinger from that direction. The ideal breeze for this delivery is from deep third man or mid off. A headwind will increase the swing off the ball but decrease the speed of the ball.

Hold the ball well out of the palm of the bowling hand in the top joints of the index and second fingers. The flat of the thumb supports the ball underneath. The seam is vertical, pointing towards the fine leg with the index and second fingers slightly across and on top of it. Your third and little fingers are positioned lightly alongside the ball. As you approach the bowling crease, gather yourself by jumping high and placing your weight onto your back foot, which is on the same side of the body as your bowling arm.

**Off Spinner**

An off spinner is a delivery which turns at slow pace after it bounces from off to leg, and because of flight creates uncertainty in the batter's mind about whether to play forward or back. Because the closed action is used, the ball curves away in the air before it spins back. It is bowled to a batter who does not play close enough to the front pad with the bat and leaves a gap through which the ball can pass and hi

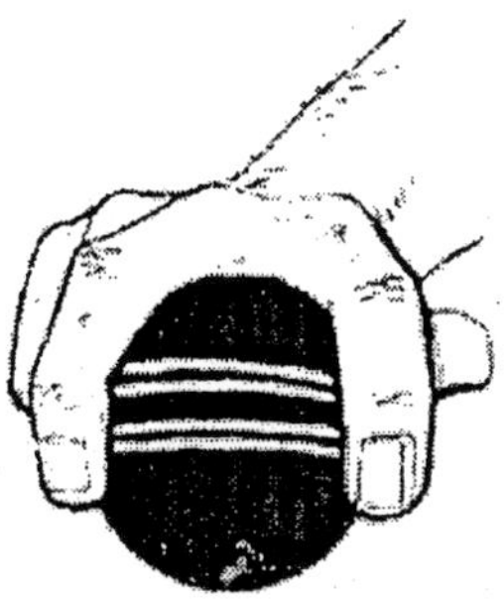

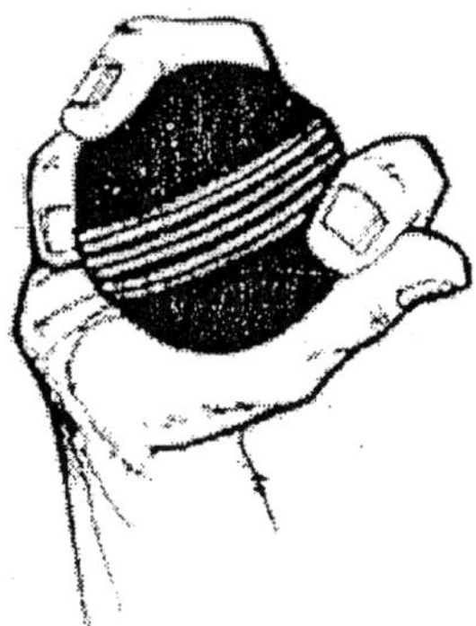

**Googly**

The googly is an off break with a leg break action. The ball is held in exactly the same manner as for the leg break, with the wrist turned down to ninety degrees. The arm is turned in an anti-clockwise direction with the back of the hand now pointing towards the batsman.

As the wrist is flicked straight, the ball will come out of the back of the hand over the third finger. There is no need to alter your action the slightest bit. Do not drop the left shoulder or point the left foot.

**Left Arm Bowling**

The left arm bowling aims the ball into the batsman, particularly if he bowls round the wicket. It is not necessary to restrict the bowler to bowling either side of the wicket, except in the case of the slow left arm orthodox leg spin, when it is generally beneficial to bowl round the wicket.

## FIELDING

Fielding in the sport of cricket is the action of fielders in collecting the ball after it is struck by the batsman, in such a way as to either limit the number of runs that the batsman scores or get the batsman out by catching the ball in flight or running the batsman out. A fielder or fieldsman may field the ball with any part of his person. However, if while the ball is in play he wilfully fields it otherwise (e.g. by using his hat), the ball becomes dead and 5 penalty runs are awarded to the batting side unless the ball previously struck a batsman not attempting to hit or avoid the ball.

**Attacking Fielding**

The ideal way of fielding is to attack whenever possible. The better the fielder, the more he will try to attack. The technique is to be on the move before the ball is hit and then to anticipate from the shot the direction the ball will take. Having decided the line, the ball is taking, try to get to it as quickly as possible. Approach the ball in a sideways manner and pick it up as it reaches the right foot, keeping your head down. The weight of the body is now on the right foot, and from that position, you get into the throwing action very quickly. The left arm and leg are pointed at the target, and the ball is thrown as you transfer the weight from the right leg to a braced left leg.

**Defensive Fielding**

To stop the ball from a hard drive is defensive fielding, no return it to the wicket keeper full toss at a smart pace, if the batsman decides to run, is attacking fielding. Get in line with ball, keep hands well open and head down. Do not take your eyes from the ball until it is firmly in your hands. The heels should be kept together. A very sound method of stopping the ball from a particularly hard shot is by turning sideways to the line of the ball and going down on the left knees, so that it touches the heel of the right foot at right angles to the line of the ball. The hands and head must be kept well down, the legs and body are now right behind the ball, and whatever it does, it should at least be stopped by you.

**Catching**

The hands pick the ball up, and they catch the ball, and in theory, they should always stop the ball. The hands are therefore extremely important, yet many people fail to use their hands properly or appear not to know how to hold them for either ground fielding or catching. Spread the fingers out as wide as possible, then with palms uppermost bring the hands together until the little fingers are touching, and then close hands until there is no gap between them.

## WICKET-KEEPING

The wicket-keeper in the sport of cricket is the player on the fielding side who stands behind the wicket or stumps being guarded by the batsman currently on strike. The wicket-keeper is the only member of the fielding side permitted to wear gloves and external leg guards.

It is essentially a specialist role although a keeper is occasionally called upon to bowl, in which case another member of the fielding side temporarily keeps wicket.

**Stance**

It is difficult to set a standard stance for wicketkeepers. Some prefer to squat on their toes, others balance on the balls of their feet. Whichever stance you adopt, it should be comfortable with your weight distributed evenly between your legs and feet. The comfortable balanced squatting stance ensures essential speedy footwork. For fast bowlers, stand back far enough to receive the average ball as it stops rising. Judge how far outside the off stump you should stand.

This will vary with different bowlers and conditions.

**Position**

A wicket keeper must stand either right up or back, there is no half way. The wicket keeper and the bowler should talk thinks over regarding methods of bowling and try to establish an understanding. Some medium-pace bowlers like to have the keeper standing close up while others prefer to have him standing back.

There are personal idiosyncrasies of the keeper who feels he is more likely to catch the ball when standing back, than up at the wicket. Other keepers feel that perhaps they could get a good stumping on the leg side, all these things should be considered by wicket keeper and bowler. It is very important that the wicket keeper stays down as long as possible only rising to meet the rise of the ball off the pitch. His body should be behind the ball whenever possible, with the fingers pointing down.

## RULES OF CRICKET

## STANDARD TEST MATCH PLAYING CONDITIONS

**Note:** All references to 'Governing Body' within the Laws of Cricket shall be replaced by 'ICC Match Referee'.

**1. Law 1 - The Players**

**1.1 Law 1.2 – Nomination of Players**

Law 1.2 shall be replaced by the following:

Each captain shall nominate his players in writing to the ICC Match Referee before the toss. No player may be changed after the nomination without the consent of the opposing captain.

**1.2 Law 1.3 - Captain**

The following shall apply in addition to Law 1.3 (a):

The deputy must be one of the nominated players.

**2. Law 2 - Substitutes and Runners**

**2.1 Law 2.5 - Fielder absent or leaving the field**

Law 2.5 shall be replaced by the following:

If a fielder fails to take the field with his side at the start of the match or at any later time, or leaves the field during a session of play, the umpire shall be informed of the reason for his absence, and he shall not thereafter come on to the field during a session of play without the consent of the umpire. The umpire shall give such consent as soon as practicable.

**3. Law 3 - The Umpires**

**3.1 Law 3.1 - Appointment and attendance**

Law 3.1 shall be replaced by the following:

The following rules for the selection and appointment of Test Match umpires shall be followed as far as it is practicable to do so:

3.1.1 ICC shall establish an 'Elite Panel' of umpires who shall be contracted to the ICC.

3.1.2 Each Full Member country shall nominate from its panel of first class umpires two umpires to an 'International Panel' and one umpire to a 'TV Panel'. (A third umpire may be nominated to the 'International Panel' with the written consent of the ICC).

**3.2 Third Umpire/TV Replays**

The following shall apply in addition to Clause 3.1:

**3.2.1 General**

(a) Save with the express written consent of the Chief Executive Officer of the ICC the Home Board will ensure the live television broadcast of all Test Matches played in its country.

(b) Where matches are broadcast the camera specifications set out in Appendix 2 shall be mandatory as a minimum requirement.

(c) Where matches are not broadcast the camera specifications set out in Appendix 3 shall be mandatory as a minimum requirement.

(d) The Home Board will ensure a separate room is provided for the third umpire and that he has access to a television monitor and direct sound link with the television control unit director to facilitate as many replays as is necessary to assist him in making a decision.

(e) In the circumstances detailed in Clauses 3.2.2, 3.2.3, 3.2.4 and 3.2.5 hereunder, the on-field umpire has the discretion whether to refer the appeal to the third umpire for a decision or not and should take a common sense approach. Players may not appeal to the umpire to use the replay system - breach of this provision would constitute dissent and the player could be liable for discipline under the ICC Code of Conduct.

**3.2.2 Run Out, Stumping and Hit Wicket Decisions**

(a) The on-field umpire shall be entitled to refer an appeal for a run-out, stumping or hit wicket to the third umpire.

(b) An on-field umpire wishing to refer a decision to the third umpire shall signal to the third umpire by making the shape of a TV screen with his hands.

(c) If the third umpire decides the batsman is out a red light is displayed; a green light means not-out. Should the third umpire be temporarily unable to respond, a white light (where available) will remain illuminated throughout the period of interruption to signify to the on-field umpires that the TV replay system is temporarily unavailable, in which case the decision will be taken by the on-field umpire. (As an alternative to the red/green light system and where available, the big replay screen may be used for the purpose of conveying the third umpire's decision.)

(d) When reviewing the TV replay(s), if the third umpire finds the batsman has been bowled rather than hit wicket or stumped, he shall indicate that the batsman was dismissed.

**3.2.3 Caught Decisions**

The on-field umpire shall be entitled to refer an appeal for a caught decision to the third umpire in the following circumstances:

**3.2.3.1 Clean Catches**

(a) Should the bowler's end umpire be unable to decide whether or not a catch was taken cleanly, he shall first consult with the square leg umpire.

(b) Should both umpires be unable to make a decision, they may consult by two-way radio with the 3rd umpire. Following such consultation, the final decision will be made and given by the bowler's end umpire, who will take into account the on-field umpires' initial views and any other advice received from the 3rd umpire.

**3.2.3.2 Bump Ball**

(a) Should the bowler's end umpire be unable to decide whether a catch was taken from a bump ball or not, he shall first consult with the square leg umpire.

(b) Should both on-field umpires be unable to make a decision, the bowler's end umpire shall be entitled to refer the decision to the third umpire to review a TV replay(s) of the batsman's stroke as in Clause 3.2.2 (b).

**3.2.4 Boundary Decisions**

(a) The on-field umpire shall be entitled to refer to the third umpire for a decision about whether the fieldsman had any part of his person in contact with the ball when he touched or crossed the boundary line or whether a four or six had been scored. A decision is to be made immediately and cannot be changed thereafter.

(b) An on-field umpire wishing the assistance of the third umpire in this circumstance shall communicate with the third umpire by use of a two-way radio and the third umpire will convey his decision to the on-field umpire by this method.

(c) The third umpire may initiate contact with the on-field umpire by two-way radio if TV coverage shows a boundary line infringement or incident as envisaged under this clause.

**3.3 Light Meters**

3.3.1 It is the responsibility of the ICC to supply light meters to the match officials to be used in accordance with these playing conditions.

3.3.2 All light meters shall be uniformly calibrated.

3.3.3 The umpires shall be entitled to use light meter readings as a guideline for determining whether the light is unfit/fit for play.

3.3.4 Light meter readings may accordingly be used by the umpires:

(a) To determine whether there has been at any stage a deterioration or improvement in the light.

(b) As benchmarks for the remainder of a stoppage, match and/or series/event.

**3.4 Use of lights**

If in the opinion of the umpires, natural light is deteriorating to an unfit level, they shall authorize the ground authorities to use the available artificial lighting so that the match can continue in acceptable conditions.

The lights are only to be used to enable a full days play to be completed as provided in Clause 16 Hours of Play, Intervals and Minimum Overs in the Day.

**4. Law 4 - The Scorers**

**4.1 Law 4.2 - Correctness of scores**

Attention is drawn to Clause 21.2.

**5. Law 5 - The Ball**

**5.1 Law 5.2 - Approval and control of balls**

Law 5.2 shall be replaced by the following:

The Home Board shall provide cricket balls of an approved standard for Test cricket and spare used balls for changing during a match, which shall also be of the same brand. Note: The Home Board shall be required to advise the visiting Board of the brand of ball to be used in the match(es) at least 30 days prior to the start of the match(es).

**5.2 Law 5.4 - New ball in a match of more than one**

**day's duration**

Law 5.4 shall be replaced by the following:

The captain of the fielding side shall have the choice of taking a new ball at any time after 80 overs have been bowled with the previous ball. The umpires shall indicate to the batsman and the scorers whenever a new ball is taken into play.

**6. Law 6 - The Bat (new law effective 1st October 2008)**

The following shall apply in addition to Law 6 (as amended in 2008):

Subject to any moratoriums that may be in place only Grade A bats shall be used in Test matches.

**7. Law 7 - The Pitch**

**7.1 Law 7.3 - Selection and preparation**

The following will apply in addition to Law 7.3:

7.1.1 The ground staff shall ensure that during the period prior to the start of play and during intervals, the pitch area shall be roped off so as to prevent unauthorised access. (The pitch area shall include an area at least 2 metres beyond the rectangle made by the crease markings at both ends of the pitch).

**7.2 Law 7.4 - Changing the pitch**

Law 7.4 shall be replaced by the following:

7.2.1: In the event of a pitch being considered too dangerous for play to continue in the estimation of the on-field umpires, they shall stop play and immediately advise the ICC Match Referee.

7.2.2: The on-field umpires and ICC Match Referee shall consult with both captains.

7.2.3: If the captains agree to continue, play shall resume.

7.2.4: If the decision is not to resume play, the on-field umpires shall consider one of the options in the following sequence:

(a) whether the existing pitch can be repaired. Repair

work will only be considered if there has been malicious damage to a non-crucial part of the pitch;

(b) whether an alternative pitch can be used;

(c) whether the match has to be abandoned.

**7.3 Law 7.5 - Non-turf pitches**

Law 7.5 shall not apply.

All matches shall be played on natural turf pitches. The use of PVA and other adhesives in the preparation of pitches is not permitted.

**8. Law 8 - The Wickets**

**8.1 Law 8.2 - Size of stumps**

The following shall apply in addition to Law 8.2:

For televised matches the Home Board may provide a slightly larger cylindrical stump to accommodate the stump camera. When the larger stump is used, all three stumps must be exactly the same size.

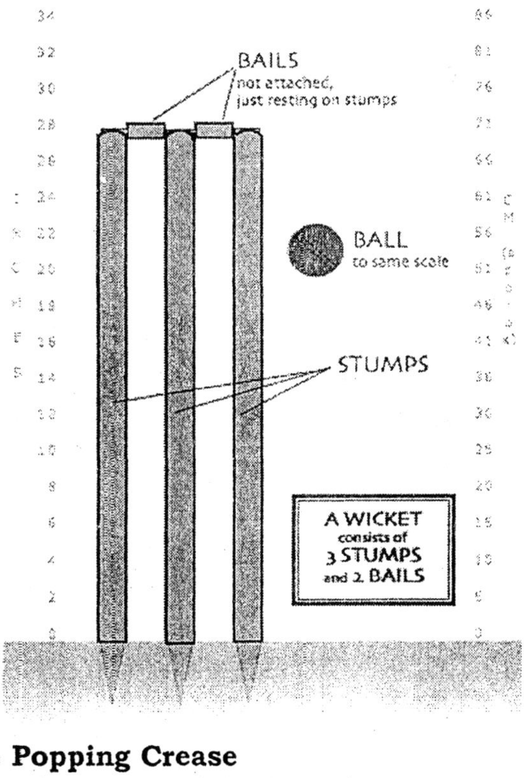


**9. Law 9 - The Bowling, Popping and Return Creases**

**9.1 Law 9.3 - The Popping Crease**

Law 9.3 shall apply, except that the reference to 'a minimum of 6 ft' shall be replaced by 'a minimum of 15 yards (13.71 metres)'.

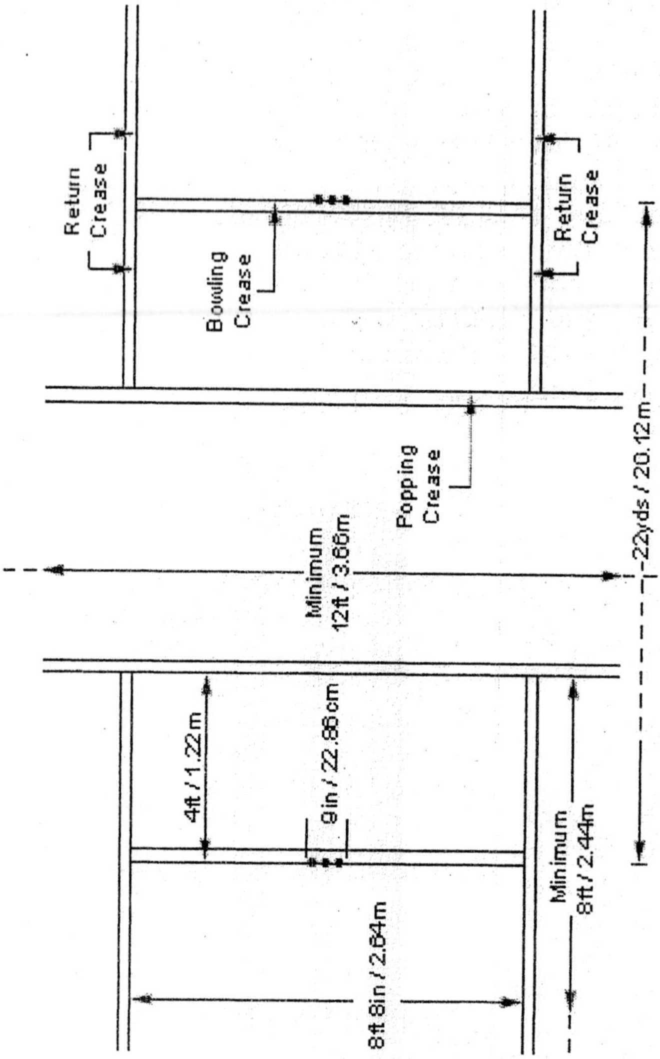


**10. Law 10 - Preparation and Maintenance of the Playing Area**

**10.1 Law 10.1 - Rolling**

The following shall apply in addition to Law 10.1:

10.1.1 Prior to tossing for choice of innings the artificial drying of the pitch and outfield shall be at the

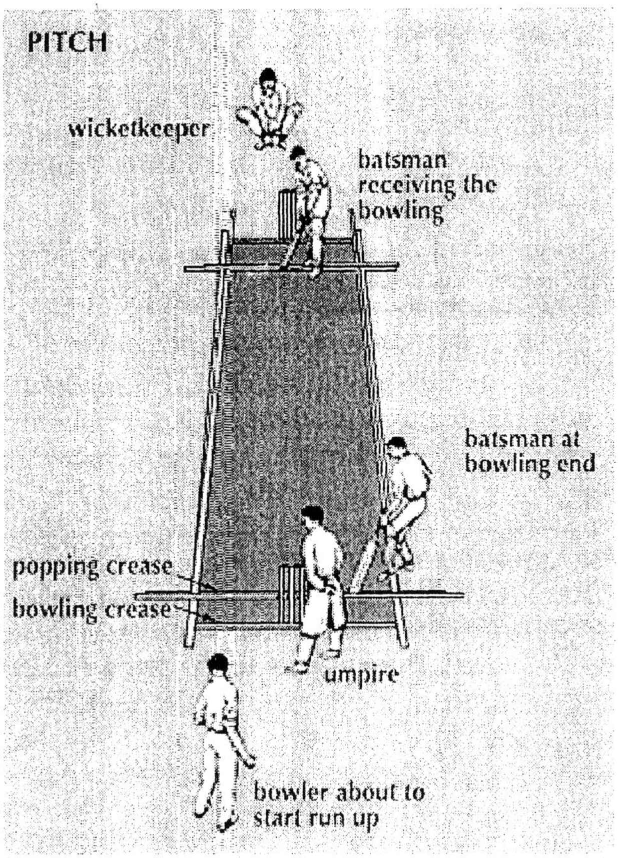


discretion of the groundsman. Thereafter and throughout the match the drying of the outfield may be undertaken at any time by the groundsman, but the drying of the affected area of the pitch shall be carried out only on the instructions and under the supervision of the umpires.

The umpires shall be empowered to have the pitch dried without reference to the captains at any time they are of the opinion that it is unfit for play.

10.1.2 The umpires may instruct the groundsman to use any available equipment, including any roller for the purpose of drying the pitch and making it fit for play.

10.1.3 An absorbent roller may be used to remove water from the covers including the cover on the match pitch.

**10.2 Law 10.6 - Maintenance of footholes**

The following shall apply in addition to Law 10.6:

The umpires shall see that wherever possible and whenever it is considered necessary, action is taken during all intervals in play to do whatever is practicable to improve the bowler's foot holes. As soon as possible after the conclusion of each day's play, bowler's foot holes will be repaired.

**11. Covering the Pitch**

**11.1 Law 11.1 - Before the match**

The following shall apply in addition to Law 11.1:

The pitch shall be entirely protected against rain up to the commencement of play.

**12. Law 12 - Innings**

Law 12 shall apply subject to the following:

12.1 Law 12.1 (a) shall be replaced by the following: A match shall be two innings per side subject to the provisions of Law 13.1.

12.2 Law12.1 (b) and 12.3 (e) shall not apply.

12.3 Matches shall be of five days scheduled duration, and of two innings per side. The two participating countries may:

(a) Provide for a rest day during the match, and/or a reserve day after the scheduled days of play.

(b) Play on any scheduled rest day, conditions and circumstances permitting, should a full day's play be lost on any day prior to the rest day.

**13. Law 13 - The Follow-on**

**13.1 Law 13.3 - First day's play lost**

If the provision of Clause 16.1.3 (b) is applied, the additional time is regarded as part of that day's play, i.e. it is the number of days remaining, and not the total number of hours available.

**14. Law 14 - Declaration and Forfeiture**

Law 14 shall apply.

**15. Law 15 - Intervals**

**15.1 Law 15.3 - Duration of intervals**

15.1.1 Luncheon Interval: The interval shall be of 40 minutes duration.

15.1.2 Tea Interval: The interval shall be of 20 minutes duration.

15.2 Law 15.8 - Tea interval- 9 wickets down

Law 15.8 shall be replaced by the following:

If at the scheduled time for the tea interval, the ninth wicket of the innings in progress is already down, or it falls at, or after that time, or falls when less than two minutes remain before that time, play will continue for a period of 30 minutes unless the players have cause to leave the field of play, or the innings is concluded earlier.

**15.3 Law 15.9 - Intervals for Drinks**

The provisions of Law 15.9 shall be strictly observed except that under conditions of extreme heat the umpires may permit extra intervals for drinks.

**16. Law 16 - Start of Play; Cessation of Play**

Law 16 shall apply subject to the following:

**16.1 Start and Cessation Times**

The Home Board shall determine the hours of play, subject to there being 6 hours scheduled play per day (Pakistan, a minimum of 5 ½ hours), and subject to:

***16.1.1 Minimum Overs in the Day***

Subject to clause 16.1.2 below:

(a) On days other than the last day, play shall continue on each day until the completion of a minimum target of 90 overs (or a minimum of 15 overs per hour) or the completion of the scheduled or rescheduled cessation time, which ever is the later but provided that play shall not continue for more than 30 minutes beyond the scheduled or rescheduled cessation time (permitted overtime). For the sake of clarity, if any of the minimum target number of overs have not been bowled at the completion of the permitted overtime, play shall cease upon completion of the over in progress. The overs not bowled shall not be made up on any subsequent day.

(b) On the last day, a minimum of 75 overs (or a minimum of 15 overs per hour) shall be bowled during the playing time other than the last hour of the match.

***16.1.2 Reduction in minimum overs***

Except in the last hour of the match, for which clause 16.1.6 makes provision, if play is suspended due to adverse weather or light or any other reason (other than normal intervals) for more than 1 hour on any day, the minimum number of overs shall be reduced by 1 over for each full 4 minutes of the aggregate playing time lost. For the avoidance of doubt, the aggregate of 1 hour shall be inclusive of any time that may have been brought forward from previous days due to playing time lost on such previous days under clause 16.1.3 (b) below.

***16.1.3 Making Up Lost Time***

*On The Day*

Subject to weather and light, except in the last hour of the match, in the event of play being suspended for any reason other than normal intervals, the playing time on that day shall be extended by the amount of time lost up to a maximum of 1 hour.

***16.1.4 Change of Intervals***

(a) If play has been suspended for any reason other than normal intervals for 30 minutes or more prior to the commencement of the scheduled or rescheduled tea interval on that day, the tea interval shall be delayed for ½ hour.

(b) Not withstanding the provisions of clause a above, the timings of intervals can be altered under Law 15.5 at any time on any day if playing time has been lost irrespective of whether the time has been lost on that day or on any previous days.

### *16.1.5 Change of Innings*

Where there is a change of innings during a days play (except where the change of innings occurs at lunch or tea or when play is suspended for any reason) 2 overs will be deducted from the minimum number of overs to be bowled.

The over in progress at the end of an innings is regarded as a completed over for the purposes of determining the minimum number of remaining overs to be bowled in the day.

### *16.1.6 Last Hour*

Law 16.6, 16.7 and 16.8 will apply except that a minimum of 15 overs shall be bowled in the last hour and all calculations with regard to suspensions of play or the start of a new innings shall be based on 1 over for each full 4 minutes.

On the final day, if both captains (the batsmen at the wicket may act for their captain) accept that there is no prospect of either side achieving a victory, they may agree to finish the match after (a) the time for the commencement of the last hour has been reached OR (b) there are a minimum of 15 overs to be bowled, whichever is the later.

### 16.2 Extra Time

The umpires may decide to play 30 minutes (a minimum of eight overs) extra time at the end of any day (other than the last day) if requested by either captain if, in the umpires opinion, it would bring about a definite result on that day [this is in addition to the additional time provided for in Clause 16.1.3 above]. If the umpires do not believe a result can be achieved no extra time shall be allowed. If it is decided to play such extra time on one or more of these days, the whole period shall be played out even though the possibility of finishing the match may have disappeared before the full period has expired.

**17. Law 17 - Practice on the Field**

**17.1 Law 17.1 - Practice on the field**

The following shall apply in addition to Law 17.1:

The use of the square for practice on any day of any match will be restricted to any netted practice area on the square set aside for that purpose.

**18. Law 18 - Scoring Runs**

Law 18 shall apply.

**19. Law 19 - Boundaries**

**19.1 Law 19.1 - The boundary of the field of play**

The following shall apply in addition to Law 19.1:

The playing area shall be a minimum of 150 yards (137.16 metres) from boundary to boundary square of the pitch, with the shorter of the two square boundaries being a minimum 65 yards (59.43 metres). The straight boundary at both ends of the pitch shall be a minimum of 70 yards (64.00 metres). Distances shall be measured from the centre of the pitch to be used.

On large grounds the aim shall be to provide the largest playing area, subject to no boundary exceeding 90 yards (82.29 meters) from the centre of the pitch to be used. Any ground which has been approved to host international cricket prior to 1st October 2007 or which is currently under construction as of this date which is unable to conform to these new minimum dimensions shall be exempt. In such cases the regulations in force immediately prior to the adoption of these regulations shall apply.

Sightscreens shall be provided at both ends of all grounds. Advertising shall be permitted on the sightscreen behind the striker, providing it is removed for the subsequent over from that end. Such advertising shall not contain flashing or flickering images and particular care should be taken by the operators that the advertising is not changed at a time which is distracting to the umpire. In addition, advertising on perimeter boards placed in front of the sightscreens is permitted save that the predominant colour of such advertising shall be of a contrasting colour to that of the ball.

**19.2 Law 19.2 - Defining the boundary - boundary marking**

The following shall apply in addition to Law 19.2:

All boundaries must be designated by a rope or similar object of a minimum standard as authorised by the ICC from time to time. Where appropriate the rope should be a required minimum distance (3 yards (2.74 metres) minimum) inside the perimeter fencing or advertising signs. For grounds with a large playing area, the maximum length of boundary should be used before applying the minimum 3 yards (2.74 metres) between the boundary and the fence.

**20. Law 20 - Lost Ball**

Law 20 shall apply.

**21. Law 21 - The Result**

Law 21 shall apply subject to the following:

**21.1 Law 21.2 - A win-one innings match**

Law 21.2 shall not apply

**21.2 Law 21.8 - Correctness of result**

Any query on the result of the match as defined in Laws 21.1, 21.3, 21.4, 21.5, 21.8 and 21.10 shall be resolved as soon as possible and a final decision made by the umpires at close of play.

**Law 21.3 – Umpire (Referee) awarding a match**

Law 21.3 shall be replaced by the following:

(a) A match shall be lost by a side which either

(i) concedes defeat or

(ii) in the opinion of the Referee refuses to play and the Referee shall award the match to the other side.

**22. Law 22 - The Over**

Law 22 shall apply subject to the addition of the

following to Law 22.5:

**22.1 Law 22.5 - Umpire miscounting**

Whenever possible the third umpire shall liaise with the scorers and if possible inform the on-field umpires if the over has been miscounted.

**23 Law 23 - Dead Ball**

Law 23 shall apply.

**24 Law 24 - No Ball**

Law 24 shall apply subject to the following:

**24.1 Law 24.1 - Mode of delivery**

Law 24.1 (b) shall be replaced by the following:

The bowler may not deliver the ball underarm. If a bowler bowls a ball underarm the umpire shall call and signal no ball, and the ball is to be re-bowled overarm.

**25. Law 25 - Wide Ball**

**25.1 Law 25.1 - Judging a Wide**

Law 25 shall apply with the following addition to Law 25.1 (Judging a wide):

For bowlers attempting to utilise the rough outside a batsman's leg stump, not necessarily as a negative tactic, the strict limited over wide interpretation shall be applied.

For bowlers whom umpires consider to be bowling down the leg side as a negative tactic, the strict limited over wide interpretation shall be applied.

**26. Batting Powerplay**

A Powerplay is a rule introduced in 2005 concerning fielding restrictions in One Day International (ODI) cricket and designed to give a temporary advantage to the batting side. In the past, there was a 15-over period at the start of an innings when only two fielders were allowed outside the 30-yard circle. This meant that attacking batsmen were likely to score runs quickly in the first 15 overs, because they were able to play aggressive shots likely to result in a boundary at a lower risk of being caught out, but would become more watchful after the end of the spell.

In an effort to keep the game more exciting during the middle overs, this rule was amended to apply only to the first 10 overs of every innings, but also in two blocks of five overs, Powerplays, which will be used at the discretion of the fielding captain.

The Powerplay was intended to add to the excitement in ODI cricket. If the batting team has got off to a very quick start, the fielding captain can choose to delay Powerplay 2 and 3, and instead spread out the field to stem the flow of runs. Powerplays may then be taken when an attacking batsman is out, or when the run rate has been reduced. Otherwise, all 20 Powerplay overs are likely to be taken at the start of the batting team's innings.

**27. Bowling Powerplay**

The bowling power play is taken by the captain of the fielding side after the 1-10 compulsory power play it is left to the fielding side captain to decide when to take the second power play. If there is a strong hitter in the crease then the captain usually denies the bowling power play and tries to get the batsmen out else if the bating team is 2 or 3 wickets down the power play is taken immediately after 10th over.

**28. The Umpire Decision Review System (abbreviated as UDRS or DRS)**

UDRS or DRS is a new technology based system currently being used on an experimental basis in the sport of cricket. The system was first introduced in Test Cricket for the sole purpose of reviewing the controversial decisions made by the on-field umpires in the case of a batsman being dismissed or not. The new review system was officially launched by International Cricket Council on 24 November 2009 during the first Test match between New Zealand and Pakistan at the University Oval in Dunedin. It was first used in One Day

Internationals in January 2011, during England's tour of Australia.

Each team is allowed to make two unsuccessful review requests per innings during a match. A fielding team may use the system to dispute a "not out" call and a batting team may do so to dispute an "out" call. The fielding team captain or the batsman being dismissed invokes the challenge by signalling a "T" with the arms. Once the challenge is invoked, acknowledged, and agreed, the Third Umpire reviews the play. While umpires may request the Third Umpire for certain close calls such as line calls and boundary calls, a challenge may be used in situations that may result in a dismissal: for example, to determine if the ball is a legal catch (making contact with the batsman's bat or glove and not touching the ground before being held by a fielder) or if a delivery made the criteria for a leg before wicket dismissal. The Third Umpire then reports to the on-field umpire whether his analysis supports the original call, contradicts the call, or is inconclusive. The on-field umpire then makes the final decision: either re-signalling a call that is standing or revoking a call that is being reversed and then making the corrected signal. Each team can go for referrals until they use their share of unsuccessful reviews. Under the DRS rule only bad decisions are reversed, in case of decisions that can go either way the original decision does not change.

**DUCKWORTH/LEWIS METHOD OF RE-CALCULATING THE TARGET SCORE IN AN INTERRUPTED MATCH**

The Professional Edition of the Duckworth/Lewis shall be used in all matches. If any match is suspended after it has started such that the number of overs available to be faced by either side is reduced from that determined when the match started, the revised target shall be computed using the latest version of CODA as distributed by ICC in accordance with the instructions provided with that software and displayed on the screen.

Where possible, arrangements shall be made for the provision of back-up capability, in case of computer malfunction, for the operation or continued operation of the Professional Edition. In the event of computer non-availability or malfunction where no such provision has been made, the Standard Edition (the method in use prior to October 2003) shall be used.The regulations given below describe only the operation of the Standard Edition, except that Clauses 4, 6 and 7 are also applicable to the Professional Edition.

# 7

# FOOTBALL

## INTRODUCTION

The game of football is played by eleven players from each team. The game starts at midfield with a free kick called the kickoff as each team is in its own half of the field. The offensive objectives are to maintain possession of the ball, keep the ball wide until near the goal, and then get the ball in front of the opponent's goal where a player can propel it between the uprights, beneath the crossbar, and completely across the goal line for a score.

The ball may be propelled with any part of the body except the hands and arms, however, the foot, body and head are the main parts of the body used. The defense's main objectives are to contain the opponents and the ball, forcing excessive passes, mark opponents in scoring position, tackle the opponent, taking the ball away whenever possible, funnel the ball to the middle of the field toward their own goal, and concentrate in front of their goal when the ball is in scoring position.

## SKILLS AND TECHNIQUES

### Gathering the Ball

This skill is very important and because of this reason it has been placed first. The ball comes to a player, and player cannot make use of it until he has got it under control. It is this ability to gain control with the minimum delay that first distinguishes a good player. When a football ball is driven against a wall, it will bounce off with almost the same velocity as it hits the wall. If the player receiving the ball allows it to bounce more than one stride away from him, it is no longer in his immediate control.

**Dribbling**

A good dribbler appears to have the ball tied to his foot at whatever speed he is running. He strokes the ball along with either the inside or the outside of both feet, but it never gets out of his reach. His body is usually well over the ball, making it extremely difficult for a would be tackler to get near enough to make a tackle.

**Kicking**

Without the correct kicking technique football might as well be just called ball. A player's feet are their main weapons on the pitch and there are a number of techniques for kicking a football that give the player a different outcome each time. For the majority of the time a football is kicked either using the inner side of the foot that runs along from toe to heel, or using the small area around the inside of the big toe.

There is also the 'sweet spot' of the foot running all the way centrally down the foot where the laces are on a traditional boot. This is the part of the foot to strike the ball with when shooting (either from the ground or using the volley technique) as it has a larger surface area and generates more power and accuracy.

**Heading**

This is one of the branches of football where the superiority of the professional over the amateur is most marked. In very few grades of amateur football does the head act as more than a straightforward defensive weapon or the scorer of an occasional goal, but in the highest class of football, the player who is unable to use his head with skill is at a serious disadvantage.

**Trapping**

Trapping is a means of bringing the ball under control with any part of the body except the arms. Trapping a ball in flight is accomplished by keeping the heel of the shoe on the ground and bringing the sole of the shoe down on the ball the instant it strikes the ground. A ball may be stopped by stepping on it lightly if it is rolling slowly, getting it between the foot and leg and the ground if it is moving fast, or clamping it between the legs and the ground if it is a high bounder or fly ball. It may be trapped between the knees or in the mid-section of body by jack-knifing over it.

**Feinting**

A dribbler who merely drives the ball on a single track against a poised opponent is not likely to get far. Apart from having no ball to control, the tackler can concentrate on a single aim, to disposes the advancing opponent, and is not likely to be outpaced. Thus, if he hopes to beat his man, the dribbler must unpoise his opponent. That is, he must carry out some preliminary feint which leads the tackler to assume that this feint is the actual move indeed.

**Passing**

Theoretically every kick, other than shots at goal, should be an attempt pass. Except in cases of emergency, this should be the aim of all kicks. The object of the pass is to send the ball to a colleagues so that it is not intercepted by an opponent, and so that it reaches the colleague at exactly the right height and speed for him to make the most of the pass. This may sound very obvious, but the number of passes that go astray, not all of them because of good interception by the opposing suggests that the art of passing is difficult to master. The modern theory of attack is simplicity itself, but in practice often proves difficult.

**Shooting**

Shooting is the most important factor in attacking play. Poor technique or players who are unwilling to shoot often lead to goal scoring opportunities being missed. Even in top level soccer, many shots pass high and wide or players can be seen to hesitate in front of goal. Thus, shooting practice should not only work on acquiring the correct techniques but on developing the right mental attitude.

Shooting practice should always resemble a real match environment. Thus, full size goals should be used as well as shooting in all types of conditions. Some coaches may want to use video analysis of players whether in match or training to study their technique. Video based statistical studies in the past have also shown that a team who has ten shots on target very rarely loses, thus showing the need for accurate shooting. A comparative analysis of 100 goal scoring shots and 100 off target shots in top European Football showed distinct differences in mental and technical skills. Poor shooting often involved one or more weaknesses in each of these domains.

## RULES OF FOOTBALL

### LAW 1 – THE FIELD OF PLAY

**Field Surface**

Matches may be played on natural or artificial surfaces, according to the rules of the competition. The colour of artificial surfaces must be green. Where artificial surfaces are used in either competition matches between representative teams of member associations affiliated to FIFA or international club competition matches, the surface must meet the requirements of the FIFA Quality Concept for Football Turf or the International Artificial Turf Standard, unless special dispensation is given by FIFA.

**Field Markings**

The field of play must be rectangular and marked with lines. These lines belong to the areas of which they are boundaries.

The two longer boundary lines are called touch lines. The two shorter lines are called goal lines.

The field of play is divided into two halves by a halfway line, which joins the midpoints of the two touch lines.

The centre mark is indicated at the midpoint of the halfway line. A circle with a radius of 9.15 m (10 yds) is marked around it.

Marks may be made off the field of play, 9.15 m (10 yds) from the corner arc and at right angles to the goal lines and the touch lines, to ensure that defending players retreat this distance when a corner kick is being taken.

**Dimensions**

The length of the touch line must be greater than the length of the goal line.

Length (touch line): minimum 90 m (100 yds)
maximum 120 m (130 yds)
Width (goal line): minimum 45 m (50 yds)
maximum 90 m (100 yds)

All lines must be of the same width, which must be not more than 12 cm (5 ins).

**International Matches**

Length: minimum 100 m (110 yds)
maximum 110 m (120 yds)
Width: minimum 64 m (70 yds)
maximum 75 m (80 yds)

**The Goal Area**

Two lines are drawn at right angles to the goal line, 5.5 m (6 yds) from the inside of each goalpost. These lines extend into the field of play for a distance of 5.5 m (6 yds) and are joined by a line drawn parallel with the goal line. The area bounded by these lines and the goal line is the goal area.

**The Penalty Area**

Two lines are drawn at right angles to the goal line, 16.5 m (18 yds) from the inside of each goalpost. These lines extend into the field of play for a distance of 16.5 m (18 yds) and are joined by a line drawn parallel with the goal line.

The area bounded by these lines and the goal line is the penalty area.

Within each penalty area, a penalty mark is made 11 m (12 yds) from the midpoint between the goalposts and equidistant to them.

**Flagposts**

A flagpost, not less than 1.5 m (5 ft) high, with a non-pointed top and a flag must be placed at each corner.

Flagposts may also be placed at each end of the halfway line, not less than 1 m (1 yd) outside the touch line.

**The Corner Arc**

A quarter circle with a radius of 1 m (1 yd) from each corner flagpost is drawn inside the field of play.

**Goals**

A goal must be placed on the centre of each goal line.

A goal consists of two upright posts equidistant from the corner flagposts and joined at the top by a horizontal crossbar. The goalposts and crossbar must be made of wood, metal or other approved material. They may be square, rectangular, round or elliptical in shape and must not be dangerous to players.

The distance between the posts is 7.32 m (8 yds) and the distance from the lower edge of the crossbar to the ground is 2.44 m (8 ft). Both goalposts and the crossbar have the same width and depth, which do not exceed 12 cm (5 ins). The goal lines must be of the same width as the goalposts and the crossbar. Nets may be attached to the goals and the ground behind the goal, provided that they are properly supported and do not interfere with the goalkeeper.

The goalposts and crossbars must be white.

**Safety**

Goals must be anchored securely to the ground. Portable goals may only be used if they satisfy this requirement.

## The Field of Play

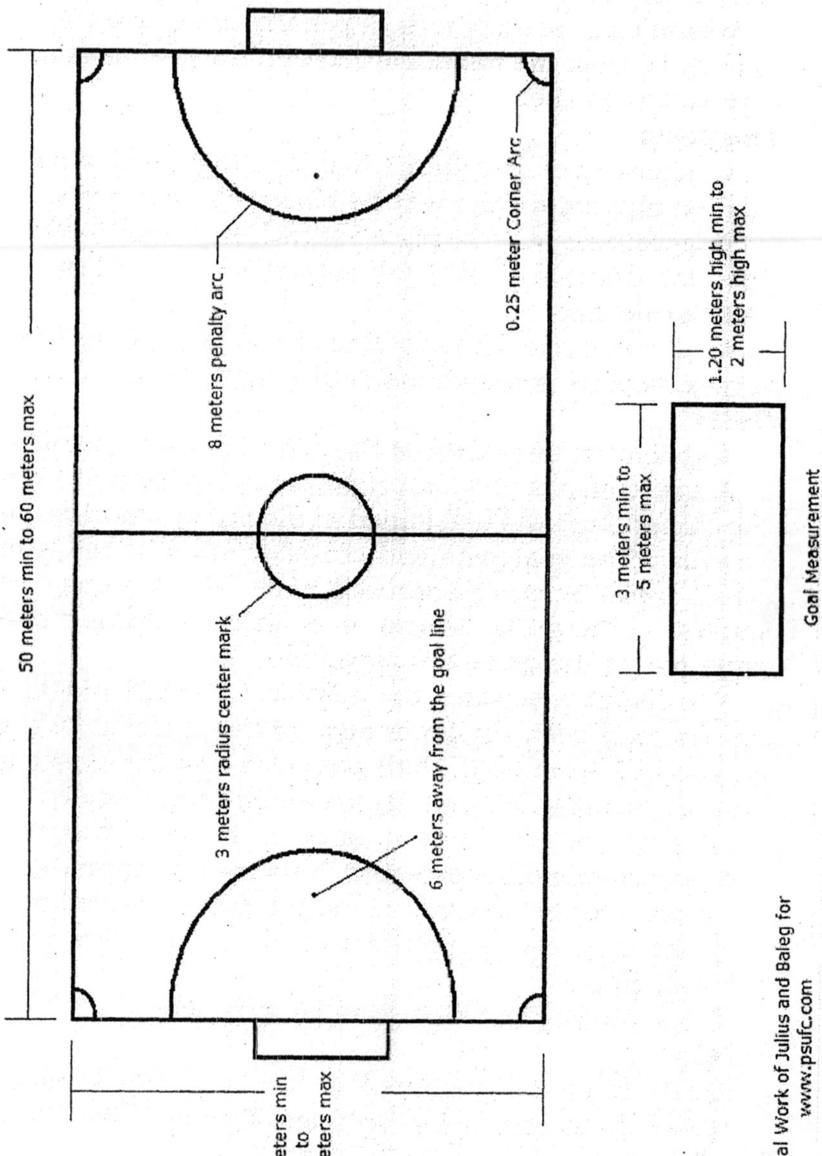

## Corner Flagpost

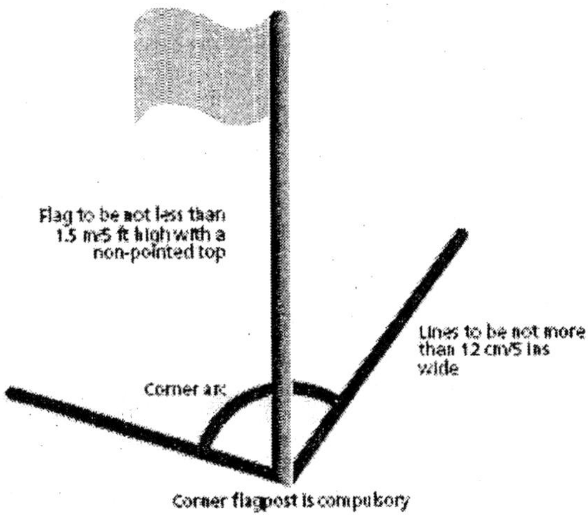


## Metric Measurements
## Decisions of the International F.A. Board

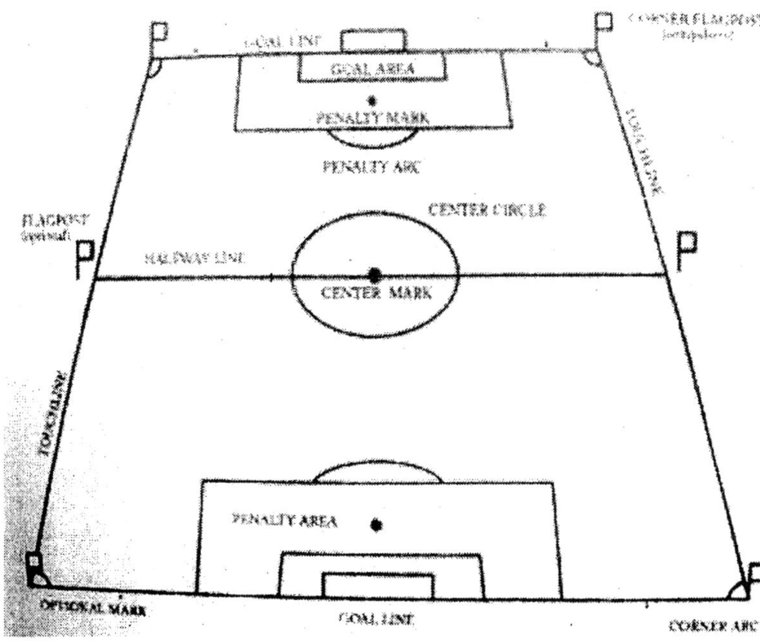

**Imperial Measurements**

**Decision 1**

Where a technical area exists, it must meet the requirements approved by the International F.A. Board, which are contained in the section of this publication entitled The Technical Area.

**LAW 2 - THE BALL**

**Qualities and Measurements**

The ball is:

- spherical
- made of leather or other suitable material
- of a circumference of not more than 70 cm (28 ins) and not less than 68 cm (27 ins)
- not more than 450 g (16 oz) and not less than 410 g (14 oz) in weight at the start of the match
- of a pressure equal to 0.6 – 1.1 atmosphere (600 – 1,100 g/cm2) at sea level (8.5 lbs/sq in – 15.6 lbs/sq in)

**Replacement of a Defective Ball**

If the ball bursts or becomes defective during the course of a match:

- the match is stopped
- the match is restarted by dropping the replacement ball at the place where the original ball became defective, unless play was stopped inside the goal area, in which case the referee drops the replacement ball on the goal area line parallel to the goal line at the point nearest to where the original ball was located when play was stopped If the ball bursts or becomes defective whilst not in play at a kick-off, goal kick, corner kick, free kick,

penalty kick or throw-in:

- the match is restarted accordingly

The ball may not be changed during the match without the authority of the referee.

## LAW 3 – THE NUMBER OF PLAYERS

### Players

A match is played by two teams, each consisting of not more than eleven players, one of whom is the goalkeeper. A match may not start if either team consists of fewer than seven players.

### Official Competitions

Up to a maximum of three substitutes may be used in any match played in an official competition organised under the auspices of FIFA, the confederations or the member associations.

The rules of the competition must state how many substitutes may be nominated, from three up to a maximum of seven.

### Other Matches

In national A team matches, up to a maximum of six substitutes may be used.

In all other matches, a greater number of substitutes may be used provided that:

- the teams concerned reach agreement on a maximum number
- the referee is informed before the match

If the referee is not informed, or if no agreement is reached before the match, no more than six substitutes are allowed.

### All Matches

In all matches, the names of the substitutes must be given to the referee prior to the start of the match. Any substitute whose name is not given to the referee at this time may not take part in the match.

### Substitution Procedure

To replace a player with a substitute, the following

conditions must be observed:

• the referee must be informed before any proposed substitution is made

• the substitute only enters the field of play after the player being replaced has left and after receiving a signal from the referee

• the substitute only enters the field of play at the halfway line and during a stoppage in the match

• the substitution is completed when a substitute enters the field of play

• from that moment, the substitute becomes a player and the player he has replaced becomes a substituted player

• the substituted player takes no further part in the match

• all substitutes are subject to the authority and jurisdiction of the referee, whether called upon to play or not

**Changing the Goalkeeper**

Any of the other players may change places with the goalkeeper, provided that:

• the referee is informed before the change is made

• the change is made during a stoppage in the match

**Infringements and Sanctions**

If a substitute or substituted player enters the field of play without the referee's permission:

• the referee stops play (although not immediately if the substitute or

substituted player does not interfere with play)

• the referee cautions him for unsporting behaviour and orders him to leave the field of play

• if the referee has stopped play, it is restarted with an indirect free kick for the opposing team from the position of the ball at the time of the stoppage

If a player changes places with the goalkeeper without the referee's permission before the change is made:

• the referee allows play to continue

• the referee cautions the players concerned when the ball is next out of play

In the event of any other infringements of this Law:

• the players concerned are cautioned

• the match is restarted with an indirect free kick, to be taken by a player of the opposing team from the position of the ball at the time of the stoppage

**Players and Substitutes Sent Off**

A player who has been sent off before the kick-off may be replaced only by one of the named substitutes.

A named substitute who has been sent off, either before the kick-off or after play has started, may not be replaced.

**LAW 4 – THE PLAYERS' EQUIPMENT**

**Safety**

A player must not use equipment or wear anything that is dangerous to himself or another player (including any kind of jewellery).

**Basic Equipment**

The basic compulsory equipment of a player comprises the following separate items:

• a jersey or shirt with sleeves – if undergarments are worn, the colour of the sleeve must be the same main colour as the sleeve of the jersey or shirt.

• shorts – if undershorts are worn, they must be of the same main colour as the shorts

• stockings

• shinguards

• footwear

Shinguards

• are covered entirely by the stockings

• are made of rubber, plastic or a similar suitable material

• provide a reasonable degree of protection

**Colours**

• The two teams must wear colours that distinguish them from each other and also the referee and the assistant referees

• Each goalkeeper must wear colours that distinguish him from the other players, the referee and the assistant referees

**Infringements and Sanctions**

In the event of any infringement of this Law:

• play need not be stopped

• the player at fault is instructed by the referee to leave the field of play to correct his equipment

• the player leaves the field of play when the ball next ceases to be in play, unless he has already corrected his equipment

• any player required to leave the field of play to correct his equipment must not re-enter without the referee's permission

• the referee checks that the player's equipment is correct before allowing him to re-enter the field of play

• the player is only allowed to re-enter the field of play when the ball is out of play

A player who has been required to leave the field of play because of an infringement of this Law and who re-enters the field of play without the referee's permission must be cautioned.

**Restart of Play**

If play is stopped by the referee to administer a caution:

• the match is restarted by an indirect free kick taken by a player of the opposing team, from the place where the ball was located when the referee stopped the match

**LAW 5 – THE REFEREE**

**The Authority of the Referee**

Each match is controlled by a referee who has full authority to enforce the Laws of the Game in connection with the match to which he has been appointed.

**Powers and Duties**

The Referee:

• enforces the Laws of the Game

• controls the match in cooperation with the assistant referees and, where applicable, with the fourth official

• ensures that any ball used meets the requirements of Law 2

• ensures that the players' equipment meets the requirements of Law 4

• acts as timekeeper and keeps a record of the match

• stops, suspends or abandons the match, at his discretion, for any infringements of the Laws

• stops, suspends or abandons the match because of outside interference of any kind

• stops the match if, in his opinion, a player is seriously injured and ensures that he is removed from the field of play. An injured player may only return to the field of play after the match has restarted

• allows play to continue until the ball is out of play if a player is, in his opinion, only slightly injured

• ensures that any player bleeding from a wound leaves the field of play. The player may only return on receiving a signal from the referee, who must be satisfied that the bleeding has stopped

• allows play to continue when the team against which an offence has been committed will benefit from such an advantage and penalises the original offence if the anticipated advantage does not ensue at that time

• punishes the more serious offence when a player commits more than one offence at the same time

• takes disciplinary action against players guilty of cautionable and sending-off offences. He is not obliged to take this action immediately but must do so when the ball next goes out of play

• takes action against team officials who fail to conduct themselves in a responsible manner and may, at his discretion, expel them from the field of play and its immediate surrounds

• acts on the advice of the assistant referees regarding incidents that he has not seen

• ensures that no unauthorised persons enter the field of play

• indicates the restart of the match after it has been stopped

**Decisions of the Referee**

The decisions of the referee regarding facts connected with play, including whether or not a goal is scored and the result of the match, are final.

The referee may only change a decision on realising that it is incorrect or, at his discretion, on the advice of an assistant referee or the fourth official, provided that he has not restarted play or terminated the match.

## LAW 6 – THE ASSISTANT REFEREES

### Duties

Two assistant referees may be appointed whose duties, subject to the decision of the referee, are to indicate:

• when the whole of the ball leaves the field of play

• which team is entitled to a corner kick, goal kick or throw-in

• when a player may be penalised for being in an offside position

• when a substitution is requested

• when misconduct or any other incident occurs out of the view of the referee

• when offences have been committed whenever the assistant referees have a better view than the referee (this includes, in certain circumstances, offences committed in the penalty area)

• whether, at penalty kicks, the goalkeeper moves off the goal line before the ball is kicked and if the ball crosses the line

### Assistance

The assistant referees also assist the referee to control the match in accordance with the Laws of the Game. In particular, they may enter the field of play to help control the 9.15 m (10 yds) distance.

In the event of undue interference or improper conduct, the referee will relieve an assistant referee of his duties and make a report to the appropriate authorities.

## LAW 7 – THE DURATION OF THE MATCH

### Periods of Play

The match lasts two equal periods of 45 minutes, unless otherwise mutually agreed between the referee and the two teams. Any agreement to alter the duration of the periods of play (for example, to reduce each half to

40 minutes because of insufficient light) must be made before the start of play and must comply with competition rules.

**Half-time Interval**

Players are entitled to an interval at half-time.

The half-time interval must not exceed 15 minutes. Competition rules must state the duration of the half-time interval.

The duration of the half-time interval may be altered only with the consent of the referee.

**Allowance for Time Lost**

Allowance is made in either period for all time lost through:

- substitutions
- assessment of injury to players
- removal of injured players from the field of play for treatment
- wasting time
- any other cause

The allowance for time lost is at the discretion of the referee.

**Penalty Kick**

If a penalty kick has to be taken or retaken, the duration of either half is extended until the penalty kick is completed.

**Abandoned Match**

An abandoned match is replayed unless the competition rules provide otherwise.

**LAW 8 – THE START AND RESTART OF PLAY**

**Preliminaries**

A coin is tossed and the team that wins the toss decides which goal it will attack in the first half of the match.

The other team takes the kick-off to start the match.

The team that wins the toss takes the kick-off to start the second half of the match.

In the second half of the match, the teams change ends and attack the opposite goals.

**Kick-off**

A kick-off is a way of starting or restarting play:

- at the start of the match
- after a goal has been scored
- at the start of the second half of the match
- at the start of each period of extra time, where applicable

A goal may be scored directly from the kick-off.

**Procedure**

- all players must be in their own half of the field of play
- the opponents of the team taking the kick-off are at least 9.15 m (10 yds) from the ball until it is in play
- the ball must be stationary on the centre mark
- the referee gives a signal
- the ball is in play when it is kicked and moves forward
- the kicker must not touch the ball again until it has touched another player

After a team scores a goal, the kick-off is taken by the other team.

**Infringements and Sanctions**

If the player taking the kick-off touches the ball again before it has touched another player:

- an indirect free kick is awarded to the opposing team to be taken from the position of the ball when the infringement occurred

In the event of any other infringement of the kick-off procedure:

**Dropped Ball**

If, while the ball is still in play, the referee is required to stop play temporarily for any reason not mentioned elsewhere in the Laws of the Game, the match is restarted with a dropped ball.

## LAW 9 – THE BALL IN AND OUT OF PLAY

### Ball Out of Play

The ball is out of play when:

- it has wholly crossed the goal line or touch line whether on the ground or in the air
- play has been stopped by the referee

### Ball In Play

The ball is in play at all other times, including when:

- it rebounds off a goalpost, crossbar or corner flagpost and remains in the field of play
- it rebounds off either the referee or an assistant referee when they are on the field of play

## LAW 10 – THE METHOD OF SCORING

### Goal Scored

A goal is scored when the whole of the ball passes over the goal line, between the goalposts and under the crossbar, provided that no infringement of the Laws of the Game has been committed previously by the team scoring the goal.

### Winning Team

The team scoring the greater number of goals during a match is the winner.

If both teams score an equal number of goals, or if no goals are scored, the match is drawn.

### Competition Rules

When competition rules require there to be a winning team after a match or home-and-away tie, the only permitted procedures for determining the winning team are those approved by the International F.A. Board, namely:

- away goals rule
- extra time
- kicks from the penalty mark

### Goal

### Offside Position

It is not an offence in itself to be in an offside position.

A player is in an offside position if:

• he is nearer to his opponents' goal line than both the ball and the second-last opponent

A player is not in an offside position if:

• he is in his own half of the field of play or
• he is level with the second-last opponent or
• he is level with the last two opponents

**Offence**

A player in an offside position is only penalised if, at the moment the ball touches or is played by one of his team, he is, in the opinion of the referee, involved in active play by:

• interfering with play or
• interfering with an opponent or
• gaining an advantage by being in that position

**No Offence**

There is no offside offence if a player receives the ball directly from:

• a goal kick
• a throw-in
• a corner kick

**LAW 11 – OFFSIDE**

Fouls and misconduct are penalised as follows:

**Direct Free Kick**

A direct free kick is awarded to the opposing team if a player commits any of the following seven offences in a manner considered by the referee to be careless, reckless or using excessive force:

• kicks or attempts to kick an opponent
• trips or attempts to trip an opponent
• jumps at an opponent
• charges an opponent
• strikes or attempts to strike an opponent
• pushes an opponent
• tackles an opponent

A direct free kick is also awarded to the opposing team

if a player commits any of the following three offences:

- holds an opponent
- spits at an opponent
- handles the ball deliberately (except for the goalkeeper within his own penalty area)

A direct free kick is taken from the place where the offence occurred.

**Penalty Kick**

A penalty kick is awarded if any of the above ten offences is committed by a player inside his own penalty area, irrespective of the position of the ball, provided it is in play.

**LAW 12 – FOULS AND MISCONDUCT**

**Indirect Free Kick**

An indirect free kick is awarded to the opposing team if a goalkeeper, inside his own penalty area, commits any of the following four offences:

- controls the ball with his hands for more than six seconds before releasing it from his possession
- touches the ball again with his hands after he has released it from his possession and before it has touched another player
- touches the ball with his hands after it has been deliberately kicked to him by a team-mate
- touches the ball with his hands after he has received it directly from a throw-in taken by a team-mate

An indirect free kick is also awarded to the opposing team if, in the opinion of the referee, a player:

**LAW 13: FREE KICK**

**Types of Free Kick**

Free kicks are either direct or indirect.

**The Direct Free Kick**

**Ball Enters the Goal**

- if a direct free kick is kicked directly into the opponents' goal, a goal is awarded
- if a direct free kick is kicked directly into the team's

own goal, a corner kick is awarded to the opposing team

**The Indirect Free Kick**

**Signal**

The referee indicates an indirect free kick by raising his arm above his head. He maintains his arm in that position until the kick has been taken and the ball has touched another player or goes out of play.

**Ball Enters the Goal**

A goal can be scored only if the ball subsequently touches another player before it enters the goal:

• if an indirect free kick is kicked directly into the opponents' goal, a goal kick is awarded

• if an indirect free kick is kicked directly into the team's own goal, a corner kick is awarded to the opposing team

**Procedure**

For both direct and indirect free kicks, the ball must be stationary when the kick is taken and the kicker must not touch the ball again until it has touched another player.

**Position of Free Kick**

Free Kick Inside the Penalty Area Direct or indirect free kick to the defending team:

• all opponents must be at least 9.15 m (10 yds) from the ball

• all opponents must remain outside the penalty area until the ball is in play

• the ball is in play when it is kicked directly out of the penalty area

• a free kick awarded in the goal area may be taken from any point inside
that area
Indirect free kick to the attacking team:

• all opponents must be at least 9.15 m (10 yds) from the ball until it is in play, unless they are on their own goal line between the goalposts

• the ball is in play when it is kicked and moves

• an indirect free kick awarded inside the goal area must be taken on the goal area line parallel to the goal line at the point nearest to where the infringement occurred

**LAW 14 – THE PENALTY KICK**

**Procedure**

• After the players have taken positions in accordance with this Law, the referee signals for the penalty kick to be taken

• The player taking the penalty kick must kick the ball forward

• He must not play the ball again until it has touched another player

• The ball is in play when it is kicked and moves forward

When a penalty kick is taken during the normal course of play, or time has been extended at half-time or full time to allow a penalty kick to be taken or retaken, a goal is awarded if, before passing between the goalposts and under the crossbar:

• the ball touches either or both of the goalposts and/or the crossbar and/or the goalkeeper

The referee decides when a penalty kick has been completed.

**LAW 15 – THE THROW-IN**

If, after the ball is in play, the thrower deliberately handles the ball before it has touched another player:

• a direct free kick is awarded to the opposing team, the kick to be taken from the place where the infringement occurred.

• a penalty kick is awarded if the infringement occurred inside the thrower's penalty area

Throw-in taken by the goalkeeper

If, after the ball is in play, the goalkeeper touches the ball again (except with his hands), before it has touched another player:

• an indirect free kick is awarded to the opposing team, the kick to be taken from the place where the infringement occurred

If, after the ball is in play, the goalkeeper deliberately

handles the ball before it has touched another player:

- a direct free kick is awarded to the opposing team if the infringement occurred outside the goalkeeper's penalty area, the kick to be taken from the place where the infringement occurred
- an indirect free kick is awarded to the opposing team if the infringement occurred inside the goalkeeper's penalty area, the kick to be taken from the place where the infringement occurred

If an opponent unfairly distracts or impedes the thrower:

- he is cautioned for unsporting behaviour

For any other infringement of this Law:

- the throw-in is taken by a player of the opposing team

**LAW 16 – THE GOAL KICK**

A goal kick is a method of restarting play.

A goal kick is awarded when the whole of the ball passes over the goal line, either on the ground or in the air, having last touched a player of the attacking team, and a goal is not scored in accordance with Law 10.

A goal may be scored directly from a goal kick, but only against the opposing team.

**Procedure**

- The ball is kicked from any point within the goal area by a player of the defending team
- Opponents remain outside the penalty area until the ball is in play
- The kicker must not play the ball again until it has touched another player
- The ball is in play when it is kicked directly out of the penalty area

**LAW 17 – THE CORNER KICK**

A corner kick is a method of restarting play.

A corner kick is awarded when the whole of the ball passes over the goal line, either on the ground or in the

air, having last touched a player of the defending team, and a goal is not scored in accordance with Law 10.

A goal may be scored directly from a corner kick, but only against the opposing team.

**THE REFEREE**

**Advantage**

The referee may play advantage whenever an infringement or offence occurs.

The referee should consider the following circumstances in deciding whether to apply the advantage or stop play:

- the severity of the offence: if the infringement warrants an expulsion, the referee must stop play and send off the player unless there is a subsequent opportunity to score a goal
- the position where the offence was committed: the closer to the opponent's goal, the more effective it can be
- the chances of an immediate, promising attack
- the atmosphere of the match

The decision to penalise the original offence must be

taken within a few seconds.

If the offence warrants a caution, it must be issued at the next stoppage.

However, unless there is a clear advantage, it is recommended that the referee stops play and cautions the player immediately. If the caution is not issued at the next stoppage, it cannot be shown later.

**Injured players**

The referee must adhere to the following procedure when dealing with injured players:

- play is allowed to continue until the ball is out of play if a player is, in the opinion of the referee, only slightly injured
- play is stopped if, in the opinion of the referee, a player is seriously injured
- after questioning the injured player, the referee may authorise one, or at most two doctors, to enter the field of play to assess the injury and arrange the player's safe and swift removal from the field of play
- the stretcher-bearers should enter the field of play with a stretcher at the same time as the doctors to allow the player to be removed as quickly as possible
- the referee must ensure an injured player is safely removed from the field of play
- a player is not allowed to receive treatment on the field of play
- any player bleeding from a wound must leave the field of play. He may not return until the referee is satisfied that the bleeding has stopped. A player is not permitted to wear clothing with blood on it
- as soon as the referee has authorised the doctors to enter the field of play, the player must leave the field of play, either on a stretcher or on foot. If a player does not comply, he must be cautioned for unsporting behaviour
- an injured player may only return to the field of play after the match has restarted

## REFEREE'S SIGNALS

# 8

# GYMNASTICS

## INTRODUCTION

Gymnastics is an activity involving performance of exercises requiring physical strength, flexibility, agility, coordination, balance, and grace. Internationally, all of the gymnastic sports are governed by the Fédération Internationale de Gymnastique (FIG) with each country having its own national governing body affiliated to FIG. Competitive Artistic gymnastics is the best known of the gymnastic sports. It typically involves the women's events of uneven parallel bars, balance beam, floor exercise, and vault. Men's events include floor exercise, pommel horse, still rings, vault, parallel bars, and high bar. Gymnastics evolved from exercises used by the ancient Greeks, that included skills for mounting and dismounting a horse, and from circus performance skills.

Other gymnastic sports include rhythmic gymnastics, the various trampolining sports, and aerobic and acrobatic gymnastics.

## GYMNASTICS FORMS

### Artistic Gymnastics

Artistic gymnastics is usually divided into Men's and Women's Gymnastics. Typically men compete six events: Floor Exercise, Pommel Horse, Still Rings, Vault, Parallel Bars, and High Bar, while women compete four: Vault, Uneven Bars, Balance Beam, and Floor Exercise. In some countries, women at one time competed on the rings, high bar, and parallel bars (for example, in the 1950s in the USSR). Though routines performed on each event may be short, they are physically exhausting and push the gymnast's strength, flexibility, endurance and awareness to the limit.

## EVENTS FOR WOMEN

### Vault

In the vaulting events gymnastics: sprint down a 25 metre (about 82 feet) runway, jump onto a beatboard or springboard (run/ take-off segment), land momentarily generally inverted on the hands on the vaulting horse or vaulting table (pre flight segment), then spring off of this platform to a two footed landing (post flight segment).

### Uneven Bars

On the uneven bars (also known as asymmetric bars, UK), the gymnast performs a routine on two horizontal bars set at different heights. These bars are made of fiberglass covered in wood laminate, to prevent them from breaking. Gymnasts often mount the Uneven Bars using a springboard.

### Balance Beam

The gymnast performs a choreographed routine up to 90 seconds in length consisting of leaps, acrobatic skills, somersaults, turns and dance elements on a padded, and sprung beam. The beam is 125 centimetres (4.10 ft) from the ground, 500 centimetres (16 ft) long, and 4 inches wide. The event requires, in particular, balance, flexibility and strength.

### Floor

In the past the Floor Exercise event was executed on wrestling mats. Today, the floor event occurs on a carpeted 12m × 12m square, usually consisting of hard foam over a layer of plywood, which is supported by springs or foam blocks generally called a "spring" floor.

## EVENTS FOR MEN

### Floor Exercise

Male gymnasts also perform on a 12m. by 12m. spring floor. A series of tumbling passes are performed to demonstrate flexibility, strength, and balance. The gymnast must also show strength skills, including circles, scales, and press handstands. Men's floor routines usually have four passes that will total between 60–70 seconds and are performed without music, unlike the women's event. Rules require that male gymnasts touch each corner of the floor at least once during their routine.

**Pommel Horse**

A typical pommel horse exercise involves both single leg and double leg work. Single leg skills are generally found in the form of scissors, an element often done on the pommels. Double leg work however, is the main staple of this event.

**Still Rings**

The rings are suspended on wire cable from a point 5.75 metres from the floor, and adjusted in height so the gymnast has room to hang freely and swing. He must perform a routine demonstrating balance, strength, power, and dynamic motion while preventing the rings themselves from swinging.

**Vault**

Gymnasts sprint down a runway, which is a maximum of 25 metres in length, before hurdling onto a spring board. The body position is maintained while "punching" (blocking using only a shoulder movement) the vaulting platform.

**Parallel Bars**

Men perform on two bars slightly further than a shoulder's width apart and usually 1.75m high while executing a series of swings, balances, and releases that require great strength and coordination.

**High Bar**

A 2.4 cm thick steel bar raised 2.5m above the landing area is all the gymnast has to hold onto as he performs giants (revolutions around the bar), release skills, twists, and changes of direction.

**Rhythmic Gymnastics**

Only women compete in rhythmic gymnastics although there is a new version of this discipline for men being pioneered in Japan.

**Trampolining and Tumbling**

Trampolining and tumbling consists of four events, individual, synchronized, double mini and power tumbling. Since 2000, individual trampoline has been included in the Olympic Games. Individual routines in trampolining involve a build-up phase during which the gymnast jumps repeatedly to achieve height, followed by a sequence of ten leaps without pauses during which the gymnast performs a sequence of aerial skills.

**Acrobatic Gymnastics**

Acrobatic gymnastics (formerly Sports Acrobatics), often referred to as acro if involed with the sport, acrobatic sports or simply sports acro, is a group gymnastic discipline for both men and women. Acrobats in groups of two, three and four perform routines with the heads, hands and feet of their partners. They may, subject to regulations (e.g. no lyrics), pick their own music.

## RULES OF GYMNASTICS

### MEN GYMNASTS

**Code of Point's**

a. To evaluate men's gymnastic exercises at all level of regional, national and international competition code of points provide a means for this purpose, and also serves following objectives:

i. It provides guidance to coaches and gymnasts in composition of competition exercises.

ii. It assures that best gymnast in any competition is selected.

iii. It provides information regarding sources from where technical information and regulation needed by judges, coaches and gymnasts at competition can become available.

**Regulations for Gymnasts, Coaches and Judges**

**Rights and Responsibilities of the Coach**

A coach has the following rights and powers:

i. During warm up period he has the right to assist gymnast or team under his care.

ii. In submitting a request in writing related to raising of apparatus and rating of new elements he has the right to assist gymnast or team under his care.

iii. In accordance with rules governing in competition to have scores of his gymnast publicly displayed immediately after his performance.

iv. He has the right to assist gymnast or team in preparation of apparatus.

v. For safety of gymnasts he has the right to be at Rings, Vault, Parallel Bars and Horizontal Bar.

vi. On rings and horizontal bar he has the right to put the gymnast to a hanging position.

A coach has the following duties and responsibilities:

i. He is required to attend every applicable victory ceremony.

ii. It is his duty to avoid any kind of undiscipline or insulting behaviour.

iii. He is expected to know code of points thoroughly and make it applicable.

iv. In accordance with Technical Regulation governing the competition the coach is required to submit team competition order and other necessary information.

v. It is his duty to start the competition without delaying it. He may misuse his rights or violate the right of any other contestant.

vi. During performance he should not talk to gymnast about his performance.

vii. During competition he should not have any kind of discussion with active judges.

viii. He should not do any abusive or undisciplined

behaviour.

ix. He should attend all victory ceremony.

**Rights and Responsibilities of the Gymnast**

A gymnast has the following rights:

i. For submitted new element he has the right to receive after submission within a reasonable time a difficulty rating in written form.

ii. He has the right to get a correct and fair judgement on his performance.

iii. At official FIG Competitions he has the right to have apparatus that fulfils specifications of FIG.

iv. To start his exercise on Rings and Horizontal Bar he has the right to get assistance for hanging position by a coach or gymnast.

v. He has the right to demand one spotter at Rings, Vault, Horizontal Bar and Parallel Bars.

vi. After falling from apparatus he has the right to take rest for not more than 30 seconds.

vii. He has the right to make any kind of changes in his equipment, to use magnesium and while taking rest after falling from apparatus to talk to his coach.

viii. He has the right to wear various protective objectives. He can wear bandages, hand guards and reasonable clothing which ensures his protection.

x. He has the right to make a request to change position of rings or horizontal bars according to his height.

xi. If he is unable to complete his exercise because of any uncontrollable reason he has the right to repeat his exercise.

xii. Before 30 seconds from beginning of his exercise he has the right to receive signal from chair of apparatus jury and a green light in official FIG competitions.

xiii. He has the right to make a request to leave the competition hall for any personal reasons. This request should be made to Chair of competition Jury.

xiv. Immediately after his performance in accordance

with rules of that competition he has the right to have his score displayed properly.

In addition to above mentioned rights a gymnast has the following duties and responsibilities:

i. It is his responsibility to wear cloths keeping following considerations in mind:

a. Clothes of same style and colour should be worn by all the competitors during a session.

b. On Pommel Horse, Rings, Parallel Bars, and Horizontal Bar he is required to wear long gymnastic pants and socks. Black, or darker shades of blue, should be colour of pants, where brown or green should be not be allowed.

c. On floor exercise and vault he should wear short pants with or without socks or long gymnastic paints with socks

d. On all apparatus a gymnastic singlet should be worn by him.

e. On all apparatus gymnasium slippers should be worn by him.

f. Gymnastic number supplied by organizers should be worn.

g. In accordance of with recent FIG Regulations on his signlet he should wear a national identification emblem.

h. A gymnastic is allowed to have only that logos, advertising and sponsorship identifiers which are permitted by recent FIG regulations.

i. At beginning of exercise as well as at end of exercise he is required to present himself in a proper manner to Chair of Apparatus Jury.

ii. Atleast 1 day before podium training he or his coach is required to submit a request in written to chair of competition jury for assessing the difficulty of a new element.

iii. He should knew code of points and conduct.

Penalties for pocr conduct of gymnast and/or coach.

a. To final score Chair of Apparatus Jury is empowered to indicate penalties.

b. In addition to specified penalty a gymnast or coast can be expelled from competition.

**Liabilities and Responsibilities of the Judges**

A. Following are the responsibilities of the Apparatus Jury:

i. In contemporary gymnastics he should be an expert and able to understand intent, purpose, application and interpretation of each rule.

ii. For judging in any competition he should have current and valid national or international judge's brevet.

iii. To carry out his duties in any competition he should have thorough knowledge of code of points, technical regulations and any other technical information.

iv. It is his duty to evaluate performance of gymnast objectively, accurately, consistently, ethically, fairly and quickly. If he has any kind of doubt benefit of such doubt should be awarded to gymnast.

v. If any instruction is given by appropriate authorities it is his duty to stick to it.

vi. At official FIG Competitions he is required to attend podium training and all meetings and scheduled instruction sessions.

**The Organization of the Apparatus Jury**

Following are included in Apparatus Jury:

A. Following should consist in Apparatus Jury for all official FIG Competition World Championships, Olympic Games, and World Cup:

i. Supplementary judges and assistants like:

ii. AB-Jury having six judges.

iii. Appointed by FIG Men's Technical Committee a Chair of Apparatus Jury having jurisdiction over both

A-Jury and B-Jury.

iv. AB-Jury having six judges.

For warm up time and for floor exercise a timer.

For Floor Exercise 2 lines judges.

Depending on requirement of competition a number of assistants such as scorer, secretary, computer operator and runners etc.

For all sessions, qualifications, team finals and all round final size and composition of Apparatus Jury should not be changed, however for international competitions, national and local competitions this can be changed. Qualification of judges as mentioned in Current Technical Regulations or Judge's regulation governing the competition should be possessed by each judge.

**Functions of the Apparatus Jury during Competition**

A. Following functions have to be performed by Chair of Apparatus Jury:

1. Not only control of warm up time is their duty but assurance of efficient running of his apparatus is also included in their duties, in addition to this following functions have to be performed by them:

i. Before 30 seconds from beginning of exercise by gymnast he is required to give a signal or a green light to indicate him that he has to begin the exercise.

ii. To observe the exercise of all gymnasts.

2. He should put work of all members of jury under his control and should co-ordinate their work.

3. Between Apparatus Jury and Chair of Competition Jury he should act as a liaison.

4. He is required to judge each aspect of each competition exercise on apparatus for which he is responsible with accuracy and efficiently.

5. For each exercise he is required to control total evaluation and final scores.

6. With approval of Chair of Competition Jury and by

rules outlined in current Technical Regulations he can change incorrect score if he finds that wrong score has been awarded to gymnast for his action.

7. He is required to perform all duties and responsibilities mentioned in various rules.

B. Following important functions should be performed by judges of A-Jury:

a) Jugde A1 should:

i. Be coordinator and member of A-Jury and should assist the chair of apparatus jury.

ii. In case of omission of any special requirement or any other start value violations he is required to inform chair of apparatus jury.

iii. In case of disagreement on start value by A-judges he should inform chair of apparatus jury about this or should submit the agreed upon start value.

iv. He is required to submit a brief report to chair of the apparatus jury relating to results of competition, citing problems, violations or any uncertainty with names of various gymnasts.

v. Within 2 months of competition in one of official FIG languages he is required to submit a report in writing about content of all exercises to President of the Men's Technical Committee and Chair of his Apparatus Jury.

**THE CODES OF POINTS**

**THE EVALUATION OF COMPETITION EXERCISES**

**General Rules**

1. Not more than 10 points should be awarded on all apparatus which forms basis for all deductions and applies only in tenths of a point. Only A-Jury and B-Jury should establish final score of the exercise.

2. Start value of an exercise should be established by A-Jury whereas registration of errors related to technique and body position should be done by B-Jury. Highest and lowest sums of execution errors should not be taken in account. To determine final score for exercise

average of four remaining sums should be subtracted from Start Value.

3. In all session of optional competition qualification, Team Final, All Around Final, Apparatus Finals rules for evaluation of exercises and determination of Final Score should be same. However, this rule does not apply to Apparatus Finals of Vault for which there are special rules.

4. Final scores earned on 6 exercises should be added up to get All-Around Score.

5. According to Current technical regulations governing the competition team score should be calculated.

6. Current Technical Regulations governing the competition should be followed while determining qualification for, and participation in the Team Final, All Around Final and Apparatus Finals.

7. Competition scoring personnel should calculate final score which before being publically should be confirmed by Chair of Apparatus Jury.

**Evaluation by the A-Jury**

a. Elements that a gymnast can perform with complete safety and with a high degree of technical mastery should be included by him in his exercise.

b. On each apparatus content of exercise should be evaluated and correct start value should be determined by A-Jury.

c. No value should be received by any unrecognized element, or in other words element which are not recognized by A-Jury should not receive any point and are ineligible for bonus points.

d. While making decisions A-Jury should keep in mind the sense of gymnastics and interest of sports. Gymnast should get advantage in case of doubt.

**Bonus Points**

i. Because of evaluation factor for performance of

difficult elements and connections A-Jury can provide up to 1.4 Bonus Points. Different Bonus Points such as D-elements, E-elements, super E-elements and connections of them are used to differentiate among the most strong exercises.

ii. Elements and connections which are performed with good technical position should be awarded with Bonus Points. Only Individual elements such as D-, E, or Super E- elements which are performed without large errors should be provided with Bonus Points. 0.10 points can be provided to D-element, 0.20 points to E-element, 0.30 points to Super-E-element.

iii. Optional connections of difficult elements which are performed without large error can be awarded with bonus points of 0.10 or 0.20 in the following manner:

For D + D—0.10

For D + E, E + E—0.20

For connection bonus an E-element should be considered equal to Super E-element.

**Instructions for the Gymnast**

a. At the expense of aestheic and technical execution a gymnast should not attempt to increase the difficulty or start value.

b. Only from basic stand position, from a short run or from a still hang mount should be commenced by gymnast. Pre-elements or intermediate elements should follow the mount. This rule applies to all vaults except in vault where specific rules stated for that apparatus apply.

c. A gymnast is adviced to perform only those elements which he is able to do accurately and with technical mastery, because he held liable for his safety. For any aesthetic and technical error B-Jury is required to deduct points.

d. At time of end of floor exercise and vault and dismounting from all apparatus gymnast should be in a standing position with both his legs together. To execute the dismount by pushing from apparatus with feet is not allowed any event except in floor exercise.

**VAULT**

**Description of a Vault Exercise**

Gymnast is required to perform 1 vault, but in case of apparatus final from different vault he has to show 2 vaults groups. With a run and from a take off from both feet to vault board with help of both legs executed with brief support with both hands on horse. Around both axes of body vault may have single or multiple turns. Gymnast is required to take his position after performing first vault and with signal of chair of apparatus jury to start his second vault.

**Information about Exercise Presentation.**

(a) During pre-flight vaults with saltos and with straddled legs are not permitted.

(b) Gymnast is required to take off forwards or backwards with help of both legs. A round off is permitted to be performed before vaulting. Safety collar may be used in such vaulting board which should be provided by competition organizer.

(c) It is advisable for gymnast to perform only those vaults which he can do safely, with high degree of aesthetic and technical mastery. Before vaults he is required to show his identification number of his intended vault.

(d) Behind horse vault should come to an end which should be in a standing position with legs both facing either away from or towards horse.

**FLOOR EXERCISE**

12m×12m should be dimension of Exercise area.

**Description of a Floor Exercise**

Floor exercise not only includes acrobatic elements but also other gymnastic elements like strength and balance parts, elements of flexibility, handstands and

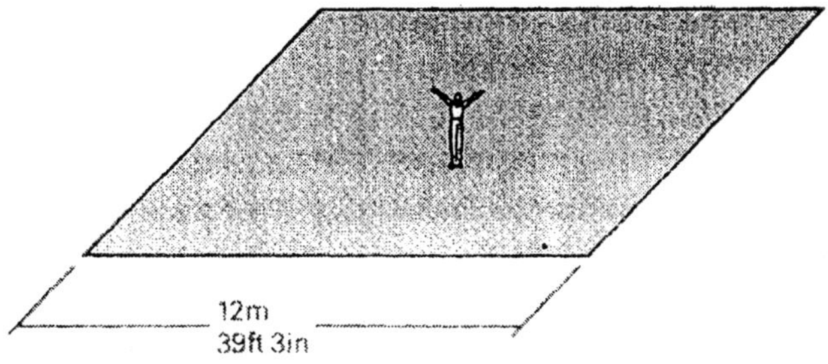


Matted area

choreographic combinations in an harmoniously manner. Performer has a time period of 70 seconds to perform his exercise for which he is allowed to use whole floor exercise area of 12m×12m.

**Presentation of Exercise**

i. A gymnast should perform only those elements which he can perform with safety and technical mastery.

ii. Within floor area he should begin his exercise. At time of beginning of exercise he should be in a standing position with both his legs together. As soon as gymnast's feet moves he is supposed to start the exercise and at same time evaluation also begins.

iii. More information related to execution and exercise construction expectation is as follows:

A. No gymnast is allowed to perform the exercise outside floor area. A-Jury is not required to evaluate any element performed outside floor area whereas B-Jury should evaluate such element in the normal fashion.

a. Boundary lines should be drawn to represent the Floor Exercise which should be considered as a part of this area. Gymnast is not allowed to step outside this line.

b. Near FX area there should be 2 line judges to control stepping outside marked floor area. These line judges should sit diagonally opposite to each other. A written advise should be given by line judges to Chair of

Apparatus Jury in case of any line violation on basis of which he would deduct points from final score of the gymnast.

c. In case of stepping outside floor area steps which should come back into area are not required to be deducted.

B. There should a timer in order to ensure that time period allowed to gymnast for presentation of his exercise should not be more than 70 seconds. Thus, maximum time of 70 seconds can be allowed however there is not any minimum time to be allowed. In order to indicate gymnast that time allowed to him is going to be finished Time Judge is required to give a warning signal at 60 seconds and to indicate finish of his time again at 70 seconds. As soon as feet of gymnast moves for first time evaluation begins and ends with his dismount in the standing position. If gymnast takes more time than allowed Chair of Apparatus Jury would receive a signal from Timer on basis of which he is required to deduct points from score of gymnast.

C. Whole available floor area is required to be used by gymnast in order to perform his exercise, in other words he should use this floor area in such a manner that all four corners of the floor should be occupied by him atleast for once.

D. Before acrobatic series or elements no gymnast is allowed to stop for 2 or more seconds.

E. Before beginning of a non-acrobatic element each acrobatic element should comes to an end in a visibly controlled landing. It should be kept in mind that during such transitions uncontrolled momentary landings are not allowed.

## POMMEL HORSE

### Description of a Pommel Horse Exercise

Pendulum swings by different types of circular swings with legs apart and together in a variety of support

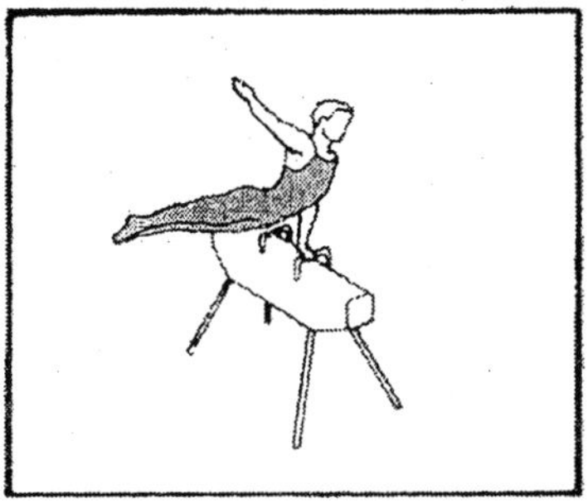

positions on all parts of horse are included in Pommel Horse. No disturbance is allowed while performance and exercise should be done with swing. In such exercise strength and hold elements are not allowed.

**Presentation of Exercise**

i. At time of beginning of exercise legs of gymnast should be together, and an approach hop or step is allowed. As soon as gymnast put his hands on horse exercise is considered to be begin.

ii. Gymnast should perform only those elements to whom he can perform safely and with technical mastery.

iii. Following are additional execution and exercise construction expectations:

a. Only swings should be there in exercise whereas no visible pauses or strength is permitted.

b. During flair and circle work no oblique positions are allowed. Only in cross support or in side support positions circles and flairs should be performed. Only in cross support or side support all turning elements should begin and finish.

c. With complete extension circles and flairs are supposed to be performed. At end of exercise lack of amplitude should be deducted as a global deduction.

**RINGS**

**Description of Ring Exercise**

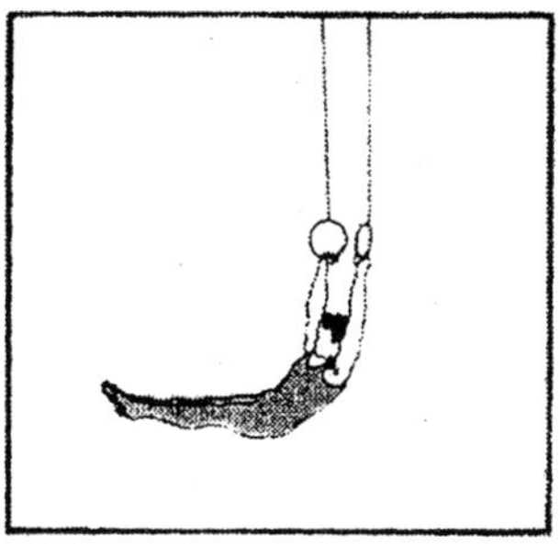

Swing, strength and hold parts in equal portions should be included in exercise on Rings. In Rings gymnast is supposed to perform exercise in a hanging position through a support position or through the handstand position. Execution with straight arms is considered best position. Change between elements of swing and strength is main feature of such exercise. Crossing and swinging of cable is not allowed.

**Presentation of Exercise**

i. Gymnast is required to jump from a still stand in order to be hanged on rings with both his legs together. For this he can have assistance from any official. As soon as gymnast leaves the floor evaluation begins.

ii. A gymnast should perform only those elements which he can do safely and with technical mastery.

iii. Swing, hold and strength elements should be in equal portions in the exercise.

iv. More execution and exercise construction are as follows:

a. With straight arms hold positions should be reached without any positional or postural corrections.

b. For atleast 2 seconds a hold position should be held.

**PARALLEL BARS**

**Description of Parallel Bar Exercise**

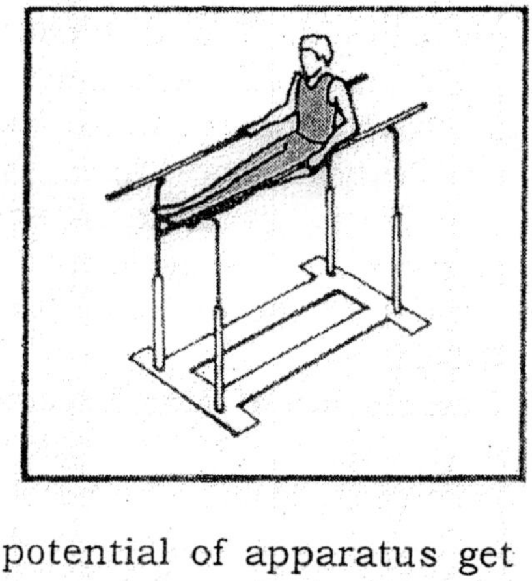

Selected swing and flight elements from available Element Groups should be include in parallel bar exercise. These elements should be performed with continuous transition through various hangs in such a manner that full potential of apparatus get reflected.

**Presentation of Exercise**

i. From a stand still with his legs together gymnast is required to start his Parallel Bar mount. As soon as any hand of gymnast touches the apparatus exercise is considered to be start whereas evaluation begins when his feet leaves the ground.

ii. For the mount a vaulting board is permitted which should be placed at height of regulation landing mats.

iii. Pre-elements are not allowed. Any element rotating more than 1800 on body axis is not allowed before grasping of rail or rails with hands.

iv. Gymnast should perform only those elements which he can perform safely and with technical mastery.

**HORIZONTAL BAR**

**Description of the Exercise**

Horizontal bar exercise includes an energetic presentation of fluid connection of swinging, turning, and flight elements which is performed alternating between elements which are performed near to and far from bar in a number of hand grips in order to indicate full potential of apparatus.

Important Information about Presentation of Exercise

i. With a good form gymnast should be jump or get help to be jumped from a still stand with his legs together to be hanged. As soon as gymnast leaves the floor evaluation should begin.

ii. Only those elements should be included by gymnast which he perform with safety and technical mastery.

iii. Following are additional execution and exercise construction presentation:

a. No interruption of any kind should be allowed during exercise;

b. Within a reasonable handstand elements from Element Group I, III and IV and basically those having hops and pirouettes on top of bar should be completed, however this rules does not apply to elements which re-grasp in double el-grip or flying hop elements.

c. Above the bar body should get rised during flight

elements.

d. Back swings in cast swings which only lead to a reverse direction and swing back down in or to a lower hang position but which do not lead to a value part are non-permissible.

**The Organization of the Apparatus Jury**

**The Jury and its Organization**

(i) To be selected as an international judge for international, continental or regional games or competition those in question must fulfil the following prerequisites:

The superior judge must be certified by the FIG and must be able to demonstrate to the satisfaction of the TC/FIG, and on the basis of good test results, good knowledge as well as good abilities and indisputable objectivity in judging. The organizers are advised here to add neutral persons. Further, the superior judges to be considered must be entered on the list of internationally certified judges.

(ii) Seating of judges in competitions between nations and other international Competitions is based on the recommendation of the FIG Technical Regulation. According to these articles the superior judge may not represent a federation involved in the competition. The number of neutral judges is based on the agreement made between the participating federations.

(iii) For meets of the FIG, Olympic Games, intercontinental, continental or regional meets or games, the jury for each event consists of five men, namely: one superior judge, and four judges, from the list of international judges, who are nominated by member organizations which take part in the competition.

(iv) The judges nominated by the participating federations must be entered on the list of internationally certified judges. Priority should be given to those who are currently certified and posses a valid FIG Brevet.

(v) Selection and Announcing of the Judges

(i) The seeding of judges of the individual nations into judges groups, according to the FIG Technical Regulations, is the responsibility of the Technical Committee and the technical directors responsible for the conduct of intercontinental, continental and regional games and competitions.

(ii) The results are to be announced to the participating federations immediately.

(iii) The personal nomination of the superior judges is under the control of the TC/FIG and the technical directors of the intercontinental, continental and regional games or meets. Nomination of judges is the responsibility of the participating federations according to the above regulations.

The TC/FIG reserves the right to unseat judges, who during previously held judges examination were proven incompetent, not objective and violated the rules and regulations.

**Formalities of Judging and General Remarks**

(i) The judges' scores will be made public for all competitions following an acoustical or optical signal. Possible corrections of judges scores should be administered by the superior judge before they are made public according to directions given by article 9 of the regulations. The final score, depending upon the circumstances will be flashed either simultaneously or following the others. The score of the superior judge is never made public.

(ii) All exercises are scored with points ranging from 0 to 10 with deductions of whole points, half points and 1/10 of a point. The final score is the average of the two middle scores of the four judges.

(iii) If a judge or superior judge brings a translator to assist him, the translator's work is limited to translating and he is forbidden to influence the superior judge or judge in any manner. Translators for superior judges are permitted to sit next to them while translators for judges may not sit next to them but only in their proximity in such a manner that when needed they may be called to their work without loss of time.

(iv) The point difference between the two middle scores may not be greater than:

0.10 with an average of 9.55 and higher
0.20 with an average of 9.00 to 9.50
0.30 with an average of 8.00 to 8.95
0.50 with an average of 6.50 to 7.95
0.80 with an average of 4.00 to 6.45
1.00 in all other cases

**Duties, Rights and Tasks of the Judges**

(i) Judges who do not take sufficient interest in such meetings, are absent, or appear late for courses and meetings, can be replaced by the director of competition.

(ii) The judges serving at an apparatus are to adhere to all parts of the Code of Points, possible written instructions of the TC/FIG, instructions obtained at judges courses and the instructions of the superior judge, and are completely responsible for the scores they award.

(iii) The judge has the right to file a written protest with the director of competition in case of arbitrary action taken against him by the superior judge.

(iv) To perform their duties, judges must possess the Code of Points, as well as any special material issued by TC/FIG otherwise they can e replaced by the directors of the competition. The officers of the federations involved assume full responsibility.

(v) They have the duty to attend the judges courses and all scheduled meetings for the competitions for which they have been selected and seeded by the TC/FIG to participate, and are to arrive punctually according to the time and directions in the work plan.

**Spotting or Assistance during Competitions**

(i) In no case may the team leader or any other official person speak with the gymnast during the performance of his exercise. If this, however, happens, the gymnast will be penalized with a deduction of 0.3 points by the superior judge.

Official person in the above sense are the team leaders, members of a team or members of an individual competition group, the local group leader or other persons who may be within the competition area.

(ii) The deduction for such assistance may range, from 0.5 to 0.7 points depending on the difficult part. This rule is applied when spotting prevented the gymnast to fall-off the apparatus or execution of an exercise part or connecting part could not have been possible without assistance.

(iii) For the prevention of accidents and for the moral support of the competitor, only one assistant will be permitted to stand, in the three different competitions, near the following apparatus: horizontal bar, parallel bars, rings and vaulting.

(iv) On the horizontal bar and the rings, a gymnast may be assisted into the hang position, but he must maintain the correct posture from the moment his feet leave the floor, i.e. the evaluation of the gymnast's exercise begins at the moment he leaves the floor.

(v) The regulation in the FIG booklet provides that all apparatus must be fixed so firmly to the podium that no shaky movements of the apparatus are possible. If an apparatus is held by the team leader or another member of the team while the gymnast is performing there will be a deduction of 0.3 points.

(vi) The presence of an additional spotter for the apparatus mentioned in section 2, in the three competitions, will cause the gymnast, without warning, a deduction of 0.3 points.

If a second spotter appears at the conclusion of an exercise, i.e. when both spotters are on the stage during the exercise, the gymnast will receive a penalty up to 0.2 points, according to the difficulty and/or risk involved in executing the dismount.

**Competition Attire**

Each competitor or each team wishing to take part in competitions of the FIG or Olympic Games or international, continental or regional games or contests must fulfil the following prerequisites for uniform when competing.

(i) On pommel horse, rings, parallel bars and horizontal bar, all competitors must perform their exercises wearing long white pants with foot-wear during all competitions.

(ii) Wearing of a shirt is compulsory during all competitions.

(iii) In competition each team must wear uniform dress of the same colour. Individual gymnasts of one nation, must adhere to this during all competitions as well.

(iv) In floor exercise and vaulting there are two possible alternatives; the competitors may wear long white pants with foot-wear or short pants with socks and shoes, socks only or perform bare footed.

(v) Failure to adhere to points 1-4, will result in a penalty of 0.3 taken from the final score of a gymnast in question.

**Combination of the Exercise (Construction)**

1. General Combination Requirements

(i) The construction of the optional exercise must differ conspicuously from the construction of the compulsory exercise. It should not necessarily be considered as an error if parts or connections from the compulsory exercise are contained in the optional exercise, but in this case the preceding or succeeding connections must be different.

(ii) Dismounts from the apparatus and at the end of the floor exercise routine must be completed in a stand with feet together. Pushing off from the apparatus with the feet to perform a dismount is not permitted.

(iii) The parts of an exercise must be connected in an elegant and fluent manner without superfluous movements, intermediate swings, repetitions of parts with the same succeeding or preceding connections, or parts which are too easy with regards to the rest of the exercise.

2. Requirements for contents of an exercise in addition to the required difficulty, the following regulations and guidelines must be adhered to:

3. Evaluation of the Combination

(i) If the dismount is not commensurate with the difficulty of the rest of the exercise, the deduction is up to 0.3.

(ii) If the construction of an exercise does not meet the general requirements deduction for each violation will be 0.3.

(iii) If from the exercise the required C-part or B-part is missing, the deduction will be 0.3.

(iv) If part of an exercise is repeated several times even though the connections before and after may be different, the deduction will be 0.2.

(v) If the optional exercise is performed exactly the same as the compulsory exercise, the gymnast will receive zero score.

## RULES FOR WOMEN GYMNASTS

### Working of Judging Panel

At FIG Competitions judgement of compulsory and optional exercise in 1a, 1b, and 2 will be decided by the following:

— 1 Head Judge — 6 Judges and — 1 Scientific Technical Collaborator:

In Competition 3 it will be decided by the following:
— 2 Head Judges — 6 Judges and — STC.

1. Seating Arrangement of the Judging Brigade

The Head Judge, STC, and Assistant sit at an angle of 90° from the middle of the apparatus in a distance which allow a correct and undisturbed observation of the exercise.

2. At Competitions between Nations and International Contests

1 Head Judge — 3 Judges and — 1 STC
or 1 Head Judge — 4 Judges — 1 STC
are able to be placed/inserted.

The STC may be form the organizing country. For the formation of the judging panel, the prescriptions of the TR, Edition 1982, 16-5 and 16-6 are to be adhered to.

3. The Determination of the Average Score

Average score is calculated in the following manner: The six scores of the judges are used for the evaluation. The highest and lowest scores are eliminated; the four middle scores are added and divided by four

In Competition 3 the scores of both Head Judges are averaged; this averages is the Average Score of both Head Judges. The difference between these scores may not be greater than what is indicated below. The score of the Head Judges has a control function and only comes into consideration, if the Base Score has to be applied.

The difference between the four middle scores may not be greater than:

Competition 1a, and 2
0.20 Pt. for scores between 9.50-10.00 Pts.
0.30 Pt. for scores between 9.00-9.45 Pts.
0.40 Pt. for scores between 8.50-8.95 Pts.
0.50 Pt. in all other cases.

In Competition 3

The difference between 5 of the 6 scores must not be greater than:

— 0.10 Pt. for scores between 9.50-10.00 Pts.

— 0.20 Pt. for scores between 9.00-9.45 Pts.

— -.30 Pt. in all other cases.

The difference between the scores of the judges and the Head Judge must also correspond with this point difference.

If there is too great a difference between these scores, a conference of all six judges follows.

In this conference either

— the unallowable value difference are clarified or

— the base score is calculated. The application of the Base Score is only able to occur with the permission of the President of FIG/WTC.

**Rights and Duties of the Judging Brigade**

Head Judge, Judge, STC and Assistants must:

— possess a Brevet;

— be inscribed on the list of international acknowledged judges;

— take part in the Judges Courses before the competition, extraordinary exceptions, which were caused by a higher power, will actually be decided by the FIG/WTC;

— Successfully have participated in an intercontinental, continental, or international course;

— Wear the prescribed competition uniform. At the Olympic Games the uniform is supplied by the Organizing Committee.

— Be at the competition site 1 hour before the beginning of the competition;

They must not leave their place during the competition or have contact with other persons.

Only the Head Judge has the right to have contact with the President of the FIG/WTc, respectively the Jury of Appeal.

They must have the knowledge of the following:

— Code of Points — Women of the FIG;

— Technical Regulations of the FIG.

Formation of the Jury of Appeal

(a) President of the FIG or his representative.

(b) President of the Women's Technical Committee of the FIG

(c) Head Judge of the respective apparatus.

The Governing Body has the right to confirm — uphold, to raise or lower a score.

Rights and Duties of the President of the FIG/WTC

i. She is responsible for the judges' Course before the Competitions.

ii. She is responsible for the special course for the Scientific Technical Collaborators.

iii. She conducts the intercontinental Course for the judges.

iv. She conducts the Protest Meeting with the Jury.

v. She has the right to consult with the Head Judge, if in her opinion the Average Scores are too high or too low in comparison to the scores on the other apparatus.

vi. In collaboration with the FIG/WTC and the Jury of Appeal she is able to:

**General Deductions for Faults**

Under general deductions for errors, one understands that it pertains to what may occur during the exercises on all apparatus.

One distinguishes:

(i) Posture errors

(ii) Compositional errors

(iii) Technical errors

(iv) Errors in behaviour of the gymnast or coach

These errors can occurs as:

(A) Medium Faults

For example:

- Distinct deviation from perfect technique amplitude, height or jumps/leaps, turns ended too late.

- Distinct posture failure such as strong knee errors

and open legs

- Strong relaxed leg or body posture
- Intermediate swing = 0.40 Pt. and more

(B) Small Faults

For example:

(i) Slight opening of the legs

(ii) Poor foot or arm work

(iii) Relaxed leg or body posture, etc. 0.20 to 0.30 Pt.

(C) Large Faults

For example:

(i) Falls

(ii) Spotting assistance.

(iii) Strong deviation from correct technique

(iv) Specific apparatus errors are found in the respective Section of each apparatus.

**UNEVEN BARS**

**Content of the Exercise**

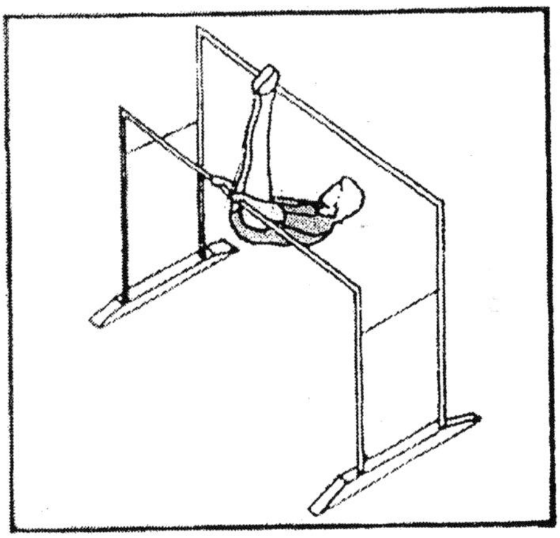

The exercise should be composed from different element groups. The difficulty parts B, C, and D should come from the following element groups.

(i) Elements from swing to handstand

(ii) Elements with turns around the breadth axis-salto turns.

(iii) Elements with turns around the longitudinal axis-pirouettes.

(iv) Upward swings or circular swings

(v) Counter, grip change, ad flight elements.

(vi) Kips

(vii) Hecht elements.

## HORSE VAULT

### Vault Groups

The vaults will be classified into the following four groups:

Group 1 — Handsprings, Cartwheels with and without longitudinal axis turn.

Group 2 — Salto forward with and without longitudinal axis turn.

Group 3 — Salto backward with and without longitudinal axis turn.

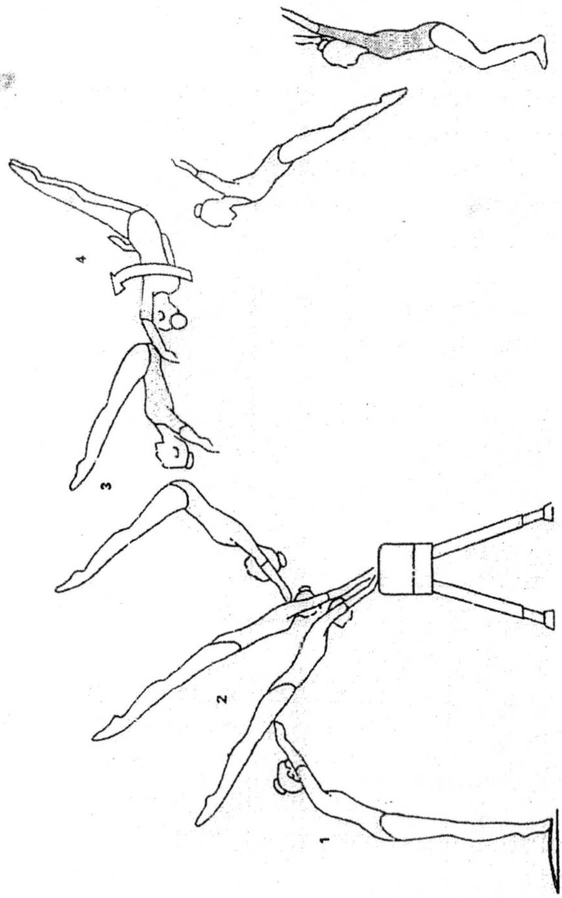

Group 4 — Vaults from a Round off.

Special Requirements

(a) In Competition 1a the gymnast has only one attempt.

(b) In Competition 1b and 2 each gymnast has the right to two attempts; the better score of both vaults is counted. The vaults may be the same or different.

(c) In Competition 3, two different vaults with different vault numbers must be shown. The Average Score will be arrived at by the averaging of the score of the vaults.

(d) The Final Average Score in Competition 3 is formulated as follows:

**BALANCE BEAM**

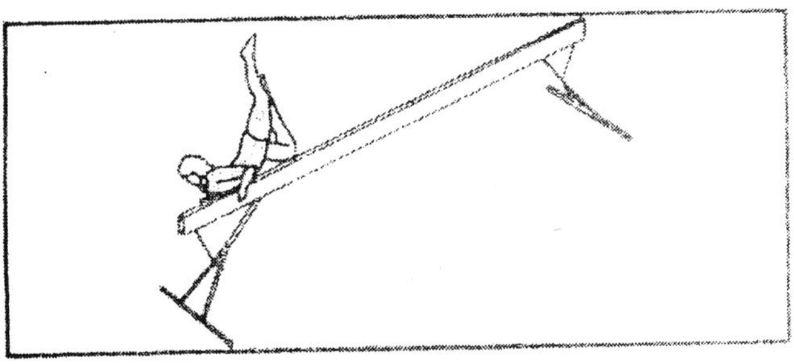

**Content of the Exercise**

The exercise must be composed from different element groups. The difficulty parts B, C and D must come from the following element groups:

— Acrobatic elements with or without flight phase in the forward, sideward or backward movement.

— Acrobatic strength elements.

— Gymnastic elements. Turns, leaps or jumps and hops, step and running combinations, balance elements in a stand, sit and lying position, body waves.

**General**

The evaluation of the exercise begins with take-off from the board or from the floor.

The duration of the optional exercise on the balance

beam may not amount to less than 1 : 10 minutes and not more than 1:30 minutes.

The exercise is ended at 1:30 minutes; further performance will not be evaluated. An interruption of 10 seconds is possible due to a fail on or from the apparatus. This will be timed separately.

Three static, typical beam elements — holds are permitted. Additional holds for concentration prior to difficult elements or connections, produce deductions.

**Specific Apparatus Deductions**

(a) Compositional Faults = Deduction

— Mount without value = 0.20 Pt.

— Exercise without high points

- too few direct connections of gymnastic and acrobatic elements = up to 0.20 Pt.

- more than 2 beam passes in succession without difficulties = each 0.10 Pt.

— Monotony in Presentation = up to 0.20 Pt.

- Domination of acrobatics = up to 0.20 Pt.

- One-sided choice of acrobatic or gymnastic elements = up to 0.20 Pt.

- Connections not corresponding to the difficulty level of the exercise = up to 0.20 Pt.

(b) Specific Apparatus Faults

— Support of a leg against the side surface of the beam = each 0.20 Pt.

— More than 3 holds = each 0.10 Pt.

(c) Absence of Special Requirements

— Without an acrobatic series = 0.20 Pt.

— Without a gymnastic series = 0.20 Pt.

— Without a 360° turn on one leg = 0.10 Pt.

— Without a gymnastic leap or jump with great amplitude = 0.10 Pt.

— Dismount not corresponding to the difficulty level of the exercise = 0.20 Pt.

For the Composition is to be noted

— Creation of high points through the direct connections of:

= 2 or several gymnastic elements

= 2 or several acrobatic elements

= 2 or several acrobatic and gymnastic elements in one series

= Leaps or jumps, turns and other gymnastic elements

—Performance of elements in the forward, sideward, and backward movement and in a side, cross, and also oblique position to the apparatus.

—Use of the entire length of the beam and in a dynamic construction of the exercise.

—Harmonious change between the groups, in particular by changing of gymnastic and acrobatic elements.

— Change between working near and far from the beam.

**Special Requirements**

— One gymnastic series of two or several elements, at least A.

— One acrobatic series of two or several elements, one of which must be an element with flight phase.

— One gymnastic turn of 360° on one leg.

— Dismount : at least B.

— One gymnastic leap or jump with great amplitude.

Value Raising Through Direct Connection of Value Parts

— Without pause, and

— Without and extra step

Following are the examples of value raising through direct connection of difficulties:

Flic-Flac, landing — take-off without pause

= Flic-Flac

Direct means: performance of elements connections

— 1/1 turn on the left leg — free leg optional } = direct

without pause placing the free leg with take-off to }

= gainer flic-flac

The value raising on beam begins with A-B connections

A- elements cannot be valued raised and serve only as a connection before B-elements for value raising.

Only acrobatic elements with flight phase can be used for value raising.

— The value raising for dismount connections begins with B + B

— For longer dismount series the same principles as for series on the beam and the dismount will be used.

## FLOOR EXERCISE

### Content of the Exercise

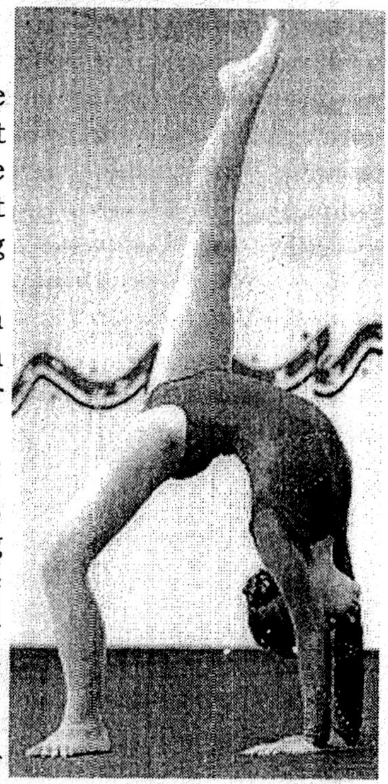

The exercise should be composed from different element groups. The difficulties B, C and D must come from the following element groups.

— Acrobatic elements with and without flight phase in forward, sideward, or backward movement.

— Gymnastic elements: turns; leaps, jumps, and hops; steps and running combinations; balance elements in stand, sitting and lying position; arm swings and body waves.

### Special Requirements

— 3 acrobatic series, one of which is an acrobatic series with two saltos or one D - salto.

— One gymnastic element: at least B.

— A dismount series: at least B.

**General**

The duration of the floor exercise may not amount to less than 1:10 minutes and not more than 1:30 minutes.

4 measures of musical lead in are permitted. These measures must belong to the floor music. It is permitted:

— Musical accompaniment with orchestra without singing.

— Musical accompaniment with piano or one other instrument.

# 9

# HANDBALL

## INTRODUCTION

Handball (also known as team handball, Olympic handball or European handball) is a team sport in which two teams of seven players each (six outfield players and a goalkeeper) pass a ball to throw it into the goal of the other team. The team with the most goals after two periods of 30 minutes wins.

Modern handball is usually played indoors, but outdoor variants exist in the forms of field handball and Czech handball (which were more common in the past) and beach handball (also called sandball). American

handball and Gaelic handball are completely different sports.

The game is quite fast and includes body contact as the defenders try to stop the attackers from approaching the goal. Contact is only allowed when the defensive player is completely in front of the offensive player, i.e. between the offensive player and the goal. This is referred to as a player sandwich. Any contact from the side or especially from behind is considered dangerous and is usually met with penalties. When a defender successfully stops an attacking player, the play is stopped and restarted by the attacking team from the spot of the infraction or on the nine meter line.

Handball is a fast moving sport so it is a given that participants be in fairly good shape before attempting to play it. There is a lot of twisting, bending, and running involved.This said it is a game played by every age group and both genders. If injury is avoided it can be played for many years.

Handball has its variants but usually it is played in a four walled room of specific dimensions. These are called the front wall, the back wall and two side walls. They are so named because they are important in the play of the game. There is a serving line where the serving player hits or serves the ball. There is a line called the short line just in front of the front wall. When served the ball must pass behind this line in order for the serve to be legal.

## RULES OF HANDBALL

Handball (also known as team handball, Olympic handball or European handball) is a team sport in which two teams of seven players each (six outfield players and a goalkeeper) pass a ball to throw it into the goal of the other team. The team with the most goals after two periods of 30 minutes wins.

Modern handball is usually played indoors, but

outdoor variants exist in the forms of field handball and Czech handball (which were more common in the past) and beach handball (also called sandball). American handball and Gaelic handball are completely different sports. The game is quite fast and includes body contact as the defenders try to stop the attackers from approaching the goal. Contact is only allowed when the defensive player is completely in front of the offensive player, i.e. between the offensive player and the goal.

## THE BASICS

### The Playing Court

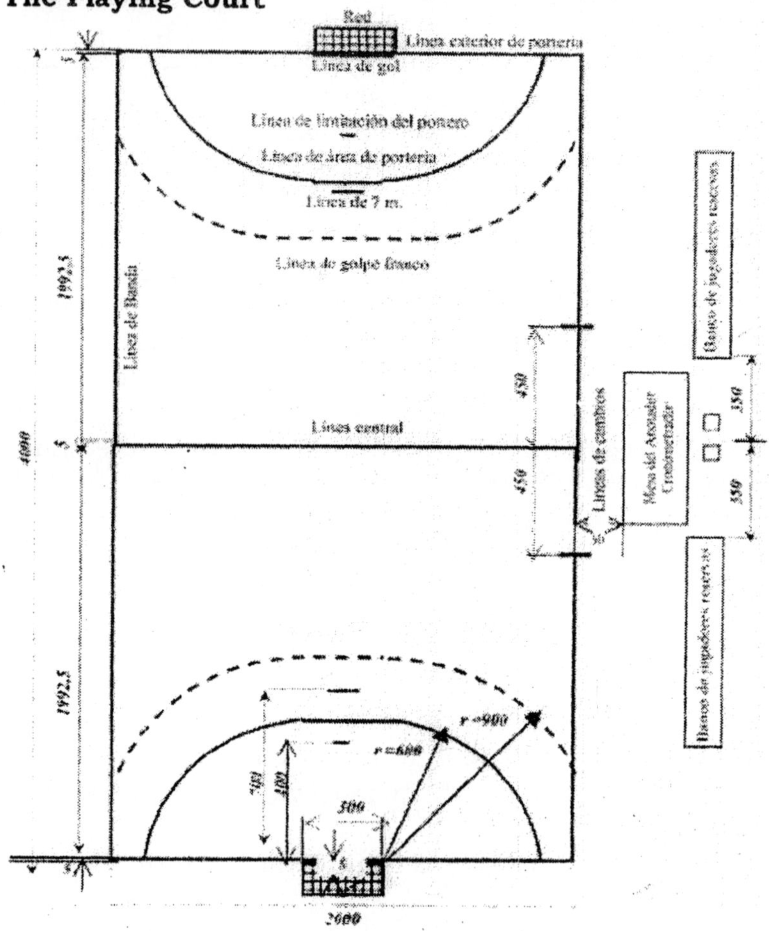

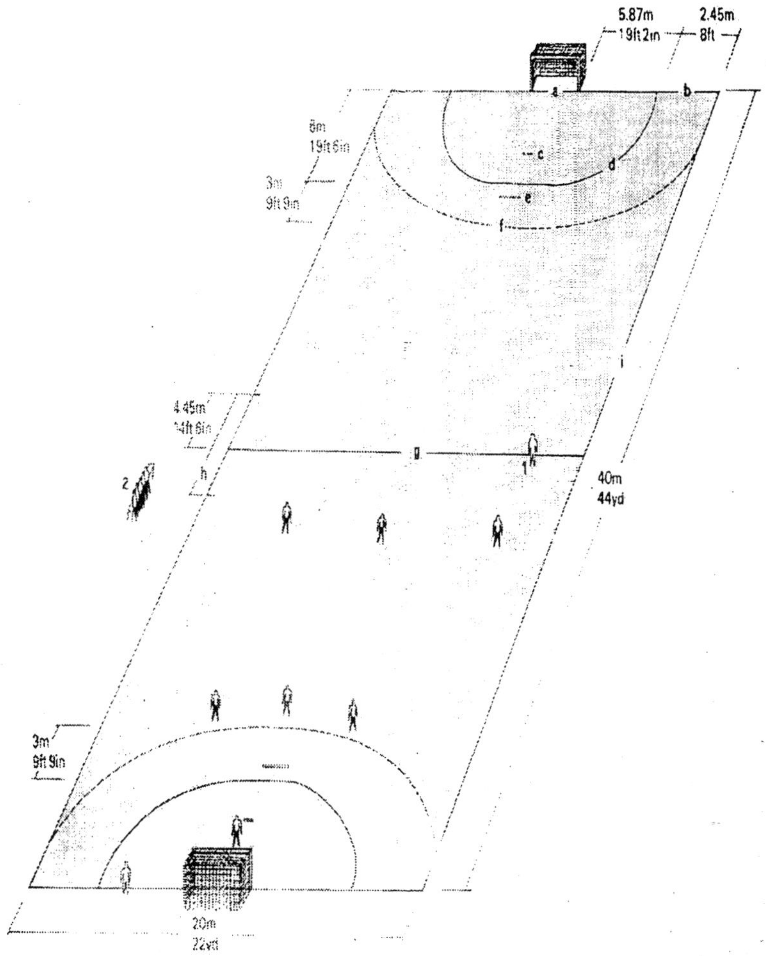


The court measures 20 meters (65' 7") by 40 meters (131' 3"). The court is larger than a basketball court, but the length may be shortened when space is limited. The goal area line, or 6-meter line (19' 8"), is the most important line. No one except the goalie is allowed to stand in the goal area. The goal opening is 2 meters by 3 meters. Players may jump into the area if the ball is released before landing in the area.

**The Ball**

Team handball is played with a 32-panel leather ball. For women, the ball is 54 to 56 centimeters and 325 to 400 grams. For men, it is 58 to 60 centimeters and 425 to 475 grams.

**Number of Players**

There are seven players on each team (six court players and one goalie). A maximum of 12 players may dress and participate in a game for each team. Substitutes may enter the game at any time through own substitution area as long as the player they are replacing has left the court.

**Uniform of the Players**

Player numbers are 1 to 20. Uniform shirts and shorts are the same color. The goalkeeper must wear a different color shirt from teammates and opponents. No jewelry is allowed.

**Referees**

There are two referees, a court referee and a goal line referee. Referees have complete authority: Their decisions are final. The referees are assisted by a timer and a scorer.

**Duration of the Game**

For players 18 years and over, the game consists of 2, 30-minute halves with 10-minute half-time. For tournament and youth games 2, 15-minute or 2, 20-minute halves. This is running time except for injury or one team time-out per half. The teams change benches at half-time. The game ends in a tie unless the game demands a winner. (Tournament rules dictate that a winner must be determined.) Overtime consists of 2, 5-minute periods).

**Passive Play**

It is illegal to keep the ball in a team's possession without making a recognizable attempt to attack and to try to score. In other words, a team cannot stall (free-throw awarded to the other team).

**Throw-Off**

A throw-off is taken by the team that wins the coin toss and chooses to start the game with the ball. Each team must be in its own half of the court with the defense 3 meters away from the ball. Following a whistle, the ball is passed from center court to a teammate and play begins. Throw-off is repeated after every goal scored and after half-time.

**Scoring**

A goal is scored when the entire ball crosses the goal line inside the goal. A goal may be scored from any throw (free-throw, throw-in, throw-off, goal-throw).

**Playing The Ball**

A player is allowed . . . -To run with the ball for 3 steps -To hold the ball for 3 seconds -Unlimited dribble with 3 steps allowed before and after dribbling (no double-dribble).

A player is NOT allowed . . .

* To endanger an opponent with the ball.
* To pull, hit or punch the ball out of the hands of an opponent.
* To contact the ball below the knee.
* To dive on the floor for a rolling or stationary ball.

**Defending the Opponent**

A player is allowed to use the torso of the body to obstruct an opponent with or without the ball. However, using the outstretched arms or legs to obstruct, push, hold, trip or hit is NOT allowed. The attacking player is not allowed to charge into a defensive player.

**Throw-In**

A throw-in is awarded when ball goes out of bounds on the sideline or when the ball is last touched by a defensive player (excluding the goalie) and goes out of bounds over the endline. The throw-in is taken from the spot where the ball crossed the sideline, or if it crossed the endline, from the nearest corner. The thrower must place one foot on the sideline to execute the throw. All opposing players must stay 3 meters away from the ball.

**Referee Throw**

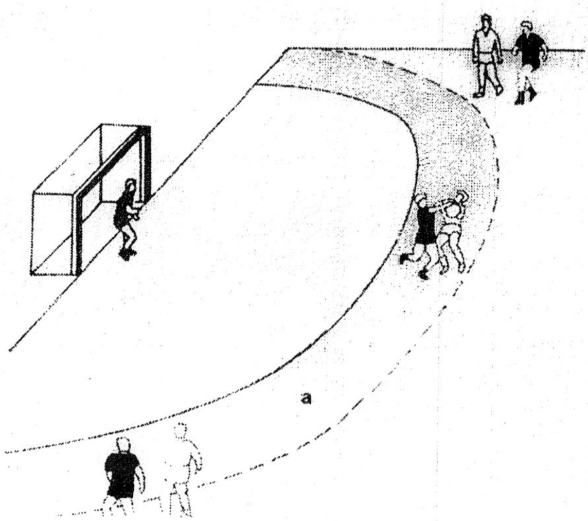

A referee throw is awarded when . . . The ball touches anything above the court after a simultaneous infringement of the rules after simultaneous possession of the ball.

The Referee throws the ball vertically between two opposing players. The jumping players may grab the ball or tap it to a teammate. All other players must be 3 meters away from the throw. The referee throw is always taken at center court.

**Free-Throw**

For a minor foul or violation, a free-throw is awarded to the opponent at the exact spot it took place. If the foul or violation occurs between the goal area line and the 9-meter line, the throw is taken from the nearest post outside the 9-meter line. The thrower must keep one foot in contact with the floor, then pass or shoot.

7-Meter Throw: The 7-meter throw is awarded when :

* A foul destroys a clear chance to score

* The goalie carries the ball back into his or her own goal area

* A court player intentionally plays the ball to his or her own goalie in the goal area and the goalie touches the ball

* A defensive player enters his or her goal area to gain an advantage over an attacking player in possession of the ball.

All players must be outside the free-throw line when the throw is taken. The player taking the throw has 3 seconds to shoot after referee's whistle. Any player may take the 7-meter throw.

**Goal-Throw**

A goal-throw is awarded when . . . The ball rebounds off the goalkeeper over the endline The ball is thrown over the endline by the attacking team.

The goalie takes the throw inside the goal area and is not restricted by the 3-step/3-second rule.

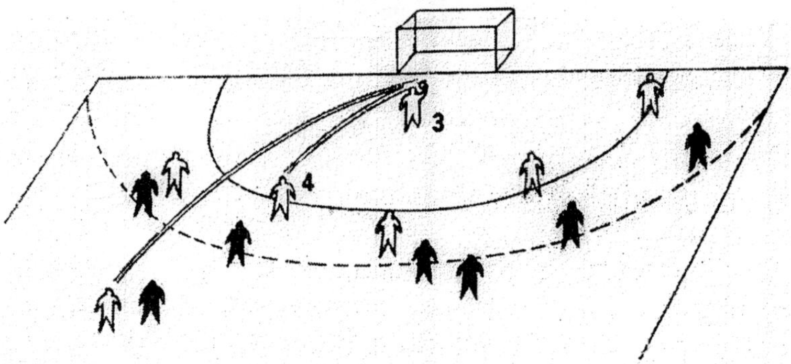


**Progressive Punishments**

Progressive Punishments: Pertain to fouls that require more punishment than just a free-throw. "Actions" directed mainly at the opponent and not the ball (such as reaching around, holding, pushing, hitting, tripping and jumping into an opponent) are to be punished progressively.

**Warnings (Yellow Card)**

The referee gives only one warning to a player for rule violations and a total of three to a team. Exceeding these limits results in 2-minute suspensions thereafter. Warnings are not required prior to giving out a 2-minute suspension. 2-minute suspensions awarded for . . . - Serious or repeated rules violations -Unsportsmanlike conduct -Illegal substitution. -The suspended player's team plays short for 2 minutes.

**Disqualification and Exclusion (Red Card)**

A disqualification is the equivalent of three, 2-minute suspensions. A disqualified player must leave court and bench, but the team can replace player after the 2-minute suspension expires. An exclusion is given for assault. The excluded player's team continues short one player for the rest of the game.

**The Goalkeeper**

(i) By changing the dress any player can become the goalkeeper and goalkeeper can become a court player.

Through team's own substitution area, goalkeeper should be substituted.

The goalkeeper enjoys the following freedom:

i. While in act of defense inside the goal area he is allowed to touch the ball with any part of his body;

ii. Inside the goal area he is allowed to move freely;

iii. At any time goal-keeper is allowed to become a court player by changing his cloths and then all rules applicable to court players will become applicable to him. As soon as any part of his body touches the floor outside goal-area line, goalkeeper is considered to have left the goal area.

iv. If he has not managed to control the ball fully he can leave goal area with ball and play it again in playing area.

**Penalty Throw**

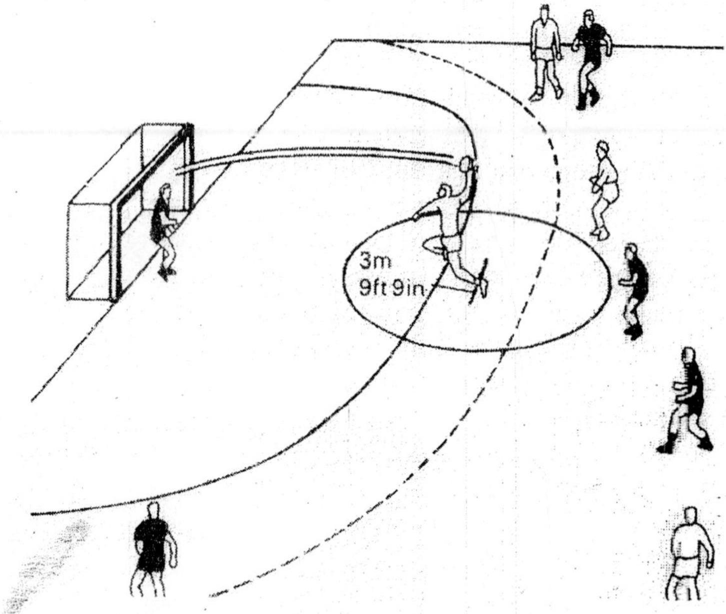


(1) In 3 seconds from whistle signal from court referee, penalty throw should be taken as a shot.

(2) In following circumstances a penalty throw should be awarded:

(a) if chance of scoring gets spoiled by infringement in any part of the court;

(b) if with the ball goal-keeper enters his goal-area;

(c) if in order to gain an advantage over opponent having possession of ball, a court player enters his own goal-area;

(d) if a court-player plays the ball in his goal-area.

(3) A free-throw should be awarded to the defending team if before ball has left thrower's hand player of

attacking team touches or crosses the free-throw-line.

(4) While the penalty-throw is being taken, the goal-keeper crosses the goal-keeper line before the ball has left the throw shall be retaken if a goal was not scored.

(5) Once the penalty throw has been taken the ball may not be played by any court-player until it has touched the goal-keeper or the goal.

(6) Whilst the penalty throw if being taken, all players of the defending team must stand at least 3 m from thrower. If a player of the defending team touches or crosses the free-throw-line before the ball has left thrower's hand the referees shall decide as follows:

(a) Goal, if the ball goes into the goal.

(b) The penalty-throw to be re-taken in all other cases.

# 10

# HOCKEY

## INTRODUCTION

Hockey is a family of sports in which two teams play against each other by trying to maneuver a ball or a puck into the opponent's goal using a hockey stick.

Field hockey is played on gravel, natural grass, sand-based or water-based artificial turf, with a small, hard ball. The game is popular among both males and females in many parts of the world, particularly in Europe, Asia, Australia, New Zealand and South Africa. In most countries, the game is played between single-sex sides, although they can be mixed-sex.

The governing body is the 116-member International Hockey Federation (FIH). Men's field hockey has been played at each summer Olympic Games since 1908 (except 1912 and 1924), while women's field hockey has been played at the Summer Olympic Games since 1980.

Modern field hockey sticks are J-shaped and constructed of a composite of wood, glass fibre or carbon fibre (sometimes both) and have a curved hook at the playing end, a flat surface on the playing side and curved surface on the rear side. While current field hockey appeared in the mid-18th century in England, primarily in schools, it was not until the first half of the 19th century that it became firmly established. The first club was created in 1849 at Blackheath in south-east London. Field hockey is the national sport of India and Pakistan.

## SKILLS AND TECHNIQUES

**Dribbling**

Dribbling is used in a number of sports, including soccer and basketball, but it also applies to the game of field hockey. When you obtain possession of the ball, it's your responsibility to dribble the ball until you can either shoot or pass.

**Passing**

Field hockey is a team sport, so you need to make sure you don't try to do everything yourself. There will be times when the defenders will be coming after you and you'll need to get rid of the ball and need to pass it along to one of your teammates.

**Shooting**

Those who possess a strong upper and middle body will be able to exert a lot of force when they take a shot but accuracy is also an important aspect of field hockey. Without accuracy, your shots will never amount to what they could if you don't practice shooting on goal.

**Defending**

There are numerous times during active field hockey play when you will need to play the defender. Even if your team currently has possession of the ball, you still need to defend against the other team and try to gain possession of the ball whenever possible to avoid the other team from scoring.

**Intercepting**

Intercepting is one of the most important field hockey skills and it can only be mastered with regular practice. Whenever your opponent has possession of the ball, it is your team's duty to try and get possession back. The easiest way to obtain possession is by intercepting passes that the opposing team attempts to make to another one of their teammates.

**Push-In**

The push-in is used for returning the ball into play after it has gone off the field over the side line. On a heavy ground there may be difficulty in sending the ball any appreciable distance. It is therefore important to get the full weight of the body behind the stroke to obtain maximum power.

**Jab**

The jab is a most useful stroke. By pushing the stick out quickly in front of the body with the left hand, the ball can be taken or kept away from an opponent when other strokes are inappropriate.

The jab can be used when the ball is near the player or when he has to reach for it. It is usually executed when the ball is not under close control.

**Tackling**

All players have to tackle opponents in possession of the ball. Half backs and backs do so more often than forwards because the very nature of their tasks is to gain possession of the ball as often as possible, in order to ply forwards with as many passes as they can.

**Push**

This stroke can be used instead of the hit for passing and for shooting at goal. It sends the ball along the ground and is especially useful on firm surfaces. The push is best used for short passes, but experts can send the ball a long distance with this stroke.

**Reverse Stop**

**To the Left Position of body**

The body will lean forward and incline slightly left. The right shoulder will have to move across in a faint hinge movement to bring the head as nearly as possible in line with the ball.

**Goalkeeping**

Perhaps the most important position in field hockey is that of the goalkeeper. Sometimes she is the only thing between the ball and the goal. Being in the direct line of fire necessitates more equipment and protection than other positions in field hockey.

**Instructions**

1. Dress properly in goalie gear so that you won't get hurt.

2. Maintain a good, ready stance in front of the goal: keep your feet together, knees bent, head up, and weight on the balls of your feet so you can easily change direction. Keep your left hand open and your right hand on your stick.

3. Be careful with your foot placement when you move

back and forth in front of the cage so that the ball won't enter the goal through your legs. Move one leg to the side with a short step and follow quickly with the other. Keep your body facing the field and your attackers so you don't turn your back on the action.

4. Stand two to three yards out from the goal when you're meeting an attacker. This closes the angle of attack. Sometimes from here, the goalie can actually interfere with the shooter's line of vision to the goal. By standing out from the goal a little bit, the goalie increases the area of shots she can defend.

5. Remember that your lower legs and feet will block most shots. To do this, bring your legs together in front of the ball. Let the ball drop in front of you and kick it out of the goal area. Try to kick it to the side of the field so your opponents don't get another shot.

## RULES OF HOCKEY

Throughout most of the world the rules set by the FIH are used. However in the United States, NCAA have their own rules for inter-collegiate competitions, and high school associations similarly play to different rules. This article assumes FIH rules unless otherwise stated.

Players are permitted to play the ball with any part of the stick other than the rounded side (back). The flat side is always on the "natural" side for a right-handed person — there are no "left-handed" hockey sticks (for actual use in play, some have been made as novelties).

### PLAYING FIELD

Width of lines should be 75mm which should be marked throughout their length;

i. Side-lines are the longer perimeter lines;

ii. Back-lines are the shorter perimeter lines;

iii. Goal-lines are the parts of back-lines between the goal posts. Outside the back-lines and side-lines, minimum run-off area should be provided.

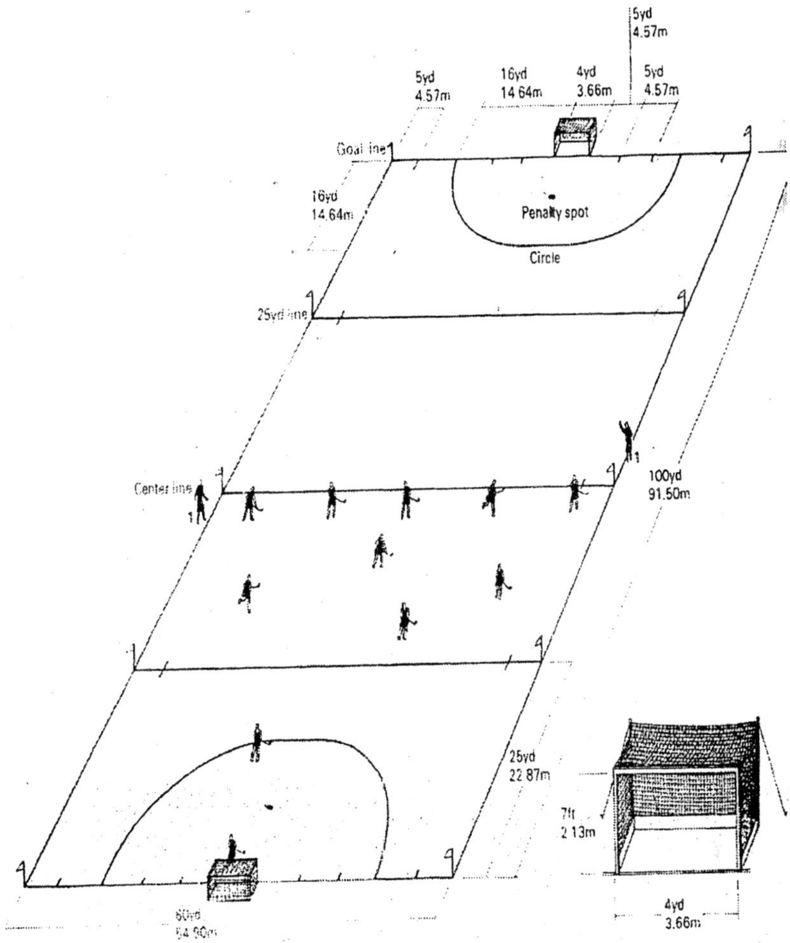


Play field should have rectangular shape with following specifications:

- Length—91.40 meters.
- Width—55 meters.
- Lines should be of white colour;

Nets

- Nets on the field should be attached at intervals of not more than 150mm.
- To rebound the ball they should be fitted loosely;

- Ball passing between them and goal-posts, crossbar, side-boards and back-boards should be prevented by them.

- mesh not more than 45 mm.

Backboards should have following specifications:

i. It should have length of 3.66 meters and height of 460mm.

ii. At the end of side-board it should be positioned on ground.

iii. Dark colour should be used to paint it from inside.

Goals

Sideboards

i. Some dark colour should be used to paint these from inside.

ii. It should have length of 1.20m and height of 460mm.

iii. They should be placed on ground in right angle direction to back-line which is fixed to back of goal-posts but their width should not be increased and should be placed at the end of backboard.

At centre of each back line:

i. there should be a goal-post and crossbar of white colour, which should have a rectangular shape of 51mm width and 75mm depth.

ii. at a distance of 3.66m vertical goal-posts should be placed.

iii. On external marks with their front face touching outer edge of back-line goal posts should be placed.

iv. 2.14 meter from ground horizontal crossbar should be fixed.

All requirements of national legal standards should be get fulfilled by shape of both posts and crossbar.

**Shooting Circle**

Following are specifications for shooting circles:

i. To meet back-lines in a quarter circle form with centres at inside front corner of nearer goal-posts, these lines should be continued without any interruption;

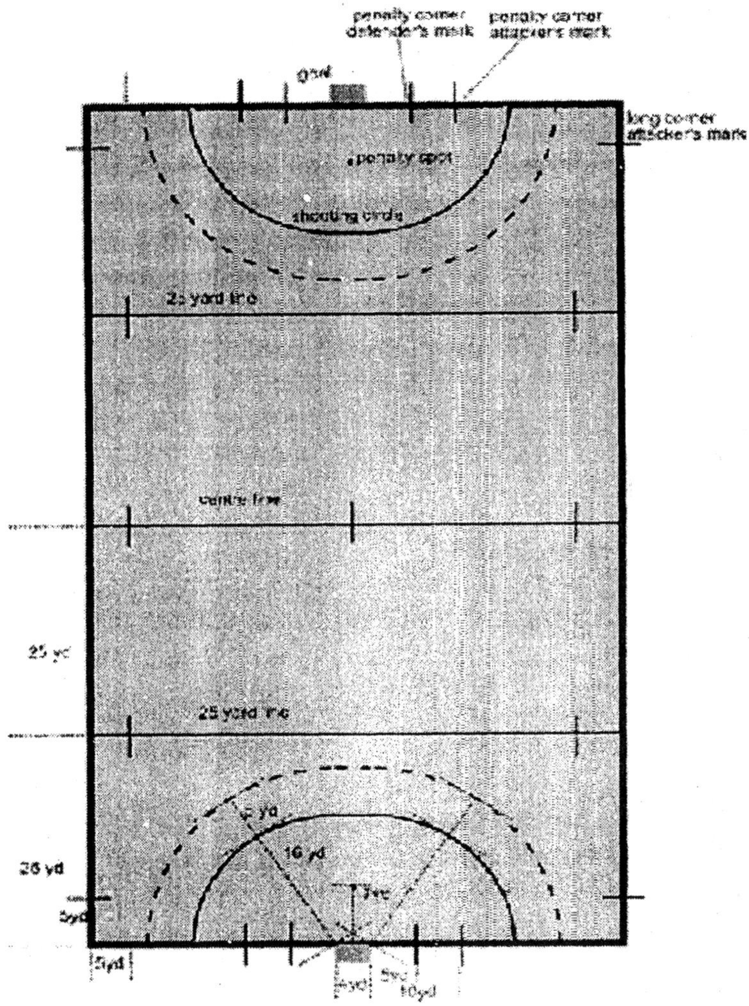


ii. 3.66 m long parallel to and 14.63m from back lines these lines should be marked inside the field. This measurement should be done from outside of back-line to outer edge of lines.

iii. Such lines are termed the circle-lines whereas space enclosed by these lines is called the shooting circles.

iv. 5 meters from outer edge of each circle-line broken lines should be marked. 300mm should be the length of each solid section whereas solid sections should have gap of length 3 metres. At top centre of circle line each broken line should be start with the solid section.

**Flag Posts**

In the following manner flag posts on the field should be placed:

i. should be placed at each corner of the field;

ii. should be safe;

iii. at a height of between 1.20 and 1.50 meters;

iv. should have flags of not more than 300m width or length.

v. should be attached to a spring base when unbreakabie;

Following other markings are done:

i. Across the field there should be centre-line.

ii. Across the field 22.90m lines should be drawn, from outer edge of nearer back line edge nearer the centre-line should be at a distance of 22.90 metres.

23-meters area is the area enclosed by 22.90 meters lines, relevant part of back-line and sidelines.

**FIELD HOCKEY POSITIONS**

Teams consist of eleven players on the field, and up to five substitutes. Substitutions are not limited but may not be made during a penalty corner. There are no set positions other than goalkeeper, but most teams arrange themselves into fullbacks, midfielders and forwards. Many teams include a single sweeper, who plays behind the fullbacks.

One player from each team is designated the goalkeeper. Goalkeepers must wear a suitable helmet with full face mask and are also permitted to wear protective padding, including large leg guards, kickers and gloves. Although goalkeepers may block or deflect the ball with any part of their bodies, and propel the ball

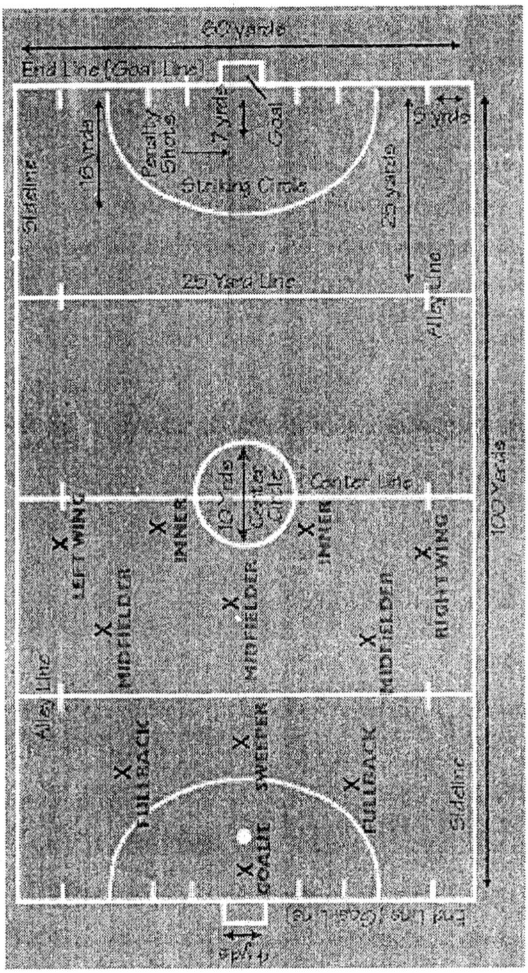


with their feet, they must always carry a stick, and normal stick rules apply. Goalkeepers are permitted to play the ball outside their defensive circle (scoring area or "D"), but must only use the stick in this circumstance.

**GENERAL PLAY IN FIELD HOCKEY**

For the purposes of the rules, all players on the team in possession of the ball are attackers, and those on the team without the ball are defenders.

The match is officiated by two field umpires.

Traditionally each umpire generally controls half of the field, divided roughly diagonally, although now experiments are being made where either umpire can make any decision anywhere on the field. These umpires are often assisted by a technical bench including a timekeeper and record keeper.

Prior to the start of the game, a coin is tossed and the winning captain can choose a starting end or start with the ball. The game time is divided into two equal halves of 35 minutes each, with five minutes for half-time. At the start of each half, as well as after goals are scored, play is started with a pass from the centre of the field. All players must start in their defensive half, but the ball may be played in any direction. Each team starts with the ball in one half, and the team that conceded the goal has possession for the restart.

Field players may only play the ball with the face of the stick. Tackling is permitted as long as the tackler does not make contact with the attacker or his stick before playing the ball (contact after the tackle may also be penalised if the tackle was made from a position where contact was inevitable). Further, the player with the ball may not deliberately use his body to push a defender out of the way.

Obstruction typically occurs in three circumstances - when a defender comes between the player with possession and the ball without first performing a legitimate tackle; when a defender's stick comes between the attacker's stick and the ball or makes contact with the attacker's stick; and also when (usually deliberately) blocking the opposition's passage to the ball.

When the ball passes over the sidelines, it is returned to play with a sideline hit, taken by a member of the team whose players were not the last to touch the ball before crossing the sideline. If it crosses the backline after last touched by an attacker, a 15 m hit. A 15 m hit is also awarded for offenses committed by the attacking side within 15 m of the end of the pitch they are attacking.

## FIELD HOCKEY SET PLAYS

### Free Hits

Free hits are awarded when offences are committed outside the scoring circles. The ball may be hit or pushed once in any direction by the team offended against. Opponents must move 5 m from the ball when a free hit is awarded, and for attacking free hits within 5 m of the circle all attackers other than the one taking the hit must also by 5 m away.

As mentioned above, a 15 m hit is awarded if an attacking player commits a foul forward of that line, or if the ball passes over the backline off an attacker. These hits are taken in line with where the foul was committed (taking a line parallel with the sideline between where the offence was committed, or the ball went out of play). If the attack commit a foul in the circle they are attacking, the defence additionally has the option to take the free hit anywhere in that circle.

**Long Corner**

A long corner is awarded if the ball goes over the backline after last being touched by a defender. Long corners are played by the attacking team and involve a free hit on the sideline five yards from the corner of the field closest to where the ball went out of play.

**Short Corner**

The short or penalty corner is a rather complicated set play that is awarded against a defending team when any offence is committed in the defensive circle, and may be awarded when a deliberate offence is committed in the defending 23 m area, or when the defending team deliberately plays the ball over the back line.

Short corners begin with five defenders (including the keeper) arranged along the backline. All other defenders must return to the centre line until the ball is in play. Attacking players begin the play standing outside the scoring circle, except for one attacker who starts the corner by playing the ball from a mark 10 m either side of the goal (the circle has a 14.63 m radius). This player puts the ball into play by pushing or hitting the ball to the other attackers outside the circle; the ball must pass outside the circle before the attackers attempt to get a shot or deflection into the goal. For safety reasons, the first shot of a penalty corner must remain under 460 mm high unless it is flicked.

**Penalty Stroke**

A penalty stroke is awarded when defenders commit a deliberate foul in the circle which deprives an attacker of possession or the opportunity to play the ball, when an accidental breach prevents a certain goal, or if defenders repeatedly "break" or start to run from the backline before a penalty corner has started. This penalty pits a single attacker against the goalkeeper, and is taken from a spot 6.4 m out and directly in front of the goal. The goalkeeper must stand with heels on

the goal line, and cannot move his feet until the ball is played. On the umpire's whistle, the striker may take one step and push or flick the ball at the goal, which the goalkeeper attempts to save. The attacker is not permitted to take more than one step, more than one shot, to fake or dummy the shot, or to move towards or interfere with the goalkeeper once the shot is taken. Hitting or dragging the ball is also forbidden. If the shot is saved, play is restarted with a 15 m hit to the defenders; if a goal is scored, play is restarted in the normal way.

**DANGEROUS PLAY AND RAISED BALLS WITHIN FIELD HOCKEY**

If the ball is raised off the ground in a manner that is, in the umpire's opinion, dangerous, the ball is turned over to the other team and they receive a free hit from the point of contact. The definition of a "dangerous ball" is a matter of interpretation by the umpires. Guidance in the rules states "a ball is considered dangerous when it causes legitimate evasive action by players" — but it also depends on the speed of the ball, the height at which it is raised, and the number of players near its path.

It is, however, legal to raise the ball when making a shot on goal (by hitting or flicking), or to make an 'overhead' pass (providing opposition players are greater than 5 m from the player, and the ball is not dangerous). The ball may only deliberately be raised using a hit if the player is shooting at goal.

Dangerous play rules also apply with relation to the usage of the stick. Players may not attempt to play at the ball above their shoulders (unless saving a goal on the goal line). It will generally be considered dangerous play to hit the ball while it is in the air; the ball must be controlled first in this circumstance.

## WARNINGS AND SUSPENSIONS WITHIN FIELD HOCKEY

Hockey uses a three-tier card system of warnings and suspensions. A Green card is a warning, while a Yellow card is a temporary suspension for a minimum of 5 minutes duration without substitution. As in association football, a Red card is a permanent exclusion from the rest of the game, without substitution, and in many circumstances will also result in the player being banned for a certain period of time or number of matches (this is governed by local playing conditions, rather than the rules of hockey). Unlike football, a player may receive more than one card of the same colour, although a second and subsequent card cannot be of a "lower" colour than one previously issued, and in the case of a second yellow card the temporary suspension would be expected to be of considerably longer duration than the first. However, local playing conditions may mandate that cards are awarded only progressively, and not allow second awards.

### Scoring in Field Hockey

The teams' object is to play the ball into their attacking

circle and, from there, hit, push or flick the ball into the goal, scoring a point. The team with more goals after two 35-minute halves wins the game

**Tie Breaker**

Conditions for breaking ties are not laid down in the rules of hockey, but many associations will follow the procedure laid down in FIH tournament regulations which mandate 7.5 minutes each way of "golden goal" extra time (i.e. the game ends as soon as one team scores). If scores are still level, then the game will be decided with penalty strokes, in much the same way that association football penalty shoot outs are conducted.

Other competitions may use alternative means of breaking a tie, for example, an extended period of golden goal extra time with a progressive reduction in the number of players each team can have on the field (usually termed "drop-offs"); if no goal is scored at the end of such extra time periods, again a result would be achieved using penalty strokes.

**FIELD HOCKEY EQUIPMENT**

Each player carries a "stick", normally a little over 3 feet (90 centimetres) long and traditionally made of wood but now often made with fibreglass, kevlar and carbon fibre composites, with a rounded handle flattening out on one side and with a hook at the bottom. New rules (2006) limit the curve of the stick so as to limit the power with which the ball can be flicked. The stick is only allowed to have a bow smaller

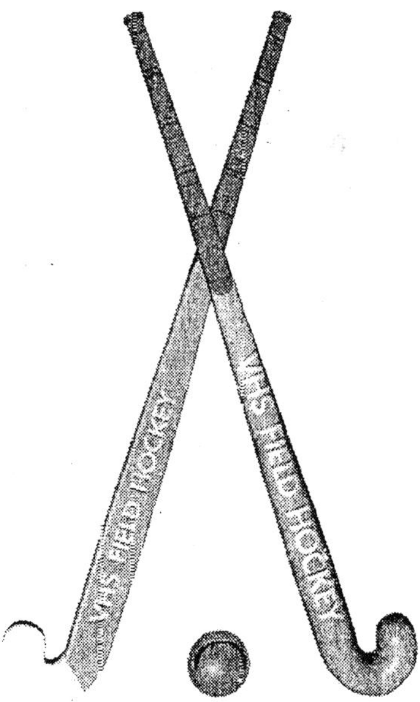

than or equal to 25 mm otherwise this is deemed to be illegal. The flat side of the hook is used to push, dribble, or hit a hard plastic ball. This ball is often covered with indentations to reduce hydroplaning that can cause an inconsistent ball speed on wet surfaces. Each field player normally wears a mouth guard and shin guards. Although the only equipment required for Goalkeepers (under FIH rules, local variants may require more) is a helmet and a stick, invariably they wear extensive protective equipment including chest guards, padded shorts, heavily padded hand protectors, leg guards, and foot guards (called "kickers").

**FIELD HOCKEY FORMATIONS**

Formations provide structure to a hockey team on the pitch. They help players understand and share the defensive and attacking responsibilities. Although higher level teams may select from a wide range of formations, teams containing inexperienced players or teams which see frequent changes to their players are likely to select from a more limited range of formations such as 4-3-3, 5-3-2 and 4-4-2. (The numbers refer to the number of players arrayed across the pitch, starting in front of the goalkeeper with the defenders, then midfield and then attack.) The 2-3-5 formation, used predominantly in Australia from relatively lowly interschool to professional interstate competitions, provides common language for many players and helps explain why "centre half" is often a name used for a player in the centre of a defence with 4 or 5 players.

Because hockey teams have 1 goalkeeper plus 10 outfield players as does association football (soccer), there are many common formations between the two sports.

One important difference in modern hockey is the absence of an offside rule. This allows attackers (often a lone attacker) to play well up the pitch, stretching the opponents' defence and using the large spaces to be found there. To counter this, defences usually keep a matching number of defenders

**MAJOR INTERNATIONAL TOURNAMENTS IN FIELD HOCKEY**

The biggest two field hockey tournaments are undoubtedly the Olympic Games tournament, and the Hockey World Cup, which is also held every 4 years. Apart from this, there is the Champions Trophy Cup held each year for the six top-ranked teams. Field hockey is also played in the Commonwealth Games. Amongst the men, India has won 8 Olympic golds and Pakistan have lifted the World Cup 4 times. Amongst the women, Australia has 3 Olympic golds while Netherlands has clinched the World Cup 6 times. Sultan Azlan Shah Hockey Tournament held annually in Malaysia is becoming a prominent Hockey Tournament where teams from around the world participate to win the cup.

# 11

# KABADDI

## INTRODUCTION

Kabaddi is a team contact sport that originated in South Asia BCE, as a form of recreational combat training. Two teams occupy opposite halves of a field and take turns sending a "raider" into the other half, in order to win points by tagging or wrestling members of the opposing team; the raider then tries to return to his own half, holding his breath and chanting "kabaddi, kabaddi, kabaddi" during the whole raid. The name — often chanted during a game — derives from a Tamil word meaning "holding of hand", which is indeed the crucial aspect of play. It is the national game of Bangladesh and the state game of Tamil Nadu, Punjab and Andhra Pradesh in India.

**Gameplay**

In the international team version of kabaddi, two teams of seven members each occupy opposite halves of

a field of 10m × 13m in case of men and 8m × 11m in case of women. Each has three supplementary players held in reserve. The game is played with 20 minute halves and a five minute halftime break during which the teams exchange sides.

Teams take turns sending a "raider" to the opposite team's half, where the goal is to tag or wrestle ("confine") members of the opposite team before returning to the home half. Tagged members are "out" and temporarily sent off the field.

Meanwhile, defenders must form a chain, for example, by linking hands; if the chain is broken, a member of the defending team is sent off. The goal of the defenders is to stop the raider from returning to the home side before taking a breath. Each time a player is out the opposing team earns a point. A team scores a bonus of two points, called a lona, if the entire opposing team is declared out. At the end of the game, the team with the most points wins. Matches are categorized based on age and weight. Six officials supervise a match: one referee, two umpires, a scorer and two assistant scorers.

## FORMS OF KABADDI

### Amar

In the 'Amar' form of Kabaddi, whenever any player is touched (out), he does not go out of the court, but stays inside, and one point is awarded to the team that touched him. This game is also played on a time basis, i.e. the time is fixed. This form of kabaddi is played in Punjab, Canada, England, New Zealand, USA, Pakistan and Australia. In the Amar form of Kabaddi, each team consists of 5–6 stoppers and 4–5 raiders. At one time, only 4 stoppers are allowed to play on the field. Every time a stopper stops the raider from going back to his starting point, that stoppers team gets 1 point. On the other hand, every time the raider tags one of the stoppers and returns to his starting point, his team gets one point.

At one time, only one of the stoppers can try.

**Sanjeevni**

In Sanjeevni Kabaddi, one player is revived against one player of the opposite team who is out, one out, one in. The duration, the number of players, dimensions of the court, etc. have been fixed by the Kabaddi Federation of India. This form of Kabaddi is the closest to the present game. In this form of Kabaddi, players are put out and revived and the game lasts 40 minutes with a 5-minute break in between. There are nine players on each side. The team that puts out all the players on the opponent's side scores four extra points for a 'Iona'. The winning team is the one that scores most points after 40 minutes. The field is bigger in this form of Kabaddi and the 'cant' different in various regions. Modern Kabaddi resembles this form of Kabaddi especially with regard to 'out & revival system' and 'Iona'. The present form of Kabaddi is a synthesis of all these forms with changes in the rules.

**Gaminee**

This is played with nine players on either side, in a field of no specific measurements. The characteristic is that a player put out has to remain out until all his team members are out. The team that is successful in putting out all the players of the opponent's side secures a point. This is akin to the present system of Iona'. After all the players are put out, the team is revived and the game continues. The game continues until five or seven 'Iona' are secured. This form of Kabaddi has no fixed game time. The main disadvantage of Gaminee is that the player is not in position to give his best performance since he is likely to remain out for the better part of the match until an Iona is scored.

## SKILLS AND TECHNIQUES

Holding breath

* Raids
* Dodging

* Movement of hand and foot
* Formation
* Safe Raid
* Holding
* Offensive Skills
* Starting a Raid
* Body Position during Raid
* Movements during Raid
* Penetration
* Misdirection
* Touching with the hand
    - o Vertical swing of arms
    - o Horizontal swing of arms
* Defensive Skills
    - o Wrist catch or Lock
    - o Crd
    - o Over the shoulder catch
    - o Ankle catch and lock
    - o Elephant stance
    - o Charging elephant
* Taunting

## RULES OF KABADDI

### RAID'S TIME

A raider shall be entitle to 30-Seconds to touch a player of the opponent team or being touched from the time he cross the gateline and back to his court. If a raider touching any defender or having touched by a defender touches the gate line with any part of his body or crosses it without infringement of these rule within 30-seconds, he shall be awarded one point. If defender (stopper) holds the raiderin his 'Fala' during and up to those 30 seconds, a point shall be awarded to the stopper. The raider has option/right to give up struggling within or the expiration of that 30 seconds period however in that case a point will be awarded to the stopper (Defender).

**Touch**

The touch means the contact by or with any part of the body of a raider or defender.

**Raid**

When a raider goes from his court into the court of the opposing team, it is called a raid. NO RAIDER SHALL BE ALLOWED TO GO AS A RAIDER MORE THAN TWO CONSECUTIVE TIMES.

**Struggle**

When a raider touches a defender or a defender touches a raider, it shall be called a struggle.

**Misconduct**

The committing of a prohibitory foul shall constitute a misconduct. Abusing and shouting onto other teammate, opponent teammate, referee, anymember of the organizing committee and member of federation constitute misconduct and there will be disciplinary action shall be taken against such player.

**Warning**

Showing of a card (Yellow, or Red) to a player by the Umpire during a match shall be treated as a warning to a player for his misconduct.

**Yellow Card**

Any player who repeats minor misconduct shall be liable for a Yellow Card. Such players shall be liable for two to five minutes suspension from the play at the discretion of the Umpire.

**Red Card**

Any player who repeats misconduct or behaves during a match or otherwise commits a major violation of these rules shall be liable for disqualification for the rest of the match/tournament at the discretion of the Umpire AND THE ONTARIO FEDERATION.

**HOLD A RAIDER**

During the struggle between Raider and the Stopper all other player of defendant return to the raider's court

until the 30 second expires. It shall be called a "hold" by the defender.

Successful Raid A successful raid shall be one when a raider, after touching any of defender reaches his court or home safely within 30 seconds.

**PLAYERS**

a. If any player played a match for any club during the season, he must play for the same club for the currency of the entire season.

b. No player shall be permitted to join and play with any other team or club or organization during the currency of the season without a written release from his respective club. The release must be signed by the Club's President and the Secretary. No club shall release any of their top Four players (top Two Raiders & Two Stoppers) to play for any other team. Federation will select top Four players from each team based on Merit (points). Top players will be considered as described in 38c & 38e. Any Two teams who participated in the Final match in the previous tournament, will not be allowed to take any released player. Any released player from any club must give priority to join the bottom team in the league. In the event, the bottom team do not wish to take the released player, then he must give priority to join the next team who is on the 2nd position from the bottom and he continues the procedure until he is signed up with a team. Released player must sign a new agreement with the new club. Player's total salary will be divided into equal payments for the total number of tournaments for the season. Any released player from any club will not be allowed at all to play for the releasing club for the entire season.

If none of the club is willing to sign up any released player for the balance of the season in that fiscal year, then the club who has released that player, must pay to the player, the amount equal to Thirty (30) percent of the remaining balance of his contract. The player must have the contract in writing to establish the appropriate amount.

c. No club shall accept any player(s) from other club whereas the player(s) has been a member of another club and he has not been fully released from his previous club. Any club that violate this rule shall be fined up to $2000.00 for a single/each violation and player could get a suspension for the entire season.

d. No club shall withhold a full release to any player(s) beyond any reason. Clubs and the player(s) have right to solve their problems among themselves. However, in case of any dispute, the Ontario Federation of Sports and Cultural Organizations has right to intervene in the matter and give their decision after hearing all related parties. The decision of the federation without prejudice shall deemed to be final.

e. Any financial dispute between releasing club and/ or the player must be sorted out among themselves before a player leaves or joins another club and at least two days prior to any tournament during the current season. No settlement shall be permitted in the field. Federation expects the full Co-operation in this matter from all the clubs.

f. Any dispute between player(s) and his club or any complaint player have against his club or dispute between Two or more clubs, that must be brought in the light of Federation at least Seven (7) daysbefore any tournament.

g. All clubs must provide the name of their players to the Federation at the time of entries/ties who lives in Canada, otherwise that player will not be allowed to play. If a player's name is given by Two teams, in that event, the President will notify the both teams. Whichever club wishes that player to play for their team, they must provide the contract to the Federation's President, signed by the player, within 24 hours once they were notified.

h. Any player who would be in breach of a contract with his club, will not be permitted to join other club until the player solves his dispute with his club and get a full release from his club (and/or federation). Whereas any kind of complaint, (including their financial payoff contracts) from the player against his club must be brought into the attention of federation to solve such dispute at least

Seven (7) days prior to any tournament to avoid any problems in the field on the day of the tournament. Panel & Executive committee reserve all rights to deliberate their final decision.

i. If through the investigation(s) and discussion(s), a player is guilty of breach of contract, then the Federation has discretion to permit (allow) such player to join other club by paying a set fine as to be determined by Federation and also payments equivalent to all monitory help his previous club had provided to the player for the season according to their contract.

j. If any club is in the breach of a contract with any player, then the matter must be brought to the Federation in writing and Federation will take views of both sides and will come up with a decision.

k. Any player who sign a contract for two clubs for the season, he will not be permitted to play in any tournament during that season.

l. A person of any race or color could participate in Kabaddi tournaments in Ontario.

m. Any player who is banned by the Ontario Sports Federation, and he wishes to play for any team/ tournament in Ontario, he must solve his dispute with local Club(s) and/or Federation at least Two (2) weeks prior to the tournament.

n. Any new player who comes to Canada to play for any individual club, and he obtain his Visa with the efforts of that individual club, in that event he must play for the same club for at least Three (3) years. The player will be free to play with any other club only if he was fully released by the same club who helped him to obtain the visa.

**NEW IMMIGRANTS**

a. New immigrant or a player with the refugee claimant status must provide a proof of their respective status to the federation two days prior to the date of first and each tournament. Refugee status must be applied before April 13th each year to be eligible to play in that year.

b. If any player's (refugee as example) claim is rejected by the Immigration, he must provide legal documents to his member club/organization for his deportation or removal order from the country so that his respective club can provide that documentation to the federation to escape from a set fine.

c. Any player who came to Canada to play Kabaddi

and/or have played on the behalf of India or Pakistan or any other country in any local or international cup and has applied as a refugee claim, he can not participate in any tournament in Ontario for 3 years.

d. All local players must represent Ontario Federation whenever required to play. If any player refuse to play on the behalf of Ont. Federation, he will be penalized for a possible suspension for up to Three (3) years or a fine of Two Thousand ($2000.00) Dollars. Any solid reason for not participating/representing federation could be considered in the federation meeting.

**GROUNDS (Kabaddi Grounds)**

a. Grounds shall be consist of a semi-soft or grassy level land. The boundary shall be drawn into a 75 Ft. semi-circle of an oval shape from the mid point for out door fields. Grounds for indoor stadiums could be adjusted accordingly with the prior approval from federation.

b. The boundary and mid-line shall be distinctly drawn in white by Three inch thick lines except the portion of mid line between the two posts which would be Four inch thick line.

c. A clear space of Thirty (30) feet shall be provided all around the play area no one will be allowed to enter during the play off.

d. In the Centre of mid - line, a Four inch thick line measuring 20 feet from inside at equal distance from both ends of the mid - line shall be demarcated to be called a 'Pala' or 'Gate-Line'.

e. Two posts, round in shape of soft or playable material with a radius of Six to Nine inches in white color shall be placed at each end of Pala or Gate-Line and these posts will not be a part of Gate-Line.

f. Raiders must stand at the side corner at the end of their respective half near the center line and opposite to their opponent team as shown in the diagram.

Stoppers must stand on the top front of the field from the center line as shown in the diagram.

g. Attached is a diagram showing measurements of the outdoor ground and positions for both Raiders & Stoppers.

**GAME**

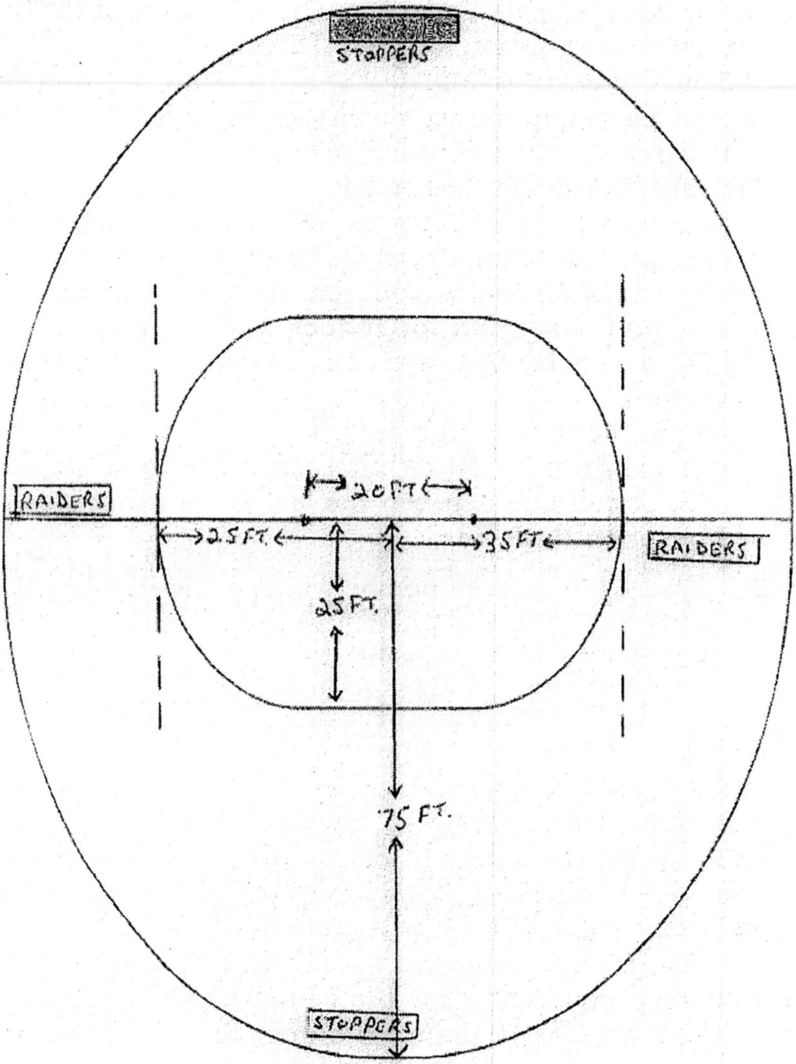

a. Kabaddi shall be played between Two teams consisting of up to Twelve (12) players (Ten participating players & Two extra or replacement players). Substitution or replacement shall only be permitted out of the list provided, at any time during the play off informing the Umpire.

b. Only one substitution for local players shall be permitted at a time during the same game. Outgoing substitute player shall not be taken in the field again in the same game. Substitution for outsider players is not permitted.

c. The duration of each league match shall be Thirty (30) minutes (e.g. 15-5-15) of actual play consisting of Two Halves of Fifteen (15) minutes each. The duration of each semi-final match shall be Thirty Five (35) minutes (e.g. 20-5-15) of actual play consisting of Two Halves. The duration offinal match shall be Forty (40) minutes (e.g. 20-5-20) of actual play consisting of Two Halves of Twenty (20) minutes each. At the half time, the teams shall change the courts and the duration of the interval shall be Five (5) minutes only.

d. The captain of the team shall: Choose the playing court side (Pala) or Raid if he wins the Toss. Be responsible to maintain the discipline in the field and take full control of his team during the play off.

e. Participating team who have less than Eight (8) players in the beginning of the match can not Enter or Replace any player before the Half time. (Except in the case of serious injury during the match, then the Federation or the Organizing committee reserve the right to exercise their options). If a replacement is permitted, the injured player will not be allowed to participate in the entire tournament on the same day.

f. The team who have less than Eight (8) players in the beginning of the match, can enter the balance of their players up to the maximum of Ten (10) players, in the

Half Time Only. If a team have less than 8 players during the match, the opponent team will be awarded with One extra point for each short player for each half of the game.

g. As soon as Umpire / Referee blow the whistle to start 2nd half of the match, no players shall be allowed to enter or replace for the rest of the match.

h. Two (2) extra players must sit on a designated spot provided at the side of their own team.

i. No team shall be allowed to enter the ground to warm up for the next match until the current match is over. The team/club will be fined Two Hundred ($200.00) dollars for the violation of this rule.

**DRESS (Langota & Shorts)**

a. Footwear will not be permitted at any time or under any circumstances during the entire game, However knee caps and anklets would be allowed. Metallic ring(s), bracelets or any kind of material which may cause injury to player or the opponent player shall not be allowed during the match.

b. Nails must be closely cut and filed prior to the matches.

c. Any kind of greasy / oily substance including Vaseline and greasy ointment, Baroza, Sticky substance, Ointment which deemed to be greasy shall be strictly prohibited on the body, hands, legs, ankles and at any part of the body before or during the match. Any infringements thereof shall be treated as a serious violation and shall be punishable amounting to a disqualification to the player for the game and player shall also face a fine of up to $1000.00 for each violation. Players shall not be permitted to play any further games until the fine is paid in full (either by the player or the club).

d. Umpires shall inspect both playing teams if it is deemed to be necessary prior to the commencement of the game and during the playoff to enforce a close observation to implicate this rule.

e. Captain of each team in the field must make an objections for any doubtful situation before starting the match. However if required organization committee and /or Federation can inspect /check Any player who repeats misconduct or behaves during a match or otherwise commits a major violation of these rules shall be liable for disqualification for the rest of the match/ tournament at the discretion of the Umpire and the Federation.

**Hold a Raider**

During the struggle between a raider and the stopper all other players of defendant team must stay at least Ten (10) feet away until point is decided. If a defender touches and keep a raider in his court and does not allow him to return to the raider's court until the 30 seconds expires, it shall be called a hold by the defender.

**Successful Raid**

A success raid shall be one a raider, after touching

any of the defender reaches his court or home safely within 30 seconds.

**CONDUCT OF PLAY: (11)**

a. A Kabbadi match shall be decided on the basis of

points of each team. The team scoring the highest points at the end of a game shall be declared winner.

b. The team winning the Toss, shall have a choice either of the court (Home) side or the first raid. In the second half of the match, the court shall be changed.

c. Arrangements for water shall be made in the clear space on the off side beyond the playing ground on the mid-line, but no player would be permitted to cross the boundary line.

d. A raider shall be allowed to touch any designated stopper player of the opposing team. All participating teams must warn their players (raiders) standing in the field that if upon touching any player of the opponent team, raider returns to his court, the raid shall be considered a successful raid and a point shall be awarded to the raider.

e. If in the opinion of the Umpire, a raider is coughed by any of the defenders of the opposing team and is unable to get out of his grip and raider signals his inability to struggle further, the Umpire shall give the point to the defender's team. 25f. If during a raid or struggle, or if there is no contact, a raider or any of the defenders goes out of the ground, the one who goes out first loses a point. If both of them go out simultaneously, no point shall be scored by any of the teams.

g. During a raid, no raider shall be cautioned by any of his own team players, otherwise the Umpire shall award a point to the defenders team. No coaching from outside shall be allowed by coaches or outside players during a play.

h. The officials of federation, one Coach and one Manager of each participating team and medical team shall be allowed inside, but at a distance of 20 feet from the boundary of the ground during the course of the game.

i. If a raider having been touched or held by any of

the defenders fails to reach his court or fails to touch the mid-line inside the pala within a struggle the defending team shall score a point.

j. No team shall delay any raid. A team taking more than 5 seconds to send raider when asked to do so by the Umpire, shall be liable to concede one point to opposing team at the discretion of the Umpire.

k. A raid having been commenced before the end of half time or close of the play shall be completed even if the time runs out during the raid.

l. In case of struggle between a raider and any of the player of the opposing team, the remaining players shall be passive temporarily and keep themselves out of the raider's way until the point is decided. If any other player of the defending teal causes any obstruction, the raider's team shall be awarded a point.

m. No other member of the federation of both participating teams in the game shall be allowed to enter in the field during the play off until the match completed.

n. First point shall be considered to be a One and a Half (1.5) point awarded to a successful raider or stopper to prevent for extra time to be given at the end of the match to decide a winner.

o. Before the end of the entire match, the Umpires will announce Two final raids from each club.

p. All Raiders from both teams must stand in the designated area for the Raiders as described in the Sketch of Kabaddi Ground.

q. A Raider must only raid on the designated stoppers as designated in the Sketch of Kabaddi Ground.

r. Any raider may also play as a stopper, as long as he joins the designated stoppers of his own team prior to the opponent raider reaches the area for designated stoppers.

**FOULS**

The followings shall be considered as fouls or illegal

tackers:

1. Twisting of the wrest, neck or ankle.
2. Strangling.
3. Gagging / Throttling.
4. Striking with the head.
5. Kicking, biting, scratching and tripping from behind.
6. Hitting with the fists.
7. Slapping with open palm or both hands.
8. Holding from costume or hair
9. Violent tacking leading to injury to the body.
10. Applying flying scissors without body hold.
11. Using abusive language, indicating words, or insulting words, etc.
12. Striking players head to the ground.
13. No player allowed to pock in the eyes.

Any players who commit these fouls shall be penalized by awarding one point to the opposite team, and also liable for further disciplinary action.

**OFFICIALS**

There shall be Two Umpires, Three scorers (One from executive member of organizing committee and One from each participating club), One coach & One manager of each team permitted during a play in the field. All others shall be required to leave the ground immediately after Umpire commence to begin the match. No supporters or any person other than the designated officials shall be permitted in the ground at half time break.

**UMPIRES**

a. There shall be two Umpires in each game. Each Umpire shall take one side of the field for the entire match.

b. The match shall start with a blow of the whistle by the Umpire. He will also blow the whistle for intervals, restart and for ending the match.

c. If there is a objection about any point, the Umpires

will discuss the objection among themselves and give the decision to the federation and that decision will be final. Objections could only be made by the team Coach or the team Manager during the match.

d. There will be a team of Six designated Umpires on the list. Each Umpire will be awarded money for Umpiring the match and the organizing committee shall be responsible to pay the money to Umpires as soon as their tournament is finished. The amount for Umpires will be decided each year between the Umpires & Federation prior to the commencement of the seasonal

**FINE TO THE TEAMS WHO DO NOT PLAYING OR SHOW UP LATE**

Any club who enter their team for any tournament before the ties take place and do not play during the tournament, such club will face a fine for a maximum of Five Hundred ($500.00) Dollars payable to the Ontario Federation of Sports and Cultural Organization.

Any team showing up late by more than Thirty (30) minutes from the scheduled time to play, (unless the weather is not suitable to play) will be penalized as follows: "A" team will pay Two Hundred Dollars ($200.00) fine.

"B" team will pay Two Hundred Dollars ($200.00) fine.

"C" team will pay Fifty Dollars ($50.00) fine.

In the event it is a rainy day, the federation will make decision to either continue or stop the tournament. The above mentioned fines shall be payable to the Ontario Federation and must be paid prior to the next tournament..

**USE OF INTOXICATION MATERIAL**

Players and Federation Officials and Umpires are strictly prohibited to Use or Consume any kind of alcohol, drugs, any toxic material during the tournament. Any player, official, Umpire or any person observed to be using Alcohol, Drugs are subject to the suspension from the entire match.

**BEST RAIDER AND BEST STOPPER**

a. One best Raider and One best Stopper will be selected for the Ontario League who could be any (local or outsider) player And One best Raider and One best Stopper will be selected from the local players. To select a best raider and a best stopper for the season and to qualify for the merit of best raider and best stopper, a player must have participated and played 75% of all tournaments organized under the supervision of the federation in Ontario only.

b. The average + percentage (%) of all points attained in all matches in all tournaments by an individual player will be calculated. Conduct, Behavior, Discipline and Co-Operation of all participating players towards the fellow Players, Umpires, Federation and the Organizing Committee will be judged by federation executive committee during the whole season and will be awarded Merit and De-Merit points and reflect the total percentage points to qualify a player to be announced the Best Raider and Best Stopper.

c. The Raiders shall be divided into Three (A, B & C) Categories. The Raider who is successful to earn more than 80% points from his total raids, will be designated as a "A" player. The Raider who is successful to earn 50% to 79.99% points from his total raids, will be designated as a "B" player.

The Raider who is successful to earn under 50% points from his total raids, will be designated as a "C" player.

d. The attainder of higher percentage points aggregated out of maximum successful raids and the conduct of play during whole season in all tournaments shall be declared the Best Raider.

e. The Stopper who make successful stops to "A" raider will be awarded with Five (5) points, and successful stops to "B" raider will be awarded with Three (3) points and successful stops to "C" raider will be awarded with One (1) point. The attainder of higher percentage points aggregated out of maximum successful stops to the Raiders and the conduct of play during the whole season in all tournaments shall be declared the Best Stopper.

f. The Best Raider will receive a Plaque and Two Hundred Dollars ($200.00) from the Federation.

g. The Best Stopper will receive a Plaque and Two Hundred Dollars ($200.00) from the Federation.

**WEIGHING THE PARTICIPATING TEAMS:**

All players participating in "B" or "C" team must take their weight at 11 a.m. in presence of Federation Officials on the day of the tournament. It is the responsibility of all participating players and their Two clubs officials to be present at that time.

If any player is late to take weight, he must pay $50.00 per hour late fine to the federation to have his weight taken after the originally scheduled time. First time, all "B" and "C" team players will take their weights in the First tournament and second time their weight will be taken on the Fourth (4th) tournament regardless of any circumstances.

e.g. : out of total Eight (8) tournaments, weight will be taken on First (1st) and Fourth (4th) tournament only. In the event any player joins the team/club after these scheduled weight days, OR did not qualify on these dates and wishes to play in the next tournament, his weight will be taken on the tournament day at 11 a.m. and fine will apply to him if he shows up later than 11 a.m. on the tournament day.

**WEIGHT MACHINE/ SCALE**

Federation will provide the weight machine/scale during tournaments. Federation will have Two (2) machines, if one is broken, then the federation will provide the 2nd machine. In the event, the machine is broker during taking the weights, then all players must take their weights again on the new machine.

Federation's Executive Committee will decide on the approval of the machine.

**QUALIFICATION FOR LOCAL PLAYERS**

In order to qualify as a local player, he must live permanently in Ontario for at least Eleven (11) months in a fiscal year, except the time he was out of country or in India. If any objection arises about his residency, and the player claims that he was out of country, he must provide a proof of Immigration Stamps on his passport and/or a used airline ticket, along with proof of address in Ontario, Banking Records, Work Records, Tax Return, Health Card, Driving Licence etc.

If any player brake this rule, his parent club will be fined up to Five Thousand Dollars ($5000.00) and the player will not be allowed to play in Ontario unless the player pays the fine of $5000.00 to his club which was paid by his club to the federation.

Any person of any race or color could participate as a player in any tournament in Ontario.

Refugee claimants in Quebec will be considered as local players in Ontario.

If any player played as a local player in B.C. or anywhere in Canada or in U.S.A., he will be considered as a outsider player. Ontario Federation will correspond with B.C. Sports Federation to obtain/confirm the list of their local players.

Junior Team: The player of the junior team could be up to 12 years of age in the currency of the same year when he wishes to participate as a player. e.g.: to participate in year 2002, the player must be born in 1990 or after. Each player's weight must not exceed 100 Lbs. to qualify to participate.

**TOURNAMENT EVENTS**

To hold a tournament event, the organizing

committee must receive entries from at least Three (3) teams for that particular event. If Three teams wishes to participate in a tournament, the tournament committee must organize that event. If there are less than Three teams, then that event will not take place during that tournament. Any teams who wishes to participate in tournaments, must inform the Federation by the end of April of the fiscal year.

**INTERNATIONAL TOURNAMENT**

To qualify to hold International Tournament, the Club must have participated in 51% of tournaments with "A" or "B" team from the time of applying for the tournament. This 51% condition is in effect after year 2004.

Ticket price and Prizes for International tournament in Ontario must be discussed every year with the Ontario Federation of Sports. Organizing tournament committee must provide reasonable proof to the federation to set the ticket price.

Coach/Manager will not be selected from the same club, for the International tournament in Ontario, who is hosting the International Tournament in the same year.

International Tournament Committee must provide light Refreshments, Soft Drinks (Juice, Gatorade etc.), Tea, Fruit, Submarines at about 5 p.m. to the team Manager / Coach . Team

Manager/Coach must provide a list of Food / Drink items to the tournament committee by 11 a.m. on the day of tournament.

# 12

# KHO-KHO

## INTRODUCTION

Kho Kho is an Indian and Pakistani sport played by teams of twelve players who try to avoid being touched by members of the opposing team, only 9 players of the team enter the field. Kho Kho and Kabaddi, in spite of popular misconception, are not the same.

In Kho-Kho, one team sits or kneels in the middle of the court, in a row, with alternate members in the row facing opposite directions. The other team may send two or three members in the court. The motive for the sitting team is to try to "tag" the opponents. The chasers can only run in one direction and cannot cut across the sitters unlike the dodgers who can run randomly and in between the sitters. They have to run round the entire row to reach the other side. The other option is to pass the chasing job to another sitter whose back is facing the chaser as the chaser is running. In this option, the chaser touches the sitter he wants ,usually nearest to the target and shouts "kho" to signify the change of guard. The objective is to tag all the opponents in the shortest time possible. The team that

takes the shortest time to tag all the opponents in the field, wins.

Kho-Kho ranks as one of the most popular traditional sports in India. The origin of Kho-Kho is difficult to trace, but many historians believe, that it is a modified form of `Run Chase`, which in its simplest form involves chasing and touching a person. With its origins in Maharashtra, Kho-Kho in ancient times, was played on `raths` or chariots, and was known as Rathera.

Kho-Kho Like all Indian games, it is simple, inexpensive and enjoyable. It does, however, demand physical fitness, strength, speed and stamina, and a certain amount of ability. Dodging, feinting and bursts of controlled speed make this game quite thrilling. To catch by pursuit - to chase, rather than just run - is the capstone of Kho-Kho. The game develops qualities such as obedience, discipline, sportsmanship, and loyalty between team members.

The rules of the game were framed in the beginning of the 20th century. At Gymkhana Poona, a Committee was formed in 1914, to frame its rules. The first ever rules on Kho-Kho were published from Gymkhana Baroda, in 1924. In 1959-60, the first national Kho-Kho championship was organised in Vijayawada (Andhra Pradesh). The Government has initiated the following awards for the game: Arjuna Award, Eklavya Award for men, Rani Laxmi Bai award for women, Veer Abhimanyu award for boys under 18, and Janaki award for girls under 16.

How the game is played Each team consists of twelve players, but only nine players take the field for a contest. A match consists of two innings. An innings consists of chasing and running turns of 7 minutes each. Eight members of the chasing team sit in their eight squares on the central lane, alternately facing the opposite direction, while the ninth member is an active chaser,

and stands at either of the posts, ready to begin the pursuit. Members of the chasing team have to put their opponent out, touching them with their palms, but without committing a foul. All the action in Kho-Kho is provided by the defenders, who try to play out the 7 minutes time, and the chasers who try to dismiss them. A defender can be dismissed in three ways: 1) if he is touched by an active chaser with his palm without committing a foul, 2) if he goes out of the limits on his own, 3) if he enters the limit late. Defenders enter the limit, in batches of three. After the third and last defender of batch is out, the next batch must enter the limits, before a `kho` is given by the successful active chaser. Defenders have full freedom of movement on both sides of the central lane, but the active chaser cannot change the direction to which he is committed. He cannot cross the central lane. An active chaser can change position with a seated chaser, by touching him from behind by palm, and uttering the word `kho` loudly, and simultaneously, chase or attack is build up through a series of `khos` as the chase continues with a relay of chasers.

At the end of the innings there is an interval of 5 minutes and an interval of 2 minutes, in between the turns. Each side alternates between chasing and defence. Kho-Kho can be played by men, women, and children of all ages. The game requires a very small piece of evenly surfaced ground, rectangular in shape, and 27m by 15m. The only equipment required are the two poles. The game lasts no more than 37 minutes.

## RULES OF KHO KHO

### KHO-KHO GROUND

**1. Endline**

The lines AB and CD running parallel to each other and equal in length to the length

of the Kho Kho fi eld are known as ENDLINES.

Note: Measurement of ENDLINES for: 14 Mts.

**2. Sidelines**

The lines AD and BC running parallel to each other and equal in length to the length

of the Kho Kho fi eld are known as SIDELINES.

Note: Measurement of SIDELINES for: - 20 Metres 20 Centimetres

**3. Field**

The limits of the Kho Kho fi eld are formed by meeting the Endlines and Sidelines at

ABC&D.

**4. Court**

The area between the post lines formed by points EFGH is known as COURT.

**5. Posts**

Two strong wooden posts, smooth all over 120 to 125 cms. Above and perpendicular to the ground, fi xed fi rmly in the free zone at tangent to the Post Lines at M and N are known as POSTS. The points M and N shall coincide with centre of the posts and shall be at a distance exactly half the width of the Kho kho Court. Their diameter shall be uniform throughout and shall measure between 9 and 10 Cms.

***Note:*** The POSTS shall not be taper. Top of the Posts shall be free from any sharp edges.

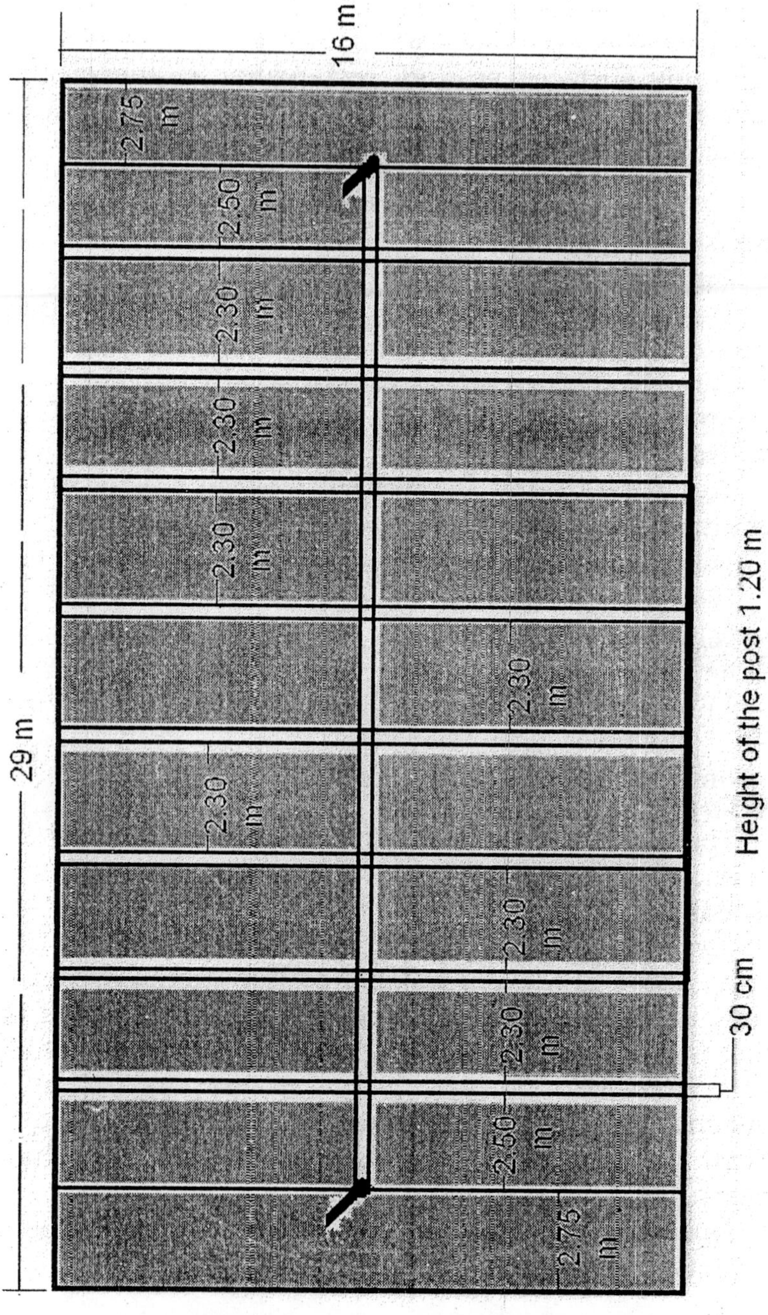
16 m
29 m
2.75 m
2.50 m
2.30 m
2.30 m
2.30 m
2.30 m
2.30 m
2.30 m
2.30 m
2.50 m
2.75 m
Height of the post 1.20 m
30 cm

**6. Central Lane**

CENTRAL LANE is a rectangle in between two Posts measuring 30Cms. × length of the court which divides the Court into two equal halves and forms Square at the intersection of Cross Lanes.

***Note:*** The length of the Central Lane: 10.70 Mts.

**7. Cross Lane**

Each of the rectangles measuring 30 Cms. x width of the court that intersects the Central Lane at right angle is known as CROSS LANE.

**8. Square**

The area 30 Cms. x 30 Cms. formed by the intersection of the Central Lane and the Cross Lane is known as a SQUARE.

**9. Lines of the Posts**

The lines which are at right angles to the Central Lane and run parallel to the Cross Lane at tangent to the Posts are known as Line of the Post or Post Lines (EF & GH).

**10. Free Zone**

The remaining portion of the fi eld on either end of the Court is known as FREE ZONE.

**11. Lobby**

The area surrounding the fi eld by a measure of 1.5 Mts. in width is known as LOBBY.

**12. Width of the Line**

Width of each line should be around 3 Cms. To 5 Cms. and is included in all measurements.

**13. Entry Zone**

The area marked in the lobby parallel to the Side Line and in the both side of Scorer's table with the outer line of the lobby measuring 1 Mt. in width and from Post Line to 3rd. Cross Lane in length is known as ENTRY ZONE. It is meant for the Runners to take entry to the fi eld for defence.

**14. Sitting Block**

Sitting Block for Reserve Players, Coach & Manager

shall be either side of the Field just outside of the Lobby adjacent to the end lines.

**15. Chasers**

The players who chase the opponents with a view to put out them and at the same time score points are known as CHASERS.

**16. Attacker**

A player who pursues the players of the opposite side i.e., defenders with a view to tag and touch them is known as an ATTACKER.

**17. Runners**

The players of the side other than the Chasers are known as RUNNERS.

**18. Defenders**

The runners who are inside the fi eld foe their turn of defence are known as DEFENDERS.

**19. To Give Kho**

To give KHO an Attacker should touch the Chaser by hand from behind him and then utter the word "KHO" loudly and distinctly.

Note: If the action of uttering the word "Kho" precedes the action of touching by hand, then it shall be deemed as a foul. Simultaneous action of touching and uttering "KHO" is not a foul. Single action of touching will not be deemed as foul. However, uttering "KHO" will be considered as foul. If an Attacker touches a chaser sitting in the Square nearest the Posts, "KHO", shall be given. If an Attacker utters any word other than the word "KHO" it will be deemed as a foul. Also uttering the word "KHO" or any other word resembling the word "KHO" by any of the Chasers will be treated as foul.

**20. Foul**

If an Attacker or a Chaser violates any Rules, it is known as a Foul.

**21. To Take a Direction**

When an Attacker goes from one Post line to another

Post line and/or after getting a Kho, he goes towards a particular Post line he is said to have taken a direction.

**22. Shoulder Line**

An imaginary line running through the centre of the shoulders of an Attacker is known as SHOULDER LINE.

**23. To Recede**

When as Attacker while going to a particular direction, touches the ground which he had already covered, he is said to have receded.

Explanation: The Ground Covered will always refer to ground covered by Rear foot in opposite direction.

**24. To Leave the Free Zone**

When an Attacker loses contact of his feet with the Free Zone and comes in contact with the Court with his feet, he is said to have left the Free Zone.

**25. To Reach the Free Zone**

When an Attacker loses contact of his feet, with the Court and comes in contact with the ground of the Free Zone by his feet he is said to have reached the Free Zone.

**26. Out of Field**

If a defender loses contact of his feet with the Field and comes outside, he is said to have gone OUT OF FIELD.

**27. Entry**

A runner is said to have entered the Field as soon as he loses the contact with the ground outside the Field with his feet and comes in contact with the ground inside the Field with his foot.

**PART-2**

**RULES OF THE GAMES**

1. The play ground (FIELD) shall be marked as shown in Part 1

2. Referee shall call both the captains for the spin of the coin (TOSS). He shall instruct one of them to call the choice of the side of the coin. He shall then declare the winner of the TOSS.

Referee shall stand at the centre of the court FACING the scoring table with Captains on either side.

B. Any 5 chasers shall occupy the Square facing the Side Lines in such a way that no adjacent chasers face the same Side Line.

The 6th chaser shall stand in either of the Free Zone to start the chase.

A. At the commencement of the turn, the fi rst batch of two Defenders shall be inside the limits (Field) and the remaining Runners shall occupy the seats meant for them.

B. After a Defender is out he shall occupy the seat meant for him.

C. After commencement of the turn, no chaser shall leave the Square without getting Kho or change the face. If he does so, it is a Foul and repetition of the same will amount to misbehavior.

3. An Attacker, as a rule, shall not cross the Central Lane to go to the other half of the court or to the Free Zone.

Crossing/touching of Central Lane by any part of the body except note is an offence. It shall be treated as Foul.

4. If a Kho is to be given, it shall be given from behind a Chaser. It shall be given in a suffi ciently loud tone so that the Defenders and the offi cials can hear. The Chaser shall not get up without getting Kho.

Note: A. An Attacker shall not give Kho by touching the arm or leg or any part of the body extended or tilled towards him by a Chaser.

B. To give Kho touching on the back of the Chaser should not be insisted upon.

5. After giving a Kho, an Attacker shall cease to be so and shall sit down immediately in the Square of the Chaser to whom he has given a Kho.

B. The natural time needed to sit on the Square after giving Kho must be allowed. However, this should not obstruct the game of Defender. If he does so it should be declared as Foul.

6. After getting a Kho Chaser will immediately be an Attacker and shall go to the half that he is facing and shall go in the direction which he has taken by going the Cross Lane or turning his shoulder towards any of the Posts. An Attacker shall take the direction according to one of the actions, which ever he has performed fi rst.

B. Defender shall be declared "OUT", if an Attacker puts him out (touches him) before leaving the SQUARE without committing foul.

7. An Attacker shall take the Direction to which he turns his Shoulder Line. When Attacker, while going in a particular direction, turns his shoulder line through more than a right angle to the direction which he has already taken it shall be a Foul.

8. Once an Attacker has taken a direction, he shall go in that direction till he reaches the Free Zone unless he gives a Kho before that. An Attacker shall not go to the other half of the court unless he turns around the Post through the Free Zone.

9. If an Attacker leaves the Free Zone, he shall go in the direction of the other Free Zone, remaining on that half of the Court where he was, when he left the Free Zone.

10. The rules about taking the direction and receding shall not be applicable in the Free Zone.

11. The chaser shall sit in a manner which shall not obstruct the Defenders. If a defender becomes out by such an obstruction he shall not be declared out.

B. The ACTION of moving/tilting shoulder thigh or any other part of the body towards a Defender who is running near the Central Lane and closer to a chaser shall be treated as a "FOUL".

12. During a turn, an Attacker may go out of court but he shall observe all the rules, about taking a direction

and receding even when he is out of court.

**Explanation**

The word "court" is to be noted. Rules of court are applicable within the area covered by or between the EXTENDED POST LINES.

Attacker will be allowed to enter the Field/Court as he wants, if he goes out of Court beyond the extended post line. He shall not be insisted to enter through the Free Zone.

13. A Defender shall not touch a Chaser. If he does so he shall be warned once in a turn. If he repeats the same, he shall be declared out.

Note: Warning to the Defender should be recorded in the Remarks Column of the Score Sheet.

14. A defender shall be declared out, if he is touched by hand by an Attacker without violating any rule or if he goes out of Field. He shall be declared out by a short blow of the whistle.

B. While chasing a Defender, if an Attacker pushes the said Defender out of field, the Defender shall NOT BE DECLARED OUT.

C. If a defender goes out of field he shall be declared out.

15. An Attacker and the Chasers shall not violate any of the rules pertaining to them.

It shall be a Foul if any rule is violated.

Note: A. If a Defender is put out as a result of such a Foul or if Foul is committed immediately as a result of the action taken in putting a defender out, the Defender shall not be declared out. The protection from being out due to a foul is applicable to the Defender who was being actually chased at the time of committing foul.

B. At the time of "Touching At Post" (POLE DIVE), dragging of rear leg and turning of shoulder line more than 90 degree will not be a foul but touching and/or crossing the Central Lane by any part of the body will be a Foul. In this case shoulder line foul should be ignored.

16. If an Attacker violates any of the rules, the Umpire shall declare a foul by blowing a short whistle continuously and shall immediately compel the Attacker to go in a direction opposite to that of which he is going. Immediately on hearing a signal given by the Umpire by his whistle, the Attacker shall take the direction indicated by the Umpire and if the Defender, being chased at that time, thereby becomes out he shall not be declared out and the Attacker shall have to follow the direction indicated by the Umpire, he need not give Kho.

**17. Advantage Rule**

If a foul committed by either the Attacker or chaser does not give any advantage whatsoever to the chasing side in their chase and disadvantage to the Defenders, it shall not be declared by the continuous short blast on whistle.

**PART-3**

**RULES ABOUT MATCHES**

1. Each team will consist of One Manager cum coach and 7 players for competition. Five players will be named for a match, only two players shall be Reserve .

2. A. An inning will consist of a chasing and defending turns which shall be of 5 minutes each for. Each match will consist of 2 innings. There shall be an interval of 5 minutes after an inning and 2 minutes break between turns for boys and girls. At the beginning of a turn 2 runners shall be inside the Field for defence.

Immediately on these 2 defenders being declared out, the next 2 runners shall be inside the Field before 2 Khos are given. Those runners who fail to enter within the period shall be declared out. The runners who may enter early shall not be declared out but called back.

2. B. Time to enter the Field (TWO CORRECT KHOS) is given to Runner. Hence Defender who is inside the

Field can be chased after One Correct Kho is given.

To Chase a new batch two Khos should not be insisted.

As soon as 1st Defender of a batch is out, the next two Runners must enter the Entry Zone.

Referee shall have the option to declare out Runners of the next batch, who have not entered the fi eld after two correct Kho's are given.

An Attacker shall not pursue a new batch after the last Defender of a batch is out in whichever manner. He must give Kho.

Runners who enter early shall be called back by the Referee.

3. The captain of the chasing team shall have the option to end the turn before the allotted time. He shall inform the Referee about the same by raising his arm and request him to stop the turn until the Referee has signaled to stop the turn, the turn is not closed. The chasing side shall not leave the Squares until the Referee has declared the turn as closed.

4. The chasing side shall score one point for each Defender out. If all six Runners are out before the completion of the turn they shall maintain the same order of defence. Order of the Runners shall not be changed during a turn.

5. In the knock out matches the side that scores more points at the end of the match shall be declared as winner. If the points are equal one more inning (one turn for each side as chasers and runners) shall be played. If again the points are equal an additional inning shall be played on minimum chase basis as follows: Referee will start the turn of his additional inning.

6. If a match is not completed for any reason, it shall be continued further at another time with the same players and the same offi cials, provided it is played in the same session, the scorers of the completed turns, of

each side shall be counted the match being continued, from the beginning of the incomplete turn.

**Clarification**

Option to give "follow on" is restricted upon 9 points only. It will be mandatory to give "follow on" if the difference is more than 9 points. In case of "follow on" the Result will be won by "an inning".

**8. Substitution**

Any number of substitutions can be allowed by the Referee on the request of Coach or Captain.

A. For chasing turn at any time during the match.

B. For Runners substitution is allowed only before they enter the field.

Note: A. During substitution the substituted chaser shall not enter the field, unless the outgoing chaser comes out of the field.

B. Substituted attacker shall not pursue the defenders directly. He must give a Kho.

**PART-4**

**OFFICIALS FOR THE MANAGEMENT OF MATCH (AUTHORITY DUTY AND RIGHTS)**

The following offi cials shall be appointed for the management of a match:

A Referee, Two Umpires, a Timekeeper and One Scorer.

**REFEREE**

1 The referee shall perform the following duties.

A. He shall check the score sheets, ground etc., and take the toss before starting the match. He shall help the umpires, to perform their duties and shall give his final decision in case of any difference between them.

B. If a player intentionally obstructs the conduct of the play or behaves in an ungentlemanly or mischievous manner or intentionally violates any of the rules, the Referee shall at his discretion penalize the defaulting players. The penalty at his discretion shall range, according to the default from warning a defaulting player or the entire team to participate in further play of the match.

C. He shall announce the warning by calling the chest number of runner or chaser and showing a "Yellow" Card. It shall be recorded by the Scorer-1 by marking the chestnumber in warning column. He shall announce the forbiddance from the participation in future play in similar way as warning but showing a "Red" Card. This will also be recorded by the Scorer-1 by marking the "F" against the chest number in defence column. Such a player shall be immediately replaced and asked to leave the arena.

**2. Umpire**

The Umpire shall move in the lobby and shall conduct the games. For any reasons, if he enters the field, he shall come back to the lobby immediately without obstructing the progress of the match. He shall give decisions and also help the other Umpire to give correct decisions. The Umpire shall declare a foul and compel the Attacker to act up to the rules, if the latter does not follow the rules.

**3. Time Keeper**

The Time Keeper shall start the turn by blowing a long whistle followed by a short after getting direction from the Referee. The end of the turn shall be declared by him by blowing a long whistle. He shall enter the lobby and declare the completion of each minute of play loudly by raising his arm holding an indicator.

**4. Scorer**

Scorer-1 shall note down and check the names and numbers of the players, shall record the performance of the players. At the end of the match he shall prepare the scores of the two sides and the Result of the match. He shall get the score sheets duly signed by all offi cials. After completing the score sheet he shall hand over to the Referee for checking and declaration of the result.

Scorer-2 shall record the order of the Defenders. He shall keep a record of the Defenders who are out and make them sit in the place provided for them. He shall execute the process of substitution and shall note down with scorer.

1. After the start of the match, if any of the offi cials is unable to offi ciate, the remaining officials shall manage the officiating till the end of the turn. If the official is unable to resume the work, he shall be replaced by a new official.

2. The officials of the match shall be appointed by the competent authority and shall function under the guidance of Referee.

**PART- 5**

**RULES ABOUT PLAYERS/ MANAGERS/COACHES**

**1. Players Uniform**

Uniform of a Kho-Kho player shall include spots/ canvas shoes (free from any metal part anywhere that may cause injury) short and vest (half sleeves) or "T-shirt" for men and Boys: shirt or "T-shirt" for women and girls.

Each player shall be numbered in front and back of his "T" shirt/shirts with number of solid color contrasting with the color of "T" shirt. The number shall be printed/stitched of size 10 cms. High and 2 cms. Wide on the back (contravention) on the lesser size will be treated as misbehavior. The numbers shall be printed to 1 to 15.

Players of the same side shall neither wear duplicate a tournament/championship. (In case the need arises. Referees will allow change of chest numbers).

Manager shall furnish scorer-1 the list of players and chest numbers.

**2. Rights & Duties of Players**

a All players must know the rules of the game and abide by the rules.

b During the game, a player may address the referee only through the team captain; the team captain may address the referee and shall be the spokesman for his players. He may also address the other offi cials but only on matters concerning their duties.

**3. Conduct of Players/Substitutes/Coaches and Managers**

The managers, Coaches & Substitutes shall sit in the place provided for them.

The following acts, are punishable:

a) Persistent addressing of officials concerning their decision.

b) Making derogatory remarks to officials.

c) Committing actions tending to influence decisions of the offi cials.

d) Making derogatory acts or personal remarks to the opponents.

e) Deliberate coaching during the game from outside the ground.

**4. Penalties**

a. For a minor offence, such as talking to opponents, spectator or offi cials, shouting, etc., a verbal warning will be given by the Referee. In case of repetition of the offence warning will be given by showing a yellow card.

b. For a serious offence, Referee may disqualify the concerned players and others from rest of the match by showing a red card.

If a player is shown red card in a match he shall be forbidden from the participation for the rest of the match and for next match also of that particular tournament. As mentioned in the rule 1, 2, 3, of Part 5 shall be taken by an Umpire and/or Referee.

The concerned shall report the matter in writing to the proper Authority (in charge of officials, Observer, Organizing Secretary, Convener, Referees Board of respective Federation/Association, Secretary General.

# 13

# SWIMMING

## INTRODUCTION

Swimming for leisure has become tremendously popular since late in the last century. The first municipal pool in the United States was built in Brookline, Massachusetts, in 1887. Soon after that, New York City built public facilities, then called baths. In the 1920s, the first boom for swimming pools occurred, with several thousand pools built in this country. At the same time, there was a great rise in estate pools, as residential pools were then called.

**SWIMMING AS A SPORT**

The development of swimming as a sport is closely connected with the further development of the capitalist mode of production. Great Britain, the most highly developed industrial state in the 19th century, became the "mother country" of modern sport. At first it was a privilege enjoyed exclusively by the ruling class, i.e., the bourgeoisie. Being forced to work twelve to fourteen hours a day it was practically impossible for the proletariat to engage in sports and on the other hand the sports clubs protected themselves against an influx

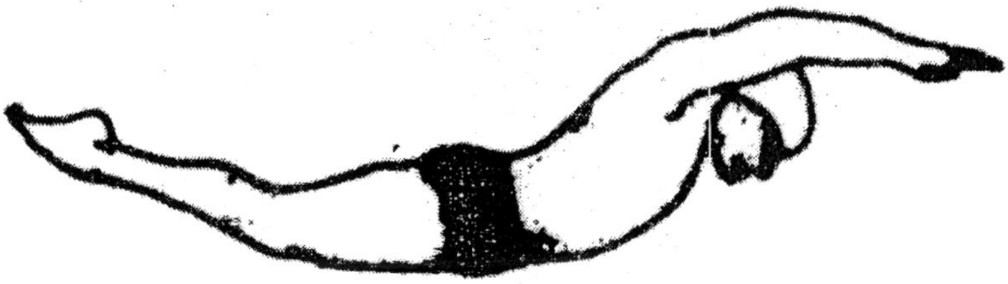

of workers by imposing high membership fees and restrictive provisions in their articles of association.

Only towards the end of the 19th century, when the working people had managed to get their working hours reduced and when extensive exploitation was replaced more and more by intensive exploitation as a result of rationalized production, did working people start going in for sports. Swimming became a popular sport among the working people because it entails little expense and brings a great deal of enjoyment. The sport began to spread also in other industrial countries in Europe. Manifold forms of physical training, which had been created by the people but which had been more or less suppressed or forgotten over prolonged periods, were modified and organized under the influence of capitalist development. Many sports clubs were also founded in Germany towards the end of the 19th century.

Swimming became an increasingly popular sport, especially among young people. The people's growing interest in this sport was also stimulated by the building of swimming pools and improved methods used in teaching swimming.

At the end of the 19th century the bourgeois swimming associations, following the example of other sports, united into a world federation. FINA (Federation Internationale de Nation Amateur) was founded in London in 1908. It consisted of ten national swimming associations. In the course of time FINA has developed into one of the world's biggest sports federations. At present it is composed of over 100 national swimming associations irrespective of the forms of state or society of the member countries.

The sports which have crystallized i the course of development of aquatic sports are swimming, waster polo, diving and synchronized swimming. The first three swimming sports are included in the programme of

Olympic events, swimming having been added to the Olympic events list in 1896 (the first Olympic Games), water polo in 1900 and high diving in 1904.

Continental federations were formed within FINA in order to stimulate international competitions. They include LEN (Ligue Europenne de Nation) which was founded in 1927 and whose members include the GDR's Deutcher Schwimmsport-Verb and, which joined LEN in 1952.

FINA's main tasks are to organize and monitor international swimming competitions (Olympic Games, world and continental cup competitions), to issue uniform statutes and rules of competition and to keep a list of world and continental records.

**SWIMMING STROKES**

**Butterfly Butterfly** is a stroke in which the swimmer

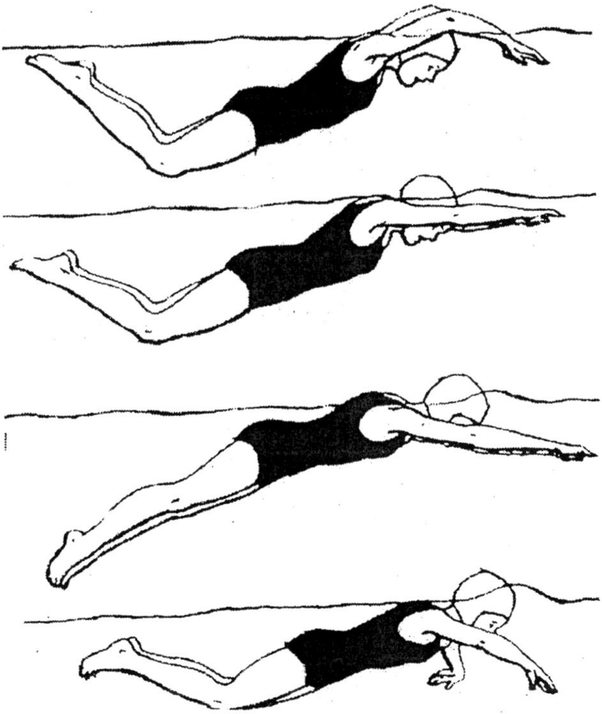

brings both hands over their head close to the water, breathing forward, "Dolphin kicking" (undulating) with both feet together in sequence, two kicks per arm stroke. All walls must be touched with two hands at the same time.

**Backstroke Backstroke** is a stroke which is similar to the front crawl, except on your back. Kicking by alternating both feet, pulling each arm one at a time, and looking straight up. At walls, flip turns are permitted, and a two-hand touch is not necessary.

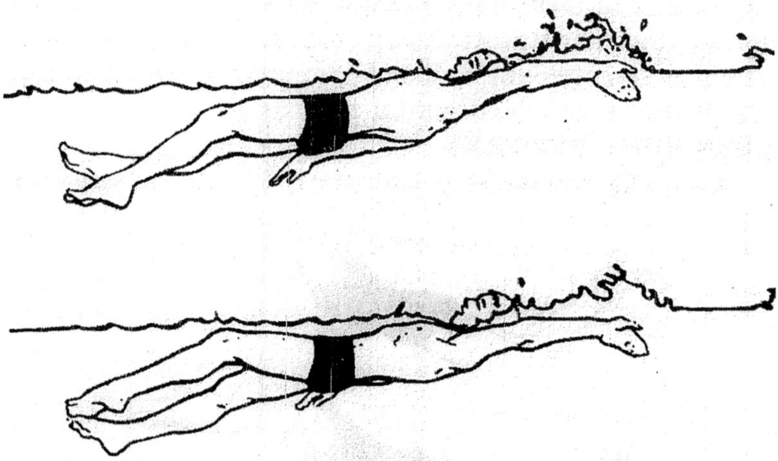

**Breaststroke** is a stroke where the swimmer kicks legs out (much like a frog, but more whip like), scoops the water in towards the chest with his or her hands and then thrusts the hands out in front just before the kick is repeated. One underwater "pull-out" is permitted after every wall, with a streamline glide, dolphin kick, and one kick to the surface. Each wall requires a two-hand (simultaneous) touch.

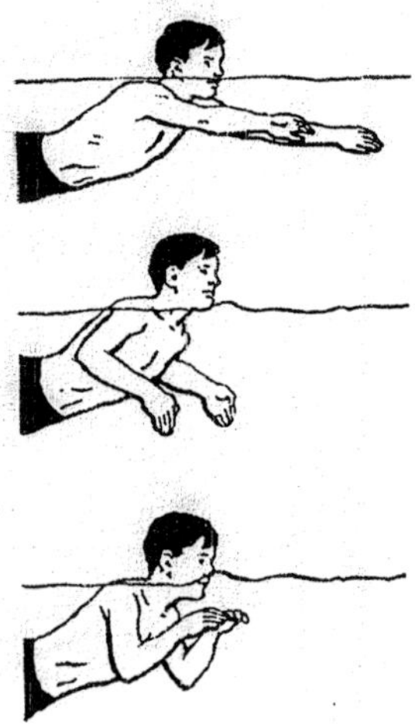

**Freestyle** is a not a defined stroke as the others are. However, as swimmers are free to choose any stroke they wish, most select the Front Crawl, as it is both the fastest and most efficient. The front crawl is a stroke where the swimmer breathes to the side, kicks by alternating both legs, and pulls with each arm at different times. Flip turns are legal. Many meets also include free relays, in which four team members each swim an equal distance of freestyle; when one member touches the wall, the next can dive off the block.

IM IM stands for individual medley, and includes, in this order: fly, back, breast, free. Open turns are required in the switch from one stroke to another, but flip turns can be made during back and free. Each stroke must be completed before moving on to the next stroke.

25:100 is the ratio for the amount swam for each stroke. 25 yards stroke to each 100 total. Many meets also include medley relays, in which four team members each swim one stroke, in the order of back, breast, fly, free. Other IM events are a 200, and 400 which is the same except that in a 200 it is 2 laps of each stroke and 400 is 4 laps of each stroke. In the 200 and 400 IM flip turns are allowed off the wall in backstroke to backstroke and freestyle to freestyle.

# RULES OF SWIMMING

## POOL

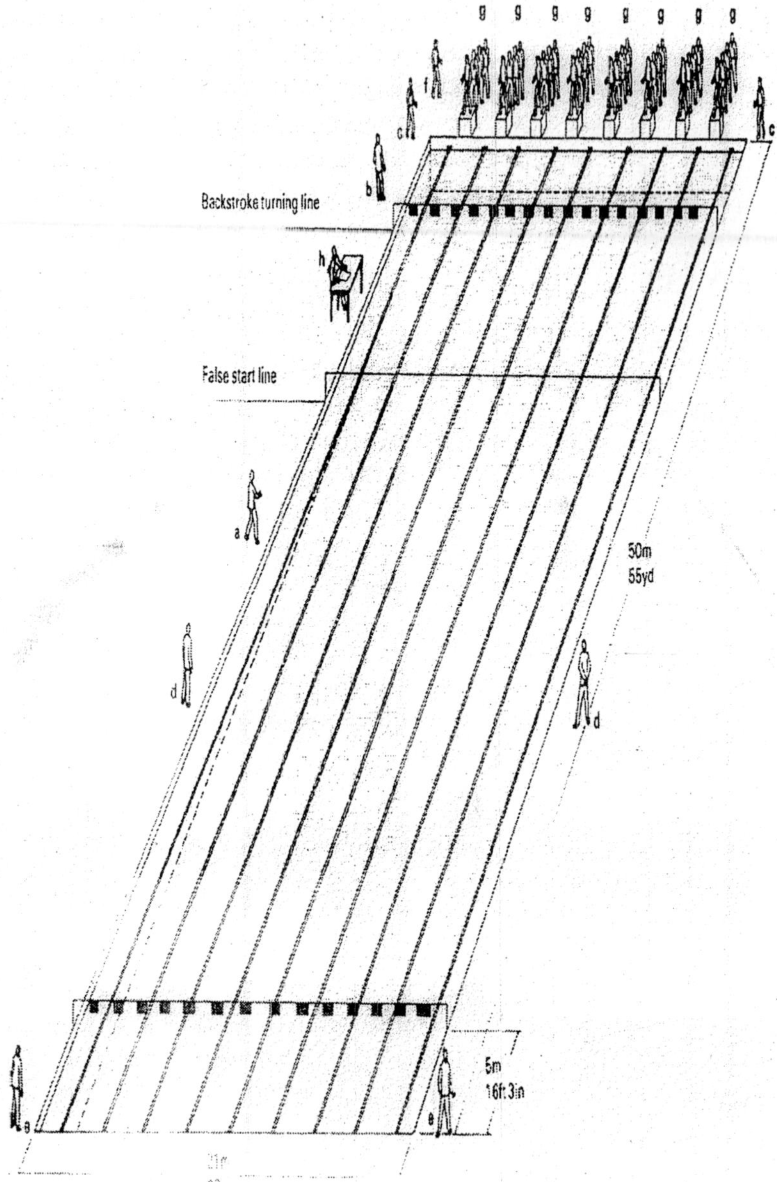

i. For Olympic Games and World Championships, Regional Games and all International Competitions specifications for pools are as follows:

i. Pool should have a length of 50m. When on starting ends or on turning end, touch panels of electronic timing equipment are used, pool should have a length which should ensures a distance of 50 meters between both panels.

ii. Against a length of 50 m above surface of water a tolerance of + 0.03m and of 0.8m below surface of water should be there.

A surveyor or other qualified official should be appointed to perform these measurements.

iii. Walls

a. These should be parallel and vertical in shape.

With surface of water in a right angle direction end walls should be constructed. End walls should be of solid material with a non-slippery surface, which should extend below surface of water 0.8m.

b. Electronic pads should have a size of at least 240cm × 90cm × 1cm which should extend 30 cm above and below the water surface.

To control individually, electronic equipment for each lane should be connected independently. Surface of touch panels should have a bright colour and line markings which should be approved for end walls.

c. Along the pool walls rest ledges are permitted, which should be above 1.2m below the surface of water and have a height of 0.15m.

d. On all 4 walls of pool, gutter should be placed. If end wall gutters have been installed they should allow for attachment of touch panels at a height of 0.3M above surface of water. Around end walls gutters there should be suitable grill or screen. To keep water at a constant level gutters should be equipped with flexible shut-off valves.

iv. There should be 8 lanes.

**CONDUCT AND OFFICIATING**

**Entries**

(i) In any combination of aquatic events conducted on a single day at the same site and where preliminaries and finals are held, no swimmer shall be permitted to compete in more than three events per day, exclusive of relays.

(ii) If a meet or event has no qualifying time standards, swimmers with no established time for an event may enter that event with no submitted time.

(iii) In meets where a combination of preliminary and final events and timed finals are held, a swimmer may compete in only three individual events per day, unless entered exclusively in timed final events on that day.

(iv) The above restrictions are effective regardless of the classification mixture and/or that separate meets re being conducted and such limitations shall be clearly stated on the entry blanks.

(v) If qualifying time standards are used they may be made in 50 meter course for long course events. or 25 yard or 25 meter course for short course events.

(vi) When timed finals are held, without preliminary heats, no swimmers shall be permitted to compete in more than 5 events per day exclusive of relays.

**FREESTYLE**

i. In such type of competition swimmer is empowered to swim in any style. However, style used by him should be different from used in individual medley or medly relay events.

ii. At completion of each length and at finish some part of swimmer's body should touch the wall.

iii. Throughout the race some part of swimmer must break the water surface. However, swimmer is not allowed to submerged during turn and for a distance of more than 15 m after start and each turn.

**BACKSTROKE**

i. Before starting signal swimmers are required to line up in water facing starting end with both their hands holding the starting grips. They should have their feet under water surface. They are not allowed to stand in or on the gutter or bend toes over lip of gutter.

ii. At signal for start and after turning swimmer is required to push off and swim upon his back during the whole race. However, he should not do this while executing a turn. Roll movement of body up to 90° from horizontal can be included in normal position on back. In such event position of head is irrelevant.

**BREASTSTROKE**

i. Body should be kept on breast from beginning of first arm stroke after start and after each turn. Swimmers are not permitted to roll onto the back.

ii. All arms should be moved at the same time and in same horizontal plane without any change in movement.

iii. During propulsive part of the kick feet should be turned in outward direction. Breaking of surface of water with feet after a down-ward dolphin kick is allowed.

iv. At each run and at completion of race swimmers should make a touch with both hands at the same time at, above, or below the level of water. Before touch head should be submerged after last arm pull, if during last complete or incomplete cycle before touch it breaks the water surface at some point.

**BUTTERFLY**

i. Body should be kept on breast and both shoulders shall be in line with normal water surface from beginning of first arm stroke after start and after each turn. Kicking on side under water is allowed. However, rolling onto back at any time is not permissible.

ii. Over water both arms should bring at same time forward and backward.

iii. To come to surface a swimmer can have one or

more kicks and one arm pull at start and at turns. After start and after each turn swimmer can be submerged completely for a maximum distance of 15 meters. From that point head should have broken the surface. Swimmer is required to be on surface till next turn or finish.

**RACE**

i. To qualify swimmer is required to cover whole distance alone.

ii. Swimmer should end his race in lane from where he started.

iii. A swimmer will not disqualify if he stands on bottom during freestyle events or during freestyle portion of medley events.

iv. During competition swimmer cannot use any device which help in increasing his speed, buoyancy or endurance.

v. If any member of team, other than swimmer designated to swim enters the water when race is being conducted, whole relay team should be disqualified from the race.

**TIMING**

i. Officials should be appointed to control Automatic Officiating Equipment. Winner should be selected on basis of time depicted by Automatic Equipment. Placing and time indicated by this equipment should be preferred over decisions of timekeepers. Decision of timekeeper will be taken into account only when this Automatic Equipment is not working properly or swimmer did not activate it.

ii. Results should be recorded only to 1/100 of a second when Automatic Equipment is used. To determine time or placement, timing to 3 digit should not be recorded or used when upto 1/1000 of a second it is available.

iii. If any swimmer is disqualified during or after an

event, it should be specified in official results. However, no time or place should be specified or announced.

## DUTIES OF OFFICIALS

### REFEREE

i. In order to ensure that FINA rules are observed properly he can intervene in competition;

ii. By raised flag and short blasts on whistle he should give a signal to swimmers indicating that event is going to be start. In same way he will indicate the flat at starter to indicate that competition should begin.

iii. He can disqualify any swimmer for breach of any rule.

### STARTER

i. He should raise a distinctive flag into vertical position as soon as referee gives the signal;

ii. He is required to stand in such a position that to all competitions he can see clearly.

### ASSISTANT REFEREE

i. It is the duty of assistant referee to ensure that in competition all officials are positioned on their respective posts. With approval of referee he can appoint substitute on place of officials who are absent or are not able to perform their duties. In some conditions he can appoint additional official also.

ii. He should lot a draw for Race Judges and should allocate them to their respective safety craft.

### TIMEKEEPERS

i. With starting signal they are required to start their watches and should stop them with instruction of Chief Timekeeper.

ii. After each finish they should record time and number of swimmer on time card and hand it to Chief Timekeeper.

Finish Judge

i. They should be placed in line with finish where they should remain to see finish clearly.

ii. According to assignment given they should record after each finish placing of swimmers.

Chief Judge

i. Each judge will be put to his position by chief judge.

ii. After race he is required to collect signed results from each judge and sent result and placing to Referee.

**RACE JUDGE**

i. To enable Race judge to see his appointed swimmer he should be placed in an escort safety craft which is assigned by random draw before start of event.

ii. It is his duty to observe that competition is being held in accordance with rules and all breach of rules is being recorded properly and reported to referee.

iii. Like referee he can order a swimmer from water upon expiry of any time limit.

**TURN JUDGES**

i. To ensure that all swimmers execute alterations in course indicated by competition information documents and pre-race briefing, turn judges are appointed.

ii. Any violation of turn procedure should be recorded by him on record sheet if race judge was informed about such violation by blasts on a whistle.

iii. They are required to hand over the signed record sheet to chief judge at completion of event.

Recorder

He is required to record withdrawals from competition, to enter results on official forms, and to maintain record for team awards.

**MEDICAL OFFICER**

i. To referee he should be responsible for all medical aspects which relates to competition and competitors.

ii. He should ensure that before beginning of competition all competitors have gone through a medical test and referee and management committee has informed about any person who is found to be unfit to play. On basis of his report referee can stop any person from participating in competition.

ii. With safety officer he is required to advise referee if according to them conditions are not suitable for competition and recommend to change course or manner of conducting the competition.

**SAFETY OFFICER**

i. He should be responsible for safety of event to referee.

ii. He should check that whole course is safe, suitable and without any obstruction.

iii. He should ensure that during competition necessary powered safety crafts have become available. Purpose of these safety crafts is to provide full safety backup to escort safety craft.

**COURSE OFFICER**

i. For correct survey of course he will be answerable to Management Committee.

ii. He should ensure that start and finish areas have marked correctly and equipments have been placed in correct position.

iii. Before start of competition he is required to ensure and inform assistant referee whether or not turn judges are in proper position or not.

**START**

i. In Open Water Competitions competitors should stand in water having such a depth from where swimming can be started with start signal.

ii. Start positions of players will be decided by draw in such a manner that lowest number should stand on left and highest number on right side.

iii. Overhead apparatus or removable equipment at water level should be used to define start line.

iii. Starter should be position in such a way that everybody can see him.

iv. Start signal should be audible and visual.

v. Men's and women's events should be treated as

separate events.

**FINISH OF RACE**

i. Rows of buoys should be drawn to indicate area leading to finish apparatus. These lines should be drawn in such a way that they get narrower while near to finish wall. To ensure that only authorised safety craft can enter or cross entrance of finish lane, escort finish lane should be positioned there.

ii. Finish Judges and Timekeepers should sit in such a manner that they can see the finish at all times. They can use whole area in which they situates.

iii. While leaving water some swimmers may require assistance. Only if any swimmer ask for such assistant should be touched or handled.

iv. As swimmers leave the water, member of medical team is required to inspect them. Swimmer should be provided a chair on which he cant sit during assessment.

v. After getting clearance from medical member, swimmers should be given access to refreshment.

# 14

# TABLE TENNIS

## INTRODUCTION

Table tennis, also known as ping-pong, is a sport in which two or four players hit a lightweight, hollow ball back and forth using table tennis rackets. The game takes place on a hard table divided by a net. Except for the initial serve, players must allow a ball played toward them only one bounce on their side of the table and must return it so that it bounces on the opposite side. Points are scored when a player fails to return the ball within the rules. Play is fast and demands quick reactions. A skilled player can impart several varieties of spin to the ball, altering its trajectory and limiting an opponent's options to great advantage.

Table tennis is controlled by the worldwide organization International Table Tennis Federation (ITTF), founded in 1926. ITTF currently includes 210 member associations. The table tennis official rules are specified in the ITTF handbook. Since 1988, table tennis has been an Olympic sport, with several event categories. In particular, from 1988 until 2004, these were: men's singles, women's singles, men's doubles and women's doubles. Since 2008 the doubles have been replaced by the team events.

## SKILLS AND TECHNIQUES

### THE GRIP

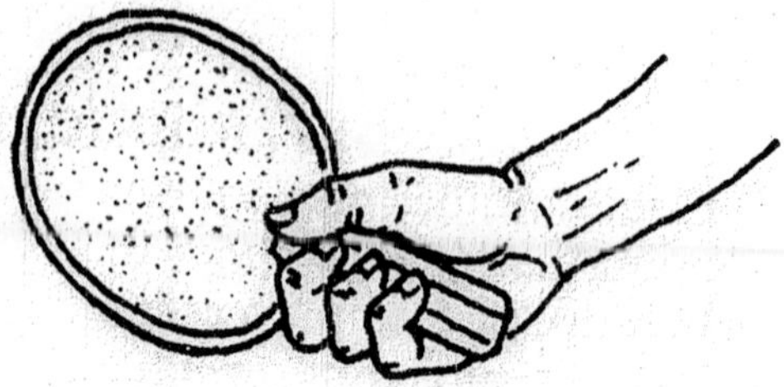

Sound strokes begin with a proper grip. Of all racket sports, table tennis is played with the smallest ball and racket and has the smallest target. Therefore, the angle at which the racket is presented to the ball during the swing must be controlled with absolute precision.

### THE SPIN

Unlike tennis, in which the dries, the volleys and the overhead smashes are usually hit flat, in table tennis, all shots, from the slow, close to the table, push returns to the 120 m.p.h. kill of a set up, require the use of spin. Though the expert has a wide range of choice in the amount of spin he uses and will vary it with the particular shot, the type of spin he uses is extremely limited, limited in fact to two. He may use either underspin or overspin, but never sidespin.

### THE SERVICE

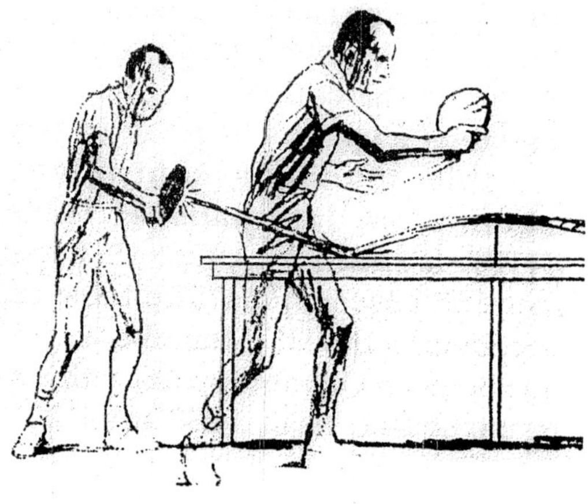

In table tennis, the serve must, before it crosses the net, bounce on the server's side of the table. The amount of power that can be applied, therefore, is quite limited. The amount of spin one can apply is also severely limited. Earlier, the server was allowed to spin the ball in his fingers before striking it, or hold it steady in his fingers to prolong contact as the bat rubbed against the firmly clutched ball.

**THE STROKES**

The most elementary stroke in the game of table tennis is so called half volley, or push, yet the one used most often, even among experts. It is the simple shot used in answer to a defensive return from your opponent when for some reason, this return does not afford the opportunity to attack.

## RULES OF TABLE TENNIS

**THE TABLE**

-Playing surface is the upper surface of table which should have rectangular shape with a length of 2.74m and width of 1.525m. This playing surface should lie 76cm above the floor horizontally;

-Sides of table top should not be included in playing surface;

-Any material can be used to construct playing surface but when a standard ball is dropped on it from a height of 30 cm it should bounce at a height of 23cm.

-A vertical net should be used to divide the playing surface into 2 equal courts. This net should run parallel with end lines, and over whole area of each court shall be continuous.

-Playing surface should be of a dark colour but should have a side line of white colour having a width of 2cm, along each 2.74m edge and a white end line having a width of 2cm along each 1.525 m edge.

-A white centre line of 3mm width should be drawn to divide court into 2 equal half-courts in doubles. This line should run parallel with side lines. Centre-line is considered as a part of each right half-court.

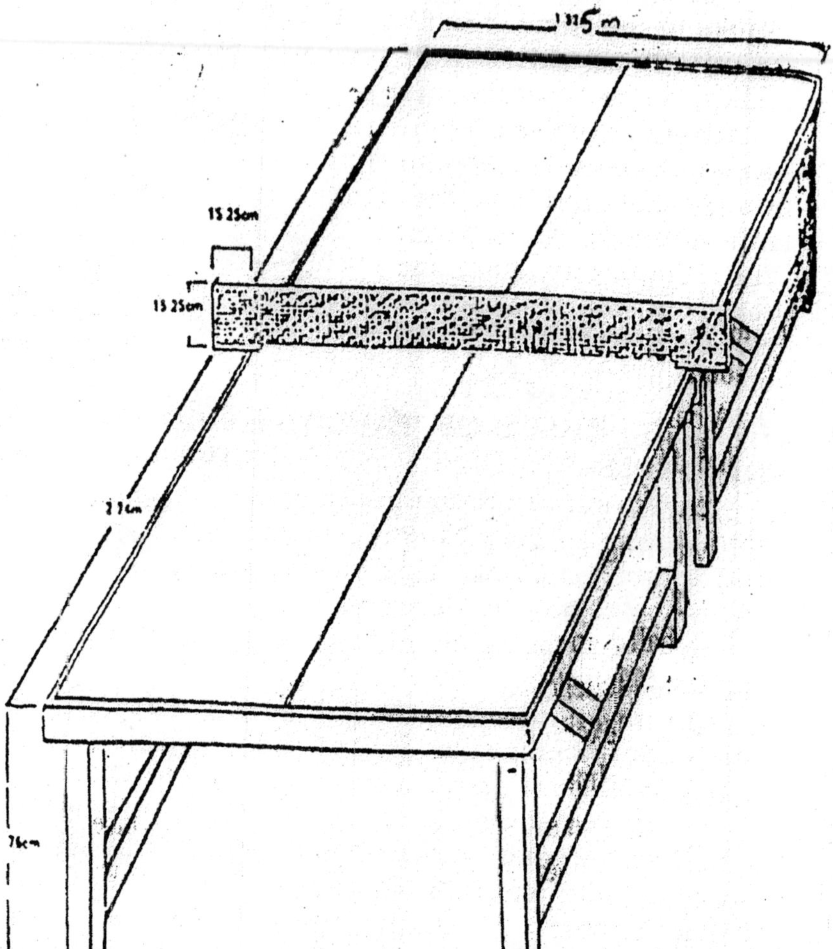

## NET ASSEMBLY

—Net, its suspension, and supporting posts including clamps which attach them to table are included in net assembly.

—A cord should be attached to suspend the net. This cord should be attached at each end to a height of 15.25cm at upright post. Outside the side line outside limits of post can be 15.25cm.

—15.25 cm above playing surface top of net should be tied.

—Bottom of net should be close to playing surface and ends of net should be near to support posts.

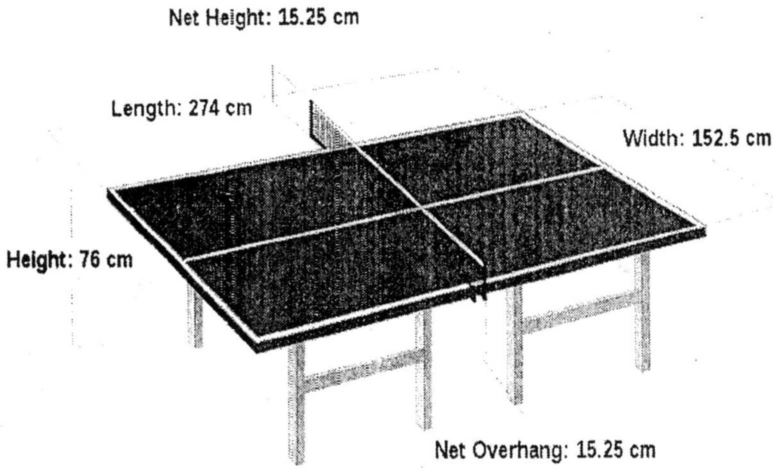


## BALL

Ball should be of spherical shape having a diameter of 38mm, its weight should be 2.5gm. It can be made of celluloid or similar plastic material and should have white or orange colour.

**RACKET**

—There is not any particular size, shape or weight prescribed for racket but it should have a flat and non-flexible blade.

—Atleast 85% of blade should be of natural wood. Within the blade an adhesive layer should be reinforce with fibrous material like carbon fibre, glass fibre or compressed paper.

Thickness of this adhesive layer should be 7.5% of total thickness or 0.33mm whichever is lower.

—Side of blade which is used to strike the ball should be covered with either an ordinary pimpled rubber or with a sandwich rubber. Ordinary rubber should have pimples outwards with not more than 2mm thickness and sandwich rubber can have pimples either inward or outward with not more than 4mm thickness.

**GAME**

Player or pair first scoring 21 points should be declared winner. If 20 points has been scored by both players or pair of players, player or pair scoring more 2 points should be declared winner.

**STARTING A GAME**

According to ITTF rule 2.13.1, the first service is decided by lot,[19] normally a coin toss. It is also common for one player (or the umpire/scorer) to hide the ball in one or the other hand (usually hidden under the table), allowing the other player to guess which hand the ball is in. The correct or incorrect guess gives the "winner" the option to choose to serve, receive, or to choose which side of the table to use. Another method is for one player to hit the ball to the other and he or she returns it or by hitting it back and forth four times and then playing out the point. This is commonly referred to as "play to serve" or "rally to serve".

**SERVICE AND RETURN**

In game play, the player serving the ball commences a play. The server first stands with the ball held on the open palm of the hand not carrying the racket, called the freehand, and tosses the ball directly upward without spin, at least 16 centimeters (approximately 6 inches) high. The server strikes the ball with the racket on the ball's descent so that it touches first his court and then touches directly the receiver's court without touching the net assembly. In casual games, many players do not toss the ball upward; however, this is technically illegal and can give the serving player an unfair advantage.

**ORDER OF PLAY**

—In case of singles firstly server is required to give a good service then only there can be a good return by the receiver. After that in this sequence both players will give good return.

—In doubles, receiver can make a good return only when server will serve a good service. If server will make a good service partner of receiver will also make a good return and in same way all players will give a good return.

**CHOICE OF ENDS, SERVING AND RECEIVING**

i. A lot should be drawn to decide which player will serve first and which will receive first. Right to make such a rests with winner of lots, he can also choose a particular end.

ii. If both players have not scored 20 points or expedite system comes into operation, after scoring of 5 points by both players receiving player becomes serving player and so on.

iii. As there are 2 players in each side in doubles, players have to decide themself who will serve first and who will receive first. Player who acts as first receiver will serve in next game.

iv. In doubles at change of ends player previously acting as receiver is required to serve and partner of previous server will be the receiver.

v. Player acting as server first in game is required to receive first in next game of match, and in last game of a doubles match players are required to change their order of receiving after scoring 10 points.

vi. Player or pair starting at one end in a game are required to start at other end in next game and in last game of match they should change ends when 10 points are scored by either player.

**Ideal Service**

—At beginning of game ball should not be in a moving position, it should be on a resting position behind end line and above level of playing surface;

—Then near vertically upwards player will throw the ball forward without twisting it in such a manner that it rises atleast 16cm after leaving palm of free hand and before being struck it does not touch anything;

—Sever should struck the ball as soon as it falls on ground so that firstly it touches his court and then after court of opponent. Ball should touch successively right half court of server and receiver in case of doubles;

—Till ball is struck by any player, racket and ball should remain above the level of playing surface;

—At time of striking of ball it should be behind end line of server but should not be farther back from part of server's body, other than his arm, head or leg which should be far from end line;

—Player is required to serve in order to ensure umpire or assistant umpire that he has made service in accordance with rules:

-in case umpire or his assistant has only some doubt regarding legality of service, they can only warn the server for first time without awarding any point;

-if umpire or his assistant has some doubt regarding legality of service for second time, point should be awarded to receiver;

—if umpire or his assistant does not consider the service a good service, receiver shall score a point. In this case they are not required to warn the server;

—In case of disabled players, umpire can ignore those services which does not satisfy rules of a good service.

**Good Return**

Game begins when server struck the ball to pass over it to opponent's court either directly or after touching net assembly.

**Clothing**

—Short-sleeved shirts and shorts of skirts, socks and playing shoes are included in Playing clothing. During play no player is permitted to wear other garments, like part of a track suit;

—To identify a player, his association, his club and advertisements, there can be numbers or lettering on back of shirt;

—Clothes should have a different colour from the ball;

—No design or lattering should be carried by clothes which can violates the rule;

—In doubles game, both players and players of same association should wear the same type of dress, however there can be some change in socks and shoes;

—Numbers which are used to identify a player should be situated in centre of back of the shirt. A panel having an area less than 600cm should be designed to contain such numbers;

## JURISDICTION OF OFFICIALS

**Referee**

In every competitions, a referee should be appointed whose identity and location should be made known to all participants or to captains of team.

Following are responsibilities of referee:

—he has to conduct the draw;

—he is required to check whether players are eligible to play or not;

—he has to decide whether or not statutory practice period can be extended;

—he has to decide whether play should be suspended in emergency or not;

—he has to take decision whether players show allow to wear track suits during match or not;

—he has to select the place where players can practice during emergency suspension of play;

—he is required to take necessary step for breach of any rule or for unsportsmanlike behaviour of any player;

—if some of duties of umpire has been delegated to some other persons, their identity and location should be made known to all participants and to their captain;

—referee or in his absence, deputy appointed to perform his duty should be present at all times during play.

**LET**

A let is a rally of which the result is not scored, and is called in the following circumstances:

* The ball touches the net in service, provided the service is otherwise correct or the ball is obstructed by the player on the receiving side. Obstruction means a player touches the ball when it is above or traveling towards the playing surface, not having touched the player's court since last being struck by the player.

* When the player on the receiving side is not ready and the service is delivered.

* Play is interrupted by the umpire or assistant umpire.

**SCORING**

A point is scored by the player for any of several results of the rally:

* Opponent fails to make a correct service or return.

* After making a service or a return, the ball touches anything other than the net assembly before being struck by the opponent.

* The ball passes over the player's court or beyond his end line without touching his court, after being struck by the opponent.

* The opponent obstructs the ball.

* The opponent strikes the ball twice successively. Note that the hand that is holding the racket counts as part of the racket and that making a good return off one's hand or fingers is allowed. It is not a fault if the ball accidentally hits one's hand or fingers and then subsequently hits the racket.

* The opponent strikes the ball with a side of the racket blade whose surface is not covered with rubber.

* The opponent moves the playing surface or touches the net assembly.

* The opponent's free hand touches the playing surface.

* As a receiver under the expedite system, completing 13 returns in a rally.

* The opponent has been warned by umpire commits a second offense in the same individual match or team match. If the third offence happens, 2 points will be given to the player. If the individual match or the team match has not ended, any unused penalty points can be transferred to the next game of that match.

**DOUBLES GAME**

In addition to games between individual players, pairs may also play table tennis. In doubles, all the rules of single play are applied except for the following.

1. A line painted along the long axis of the table to create doubles courts bisects the table. This line's only purpose is to facilitate the doubles service rule, which is that service, must originate from the right hand "box" in such a way that the first bounce of the serve bounces

once in said right hand box and then must bounce at least once in the opponent side's right hand box (far left box for server), or the receiving pair score a point.

2. Players must alternate hitting the ball. For example, if A is paired with B, X is paired with Y, A is the server and X is the receiver. The order of play shall be A → X → B → Y. The rally proceeds this way until one side fails to make a legal return and the other side scores.

3. At each change of service, the previous receiver shall become the server and the partner of the previous server shall become the receiver. For example, if the previous order of play is A → X → B → Y, the order becomes X → B → Y → A after the change of service.

4. In each game of a doubles match, the pair having the right to serve first shall choose which of them will do so. The receiving pair, however, can only choose in the first game of the match. When the first server is chosen in the second or the latter games of the match, the first receiver of the game is the player who served to the first server of the game in the preceding game. For example, if the order of play is A → X → B → Y at beginning of the first game, the order begins with X → A → Y → B or Y → B → X → A in the second game depending on either X or Y being chosen as the first server of the game.

5. When a pair reach 5 points in the final game, the pairs must switch ends of the table and the team that receives the service must switch receiver. For example, when the last order of play before a pair score 5 points in the final game is A → X → B → Y, the order after change shall be A → Y → B → X if A still has the second serve. Otherwise, X is the next server and the order becomes X → A → Y → B.

Singles and doubles are both played in international competition, including the Olympic Games since 1988 and the Commonwealth Games since 2002. In 2005, the ITTF announced that doubles table tennis only was featured as a part of team events in the 2008 Olympics.

**Competition**

Competitive table tennis is popular in Asia and Europe and has been gaining attention in the United States. The most important international competitions are the World Table Tennis Championships, the Table Tennis World Cup, the Olympics and the ITTF Pro Tour. Continental competitions include the European Championships, Europe Top-12, the Asian Championships and the Asian Games. Chinese players have won the men's World Championships 60% of the time since 1959; in the women's competition, Chinese players have won all but three of the World Championships since 1971. Other strong teams come from East Asia and European countries, including Austria, Belarus, Germany, Hong Kong, Japan, South Korea, Singapore, Sweden, and Taiwan.

There are also professional competitions at the clubs level. The national league of countries like China (the China Table Tennis Super League), Germany, France, Belgium and Austria are some highest level examples. There are also some important international club teams competitions such as the European Champions League and its former competition, the European Club Cup, where the top club teams from European countries compete.

# 15

# TENNIS

## INTRODUCTION

Tennis is a sport usually played between two players (singles) or between two teams of two players each (doubles). Each player uses a racket that is strung to strike a hollow rubber ball covered with felt over a net into the opponent's court. Tennis is an Olympic sport and is played at all levels of society at all ages. The sport can be played by anyone who can hold a racket, including people in wheelchairs.

The modern game of tennis originated in the United Kingdom in the late 19th century as "lawn tennis" which has close connections to various field/lawn games as well as to the ancient game of real tennis. Up to then,

"tennis" referred to the latter sport: for example, in Disraeli's novel Sybil (1845), Lord Eugene De Vere announces that he will "go down to Hampton Court and play tennis. As it is the Derby [classic horse race], nobody will be there". After its creation, lawn tennis spread throughout the upper-class English-speaking population before spreading around the world.

Tennis is enjoyed by millions of recreational players and is also a hugely popular worldwide spectator sport, especially the four Grand Slam tournaments: the Australian Open played on hard courts, the French Open played on red clay courts, Wimbledon played on grass courts, and the US Open played also on hard courts.

## SKILLS AND TECHNIQUES

### Grip

Racquet grip is a very essential part of stroke, because a faulty grip will ruin the finest serving. It is a natural

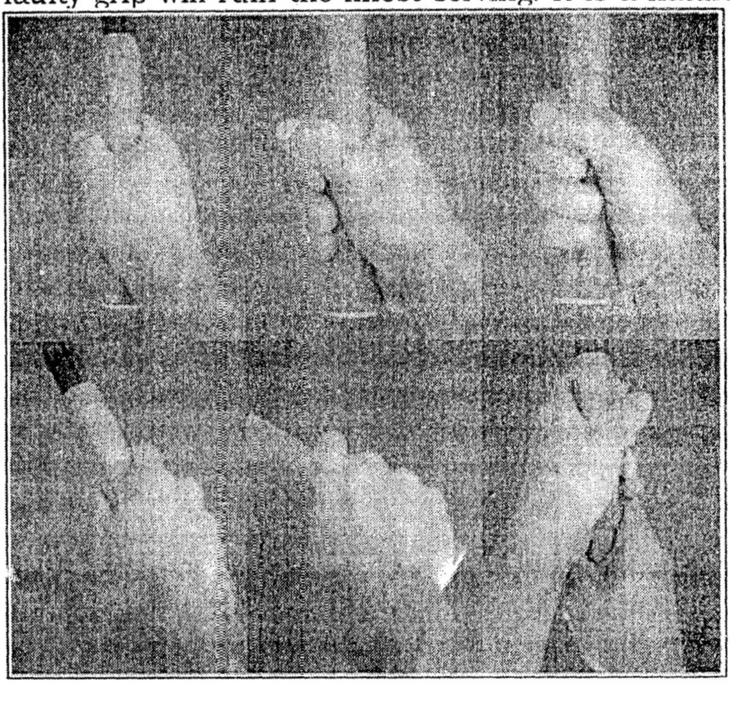

grip for a top forehand drive. It is inherently weak for the backhand, as the only natural shot is a chop stroke.

To acquire the forehand grip, hold the racquet with the edge of the frame towards the ground and the face perpendicular, the handle towards the body, and "shake hands" with it, just as if you were greeting a friend. The handle settled comfortably and naturally into the hand, the line of the arm, hand, and racquet are one. The swing brings the racquet head on a line with the arm, and the whole racquet is merely an extension of it.

The backhand grip is a quarter circle turn of hand on the handle, bringing the hand on top of the handle and the knuckles directly up. The shot travels ACROSS the wrist.

All tennis strokes, should be made with the body' at right angles to the net, with the shoulders lined up parallel to the line of flight of the ball. The weight should always travel forward. It should pass from the back foot to the front foot at the moment of striking the ball. Never allow the weight to be going away from the stroke. It is weight that determines the "pace" of a stroke; swing that, decides the "speed."

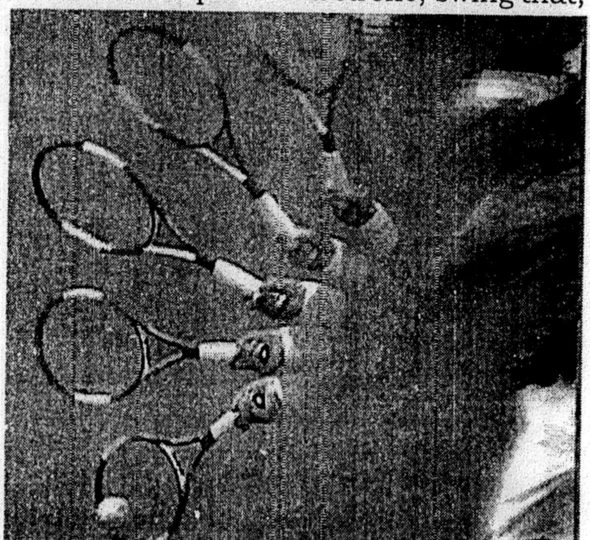

**Forehand Drive**

Forehand drive is generally the first stroke learned in tennis, probably because it is the easiest to master, once you can hit a forehand and underarm serve, you can play a game.

The easiest grip to use is the Eastern forehand. Start in the ready position, i.e., the position that is going to make it easier for you to get off the mark quickly, so that you can get to the right place at the right moment for hitting the ball. When in the ready position, support the racket with your free hand at the throat and start with a relaxed forehand grip.

**Backhand Drive**

The tennis backhand is executed from the side opposite of the forehand side. So if you are right-handed, your backhand is executed from the left side of your body and if you are left-handed, your backhand is executed from the right side of your body.

In order to execute a tennis backhand, you must bring your natural hitting hand around your body before hitting the tennis ball. The tennis backhand may seem awkward at first, but as you practice and familiarize yourself with this stroke it will become a welcomed alternative to the foundation of your tennis techniques and skills.

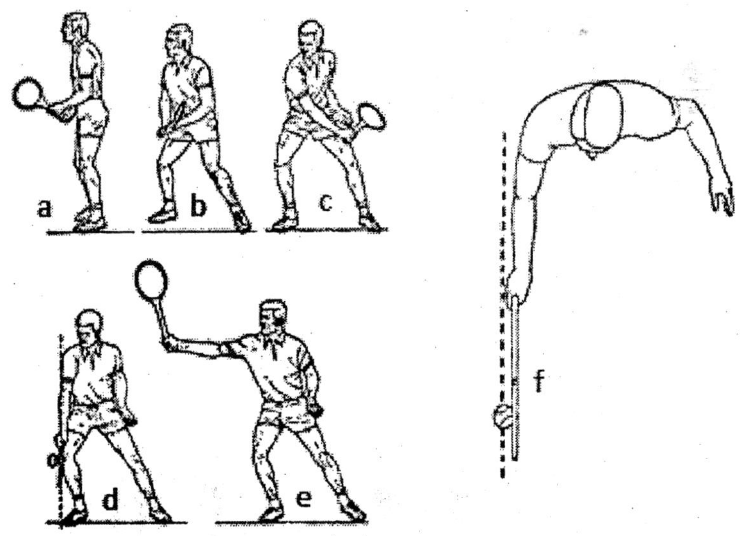

**Service**

The tennis serve initiates every point. The tennis player that is serving is termed the server and the other tennis player is termed the receiver. By rule, you can opt to serve anyway you see fit, it is your choice.

Technically though, competitive tennis players achieve and maintain the most effective results by tossing the ball straight up high above the head while rotating the tennis racquet with a full motion swing aiming to strike the ball to the diagonal service area on the opposite end of the tennis court.

**Tennis Lob**

Uniquely termed in tennis, the lob is mainly used as a defensive technique to turn the momentum of a point into an offensive play. Did that make sense? Let me attempt to clarify.

What is a lob? A lob is a high arching shot with additional hang time that is initiated by a forehand, backhand, or at times a volley. With the lob technique, a tennis competitor has the ability to change the course of a point and keep an opponent off balance during game play.

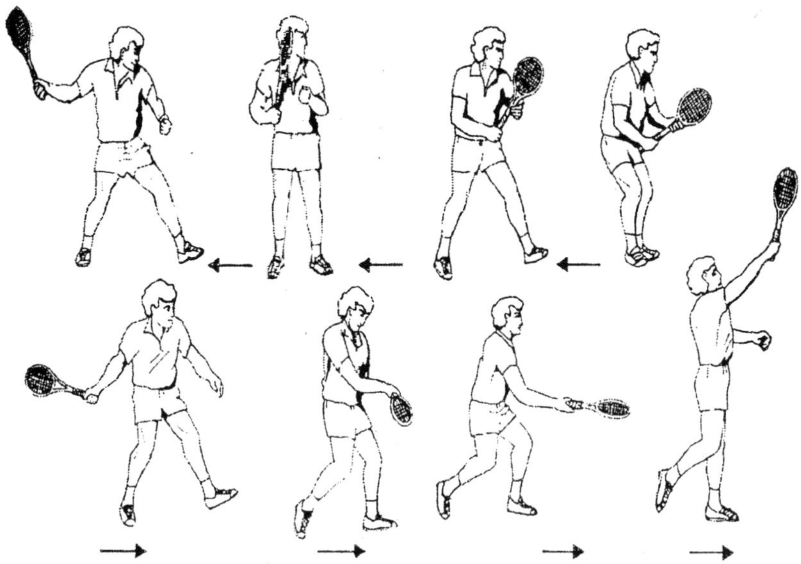

As a competitor, your goal is to win each an every point. From time to time tennis athletes find themselves out of position or vulnerable during game play. This is when the lob technique comes in handy and can change the direction of that point.

**Tennis Overhead Smash**

Similar to a serve, the overhead tennis technique is designed to earn points by striking the tennis ball as it floats in the air over the head to the forehand or backhand side of a tennis athlete's body. Generally, this is the response to an unsuccessful lob attempt where the tennis competitor that initiated the lob pays dearly.

Good smashers have good footwork and really reach up and go for the ball. The smash differs from the serve because it has a much shorter take back. Instead of the racket extending right out at the back of the body, it is just taken straight behind your shoulder into the back scratching position. This is necessary, as the smash requires more precise timing and the ball on the smash if falling from a greater height on the service place up.

**Tennis Volley**

Simply put, the volley is a short punch technique with little or no back swing from a tennis athlete's forehand or backhand side. If you are the type of player who enjoys going on the attack to instigate fast-paced action, the

volley is probably one if not your favorite tennis skill that intensifies your game.

Other than a serve or an overhead, every shot a player executes before the ball bounces on the court is considered a volley. This skill is frequently attempted as a reaction to an out-of-position jam where a tennis athlete is unable to play the bounce.

## RULES OF TENNIS

### 1. THE COURT

The court shall be a rectangle, 78 feet (23.77 m) long and, for singles matches, 27 feet (8.23 m) wide. For doubles matches, the court shall be 36 feet (10.97 m) wide.

The court shall be divided across the middle by a net suspended by a cord or metal cable which shall pass over or be attached to two net posts at a height of 3 ½ feet (1.07 m). The net shall be fully extended so that it completely fills the space between the two net posts and it must be of sufficiently small mesh to ensure that a ball cannot pass through it. The height of the net shall be 3 feet (0.914 m) at the centre, where it shall be held down tightly by a strap. A band shall cover the cord or metal cable and the top of the net. The strap and band shall be completely white.

- The maximum diameter of the cord or metal cable shall be 1/3 inch (0.8 cm).
- The maximum width of the strap shall be 2 inches (5 cm).
- The band shall be between 2 inches (5 cm) and 2 ½ inches (6.35 cm) deep on each side.

For doubles matches, the centres of the net posts shall be 3 feet (0.914 m) outside the doubles court on each side.

For singles matches, if a singles net is used, the centres of the net posts shall be 3 feet (0.914 m) outside the singles court on each side. If a doubles net is used,

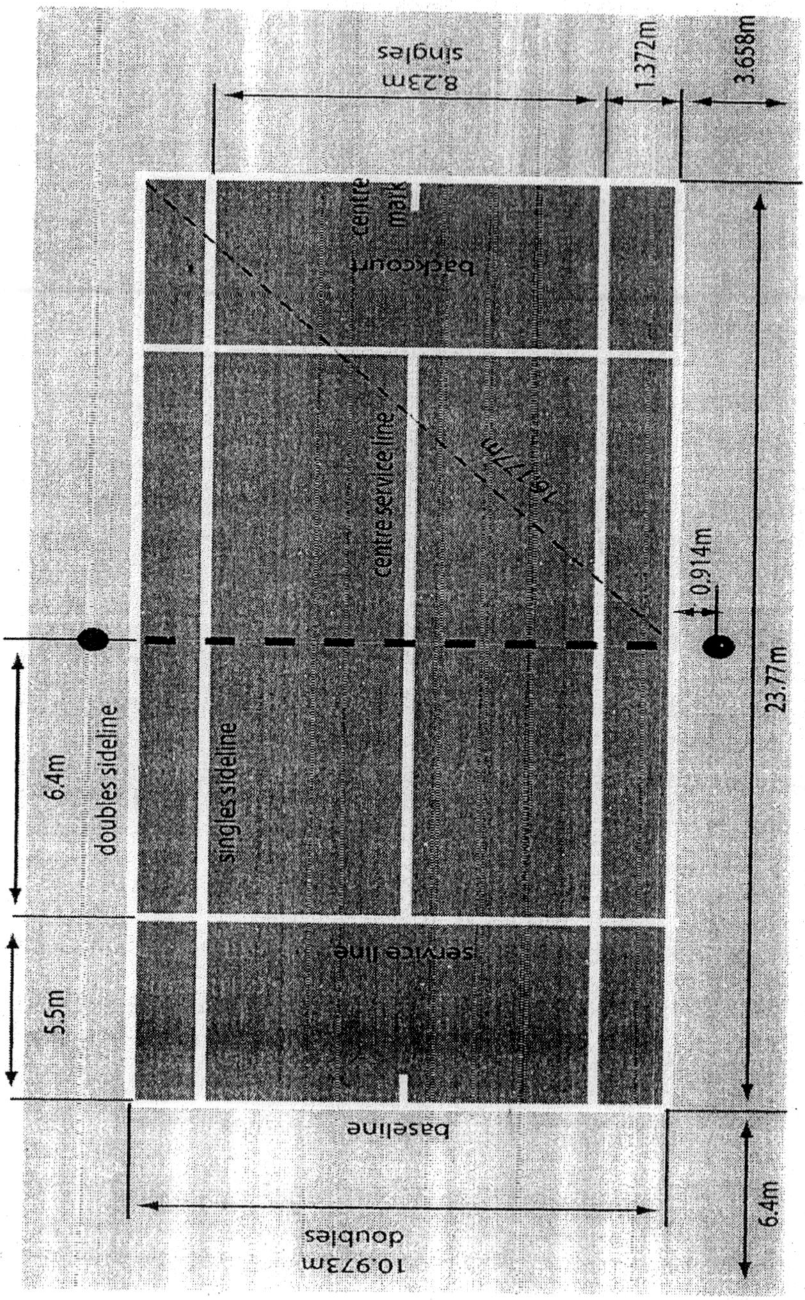
8.23m
singles
1.372m
3.658m
centre
mark
backcourt
centre service line
0.914m
23.77m
6.4m
doubles sideline
singles sideline
5.5m
service line
baseline
10.973m
doubles
6.4m

then the net shall be supported, at a height of 3 ½ feet (1.07 m), by two singles sticks, the centres of which shall be 3 feet (0.914 m) outside the singles court on each side.

- The net posts shall not be more than 6 inches (15 cm) square or 6 inches (15 cm) in diameter.
- The singles sticks shail not be more than 3 inches (7.5 cm) square or 3 inches (7.5 cm) in diameter.
- The net posts and singles sticks shall not be more than 1 inch (2.5 cm) above the top of the net cord.

The lines at the ends of the court are called baselines and the lines at the sides of the court are called sidelines.

Two lines shall be drawn between the singles sidelines, 21 feet (6.40 m) from each side of the net, parallel with the net. These lines are called the servicelines. On each side of the net, the area between the serviceline and the net shall be divided into two equal parts, the service courts, by the centre serviceline. The centre serviceline shall be drawn parallel with the singles sidelines and half way between them.

Each baseline shall be divided in half by a centre mark, 4 inches (10 cm) in length, which shall be drawn inside the court and parallel with the singles sidelines.

- The centre serviceline and centre mark shall be 2 inches (5 cm) wide.
- The other lines of the court shall be between 1 inch (2.5 cm) and 2 inches (5 cm) wide, except that the baselines may be up to 4 inches (10 cm) wide.

All court measurements shall be made to the outside of the lines and all lines of the court shall be of the same colour clearly contrasting with the colour of the surface.

**2. PERMANENT FIXTURES**

The permanent fixtures of the court include the backstops and sidestops, the spectators, the stands and seats for spectators, all other fixtures around and above the court, the chair umpire, line umpires, net umpire and ball persons when in their recognised positions.

In a singles match played with a doubles net and singles sticks, the net posts and the part of the net outside the singles sticks are permanent fixtures and are not considered as net posts or part of the net.

**3. THE BALL**

The International Tennis Federation shall rule on the question of whether any ball or prototype complies with Appendix I or is otherwise approved, or not approved, for play. Such ruling may be taken on its own initiative, or upon application by any party with a bona fide interest therein, including any player, equipment manufacturer or National Association or members thereof. Such rulings and applications shall be made in accordance with the applicable Review and Hearing Procedures of the International Tennis Federation.

**4. THE RACKET**

The International Tennis Federation shall rule on the question of whether any racket or prototype complies with Appendix II or is otherwise approved, or not approved, for play. Such ruling may be undertaken on its own initiative, or upon application by any party with a bona fide interest therein, including any player, equipment manufacturer or National Association or members thereof. Such rulings and applications shall be made in accordance with the applicable Review and Hearing Procedures of the International Tennis Federation.

**5. SCORE IN A GAME**

**a. Standard game**

A standard game is scored as follows with the server's score being called first:

No point - "Love"
First point - "15"
Second point - "30"
Third point - "40"

Fourth point - "Game"

except that if each player/team has won three points, the score is "Deuce".

After "Deuce", the score is "Advantage" for the player/team who wins the next point. If that same player/team also wins the next point, that player/team wins the "Game"; if the opposing player/team wins the next point, the score is again "Deuce". A player/team needs to win two consecutive points immediately after "Deuce" to win the "Game".

b. Tie-break game

During a tie-break game, points are scored "Zero", "1", "2", "3", etc. The first player/team to win seven points wins the "Game" and "Set", provided there is a margin of two points over the opponent(s). If necessary, the tie-break game shall continue until this margin is achieved.

**6. SCORE IN A SET**

There are different methods of scoring in a set. The two main methods are the "Advantage Set" and the "Tie-break Set". Either method may be used provided that the one to be used is announced in advance of the event. If the "Tie-break Set" method is to be used, it must also be announced whether the final set will be played as a "Tie-break Set" or an "Advantage Set".

**a. "Advantage Set"**

The first player/team to win six games wins that "Set", provided there is a margin of two games over the opponent(s). If necessary, the set shall continue until this margin is achieved.

**b. "Tie-break Set"**

The first player/team to win six games wins that "Set", provided there is a margin of two games over the opponent(s). If the score reaches six games all, a tie-break game shall be played.

**7. SCORE IN A MATCH**

A match can be played to the best of 3 sets (a player/

team needs to win 2 sets to win the match) or to the best of 5 sets (a player/team needs to win 3 sets to win the match).

**8. SERVER & RECEIVER**

The players/teams shall stand on opposite sides of the net. The server is the player who puts the ball into play for the first point. The receiver is the player who is ready to return the ball served by the server.

Case 1: Is the receiver allowed to stand outside the lines of the court?

Decision: Yes. The receiver may take any position inside or outside the lines on the receiver's side of the net.

**9. CHOICE OF ENDS & SERVICE**

The choice of ends and the choice to be server or receiver in the first game shall be decided by toss before the warm-up starts. The player/team who wins the toss may choose:

a. To be server or receiver in the first game of the match, in which case the opponent(s) shall choose the end of the court for the first game of the match; or

b. The end of the court for the first game of the match, in which case the opponent(s) shall choose to be server or receiver for the first game of the match; or

**10. CHANGE OF ENDS**

The players shall change ends at the end of the first, third and every subsequent odd game of each set. The players shall also change ends at the end of each set unless the total number of games in that set is even, in which case the players change ends at the end of the first game of the next set.

**11. BALL IN PLAY**

Unless a fault or a let is called, the ball is in play from the moment the server hits the ball, and remains in play until the point is decided.

## 12. BALL TOUCHES A LINE

If a ball touches a line, it is regarded as touching the court bounded by that line.

## 13. BALL TOUCHES A PERMANENT FIXTURE

If the ball in play touches a permanent fixture after it has hit the correct court, the player who hit the ball wins the point. If the ball in play touches a permanent fixture before it hits the ground, the player who hit the ball loses the point.

## 14. ORDER OF SERVICE

At the end of each standard game, the receiver shall become the server and the server shall become the receiver for the next game. In doubles, the team due to serve in the first game of each set shall decide which player shall serve for that game. Similarly, before the second game starts, their opponents shall decide which player shall serve for that game.

## 15. ORDER OF RECEIVING IN DOUBLES

The team which is due to receive in the first game of a set shall decide which player shall receive the first point in the game. Similarly, before the second game starts, their opponents shall decide which player shall receive the first point of that game.

The player who was the receiver's partner for the first point of the game shall receive the second point and this rotation shall continue until the end of the game and the set.

## 16. THE SERVICE

Immediately before starting the service motion, the server shall stand at rest with both feet behind (i.e. further from the net than) the baseline and within the imaginary extensions of the centre mark and the sideline.

The server shall then release the ball by hand in any direction and hit the ball with the racket before the ball hits the ground. The service motion is completed at the moment that the player's racket hits or misses the ball.

**17. SERVING**

When serving in a standard game, the server shall stand behind alternate halves of the court, starting from the right half of the court in every game.

In a tie-break game, the service shall be served from behind alternate halves of the court, with the first served from the right half of the court.

The service shall pass over the net and hit the service court diagonally opposite, before the receiver returns it.

**18. FOOT FAULT**

During the service motion, the server shall not:

a. Change position by walking or running, although slight movements of the feet are permitted; or

b. Touch the baseline or the court with either foot; or

c. Touch the area outside the imaginary extension of the sideline with either foot; or

d. Touch the imaginary extension of the centre mark with either foot.

**19. SERVICE FAULT**

The service is a fault if:

a. The server breaks rules 16, 17 or 18; or

b. The server misses the ball when trying to hit it; or

c. The ball served touches a permanent fixture, singles stick or net post before it hits the ground; or

d. The ball served touches the server or server's partner, or anything the server or server's partner is wearing or carrying.

**20. SECOND SERVICE**

If the first service is a fault, the server shall serve again without delay from behind the same half of the court from which that fault was served, unless the service was from the wrong half.

**21. WHEN TO SERVE & RECEIVE**

The server shall not serve until the receiver is ready. However, the receiver shall play to the reasonable pace of the server and shall be ready to receive within a reasonable time of the server being ready.

A receiver who attempts to return the service shall be considered as being ready. If it is demonstrated that the receiver is not ready, the service cannot be called a fault.

**22. THE LET DURING A SERVICE**

The service is a let if:

a. The ball served touches the net, strap or band, and is otherwise good; or, after touching the net, strap or band, touches the receiver or the receiver's partner or anything they wear or carry before hitting the ground; or

b. The ball is served when the receiver is not ready.

**23. THE LET**

In all cases when a let is called, except when a service let is called on a second service, the whole point shall be replayed.

**24. PLAYER LOSES POINT**

The point is lost if:

a. The player serves two consecutive faults; or

b. The player does not return the ball in play before it bounces twice consecutively; or

c. The player returns the ball in play so that it hits the ground, or before it bounces, an object, outside the correct court; or

d. The player returns the ball in play so that, before it bounces, it hits a permanent fixture; or

e. The receiver returns the service before it bounces; or

f. The player deliberately carries or catches the ball in play on the racket or deliberately touches it with the racket more than once.

**25. A GOOD RETURN**

It is a good return if:

a. The ball touches the net, net posts/singles sticks, cord or metal cable, strap or band, provided that it passes over any of them and hits the ground within the correct court; except as provided in Rule 2 and 24 (d); or

b. After the ball in play has hit the ground within the correct court and has spun or been blown back over the net, the player reaches over the net and plays the ball into the correct court, provided that the player does not break Rule 24; or

c. The ball is returned outside the net posts, either above or below the level of the top of the net, even though it touches the net posts, provided that it hits the ground in the correct court; except as provided in Rules 2 and 24 (d); or

d. The ball passes under the net cord between the singles stick and the adjacent net post without touching either net, net cord or net post and hits the ground in the correct court, or

e. The player's racket passes over the net after hitting the ball on the player's own side of the net and the ball hits the ground in the correct court; or

f. The player hits the ball in play, which hits another ball lying in the correct court.

**26. HINDRANCE**

If a player is hindered in playing the point by a deliberate act of the opponent(s), the player shall win the point.

However, the point shall be replayed if a player is hindered in playing the point by either an unintentional act of the opponent(s), or something outside the player's own control (not including a permanent fixture).

**27. CORRECTING ERRORS**

As a principle, when an error in respect of the Rules of Tennis is discovered, all points previously played shall stand. Errors so discovered shall be corrected as follows:

a. During a standard game or a tie-break game, if a player serves from the wrong half of the court, this should be corrected as soon as the error is discovered and the server shall serve from the correct half of the court according to the score. A fault that was served before the error was discovered shall stand.

b. During a standard game or a tie-break game, if the players are at the wrong ends of the court, the error should be corrected as soon as it is discovered and the server shall serve from the correct end of the court according to the score.

c. If a player serves out of turn during a standard game, the player who was originally due to serve shall serve as soon as the error is discovered. However, if a game is completed before the error is discovered the order of service shall remain as altered. In this case, any ball change to be made after an agreed number of games should be made one game later than originally scheduled. A fault that was served by the opponents(s) before the error was discovered shall not stand.

In doubles, if the partners of one team serve out of turn, a fault that was served before the error was discovered shall stand.

d. If a player serves out of turn during a tie-break game and the error is discovered after an even number of points have been played, the error is corrected immediately. If the error is discovered after an odd number of points have been played, the order of service shall remain as altered.

A fault that was served by the opponent(s) before the error was discovered shall not stand.

In doubles, if the partners of one team serve out of turn, a fault that was served before the error was discovered shall stand.

e. During a standard game or a tie-break game in doubles, if there is an error in the order of receiving, this shall remain as altered until the end of the game in which the error is discovered. For the next game in which they are the receivers in that set, the partners shall then resume the original order of receiving.

f. If in error a tie-break game is started at 6 games all, when it was previously agreed that the set would be an "Advantage set", the error shall be corrected immediately if only one point has been played. If the error is discovered after the second point is in play, the set will continue as a "Tie-break set".

g. If in error a standard game is started at 6 games all, when it was previously agreed that the set would be a "Tie-break set", the error shall be corrected immediately if only one point has been played. If the error is discovered after the second point is in play, the set will continue as an "Advantage set" until the score reaches 8 games all (or a higher even number), when a tie-break game shall be played.

**28. ROLE OF COURT OFFICIALS**

For matches where officials are appointed, their roles and responsibilities can be found in Appendix V.

**29. CONTINUOUS PLAY**

As a principle, play should be continuous, from the time the match starts (when the first service of the match is put in play) until the match finishes.

a. Between points, a maximum of twenty (20) seconds is allowed. When the players change ends at the end of a game, a maximum of ninety (90) seconds are allowed. However, after the first game of each set and during a tie-break game, play shall be continuous and the players shall change ends without a rest.

At the end of each set there shall be a set break of a maximum of one hundred and twenty (120) seconds.

The maximum time starts from the moment that one point finishes until the first service is struck for the next point. Event organisers may apply for ITF approval to extend the ninety (90) seconds allowed when the players change ends at the end of a game and the one hundred and twenty (120) seconds allowed at a set break.

b. If, for reasons outside the player's control, clothing,

footwear or necessary equipment (excluding the racket) is broken or needs to be replaced, the player may be allowed reasonable extra time to rectify the problem.

c. No extra time shall be given to allow a player to recover condition. However, a player suffering from a treatable medical condition may be allowed one medical time-out of three minutes for the treatment of that medical condition.

A limited number of toilet/change of attire breaks may also be allowed, if this is announced in advance of the event.

d. Event organisers may allow a rest period of a maximum of ten (10) minutes if this is announced in advance of the event. This rest period can be taken after the 3rd set in a best of 5 sets match, or after the 2nd set in a best of 3 sets match.

e. The warm-up time shall be a maximum of five (5) minutes, unless otherwise decided by the event organisers.

# 16

# VOLLEYBALL

## INTRODUCTION

Volleyball is an Olympic team sport in which two teams of six players are separated by a net. Each team tries to score points by grounding a ball on the other team's court under organized rules.

The complete rules are extensive. But simply, play proceeds as follows: A player on one of the teams begins a 'rally' by serving the ball (tossing or releasing it and then hitting it with a hand or arm), from behind the back

boundary line of the court, over the net, and into the receiving team's court. The receiving team must not let the ball be grounded within their court. They may touch the ball as many as three times. Typically, the first two touches are to set up for an attack, an attempt to direct the ball back over the net in such a way that the serving team is unable to prevent it from being grounded in their court.

A number of consistent techniques have evolved in volleyball, including spiking and blocking (because these plays are made above the top of the net the vertical jump is an athletic skill emphasized in the sport) as well as passing, setting, and specialized player positions and offensive and defensive structures.

## SKILLS AND TECHNIQUES

Competitive teams master six basic skills: serve, pass, set, attack, block and dig. Each of these skills comprises a number of specific techniques that have been introduced over the years and are now considered standard practice in high-level volleyball.

**Serve**

A player stands behind the inline and serves the ball, in an attempt to drive it into the opponent's court. His or her main objective is to make it land inside the court; it is also desirable to set the ball's direction, speed and acceleration so that it becomes difficult for the receiver to handle it properly. A serve is called an "ace" when the ball lands directly onto the court or travels outside the court after being touched by an opponent.

In contemporary volleyball, many types of serves are employed:

- **Underhand:** a serve in which the player strikes the ball below the waist instead of tossing it up and striking it with an overhand throwing motion.
- **Sky Ball Serve:** a specific type of underhand serve occasionally used in beach volleyball, where the ball is hit so high it comes down almost in a straight line.
- **Topspin:** an overhand serve where the player tosses the ball high and hits it with a wrist span, giving it topspin which causes it to drop faster than it would otherwise and helps maintain a straight flight path.
- **Float:** an overhand serve where the ball is hit with no spin so that its path becomes unpredictable, akin to a knuckleball in baseball.
- **Jump Serve:** an overhand serve where the ball is first tossed high in the air, then the player makes a timed approach and jumps to make contact with the ball, hitting it with much pace and topspin.

**Set**

The set is usually the second contact that a team makes with the ball. The main goal of setting is to put the ball in the air in such a way that it can be driven by an attack into the opponent's court. The setter coordinates the offensive movements of a team, and is the player who ultimately decides which player will actually attack the ball.

**Pass**

Also called reception, the pass is the attempt by a team to properly handle the opponent's serve, or any form of attack. Proper handling includes not only preventing the ball from touching the court, but also making it reach the position where the setter is standing quickly and precisely.

**Attack**

The attack, also known as the spike, is usually the

third contact a team makes with the ball. The object of attacking is to handle the ball so that it lands on the opponent's court and cannot be defended. A player makes a series of steps (the "approach"), jumps, and swings at the ball.

**Block**

Blocking refers to the actions taken by players standing at the net to stop or alter an opponent's attack.

A block that is aimed at completely stopping an attack, thus making the ball remain in the opponent's court, is called offensive. A well-executed offensive block is performed by jumping and reaching to penetrate with one's arms and hands over the net and into the opponent's area. It requires anticipating the direction the ball will go once the attack takes place. It may also require calculating the best foot work to executing the "perfect" block.

**Dig**

Digging is the ability to prevent the ball from touching one's court after a spike or attack, particularly a ball that is nearly touching the ground. In many aspects, this skill is similar to passing, or bumping: overhand dig and bump are also used to distinguish between defensive actions taken with fingertips or with joined arms.

## RULES OF VOLLEYBALL

### PLAYING SURFACE

a. Play should be conducted only on a flat, horizontal and uniform surfaced area which should be safe for players. Play should not be conducted on rough or slippery surfaces. Only surface of wood or synthetic surface should be used in FIVB World and official Competitions. Any above mentioned surfaces can be used, however, they should be approved by FIVB.

ii. Surface of light colour should be used in indoor courts.

iii. In FIVB World and Official Competitions, lines of white colour should be drawn, whereas in playing court and free zone lines of other colours should be drawn.

**Playing Area**

Playing court and Free Zone jointly are termed as Playing Area. This area should be of rectangular shape and have symmetry.

**Lines**

a. Boundary Lines: Playing court should be marked by two sidelines and two end lines. These lines should be drawn inside the dimensions of Playing Court.

b. Attack Line: To mark the front zone an attack line should be drawn on each court. Rear edge of this line should be drawn 3 m back from axis of centre line.

c. Centre-Line: To divide the playing court into equal parts, centre line is drawn. This line divides the court into two parts measuring 9×9 m each.

All lines should have a width of 5m, which should have a light colour, but different from floor's colour and any other lines.

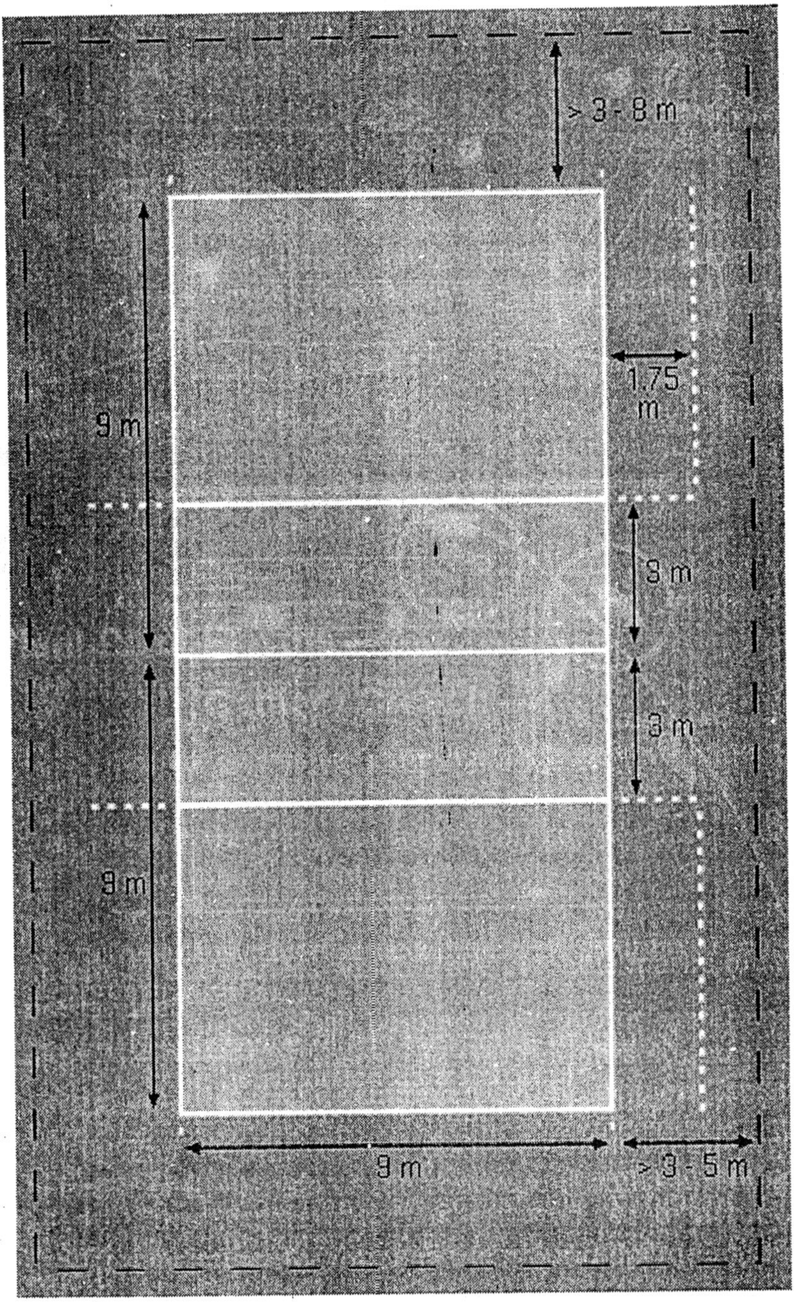

> 3 - 8 m
1.75 m
9 m
3 m
3 m
9 m
9 m
> 3 - 5 m

**Dimensions**

Playing court should have a rectangular shape which should be 18m long and 9m wide. It should be surrounded by a free zone which should have a width of 3m.

Space above the playing area which is without any obstruction is known as Free Playing Space. This space should be situated at a height of 7 m from playing surface.

In FIVB World Competitions these specifications can change. Free zone should situates 5m from sidelines and 8m from end lines, whereas free playing surface should situate at a height of 12.5m from playing surface.

**Weather**

Minimum temperature should not be less than 10°C or 50°F. However, for FIVB Competitions minimum temperature should not be less than 16°C and maximum temperature not less than 25°C.

**Lighting**

There should be proper lighting provision on court. In FIVB World and Official Competitions lighting of 1000 to 1500 luxes measuring at a height of 1m from playing surface should be done.

**THE NET**

**Structure of Net**

Net of 1m width and 9.50 length should be used in play. Net should be made of 10cm square black mesh. A 5cm wide horizontal band should be there on its top, which should be made up of two-fold white canvas sewn along its full length. For keeping its top taught, each extreme end of band should have a hole through which a cord can be passed which fastened the band to the posts. To fasten the net to posts and keeping its top taught, a flexible cable should be there in band.

To fasten net to the posts and to keep its lower part taut, a rope should be threaded through meshes at its bottom.

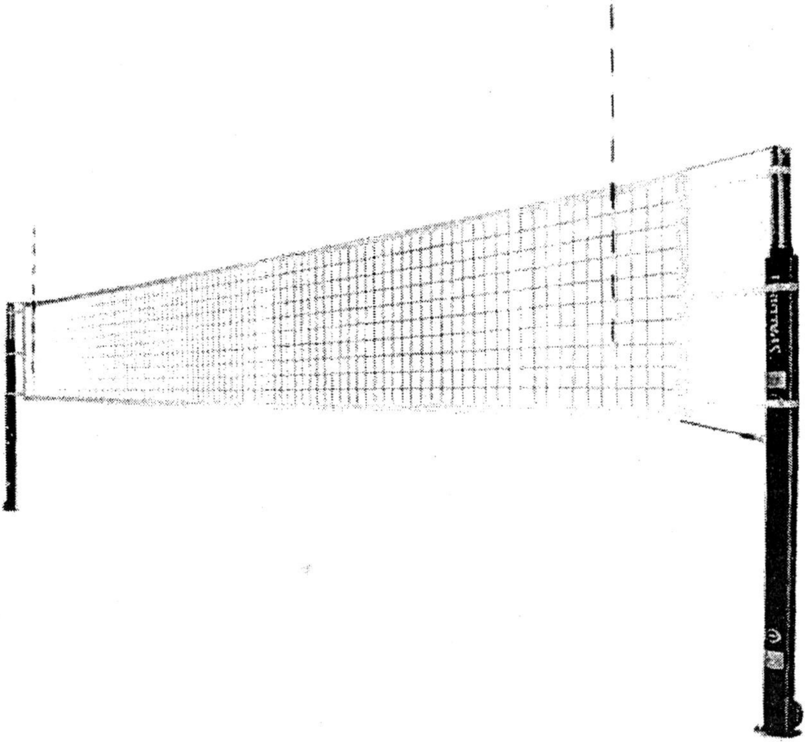

**Height**

Over the centre line a net should be placed vertically in such a way that its top is set at a height of 2.43 m for men and 2.24 m for women.

Height of net should be measured from centre of the court. It should not be placed at more height that prescribed.

**Vertical Side Markers**

At each end of net vertical to side lines and centre line two movable tapes of 5cm width should be marked. Two flexible stick should be fastened to the net which should be parallel to tapes and just outside them. These sticks should be placed at a distance of 9.40 m from each other. These sticks should have a length of 1.80 m and a radius of 5mm. These should be made of fibreglass or similar material and should extend to 80 cm above top the net. These should have rods of contrasting colour having sections of 10cm width.

**Volleyball Post**

i. Posts should have rounded shape. No wire should be used to fix it to ground.

i. At a distance of .50-1.00 m outside the sideline posts should bc placed. These posts are placed to support the net, which should have a height of 2.55m. These should be flexible.

**Antenna**

An Antenna is a flexible rod of fibreglass or similar material. It should have a length of 1.80m and diameter of 10mm. These should be fastened at outer edge of each side-band, and shculd be placed on opposite sides of net.

Over the net top 80 cm of each antenna should extend which should be marked with 10 cm stripes of contrasting colour.

These are considered to be part of the net which limits the crossing space.

**Ball**

Ball should have spherical shape. It should be made up of flexible leather or synthetic leather case inside which a bladder of rubber or similar material should be placed. It can be of a single colour or of multiple colours.

Weight of ball should be between 260 to 280 g and circumference between 65 to 67cm. Its inside pressure should be between 0.30 to 0.325 kg/cm$^2$.

**Features**

Circumference, weight, pressure, type, colour etc.

of all balls used in a match should be same.

In FIVB World and Official Competitions, only FIVB approved balls should be used.

Three-Balls System

3 balls should be used in FIVB World and Official Competitions. 6 ball retrievers should be stationed, one at each corner of free-zone and one behind each referee.

**Rights and Duties of Players**

a. All players should have thorough knowledge of rules of game.

b. Only team captain has the right to interact with referee. Captain will also act as spokesman for his players. He can also address the umpire for matters relating to his duties.

**Penalties**

i. A penalty can be awarded for any serious offence, by result of which offending team can loose the service or opposing team can get a point. A player can be disqualified from the match who commits a foul for more than once.

Player making bad comments to officials, opponents or spectators can be disqualified by referee without any prior warning.

ii. Player should be warned who is either talking to his opponent, spectator, or officials or shouting during play.

**Behaviour of Players, Substitutes and Coaches**

Players are not allowed to behave in any of following way:

i. to make comments on opponents;

ii. to make uncivil comments on officials;

iii. to go out of court during an interruption of play without taking permission of referee;

iv. to disagree with decisions of officials;

v. to insist an official to change the decision to act in an uncivil way;

**Equipments of Players**

Following different equipments are used by players:

a. A jersey, shorts, shoes and socks are included in uniform of players. These should be neat and clean.

b. Players should wear light, pliable and flat shoes which should be of rubber or leather.

c. Jerseys of all the players should be numbered through 1 to 8. These numbers should be of different contrasting colour than colour of jersey and should be placed a height of 10 cm on chest and at 15 cm on back.

**Non-Permissible Objects and Uniforms**

a. No player is allowed to wear any harmful object or object which can provide any kind of advantage to any player;

b. Colour of uniform of all players of a team should be same. Jersey without number should not be used.

**Variations**

a. If by chance colour of uniform of both teams are same, home team is required to change its dress. If a neutral site is involved, the team listed first on the score-sheet shall change uniforms.

b. Players can play in their training suits if first referee authorise to do so because of cold weather. This is possible only when they are of same colour, design and numbered properly.

**Team Captain**

Team captain is required to do the following things before commencement of match:

i. to sign the scoresheet;

ii. to act as representative of his at time of toss.

At end of match he will thanks the referees and signs the score sheet to ratify the outcome.

**Rights and Liabilities of the Team Captain**

i. As mentioned earlier he will act as a spokesman of his players, so he will submit any question or request of his players to the referee;

ii. He can make a request to referee to change his uniform and any equipment;

iii. He can ask first referee to verify the net, floor, ball and positions of opponents;

iv. He can demand legal interruptions in the game.

**Fundamental Liabilities**

a. All the participants are required to agree with decisions of referee. If they have any kind of doubt captain of team can submit a request for clarification of his judgment.

b. All the participants should have complete knowledge of rules of the game;

c. All participants should behave in a respectful manner with all officials and opponents.

**Liabilities of the Coach**

a. He is required to hand over a completed and signed Line-Up Sheet to referee before beginning of each set;

b. Before game, he will note down and verify the names and numbers of players on score sheet and will sign it;

c. He can sit on player's bench near the scorer during the match.

d. Before match he can direct warm-up sessions of his players.

**Liabilities of the Assistant Coach**

a. If because of any reason coach is not able to present at field, his assistant can perform his responsibilities. For this, permission of first referee should be taken.

b. He can sit on bench of player.

**Team Coaches, Manager and Captains**

The coach or captain has the right to request a time-out substitution. During a time-out he has the right to speak to players but may not enter the court.

**Team**

**Number of players**

i. Not more than 6 players can be included in a team. However, 6 substitutes are also allowed. Before commencement of game names and numbers of all players should be recorded properly on Score Sheet. Player whose name does not appear in Score Sheet will not allowed to participate in the game.

ii. A player cannot be substituted for more than once in any set. As soon as substitute enters the court, substituted player should leave the court. Further, substitute can be replaced only be player substituted previously.

**Players Substituted**

Captain or coach of the team can request referee or umpire to substitute any player during period ball is dead.

Upto 6 substitutions can be made in each set. Substitute is required to report scorer in playing strip before joining the game, and should enter into court as soon as he is ordered to do so. If he does not enter court immediately after receiving order to do so, a time out should be charted out. A team can lose the service or opponent can be

**Legal Substitution**

a. Any player can be substituted only at time when ball is dead and before biow of whistle for service;

b. Following specifications should be kept in mind related to substitution of players:

i. Only for once player of starting line-up can leave the game Player of starting line-up is allowed to leave the game only for one time.

**Procedure for Legal Substitutions**

Following procedure should be followed to substitute a player:

a. Referee has the right to accept or reject the request of substitution;

b. Coaches cannot speak to their players at time of substitution;

c. If request of substitution is accepted by referee,

substitute player will enter from side line by raising his hand or numbered cards. At the same time player having same number of card should stand in front of his substitute. On signal of second referee, substitute will enter into the court and will take numbered cards from substitute.

**Location of Players**

Following provisions should be followed during serving of ball:

Players of both teams must be within their courts in two lines of three players, taking positions as follows:

The three players at the net are front line players, occupying from right to left, position 2, 3 and 4, while the three players in the back are back line players, occupying from right to left, positions 1, 6 and 5.

The positions of the players on the court must conform to the rotational order recorded on the score sheet; namely:

In the front line, 3 must be between 2 and 4, and in front of 6. In the back line, 6 must be between 1 and 5, and behind. Consequently, 2 must be in front of 1, and 4 must be in front of 5. Once the line-up sheet has been given to the scorer no change of line-up is authorized, unless there has been an error or omission by the scorer.

Any discrepancy between the line-up sheet and the actual position of the players on the court must be corrected before the start of the game according to the line-up sheet, without penalty. However, if one or more players on the court is not identified on the line-up sheet, the team is requested to correct the mistake according to the line-up sheet without penalty.

But if the coach of the team wishes to keep the players on the court, he must requested the substitutions of the player. In this case, this team will be charged the necessary substitution.

In following manner position of players are

determined and controlled by position of their feet contacting the ground:

i. Each right or left player should have any part of his foot closer to respective side line. Feet of centre player who belongs to same line of players should have his foot farther from these players;

ii. Each front line player should have any part of his foot near to centre line, and foot of his corresponding backline teammate should be farther from him.

Players are free to move about and to have any position on their own court and free zone after serving of ball.

Within their playing area, players can move anywhere except under net on court of their opponent.

Throughout the set rotation order should be same as indicated by score sheet. Rotation order can be changed but only at beginning of each set which should be recorded on Score Sheet.

**Selection of Captain**

a. A team consists of a captain who is regarded as sportsman and representative of team;

b. Coach or captain will select other captain out of existing players if because of any reason he cannot continue to play;

c. Captain should wear a ribbon or strip which will distinguish him from other players. This strip should measure 8cm × 2cm and should have different colour from jersey. It should be placed on left side of captain's uniform. Player's Strip

i. Through 8 to 15 players' jerseys should be numbered. These numbers should be placed at a height of 15cm on back.

In international matches, the captain shall wear a badge on the left side of his chest, measuring 8cm. by 1.5cm. in a different colour to that of the jersey.

ii. A player should wear a jersey, shorts, and light

shoes. They cannot wear any headgear or any kind of injurious article. Referee can allow any player to play barefooted, if player makes any request for the same.

iii. Uniform of all players of a team should be same. They can wear training suits if referee allow them because of cold weather.

**Officials and their Duties**

Presence of following official is must in a game:

1 referee;

1 umpire;

1 scorer;

2 linesmen.

**Umpire**

Umpire will sit on that side of court from which he can face-out the referee properly.

Following are included in duties of umpire:

a. He is required to indicate when ball touches vertical side markers and goes outside them;

b. Whenever a player crosses the centre line or has illegally played the ball within the attack zone, he should blow the whistle.

c. He will give his judgment when ball contacts with the net, except those over or near the top of the net;

d. He supervises the conduct of coaches and substitutes on the bench.

e. He times the duration of the times-out.

f. He watches for contact of the ball with any foreign objects.

g. He verifies at the beginning of each set that the initial positions of each team correspond exactly to the order of rotation as shown on the score sheet.

h. He gives his opinion to the referee in all matters, when requested.

i. He checks that the rotational order and positions of the receiving team are correct at the time of each service.

j. He calls the attention of the referee to any

unsporting actions.

k. He authorizes substitutions if requested by team captains or coaches.

**Linesmen**

**Position**

a. In International matches atleast 4 linesmen should be appointed who should stand in free zone between 1m to 3m from each corner of the court, on the imaginary extension of line they control. From service corner, back lines should be controlled and from opposing corner, side lines should be controlled.

b. If instead of 4, only 2 linesmen have been appointed, they should stand diagonally opposite each other, one at each end of playing court at corner away from service zone.

**Responsibilities during the Match**

If only 2 linesman have been appointed, they should sit at diagonally opposite corners of the court at a distance of 1 meter in indoor games while 3m in outdoor games. Each linesman has to keep a watch on side lines and end line nearest to him and to give signal to referee. They should raise their flag in while ball is out and drop in downward direction when ball is in.

When any player of receiving team gets touched by an Out Ball, Linesman can be requested by the referee to indicate this by giving signal from his flag.

Linesman will indicate to referee errors made by players while making the service or in a situation when ball goes out of vertical side markers completely.

**Referee**

Referee has full control over the game and every player is required to respect his decision. From beginning of play to end of match all players are considered to be under authority of Referee.

He is required to answer all the questions of players and can overrule decision of other officials when he is not satisfied by their judgment. In order to clear view of the game he should be positioned at a height of 50cm above one end of the net. Players, coaches and managers behaving in an unsportsmanlike manner can be penalised.

**Location of First and Second Referee**

a. For First Referee a stand at one end of net is made. He should be suited at a height of 50cm above the level of upper edge of the net.

b. Second Referee will stand in opposite site from where he can face the first referee. He should be along the extension of front zone of receiving team at moment of service.

**Right of First Referee**

a. He can give judgment on any matter relating to game;

b. He has the power to direct the whole match from beginning to end and issue directions to all officials in performing their duties.

c. He has to decide whether the playing court is in proper condition for play or not.

d. His decisions are final and are binding on all the players. He can overrule of any official if he is not satisfy with their judgment.

e. It is the responsibility of both first and second referee that ball to be used fulfils all specifications. No ball which does not fulfils specifications should be used.

**Duties of the First Referee**

First Referee will perform following duties during the match:

i. He will give signal and will penalise fouls committed by players;

ii. Only he can decide upon faults involving the server, the positions of the serving team, screening, the contact of the ball when in service trajectory, the faults in contacting the ball, the faults over the net and its horizontal bank, whether a simultaneous fault was committed or not and so forth.

iii. If captain is not agree with explanation of rules given by referee, at end of match first referee is required to give his authorisation to register this protest.

First Referee has to perform following duties before commencement of match:

i. He is required to control warm-up of team;

ii. He will perform toss up for service and court;

iii. Verify the condition of playing court as well as of all equipments to be used.

**Duties of the Second Referee**

On following occasions he should blow his whistle and give signal:

i. when ball touches the antenna on his side of court or crosses the net outside of crossing space;

ii. when any team committed positional foul;

iii. when under upper edge of the net a player touches either net or antenna;

iv. when back line player commits illegal attack-hit or blocking;

v. when any player get injured;

vi. when ball touches any outside object;

With help of Line-Up Sheet second referee will check the actual positions of players before beginning of each set.

**Power of the Second Referee**

Second Referee is considered to be the assistant of First Referee. He can replace First Referee if and only if because of any reason First Referee is not able to continue.

He has the right to perform the following:

a. Before and during all sets he verifies the position of players who are sitting on player's bench, and will make report to first referee about any misconduct of players;

b. Time-outs and substitutions made by a team are under his control and he will report First Referee and Coach about this during any interval;

c. He will supervise the conduct of all players and make a report to first referee for misconduct of any player;

d. He has the right to accept or reject request for interruption of game;

e. He make control on warming-up period of substitutes;

f. Whether surface of playing court should be dried up or not, should be decided by him;

**Scorer**

On opposite side of court to Referee and behind the umpire, Scorer should be positioned to perform the following duties:

a. He will record names and numbers of all players and substitutes on Score Sheet before beginning of each match.

b. He will record score, substitutions and number of time-outs requested during each set carefully.

c. He should announce number of time-outs requested during each set as soon as new request for a time-out has been made by any team;

d. He will verify that rotation order has not changed throughout the game;

e. He will record location of players on court before beginning of each set. On Score Sheet position of team serving first should be recorded first.

**Location**

Scorer's table should be positioned in opposite side from where he is facing the first referee.

**Rights and Powers**

a. During the game interruptions he can give signal to referee for errors in teams' line-ups or in team's service order;

b. He helps second-referee in doing registrations on

score sheet, controlling legal interruptions and in making report to first referee, coaches and public.

**Change of Courts**

a. Before beginning of each set teams should change their ends, whereas substitute players and other team members have to change their benches.

b. Team should change their courts as soon as one of scores 8 points, however no player should get any kind of instruction from referee and players should not change their positions. Player serving before change will serve again this time.

If teams have forgotten to change courts at proper time, they should do it as soon as they come to known the fact. Score should not be changed after change of court.

**Interval Between Sets and Changes of Courts**

Between sets an interval of not more than 2 minutes is allowed, whose duration increases to 5 minutes between fourth and fifth sets. The teams must line-up on their end lines at the moment they are called by the first referee to resume the match.

**Substitutions**

i. Play can be stopped for not more than 3 minutes if an injured player is to substitute, and this period should not be considered as a time-out. This stoppage should be allowed only if it is not possible to replace the injured player. Referee will stop the play as soon as any player get injured.

ii. Play should be started again immediately after injured player has substituted and no player is allowed to get any kind of advice from coach.

**Change of Service**

When serving team commits any foul, service should be changed.

**Side-Out**

With call out of Side-Out, service order should change.